CRICKET IN PAKISTAN

NATION, IDENTITY, AND POLITICS

CRICKET
IN PAKISTAN

NATION, IDENTITY, AND POLITICS

ALI KHAN

OXFORD
UNIVERSITY PRESS

OXFORD
UNIVERSITY PRESS

Oxford University Press is a department of the University of Oxford.
It furthers the University's objective of excellence in research, scholarship,
and education by publishing worldwide. Oxford is a registered trade mark of
Oxford University Press in the UK and in certain other countries

Published in Pakistan by
Oxford University Press
No. 38, Sector 15, Korangi Industrial Area,
PO Box 8214, Karachi-74900, Pakistan

ISBN 978-0-19-070884-9

Typeset in Adobe Garamond Pro
Printed on 68gsm Offset Paper

Printed by Delta Dot Technologies (Pvt.) Ltd., Karachi

Acknowledgements
Cover Photograph: Pakistani children play cricket in a closed market during a strike.
(000_UN0LL), ARIF ALI / AFP

Contents

Acknowledgements

This book has taken several years of research, writing, and re-writing; but it is in fact the outcome of a lifetime of love and engagement with the game of cricket that began while watching Sir Vivian Richards, the legendary West Indian cricketer, score 291 at the Oval against England in 1976. Along the way there are many who have contributed to the final manuscript as you now read it.

My friends and colleagues were a constant source of encouragement and feedback. In particular, I received constant encouragement and feedback on entire drafts from Sadaf Ahmed and Marie Lall. Souvik Naha, Kingshuk Chatterjee, Chris Valiotis, Ali Nobil Ahmad, Shabbir Ahsen, Ammara Maqsood, Ali Usman Qasmi, Umair Javed, Marta Bolognani, Sameen Mohsin, Asma Faiz, Ali Raza, and Mohammad Waseem—all provided me with important advice and ideas. Christophe Jaffrelot pushed me to write the book after a discussion over dinner. I am indebted to my copyeditor Ateeb Gul—despite being struck by Covid, he worked tirelessly to ensure that the manuscript was carefully vetted. Robert Curphey, the archive and library manager at the Marylebone Cricket Club (MCC) at Lord's, facilitated my work enthusiastically helping find materials and books throughout my secondary research. I consulted Osman Samiuddin's work often, and he was kind enough to answer my regular queries. Kamila Hyat, Mazher Arshad, Umar Farooq Kalson, and Ahmer Naqvi provided unique feedback and insight.

I would not have been able to carry out much of the fieldwork without the help of officials at the Pakistan Cricket Board (PCB). Chairman Ehsan Mani and Chief Executive Wasim Khan were generous with their time as was former Chief Operating Officer Subhan Ahmed. Hissan Ur Rehman and Imran Ahmad Khan, previously my students and now making their names at the cricket board, were always on hand to provide insight and perspective. Yahya Ghaznavi's extensive knowledge on the history of Pakistan cricket helped me immensely in filling important gaps. I am also thankful to all the cricketers, former and current, who spoke to me openly about their experiences with cricket.

My university Lahore University of Management Sciences (LUMS) provided initial research support through a Faculty Initiative Fund (FIF) grant and then a generous sabbatical during which I was able to complete my manuscript.

My family have unequivocally supported me in all my ventures. My wife Mariyam and daughter Alena are a constant source of support and happiness. Minnoo, Bhayya, Sara, Aalia, Omar, and Faiza have all in their way provided me the environment in which I could thrive. But undoubtedly the biggest influence on me has been my father, Shaharyar M. Khan, affectionately known to all as Mian, and who has been responsible for what I have achieved today and who inculcated in me a love of this most mesmerizing and complex sport. Thank you!

Introduction

What do they know of cricket who only cricket know?[1]
— C.L.R. James

In his magisterial work on cricket and society in the West Indies, C.L.R. James exhorted the reader to see cricket not simply as a sport but as part of a much wider social and political reality. Unfortunately, the great Trinidadian Marxist's plea for sport to be understood in all its many social, political, and cultural aspects remains largely unheeded. Despite the endless flow of televised images, commentary, and advertising selling evermore garish and extreme incarnations of limited-overs cricket, surprisingly little of any substance has been written about its importance in Pakistan.

As Pakistan's most popular sport by far, cricket has played a significant role in defining the culture and history of the country, thus becoming an essential part of its post-colonial identity and national pride. Pakistan has a 'hegemonic sports culture,' one that 'dominates a country's emotional attachments.'[2] In Pakistan, cricket has often been ascribed great power as a national symbol of unity, able to integrate a multi-ethnic, culturally diverse, and stratified society. As Khan states in his book on cricket acting as a bridge of peace between perennially hostile neighbours India and Pakistan: 'In Pakistan it [cricket] is the strongest unifying force amongst its people, young and old, rich or poor, man or woman, Shia or Sunni, Pathan or Sindhi. It brings a unity in peacetime only achieved in times of war.'[3] Cricket therefore has come to represent Pakistan.

But as James most clearly implies, cricket has also come to act as a microcosm or reflection of society—its politics, history, culture, and aspirations. In Pakistan, cricket is a metaphor for modern life—from the youthful exuberance, energy, and innovation of a young nation, to increasing religiosity, aspects of corruption, and global relations. No other sphere of life articulates Pakistan's history, culture, society, and economy more precisely than the cultural practice of cricket. But, cricket, like other sports, is also a multi-billion-dollar industry with far reaching social and economic consequences. It is thereby able to create and communicate meaning, giving it the ability to affect the culture of the society in which it is embedded. Sport defines cultures, drives economies, and shapes politics.

A closer analysis of these dialectical discourses of cricket in Pakistan—the ability to affect society and to be affected by and represent it—consequently produces a blueprint of those important and valued behaviours that are the foundation of the larger culture in which the sport is embedded. An analysis of cricket therefore allows for a unique and privileged insight into political and sociological issues such as race, cultural change, national identity, and self-realization. This book looks at the way the history, politics, economics, and society of the region have transformed cricket, making it a part of a popular culture that represents Pakistan. But simultaneously, cricket has also shaped the very influences that sculpted it, thereby allowing the exploration and analysis of the intricate relationships between sport, culture, politics, identity, and regional cooperation through the unique lens of Pakistani cricket.

Given the economic, political, cultural, and emotional significance of cricket in South Asia and its linkages to wider historical processes that have shaped the region since the 20th century, there is a conspicuous lack of material examining cricket within the broader historical and social context. Wagg emphasizes the point stating that while there is a substantial corpus of literature on the history, sociology, and social anthropology of sport, in the context of South Asia sport has been a marginal presence. Even post-colonial writings rarely touch on sport as an area of significance, concentrating instead on literature.[4] This is perplexing since the impact of sporting personalities such as the Australian Donald Bradman or the West Indian Vivian Richards or the Indian Sachin Tendulkar or Pakistan's Imran Khan is second to none within their respective societies.

There are notable exceptions to the scarcity of research on cricket in South Asia, particularly in the work of the Indian academics Boria Majumdar,[5] Mihir Bose,[6] Ramchandra Guha,[7] and Kausik Bandyopadhyay[8]—all of whom have written detailed accounts of Indian cricket embedded within the space of a wider society. Mike Marqusee's *War Minus the Shooting* is part-travelogue/part-incisive social observation on the politics and culture of the Subcontinent during the time of the 1996 cricket world cup.[9]

However, when it comes to academic material on cricket in Pakistan the cupboard is quite bare, with the notable exception of Chris Valiotis's *Cricket and Identity in Pakistan and Anglo-Pakistan*[10] which looks at the role of cricket and national identity amongst Pakistanis and the Pakistani diaspora. Apart from this, there have been a few comprehensive accounts of the history of Pakistan cricket, most notably the work of Peter Oborne,[11] Osman Samiuddin,[12] and by Oborne and Heller.[13] These commendable works have succeeded in documenting the history of cricket in Pakistan. However, they are written in a descriptive and journalistic style and while they touch on the wider social milieu in which cricket is embedded, their focus is not directed at an analysis of cricket and its wider implications and interactions with society, politics, and culture. Other cricket-related books that centre on Pakistan deal largely with cricketing affairs and include further histories of the game, numerous player autobiographies,[14] and tour diaries. Most academic analysis of cricket in Pakistan has appeared as the occasional chapter in edited volumes or as part of a larger compendium on cricket.[15]

As an area of academic research Pakistan has garnered a growing corpus of work, particularly in the last decade, with the majority of this research concentrated on issues of religion, terrorism, and politics.[16] However, for a country of its size, diversity, and global importance, there are still extensive gaps in the academic literature. One such gap exists in the vast domain of popular culture of which sport is a significant portion. It is my contention that the study of cricket in Pakistan is crucial to understanding the wider culture, politics, identity, and regional relations of Pakistan, all of which are thematic occupations in this book. As I have pointed out earlier, despite the centrality of cricket to the history, culture, and society of Pakistan, there are very few books that examine cricket's central position in the imagination of the Pakistani society. My attempt with this book has been to throw in, in Majumdar's words, 'a few stepping stones across a stream,'[17] to help the process of building scholarship on sport in South Asian society and particularly on the vast untapped area of cricket and society in Pakistan.

The research for this book was based on a variety of qualitative methods of data collection. Between 2004 and 2006 and then again between 2015 to 2017, I was able to gain a high level of access to the Pakistan Cricket Board— the official administrators of the game in Pakistan. During this period, I carried out participant observation during several of Pakistan's international matches. It also allowed the undertaking of in-depth interviews with board officials, cricketers (former and current), journalists, and fans. Moreover, being based in Lahore which doubles as Pakistan's cricket headquarters enabled me to interview cricket historians, club cricketers, and coaches based in the city. The vast majority of interviewees were eager and enthusiastic about sharing their views on a subject that is so close to the hearts of millions in Pakistan. The only difficulties that were faced occurred during questions on match-fixing where players, officials, and journalists were genuinely concerned about their safety if word got out on revelations concerning the people involved. In such cases, multiple visits and the gradual building of trust allowed important information to be pieced together. I have purposely left out names in passages where information given was sensitive.

Apart from field-based interviews, I undertook a considerable amount of secondary research that involved archival work at the MCC library at Lord's Cricket Ground—the original headquarters of the game. The library holds rare journals and magazines on cricket, historical documents, published autobiographies and diaries of former and current cricketers, and the minutes of the meetings of the International Cricket Council (ICC), the global cricketing administrator. The autobiographies and biographies allowed me to document the views of the many cricketers who were not available for interviews but whose perspectives were essential for the book.

Finally, I believe that much of the research is also based on a lifetimes' love for and engagement with the game of cricket that has allowed the accumulation of knowledge of years of playing, watching, and interacting with the game. When you have woken up at odd hours of the night to hear famous victories on the radio or have seen Pakistan raise the World Cup against all odds or experienced the atmosphere of an incredible Indo-Pak match, then you *live* your research rather than simply undertake it. It is a unique emotional attachment.

CRICKET IN PAKISTAN: NATION, IDENTITY, AND POLITICS

Two-way Reflections—Cricket in Society, Society in Cricket

'A hard country,' 'paradox,' 'descent into chaos,' 'on the brink'[18]—these are just some of the adjectives that have been used to describe Pakistan. A sense of endemic disarray seems to have persisted from its difficult birth in 1947 when a million people perished in the violence accompanying Partition[19] and a further 20 million were displaced.[20] How did Pakistan even survive in 1947 amidst floods of refugees, a threadbare government machinery, a loss of qualified personnel and finance, and barely any industry and international support is a fascinating question to ask. But against all odds, it not only survived but has had periods of relative prosperity as well. The story of its cricket is similar. A country that had no domestic cricketing structure won a Test match in its very first series against India in 1952. Two years later, on its first tour to England, Pakistan registered a win against the country that had introduced the game to them. In contrast, it would take India twenty years to register a first Test victory over England. New Zealand took twenty-six years to register a win. Pakistan (and Pakistani cricket), therefore, can rightly be described as an enigma.

Chapter 1 of this book grapples with this paradox called Pakistan, examining the nature of its cricket team and linking it to the wider political, economic, and cultural environment within which cricket is to be found. From the adoption of a cultural practice that was so strongly associated with a specific country of origin and more particularly so closely associated with the British Empire by the elite to the mass spread of the game post-Partition, cricket's democratization or vernacularization, as Appadurai refers to it,[21] provides the first of several conundrums. As radio and television coverage—in a low literacy country like India (or, in this case, Pakistan)—propelled the game to different parts of the country and a much more diverse population, the rapidly fluctuating political and economic transformations in the country were reflected in the nature of the cricket team.

When Pakistan began its cricketing journey, it was led by the Oxford educated Abdul Hafeez Kardar and consisted of a team almost entirely comprising middle class, college graduates from the urban centres of Karachi and Lahore. In the 1970s and 1980s, Pakistan was regarded as 'impossibly glamorous'[22] in large part due to Imran Khan's international playboy reputation and Benazir Bhutto's time in Oxford. The cricket team too consisted of global superstars who played in Australia and England when not on international duty. Fast forward to 2004: Pakistan was being led by Inzamam-ul-Haq, the son of a muezzin, who captained a team of players from all over Pakistan and from much less privileged backgrounds—sons of daily wage labourers, night watchmen, small farmers. These changes in the composition of the Pakistan cricket team reflected the wider socio-political changes that Pakistan was going through along the way.[23]

By 2009, the country was increasingly politically isolated, and international cricket in Pakistan had been halted. But throughout the decades, the rising chaos in Pakistan's political and economic systems has not prevented Pakistan cricket from confounding its critics. In the 1980s, as urbanization and population growth increased exponentially, space became a premium—school grounds disappeared and less and less cricketers came to the national team through the school route. In its place came a specifically Pakistani innovation—tape-ball cricket—which drove the game forward in unusual ways. In fact, it is this lack of formal structures, and the very anarchy of Pakistan cricket as Cashman suggests,[24] that holds the secret to Pakistan's success. Pakistan was youthful, exuberant, unfettered, and dazzling. But it was also corrupt, undisciplined, disorderly, and chaotic. Just like its cricket.

Chapter 1 introduces us to how socio-political transformations in Pakistan were reflected in the changing nature of the cricket team giving the team its distinct nature. Furthermore, the contradictory tendencies in both society and sport are what make cricket and Pakistan uniquely fascinating.

National Politics and the Appropriation of Cricket

But the book deals with more than cricket as a reflection of the society, contending instead that there is a two-way relationship—with cricket not only *reflecting* changes in wider society but also *affecting* certain social, political, and economic changes. However, in an attempt to ignore this two-way exchange, one of the most common retorts in modern sport is to 'keep politics out of sport,' as if the purity of sport is contaminated by the Machiavellian nature of politics. But much of this book looks at the effects of wider influences like politics on cricket and vice versa. As Majumdar stated: 'sport is not only political, it is politics.'[25]

Chapter 2 of this book examines the Faustian deal that was struck early on between politics and cricket. In the absence of a domestic structure for cricket as well as no financial or organizational support, cricket in Pakistan turned to individual benefactors who were also important political patrons. It allowed cricket to survive and thrive, but the resulting patron-client relationship led to the involvement of the state in how cricket was organized.

More importantly, as cricket spread across the country, successive governments saw it as a means of nation building and identity construction leading to cricket being appropriated by both civilian and military governments. For a new country struggling to find something to act as a marker of identity, cricket as a collective cultural expression was ideal. As Houlihan and Hill both point out, sport has been recognized as having a role to play in the consolidation of certain nationalisms or the promotion of the interests of particular nation states.[26] Interestingly, in Pakistan, authoritarian leaders—such as the military generals Ziaul Haq and Pervez Musharraf who between them constituted sixteen years of direct rule—often used cricket to help validate their rule and thereby exploited it more actively for advancing, for example, foreign relations. Democratically elected governments with less need to demonstrate their legitimacy appear to have been less active. Were better administrators appointed by military governments as a result of the necessity of using cricket to provide them legitimacy at home and abroad? Did civilian governments use political patronage to make appointments, thereby bequeathing their legacy of kleptocracy and corruption?

Regardless, the political environments impacted cricket in a variety of ways. By looking at the contrasting impacts that occurred as a result of political interference—which are not always negative—the chapter also examines the importance of leadership in a South Asian context and how tendencies towards authoritarianism, centralization, competence, and incompetence are the result of a wider political culture in Pakistan.

If the first chapter dealt with the reflection of society on the nature of Pakistani cricket, the second looks more specifically at the impact of national politics on cricket in Pakistan.

Local and Global—Match-Fixing, Corruption, and Redemption

In addition to local political factors, from the late 1980s onward global political and economic changes too opened cricket up to new influences. This was a decade when change swept through the world's political and social systems. Transformations were occurring globally. Pakistan entered a decade of democracy following a decade of military dictatorship. Unfortunately, with civilian rule came declining governance and increasing corruption. Cricket too saw tumultuous changes. The balance of power in the global control of cricket shifted dramatically towards South Asia bringing rapid commercialization of the sport in the Subcontinent. One of the ways that the confluence of local and global factors manifested itself was in the form of match-fixing, a vice that damaged the credibility of the game globally and in Pakistan. Match-fixing highlighted the increasingly acute contradictions between cricket's moralistic ideology and the reality of its political economy in the age of late capitalism. Commercialization battered cricket's old ethos, replacing it with a new set of values, what Appadurai calls the 'transcendence of traditional cricketing norms and values' where making money features more prominently than the 'spirit of the game' or its nationalist concerns.[27] Beckles argues the same in his analysis of West Indies cricket, claiming that globalization has stripped the nationalist identity of players, thereby making them hostage to market processes.[28] This is captured most starkly in the Twenty20 practice of auctions where players are sold to the highest bidder. Lists are then published with sold players and the price they garnered and those unwanted ones who remain unsold.

Money also brought in its wake new promises of and desires for upward mobility and modernity. Inevitably, it attracted the attention of criminal networks. The heady days of greed, fame, and excess, promoted rather than discouraged by maladaptive leadership, brought scandal. Redemption and catharsis would only come via another aspect that had gained increasing currency in Pakistan at the same time—the spectre of increasing religiosity. As a result, global influences such as commercialization may have facilitated the emergence of modern day match-fixing, but at a more local level the analysis in Chapter 3 locates fixing in a broader national environment of endemic corruption in Pakistan.

Keys states that scholars and journalists, writing exposés of new and deeper levels of corruption in international sport, continued to adopt tones of ill-informed outrage at how far sport had strayed from its allegedly pure roots.[29] The fact is that, as the book argues, sport is part of the wider culture and inevitably will be influenced by the wider political, economic, and cultural environment, whether in Russia or in Pakistan. The predominant social themes of religiosity, corruption, accountability, leadership, and changing values are intimately captured in the analysis of match-fixing in cricket in Pakistan and are at the heart of Chapter 3 on corruption and redemption.

Global Relations: Cricket in a Colonial and Post-Colonial Context

While global factors affected Pakistan cricket through increasing commercialization and the incidence of match-fixing, the two-way interaction between cricket and the wider society means that cricket in Pakistan would also impact Pakistan's global relations. Inevitably, the great importance attached to cricket in Pakistani society means that it would have a major role to play in the country's international relations and image. Nowhere is this more critical than in Pakistan's bilateral relations with neighbouring India and also with England, its former colonial master—these discourses constitute the subjects of Chapters 4–6 of the book.

In the case of England, because of the link to the Empire, the cricketing association is framed by the historical colonial relationship and highlights the issue of race. History necessitates that cricket be placed within a broader colonial context. In Pakistan's case, the interaction with England was made antagonistic by the fact that by the 1980s, as Searle points out, the cricket playing subject became more 'than the equal, the master and destroyer too. The coloniser's game becoming his nemesis.'[30] Specifically, Chapter 4 looks at how cricketing relations between England and Pakistan were influenced by and reflect bilateral relations between the two countries as well as their past intertwined colonial and post-colonial histories. But changing dynamics within the cricketing world also caused conflict in bilateral relations producing a two-way dynamic.

The England–Pakistan cricketing relationship came to be defined by a tension between colonial arrogance on the one side and a desire for decolonization on the other, 'from a game played and controlled by white English and colonial elites, to a sport carrying the aspirations of national independence and democratic ownership.'[31] The fact that a colonial mindset was built not only on the belief in the supremacy of their military, political, and economic systems but also on a moral superiority led to orientalist discourses that stereotyped Pakistani cricket and Pakistan as a nation.[32] With the global governance of the game as well as cricketing success beginning an unprecedented shift away from the West—in this case represented by the vestiges of the British Empire—the orientalist disdain of the past was replaced by outright racial hostility by English cricket, the media, and the crowds towards Pakistan. Moreover, Pakistan's global reputation as a conservative Islamic nation trumped even the orientalist discourse in terms of negative perceptions towards Pakistan. Eventually, though, the effects of globalization and multiculturalism affecting both England and Pakistan meant that new equilibriums were accepted, thus leading to a stabilization of relations.

In order to analyse these changing dynamics and how these contrasting viewpoints changed over the decades, Chapter 4 refers to a series of confrontations over umpiring, ball tampering, and touring. An examination of these encounters highlights the prevailing attitudes and relations of England and Pakistan towards one another as well as how these perceptions have changed over the last seventy years as a result of political, social, and cultural changes in both countries.

Sibling Rivalry

Over the years, arguably the country that has played the most important role in Pakistan's national narrative is its neighbour, India. The relationship is complex, contradictory, and globally influential. The countries were born of one at the time of decolonization. Partition brought with it violence that was unprecedented in scale and method.[33] Apart from the killings, millions were displaced as they moved between the new nations of Pakistan and India in one of the largest ever movements of people.[34] Since then, the two countries have been involved in a number of wars, conflicts, and military and political stand offs. The India–Pakistan border is amongst the most militarized and dangerous in the world. The presence of nuclear weapons on both sides adds an element of finality to the options. The conflicts that have occurred between the two postcolonial nations have often dominated global political events. Relations between India and Pakistan have repercussions beyond their own borders and more than anywhere else in the world, cricket far from simply being a sport extends well 'beyond the boundary' to encompass politics, economics, and culture.

Cricketing relations between India and Pakistan, therefore, are crucial to understanding the wider relations between the two countries. Not only does cricket reflect the culture, national identities, and aspirations of both countries, it also impacts significantly on their political relations. If we factor in the fact that up to a billion people in South Asia watch bilateral India–Pakistan matches, we realize the significance of cricket in these two neighbouring countries.

Chapters 5 and 6 in the book examine the deeply contradictory nature of Indo-Pak relations addressing in particular the conundrum of how, following the horrors of Partition and the resultant turmoil which triggered off hatred, distrust, and prejudice in almost every sphere of activity in the Subcontinent, did the Pakistan team tour India in the first bilateral exchange between the two countries only five years later? Moreover, how is it that, following Partition, two wars, multiple border skirmishes, support for insurgencies, and testing nuclear devices, did cricket continue to provide opportunities for deeply emotional reunions? The frequently hostile relations between the states often remained at odds with the cricketing relations between the boards, players, and fans. Chapters 5 and 6, therefore, examine the undulating political relations between India and Pakistan, juxtaposing that with the cricketing relations that existed sometimes in contrast to the political grain and sometimes hostage to the wider situation.

I examine specific occasions in the Indo-Pak cricketing rivalry to see how they facilitated political and cultural relations between the countries. On several occasions, in the midst of heightened political tension, cricket facilitated better relations. The deeply collective and emotional nature of a sporting rivalry provides memorable occasions that were able to challenge dominant state narratives. In the case of India and Pakistan, there have been unforgettable instances that have resonated well beyond the cricket field. These instances are analysed in light of their impact on the overarching India–Pakistan relationship.

When thinking of India and Pakistan, the dominant view is of enmity. But there is also a deep bond that has existed throughout the last seven decades. The collective histories and culture remain at odds with the political relations between the nation states. The two countries share similar languages, music, dress, customs, and cuisines, and when their citizens meet abroad they slip easily into camaraderie. Indian films remain part of culture across the border and Pakistani television serials and musicians have been popular in India. Until recently, a citizen of either country visiting the other was soon overwhelmed with the hospitality showered upon them by anyone discovering where they were from. Chapter 5 shows that there are occasions where the two countries have established friendly relations and also discusses benefits of such collaboration.

As we look forward, the signs of better relations between Pakistan and India appear distant. Writing in 2008, Jon Gemmell would state that 'one of the most encouraging developments in international cricket has been the rapprochement between India and Pakistan.'[35] Sadly, bilateral relations have been suspended since 2012. Politics has trumped sport as the current worsening of bilateral ties robs the cricketing world of its most captivating rivalry while simultaneously severing an avenue of people-to-people interaction. As cricketing tours between the countries stop, walls go up and exchanges elsewhere follow suit. Some impacts are unfortunate as Indian films in Pakistan disappear from cinemas and Pakistani television serials are dropped from cable networks in India. Other changes are more personal. Families and friends find travel ever more restrictive. Mohammed Hanif, the Pakistani author, writes of more tragic circumstances:

> I took a flight back from India after the 2008 Mumbai attacks. Almost all the passengers returning to Pakistan had been dragged out of their hospital beds. Some of them were in their hospital gowns, others clutching plastic bags full of medicines and half-used IVs, yellow tubes hanging from their arms. They were under treatment in various Indian hospitals for life-threatening diseases and had to leave their hospital beds and rush home as India and Pakistan were on the verge of yet another war.[36]

Less than a year earlier, Pakistan and India had played their fourth series in four years. It was meant to be the start of a more mature and steady relationship.

When one thinks of Pakistan, inevitably a variety of themes come to mind. Colonialism, Partition, new nation, Islam, India, corruption, terrorism, Imran Khan, Malala Yousafzai—these are some of the most prominent among them. But what connects all of these topics is cricket. Their role in Pakistan is reflected in their role in cricket in Pakistan and an analysis of it leads us to a unique insight into Pakistan.

It is fitting that Pakistan's current Prime Minister is Imran Khan, one of the greatest cricketers of Pakistan. He owes much of his popularity to his prowess as a cricketer and as a leader in the field of cricket. But such is the power of cricket that Pakistan elected him as Prime Minister (even his election symbol was a cricket bat). Malala Yousafzai—Nobel laureate of the Peace Prize 2014—who was shot by the Taliban in 2012 for speaking out on women's education, became a symbol of defiance and girls' right to education. Malala has rubbed shoulders with world leaders but her excitement at meeting the Pakistan cricket team in 2016 in Birmingham was on a different scale altogether. In March 2020, as the Covid-19 virus spread across the world, Pakistan's international Twenty20 league continued unaffected. Crowds packed into stadiums and rumours abounded that the government and the media were not reporting cases until the tournament ended. Ultimately, reality intruded, and the tournament was halted and finished later in the year. But such is the importance of cricket that it literally takes on a life and death role. How does one understand the enigma that is Pakistan? Maybe like its cricket team Pakistan often defies description. But if anything goes to the heart of the nation, it is cricket.

1

The Nature of Pakistan Cricket

*Mercurial—(of a person) subject to sudden or
unpredictable changes of mood or mind.*

On 4 June 2017, the outdoor spaces across Pakistan, where large screens had been mounted for the highly anticipated clash between Pakistan and India, had emptied out hours before Pakistan succumbed feebly to India. Another loss to their great rivals in an international tournament had left a pall of gloom hanging over the country. Pakistan had been at its worst—poor fielding, wayward bowling, and inept batting. Such had been the scale of defeat in their first match of the Champions Trophy in England that Pakistan faced elimination unless they won every subsequent match. Disappointed fans back in Pakistan did not break TV sets or burn effigies. Of late, Pakistan has only rarely defeated India and, realistically, few expected Pakistan to win the match. But the manner of the defeat—the one-sidedness of it—left even the staunchest fans shaken. In fact, there was disappointment throughout the cricketing community, as neutral observers and even Indian supporters mourned how one of cricket's greatest rivalries was now almost irrelevant.

Exactly two weeks later, on 18 June 2017, Pakistan stood as champions, having comprehensively defeated India in the final—out-bowling, out-batting, and out-fielding the favourites. En route, they had beaten the

1

number-one ranked South Africa, Sri Lanka, home-favourites England, and then the tournament favourites, India. It was a turnaround of gargantuan proportions and one that only Pakistan could have achieved. Cricket lovers immediately cast their minds back twenty-five years when a similar scenario emerged during the 1992 World Cup in Australia. Then, Pakistan had also almost been eliminated, being saved only by the weather and an abandoned match. Following that, every subsequent game they played was a knockout. At the conclusion of the tournament, Pakistan had won the World Cup, defeating England in Melbourne.

Even in the recently concluded World Cup of 2019, Pakistan had suffered one of the heaviest possible defeats in their opening match and followed up with a further defeat in the subsequent match. As every match became a knockout, Pakistan won their subsequent matches but, on this occasion, failed to qualify for the semi-finals by a whisker. En route, however, they did defeat both the teams that ultimately met in the final. Since officially becoming part of the cricketing fraternity in 1952, Pakistan has taken on the reputation of a team so mercurial that it redefines the meaning of an unpredictable nature. One is reminded of Henry Wadsworth Longfellow's famous poem about the little girl who had a curl in the middle of her forehead: 'When she was good / She was very, very good, / And when she was bad she was horrid.'

To understand the nature of cricket in Pakistan, it is essential to trace its roots, its early influences, and the forces that subsequently moulded it. From this foundation I explain how cricket in Pakistan has taken on the particular national characteristic so vividly highlighted above. This will take into account the social, economic, and political factors that have influenced it, for over the years specific cricketing cultures have developed in all cricket-playing nations, partly through the way they played their cricket and partly through a view that what's bred in the bone comes out in the flesh. In other words, cricket reflects a nation's cultural heritage and character: its history, its personality, its culture, its social make up, its insecurities, its politics, and its religious commitment. This chapter looks at the different influences that have shaped Pakistan cricket, concluding with an analysis of the reasons for Pakistan's 'mercurial' nature.

THE DIFFUSION OF CRICKET TO THE SUBCONTINENT

Diffusion, in contrast to innovation, is an external type of change. It occurs when an idea is transferred from one cultural context to another. It is also far more common than innovation, for if we all depended on our own innovations rather than borrowing the traits of others, our progress, built as it is on our cumulative knowledge, would be much slower. But not all traits diffuse from one culture to another—some are rejected immediately while others die a slower death. Some are enthusiastically accepted and subsequently prosper. Cricket, as Kaufman and Patterson point out,[1] is a classic example—accepted in some colonies (India, West Indies), rejected in others (Canada, USA), and famously syncretized in yet others (Trobriand Cricket[2]). How the game was taken up and how it spread in the Subcontinent tells us much about its initial character and how that changed as it diffused to a wider population.

Beyond British shores, the game spread through hegemonic colonialism. Throughout the late 19th and early 20th centuries, this quintessential English sport was spread across the empire to act as an 'innocuous outlet for mass frustrations, while facilitating the transmission of values like respect for authority, especially that of Whites, deferred gratification, and team spirit; the inculcation of norms such as unquestioned acceptance of the decisions of authority figures in particular Whites' (this was embodied in the term, 'it's not cricket').[3]

The British thus took the game wherever they went, playing amongst themselves, before allowing the 'natives' to join in, initially in a limited capacity. It arrived in Australia almost as soon as colonization began in 1788. It was introduced to the West Indies and India in the first half of the 18th century. New Zealand and South Africa followed in the early years of the 19th century. Cricket had even travelled to North America via the English colonies very early in the 17th century and was in fact popular until the 19th century when interest waned rapidly.[4]

The relationship between national identity and an important and originally imported cultural activity in countries that were once territories within the British Empire saw each of these colonies develop their own specific cricketing cultures. Australia, for example, lacked the rigid class divisions that marked the 'players' and 'gentlemen'[5] in England, and played the game without the elite infused honour code of the home country. Cricket also represented for a nascent Australian nation the first opportunity to match itself against the mother country. Others followed suit against their former imperial masters. In the West Indies, cricket was well established by the early 1800s. Initially, it was played exclusively by the colonizers, often by military men garrisoned there to thwart black uprisings on land and French incursions by sea.[6]

Within 30 years elite clubs had been founded where private games were played and watched by the plantation owners and growing number of white middle class administrators, lawyers, merchants and accountants, where influence was now superseding that of the old families as the price of sugar fell. All these men shared a common goal—the preservation of a colonial, hierarchical, capitalist society—and so West Indies cricket was born into the tradition of white authority—British authority. Cricket was a social tool to sustain the empire.[7]

The spread of cricket in the West Indies beyond the white elite occurred gradually. Lister explains how, like other aspects of colonial life, cricket required ancillary labour.[8] Grounds needed to be maintained, pitches needed to be prepared, and balls struck needed to be retrieved from the neighbouring cane fields. This was black man's work—and in the first decades of the 19th century such menial tasks were the initial black connection to West Indies cricket. But by the early 1900s the West Indies team already had two black players, making it racially integrated well before baseball teams in the United States were.[9] In the West Indies, the struggle was not so much integration as much as who would lead the team. It would take until 1959 before a black man captained the West Indies—126 years after abolition of slavery in the British Empire.[10]

In the West Indies, the sport was initially controlled by whites—and while the early history of cricket in the West Indies is primarily a history of white and middle class players and white organizations, blacks soon embraced the game. Emancipation from slavery democratized the game in the West Indies. In contrast to the West Indies, India and Pakistan—two other British colonies where cricket took root—had captains of colour when they began their international journey: Cottari Kanakaiya 'C.K.' Nayudu in India and Abdul Hafeez Kardar for Pakistan. The attitudes of the colonizers towards the co-opted elite in the Subcontinent were significantly different to their attitudes towards slaves in the West Indies.

However, it is significant that prior to Partition, India's first captain for the tour to England was to be either the Maharaja of Patiala or the Maharaja of Vizianagaram. Both had patronized cricket in India and now expected to be rewarded through captaincy. Ultimately, however, both withdrew from the tour on grounds of health. The Maharaja of Porbandar Natwarsinhji Bhavsinhji was made captain and Prince Ghanshyamsinhji Limbdi (aka K.S. Limbdi) vice-captain. Once in England, both newly appointed captain and vice-captain stepped down in favour of India's most accomplished cricketer of the time—C.K. Nayudu.[11] However, it was clear that the colonial authorities wanted aristocracy at the helm of affairs in cricket as well as elsewhere in the Subcontinent. Moreover, the princes having supported cricket during its embryonic period expected to be rewarded with opportunities for greater interaction with the colonial masters. None of the Maharajas—Patiala, Vizianagaram, or Porbandar—were known for their cricketing skill. The Maharaja of Vizianagaram would subsequently replace Nayudu on India's second tour to England and a third tour saw the Nawab of Pataudi Iftikhar Ali Khan become captain in 1946. It was not until independence was achieved and Lala Amarnath would become captain that the crown slipped away from the aristocracy. For Pakistan of course, captaincy only came post-independence and even then it was the Oxford educated Abdul Hafeez Kardar who led the team. Local elite social groups in India and Pakistan were often drawn into the cultural hegemony of the British and attempts to maintain this hegemony survived in the form of attempts to ensure that the leadership of the team remained in the hands of these local elites.

The appointment of a black captain and independence for Islands in the Caribbean further increased the central role of black players in West Indies cricket. Cricket bound together the islands and territories scattered over thousands of miles of sea. Cricket became a symbol of unity and power, particularly in the 1970s. For India and Pakistan, captaincy was a more seamless process despite the early Indian experience. Both examples also highlight how colonial attitudes towards 'natives' in the West Indies and India were a reflection of the indigenous historical and political contexts.

THE SPREAD OF CRICKET IN PAKISTAN

As in the West Indies, the game came to the Subcontinent along with colonial rule, spread via soldiers and sailors. The first Indians to take to the game were the Parsis of Bombay. Descended from Persian Zoroastrians, the Parsis—so often the bridge between colonials and the natives—were a small, educated, prosperous, and Westernized community which took enthusiastically to the game. Kidambi points out that the passion for cricket among the Parsis was part of a significant transformation within the community in the late 19th century.[12] At the heart of this transition was a distinctive project of self-fashioning on the part of the Parsi community, particularly in Bombay, that saw them express their 'Britishness' in a range of everyday practices.[13] Similarly, the Parsis had also been the pioneers of South Asian theatre and cinema. Guha reports that at least thirty Parsi clubs were formed in the 1850s and 1860s.[14] The Hindus started playing cricket 'in a spirit of competitive communalism, for in Bombay they had long standing social and business rivalry with the Parsis'[15] and by 1866 'Bombay Union,' the first Hindu club, was established. Muslim suspicions over British influences, most notably highlighted in their refusal to adopt Western education,[16] meant that it would take another twenty years for a Muslim cricket club to be established in 1883.

This spread of cricket from the British to the wider Indian society comprising ethno-religious communities was, according to Kaufman and Patterson, the reason for its subsequent popularity and later mass appeal.[17] They identify three mechanisms for the success of cricket in the Subcontinent. Firstly, the colonial elites encouraged their indigenous elite subjects to play the game as a way of 'civilizing the native' in their own image and strengthening the empire. As Appadurai states: 'On the whole, from about 1870 to 1930, in the high period of the Raj, there is no doubt that for Indians to play cricket was to experiment with the mysteries of the English upper class life.'[18] Secondly, the indigenous elites who took on the game and patronized it, emulated their colonial masters by also gradually involving their own upper-middle and lower middle rungs of society in the game. The very rigid social hierarchy in the Subcontinent, according to Kaufman and Patterson, helped in popularizing the game amongst the locals. This stands in contrast to the social environment in Canada and the United States where the vision of a more egalitarian society saw the elite separate themselves (and cricket) from the wider society. Finally, the rigidity of the social system in the Subcontinent with opportunities for upward mobility so constrained meant that cricket 'provided those of the lower castes some means of symbolic competence—that is, by competing against those of other castes, races, and classes, low caste cricketers could assert themselves in ways not permitted in ordinary society.'[19]

Initial matches against the 'Europeans'—as they were known—were so one sided that they were billed 'Natives with Bats versus Officers with Umbrellas.'[20] But by 1912 a quadrangular involving Europeans, Hindus, Parsis, and Muslims had been established and crowds upward of tens of thousands would congregate to support their teams in Bombay. In 1937, a fifth team amalgamating the myriad other communities in the Subcontinent was added under the rubric 'The Rest' to put in place the 'Pentangular.' The tournament ran until 1946 and played an important role in the early development of cricket in the Subcontinent.[21] Guha talks of deserted streets during the Pentangular, tickets selling in black with every inch of space being occupied in the stadium. There was a 'frenzy of activity'[22] as the city came to a standstill. Success spawned further success as similar tournaments sprung up in Karachi in 1916, in Delhi in 1937, and in Lahore where the large Sikh population saw them field a team against Hindus and Muslims.[23]

The fact that the Parsi community had taken to cricket so enthusiastically also meant that Karachi, like Bombay which is another port city with a sizeable Parsi community, had a well-established cricketing setup leading up to Partition. The quadrangular tournament in Karachi involving Hindus, Muslims, Parsis, and Europeans was particularly well organized producing both players and administrators. Moreover, the presence of wealthy Parsi, Hindu, and Bohra merchants also meant that there was ample patronage for the game in the city. Lahore, in contrast, while an important centre for cricket in Northern India, saw its importance grow more significantly post-Partition. The early importance of Lahore and Karachi prior to 1947 meant that after Partition cricket was initially confined in its outreach. As pointed out, in the immediate post-Partition period there was little opportunity for dissemination of cricket in Pakistan:

> The game was largely the preserve of the wealthy elite, belonging to the network of college alumni steeped in the traditions of British education, language, and culture. Cricket in the 1950s has been described as a 'social outing' for the college and university alumni of both Lahore and Karachi, who often attended matches 'to be seen' and to mix with each other. Few players from lower—to lower—middle class backgrounds had the opportunity to play first class cricket, and the sport only had limited popular following.[24]

In its formative years in Pakistan, cricket was almost exclusively a middle class sport. Even in the major urban centres of Lahore and Karachi, cricket was played by the middle classes and had not spread to the urban poor. It was unknown amongst the rural peasantry, nor (with a handful of exceptions) was it taken up by the aristocracy and the landowning class. In fact, unlike the original game whose roots are found in rural England, the South Asian variant was initially a firmly urban phenomenon. Part of this also reflects the early importance of schools, universities, and clubs in the absence of a first class setup for cricket which was not established until 1953—a year after Pakistan played its first official international match. In fact, Lahore's growing importance as a centre for cricket was built upon the contribution of two publicly funded universities in particular: Government College and Islamia College—and, to a lesser extent, Aitchison College.

> Lahore had a vigorous collegiate system, modelled on the educational institutions of Britain. Three of its colleges, Aitchison, Government and Islamia, promoted the disciplinarian approach to cricket and other sports inherited from British muscular Christian educators.[25]

The rivalry between Government and Islamia was instrumental in moulding some of the greatest players of the early years of Pakistan cricket. Lahore's open spaces and parks—especially the areas of Minto and Zaman Parks—were also more conducive to the growth of clubs in the city and both club cricket and the collegiate variety would attract intense rivalries and large crowds. When Pakistan won its first Test Match against England in 1954, ten of the eighteen players in the squad were from either Government College or Islamia College.[26] Karachi, in contrast, with an absence of grounds and a massive influx of refugees from India, struggled to maintain its early cricketing ascendancy. Regardless, Karachi fell back on a highly competitive school tournament, a legacy from its pre-Partition days. Samiuddin quotes the Pakistani cricket journalist Qamar Ahmed as saying: 'When Pakistan went to India on their first tour and won a Test Match so soon, it was because of the breeding ground of schools, universities and clubs.'[27]

THE FIRST EXPANSION

The nascent domestic system that had been in place since 1953 saw a significant change in late 1958. This modification had a significant impact on initiating the spread of the game beyond the middle-class pool of the urban centres of Lahore and Karachi. The impetus though, was political. At Partition, the Eastern wing of Pakistan was not only more populous than the Western wing; it was also more linguistically and culturally homogenous. In order to 'safeguard the centre from a populist Bengali challenge,'[28] Operation One Unit was enforced in October 1955, leading to the amalgamation of the four diverse provinces of West Pakistan into one unit. Now West Pakistan would be one, not four, disparities, to counter one East Pakistan.

In cricketing terms, the dissolution of the provinces saw cities and divisions stepping in so that by the early 1960s teams from smaller centres such as Hyderabad, Sargodha, Multan, Khairpur, Peshawar, and Quetta were playing first class cricket. The structural change would not have an immediate effect as the smaller centres struggled to catch up with the established cricketing nurseries of Lahore and Karachi. For the next two decades, the middle classes from Lahore and Karachi continued to dominate the national team and in as late as the 1976–77 tour of Australia and the West Indies, the Pakistan squad of nineteen was made up of eleven players from Karachi and eight players from Lahore.

Of Pakistan's 79 Test Cricketers until the start of the series against India (in 1978), 38 were born either in Lahore or Karachi (27 in Lahore, 11 in Karachi). Another 30 of the 79 were born in Pre-Partition India but moved to either of the two cities so that together the two produced 80% of the country's Test cricketers till then.[29]

But the decentralization that began with the One Unit policy meant that the seeds had been planted more widely and by the 1980s they began to produce a much more diverse pool of players.

However, political changes were not the only factor driving the spread of the game. By the late 1970s, the cricket team itself was beginning to meet with substantial success and several players achieved international repute. There were significant series-levelling victories against Australia in 1976–77 and then a watershed defeat of arch-rivals India in 1978–79. Pakistan reached the semi-finals of the Cricket World Cup in 1979, 1983, and 1987, before defeating England in the final of the 1992 competition.

Significantly, both the 1977 win in Australia and the subsequent series win against India in 1978–79 were relayed live on Pakistan Television (PTV). The initial popularization of cricket via the media had in fact come primarily through radio coverage. Newspaper circulation was limited and, in a country that at the time had a literacy rate of 15 per cent, the reach of the print media was severely reduced. But from the mid-1950s, the spread of cheap transistor radios and radio broadcasts to both urban and rural markets was a significant step forward. And for Radio Pakistan, cricket was on the agenda early as it was seen as an instrument both of entertainment and nation building. Interestingly, the perception of cricket being an 'elite' sport saw live TV and radio commentary confined to English with only short summaries in Urdu. Despite this, the familiarity of the population with cricket did increase as more and more people became acquainted with the sport and its vocabulary. Urdu commentary, in fact, did not come to share the stage until 1978 when General Ziaul Haq, recognizing the populist appeal of the decision, insisted that 30 minutes of English commentary be followed by 30 minutes of Urdu.[30]

It was, however, the advent of television—a medium that did not require proficiency in English or Urdu—that opened the floodgates and audiences 'began to identify with the nation's players irrespective of their ethnic and political affiliations.'[31] Pakistan Television (PTV) began cricket broadcasting in the late 1960s and its initial attempts were limited and cautious. This was transformed in the 1970s under the vision of two brothers, Akhtar and Athar Viqar Azeem who joined PTV and revolutionized cricket coverage at a time when the team itself was becoming increasingly popular as well.[32] From Australia, the live transmission in 1977 was a first ever for PTV which went on to relay the entire India series that followed. Television began to displace radio as the medium for coverage. Millions began tuning in—usually crowds of 8–10 around a single screen making it a deeply communal event.[33] Cricketers such as Imran Khan, Majid Khan, Asif Iqbal, and Zaheer Abbas became superstars and money poured into the game. By 1986, a TV audience of one billion saw Javed Miandad hit a last ball six to defeat India in Sharjah.[34]

Venues for watching live international cricket also expanded. During the 1978–79 tour by India, a first test match was played in the industrial hub of Faisalabad. In the same year a formidable West Indies team, world champions at the time and brimming with superstars, toured Pakistan and played in the cricketing outposts of Sukkur, Sahiwal, and Bahawalpur. By 1987, Pakistan co-hosted a World Cup with India with matches being played throughout Pakistan including in Hyderabad, Gujranwala, and Peshawar. Domestic matches were played at new venues in Multan, Sialkot, and Sargodha. The game was spreading beyond the major cities and within a decade, players began to emerge from these new grassroots.

The popularization of cricket was clearly stimulated by the success of the national team and the developments in media and communication that coincided with that success. The rural and lower-class urban communities, previously lacking exposure to the game, grew more in touch with cricket rules and customs once networks of communication expanded to include them. Radio and television broadcasts of cricket into traditional community and market spaces were crucial factors behind the game's dissemination.[35] Cricket spread to areas in which it had never previously existed, where it discovered the ability to attract and unify people of all classes, ethnicities, and religions.

In England, cricket's popularity narrowed, particularly after the Second World War, as the working class turned increasingly to football. Cricket was displaced as the dominant national sport, receding in the national consciousness and losing recognition among the masses, its appeal concentrating in a narrow middle-class base. In contrast, and as elsewhere on the Subcontinent, the three decades since 1980 witnessed an incredible expansion in the game, both socially and geographically.[36] Suddenly the game was followed with a fervour and zeal that is commonly associated with the way Brazilians follow their football. Such was the level of cricket's adoption in the Subcontinent that it prompted Ashis Nandy to call cricket 'an Indian game that was accidentally discovered by the British.'[37]

The cricketers of the 1970s were a transformative generation bringing about the success that the growth in the media and the geographical spread of the game was able to capitalize on. They were also products of specific political and social factors of that time period which need to be taken account of if we are to understand the nature of the cricket team and the way they played the sport.

THE CULTURALLY LIBERAL 1960S AND 1970S

The 1960s and 1970s were socially and culturally 'liberal' decades. During this period, Pakistani cinema, for example, developed an urban focussed and modern narrative which continued to flourish into the 1970s when cinema reached its most prolific period. Under a liberal censor regime during the Ayub Khan years (1958–1969), Pakistan made some of its most avantgarde films. Under Zulfikar Ali Bhutto's first ever elected civilian government, the censors were still more generous and, by 1974, Pakistan was making more than 100 films annually. Folk culture, poetry, singers, intellectuals, and music were celebrated, and a more pluralistic vision of Islam was emphasized.

Pakistan was an open and welcoming destination, attracting tourists and other distinguished Western celebrities including Dizzy Gillespie (1956), Che Guevara (1959), Queen Elizabeth (1961), Jackie Kennedy (1962), and Buzz Aldrin and Neil Armstrong (1970). The country even became an intermediate destination on the 'Hippie Trail' that stretched from Turkey, through Iran, Afghanistan, Pakistan, and into India. In Pakistan, the Sufi shrines were a popular destination for the traveling hippies as well as for middle class Pakistani youth who had begun to frequent them as well.[38]

Tourism boomed with Karachi airport becoming amongst the busiest in the region. Alcohol was widely available in urban centres and Karachi's nightclubs openly advertised their latest 'Dinner, Dance and Cabaret' promotions. Advertisements for Pakistan International Airlines (PIA) and various tobacco companies often highlighted women as independent and self-assured. Posters of glamorous film stars adorned the streets of Lahore. Pakistan was a youthful, confident, and optimistic nation. This middle-class, urban youth-driven liberal culture continued into the 1970s.

By the early 1970s, young men's hair that had remained somewhat short till even the late 1960s, started to grow longer (along with thick side burns); and women's kameez (shirts), grew shorter in length—all inspired by Hollywood films of the time, and Pakistani film artistes such as Waheed Murad and Shabnam; and also by some famous Indian film stars (particularly Rajesh Khanna and Mumtaz) whose films young Pakistanis watched by driving into Kabul (from North Pakistan).[39]

By the time it became an international force in the 1970s, the cricket team was dominated by glamorous and charismatic characters, many of whom spent their summers playing in England where they were introduced to a Westernized lifestyle which several took a particular liking to. Stories of late nights, nightclubs, and alcohol regularly made the rounds and yet aided by the success of the team, these reports simply added to the allure of the players. More lowkey members became greatly respected players for their English county teams. Pakistani cricketers were very much part of an international community of players and they regarded themselves as part of a professional international cadre. Heller and Oborne note:

> It is worth adding that by joining English county cricket, Pakistan's cricketers became part of a very strong community with a distinctive social life. They were never expected to violate their religious principles, but they were expected to 'do their turn' at the bar, and to accept drinkers, gamblers and womanisers as friends and colleagues.[40]

Unsurprisingly, at this point, the cricket team reflected the time—made up of young men from the major metropolitan centres of Lahore and Karachi, they exuded an educated, urbane, and glamorous vibe on and off the field. It is therefore unsurprising that, for example, a celebratory photograph taken in 1976 shows a relaxed captain, Mushtaq Mohammad, enjoying a beer after winning a match in Karachi. Another series of photographs taken during the 1977 tour to the West Indies shows three Pakistani cricketers in cowboy hats at a karaoke session. The headline, 'Check de Pakistani Face-Man Dem'; and below, the colourful photographs with the question, 'Are these movie stars? No ... they are touring Pakistani cricketers.' Yet another has players dancing at a nightclub after a famous victory in the same series in 1977. This scenario would soon be unthinkable. But in the 1970s, Pakistan had a team of superstars whose global reach through their involvement in the English county circuit and the breakaway Australian World Series league only increased their status. In fact, at this point it was Pakistan and not India that had the 'global' cricketers. Fewer Indians played county cricket in England and none joined the World Series Cricket league.

This batch of cricketers was the first to fully represent this new country. Its predecessors were largely products of pre-Partition India. It was these superstars from the 1970s who were transformative in the way they changed the nature of Pakistan cricket. Up until the late 1970s, South Asian teams had tended to avoid friction and confrontation with opponents, particularly England and Australia. Avoiding defeat was considered the achievement to be aspired to. Many of the cricketers of the 1950s and 1960s had been passive and were treated with disdain by their opponents. However, the cricketers of the 1970s were a different breed. More regular international cricket, playing in the English county league, and being part of the breakaway Australian World Series Cricket league had given them international exposure and broken the sense of inferiority that stalked previous players. Driven by a group of liberated, strong-minded senior players, the Pakistan team was cocky and confident, willing to give as much as they got on the field.

This demand for equality irked the traditional powers in the game, particularly England and Australia, who found it difficult to accept that they were being challenged by a team of upstarts. These traits—aggressive, cocky, swaggering, and brash—would characterize Pakistan cricket for decades to come and would set them apart from their South Asian counterparts of the time. Like the cricketers, Pakistan at this time was a confident, youthful, hopeful, and energetic country. It would remain so even though earlier changes (geographical spread of cricket) began to have an impact alongside current major social and political upheavals. The cumulative effect would bring a transformation in the nature of the team and the way they played cricket.

Socio-Political Transformation in Zia's Tenure

In July 1977, General Muhammad Ziaul Haq toppled the democratically-elected Prime Minister Zulfikar Ali Bhutto and immediately initiated a process of sweeping Islamization which drastically changed the cultural and political identities of the society. Committed to enforcing his interpretation of the 'Nizam-i-Mustafa' or 'Rule of the Prophet,' Zia introduced several draconian laws in the name of religion, Islamizing an increasing number of social and governmental aspects of Pakistani life.

Nearly 12,000 madrasas were created, many of which were militarized and which bequeathed a jihadist legacy.[41] The legal system and the penal code were amended and school curriculums and textbooks were reviewed and overhauled to remove 'un-Islamic' material. Offices, schools, and factories were required to offer praying space and an ordinance was issued banning eating, smoking, and drinking in public places during Ramadan.

Women suffered in particular. Co-education schools and colleges were forced to adopt a policy of gender segregation. Sportswomen were not allowed to participate in international events and women were banned from appearing in television commercials unless the advertised product was for domestic use (detergents, sewing machines, etc.). All women who appeared on television and other media had to wear the national high-collared dress, and a *dupatta* (scarf) or *chadar* (shawl) over their heads.[42] By 1979, the national television network ceased playing any music other than patriotic songs. In the same year, apparently offended by the 'immorality' on view in films, Zia passed an ordinance that cancelled the censor certificates of all films made prior to the imposition of martial law. Under Zia's rule, all entertainment, particularly Indian entertainment, was labelled as *fohsh*, or vulgar. Classical Indian music and dance were banned, and colleges were instructed to shut down their music societies.

Zia's Islamization sought to create an identity that stood in contrast to that of India and a major effort was made to distance Pakistani culture from the ancient South Asian influences of the more distant past. The result was an artificial split between Indian and Pakistani cultures. This was in stark contrast to Bhutto's regime which had stressed on common indigenous South Asian roots. As a result, by the time Zia was killed in an air crash in 1988, Pakistani society stood considerably changed to what it was prior to 1977.

Following Ziaul Haq's death, Pakistan witnessed a transition of power from a military dictatorship to a democratic system. Yet, during the 'decade of democracy' in the 1990s, none of the democratic regimes showed the strategic vision and acumen that were required to effectively challenge Zia's policies. The policies of Islamization remained. Religious radicals were given a free hand in establishing madrasas, securing funding from abroad, proselytizing, and agitating against secular forces—all of this without any serious interference by state authorities; in fact, in many cases, with the willing participation or support of various parts of the bureaucracy. As Lall points out, the Islamization process radicalized Pakistani society between 1977 and 1988 and was never reversed.[43] Democracy, then, did not reverse Zia's 'doleful' legacy.[44]

The seeds planted from the late 1970s onwards had an enormous impact on society from the mid-1990s onwards, as 'Zia's children'—those born during Zia's Islamization years—grew up. Society had shifted towards conservatism and even religious radicalism when the extremist and sectarian outfits that the state had constructed in the 1980s (for the 'Afghan Jihad') became active within Pakistan, triggering a brutal sectarian war in the Punjab. The gender discrimination in the Hudood Ordinance remained largely unchallenged and the persecution of Ahmadi and Christian minorities besmirched Pakistan's international reputation. Various old and new Islamic evangelist organizations began to assert themselves, concentrating on bagging clients and enthusiasts from the country's urban middle and lower middle classes. The social and political changes occurring from the late 1970s onwards combined with the spread of the game due to the team's success, the geographical spread of the game to smaller centres, and the amplifying effect of the media—all had a significant impact on the nature of the cricket team.

IMPACT OF THE SOCIO-POLITICAL CHANGES ON THE TEAM

The personality of the team changed as it became more representative of the nation. Economic and demographic changes were seeing cricket ease out of the grasp of the middle classes. University cricket began to decline and graduates increasingly took up positions in the commercial sector to be replaced in the cricket team by individuals with relatively less formal education. School cricket also weakened as population pressure and a push to prepare students for professional services led to more and more school grounds being built over by classrooms and sport being increasingly marginalized. Clubs began to recruit from a new pool of urban youth and the rural poor. Many of these individuals were also brought up in a time when society had moved to a more conservative environment, initiated under Zia and continued in the democratic decade that followed. For these individuals, religion had a more central position in their lives as compared to the cricketers of the 1970s. Moreover, born and brought up in a time when Islamization was being instituted, religious metaphors and language came much more naturally to the new generation. During a particularly evident period the strength of Islamic evangelism reached deep into the team itself before evaporating in that particular manifestation (see Chapter 3).

This new generation of cricketers played the game with a captivating and intuitive talent. Many of these players came not from Lahore and Karachi but from the smaller centres in Punjab—Mushtaq Ahmed was from Sahiwal, Inzamam-ul-Haq from Multan, Shoaib Malik from Sialkot, Aaqib Javed from Sheikhupura, and Waqar Younis from Burewala. Several were from poor backgrounds—Yousuf Youhana was the son of a sweeper, Shoaib Akhtar's father was a night watchman, and Mushtaq Ahmed's father was a daily wage labourer.

When I interviewed Mushtaq Ahmed, he was interacting with a group of school children who had come for a visit to the National Cricket Academy (NCA). 'Mushy' was no longer a player but was the head of the NCA. Today he lives in a plush area of Lahore and was an important part of the winning World Cup team of 1992. He represented Pakistan for many years, was implicated in the match-fixing report, played with great success in the English county system, and then took on a variety of coaching roles for Pakistan. Mushtaq also epitomized the rise of the new type of cricketer. Born in Sahiwal, but having played county cricket in England for over a decade, he now speaks English with a British Asian accent:

> My father would earn Rs. 100 a day and would often skip dinner so that his eight children—four sons and four daughters—would have more to eat. We had a few buffaloes which I would tend to but often I would avoid this work as well as school so that I could watch cricket on TV or practice being my favourite cricketers. I batted with the swagger of the great West Indian Viv Richards. I mastered the bowling action of Abdul Qadir. When I was selected to play for Pakistan I had never travelled in an airplane. I didn't even know how to operate the lift in the hotel the players were staying at and kept going up and down!

As this brand-new cricketing passion spread through the wider masses driven by television, a successful team, and an extraordinarily charismatic leader in Imran Khan, the most significant change occurred in the previously resistant North-West Frontier Province (renamed Khyber Pakhtunkhwa in 2010). The tribal people had refused to play cricket before independence because they associated the sport with a brutal, foreign occupation. This hostility vanished after 1980.

Initially, Pakistan saw the emergence of cricketing stars of Pashtun heritage[45] and then of players from the region itself. Of these players, Imran Khan, who has often emphasized his Pashtun roots, was one of Pakistan's greatest cricketers; Shahid Afridi arguably the most popular for his explosive batting; and Younis Khan Pakistan's highest run getter. Thus, in an area which since the invasion of Afghanistan in 2001 has been devastated by drones and the Taliban, cricket has gone from strength to strength. Even amidst the lack of a cricketing structure the region has increasingly produced talented players. The fact that many were willing to endure any hardship to play the game of cricket has led them to being resilient and hardened cricketers. Today cricketers are emerging from the Federally Administered Tribal Areas (FATA) including from the notorious Waziristan region, once completely under the control of the Taliban until the army conducted a clean-up operation in 2012. A FATA team which covers ten districts including South and North Waziristan has been playing first class cricket since 2015–16.

The Taliban, driven by a puritanical hostility to sports and games, particularly games with connections to colonial powers, had initially attempted to crush the sport: 'His [Maulana Fazlullah] fighters came to the village of Null and said: "Stop this nonsense. It's a waste of time to do these sports. Pick up your gun".'[46] But cricket would not be suppressed and as soon as the Taliban were driven out of the valley, cricket flourished. Oborne adds that outside of the Swat valley there was less hostility from the Taliban towards cricket and many actually enjoyed the game.

It appears that the local Taliban were won over by the game as it gained more and more adherents in the Frontier province including in the Afghan refugee camps in and around Peshawar. They had banned the game in 1996 but lifted the ban by 2000. It is here that the seeds of Afghan cricket were first laid and which have now produced the most exciting newcomer to international cricket. Many of Afghanistan's current national cricketers learnt their cricket in Pakistan before taking it back to their homeland. Even within Afghanistan, the Taliban were persuaded to change their stance on cricket. Wagg writes that by 2001, the Taliban permitted the playing of cricket and even paid for the Afghan team's equipment during their tour to Pakistan the same year.[47] The tour was apparently an attempt, at the behest of the Pakistan government, to soften the Taliban's reactionary image and portray a more forward-looking, modern viewpoint which would promote the regime at home and provide some acceptance abroad.[48] Cricket, according to Rumford, became the Taliban's gateway to creating a space within a global culture, a rarely acknowledged attempt at embracing global modernity.[49] Today cricket is played with a unique fervour throughout Khyber Pakhtunkhwa and FATA—in rural villages, obscure towns, remote valleys, and over the border into Afghanistan.

> It is played on riverbanks, on mountain plateaux, in graveyards, on barren earth—basically anywhere with a flat surface. It is played with rough-hewn planks, with wooden balls, with tennis balls, with compressed melted footballs, with anything that can bounce.[50]

Clearly, this newer generation of cricketers learnt their cricket in a very different environment to the schools and universities of earlier generations. Most of the newer cricketers practiced on dusty *maidans* (open spaces) or in under-funded state schools. They learnt the game by copying the heroes they saw on television rather than through coaching at school or university. The success of the team, and the fact that it was increasingly beamed across Pakistan on television, meant that there was a burgeoning enthusiasm for the game, and a very large and youthful population of talented individuals were always likely to be thrown up. These individuals played the game with a natural flair and intuitiveness which brought a fearlessness to their game. The fact that few of the players had received any early coaching meant that their untamed talent would remain explosive and unpredictable; this lesser dependence on preparation and meticulousness meant a reliance on instinct rather than forethought and planning. The consistency that could have complemented their natural talent would need greater coaching and structure than cricket in the *maidan* could provide.

The changing demographic did, though, lead to an increased insularity as these individuals lacked the social and language skills to build up a rapport with players from opposing teams. Therefore, in stark contrast to their colleagues of the 1970s and 1980s, the players of the 1990s and 2000s were more isolated from the international cricketing community. Not only did they not play much county cricket in England, they were also barred from the cash rich Indian Premier League which drew cricketing stars from all nations except Pakistan (see Chapters 5 and 6).

There was another innovation during the early 1980s that had a major impact on the nature of Pakistani cricket. Tape-ball cricket has played a crucial role in moulding the character of generations of Pakistani cricketers from the 1980s onwards. Yet its influence on cricket in Pakistan has rarely been recognized.

For two decades after Partition, cricket was played in clubs, schools, and universities. This was formal, organized cricket, with proper equipment and grounds. But from the 1970s, Pakistan and its cities saw an explosive urban growth and Karachi in particular expanded rapidly. As Pakistan's urban population increased, driven by rural–urban migration and natural increases, space began to run short. Schools built additional classrooms over their sports grounds and public grounds became scarcer. This led to a decline in club and school cricket and, in conjunction with the expensiveness of cricket equipment, necessity became the mother of invention. In Karachi it was new residential areas, including for example the middle-class locality of Nazimabad, that had vast empty spaces and wide, sparsely populated avenues which became cricketing venues. It is rumoured[51] that it was in Nazimabad that electrical tape was first stretched across a tennis ball, allowing fast bowlers to propel the ball at high speed without getting loopy 'tennis ball' bounce. As the tape frayed, the ball mimicked swing. Spinners dispensed with flight and began producing the *doosra* (or the mystery ball). It produced some of Pakistan's most legendary fast bowlers: Wasim Akram, Waqar Younis, Shoaib Akhtar, and Mohammad Amir. Actions and techniques changed as tape-ball players emerged onto the 'conventional' cricket scene. The bowlers flourished, even though it also led to the proliferation of illegal bowling actions. Batsmen emerged less often. Matches were played at a frenetic pace, typically 4–15 overs in duration, with 20 runs per over being achievable—and this rarely prepared the batsmen for 'occupation of the crease.'

According to Hussain, the emergence of tape-ball cricket was given further impetus by the broadcasting of day–night cricket from Australia, in 1979, by PTV.[52] Inspired by the massive lights that international cricketers played under in Adelaide, Sydney, and Melbourne, Karachi began using street lights and coloured clothing to start their own version of night cricket. A typical street game might be played in a narrow lane, not more than 15 feet wide, with houses on both sides. If you are lucky, there will be a vacant plot on one side. Lighting for night matches is provided by 1000-watt hanger-lights: yellow tubes that are hung overhead (and one of the players almost always has to be a makeshift electrician). Often, there is only enough light to cover the pitch, the bowler ghosting in from the darkness into the batsman's view. Matches are four to six overs long, but usually between eight and fifteen overs in tournaments.[53] By the 1990s, tape-ball cricket, aided by the demise of both school and club cricket, had spread so wide that 'virtually every modern Pakistani Test cricketer has played tape ball before regular cricket.'[54] Pakistan's older generation may have learnt their cricket at school, but the modern ones mostly picked it up off the streets.

But while tape-ball cricket expanded the game enormously, it did so in an unfettered and unbridled manner. It was a game of high intensity, innovation, and energy—and those who played it, played it with a rare passion. The laws of the game were simplified: there was no room for the leg before wicket and umpires had a minimal role to play. Those who played this form of cricket had rarely received any formal coaching. As with their earlier *maidan* counterparts, they saw their heroes on television and tried to emulate them in their local matches.

With both—players from the *maidan* and street-based, tape-ball cricketers—the role of coaching is minimal. This contrasts with the older style of cricket where players emerged from a more structured environment, mainly through school and university where coaches would hone the talent of their pupils before they progressed to playing at the club and domestic levels. This more conventional route certainly has its advantages, one of which is a more consistent level of performance, based as it were on mentorship, drills, practice sessions, and refining techniques. Several of the Pakistani players of the 1970s not only came through the university and school coached route but also refined their skills further in England.

However, one can imagine coaching to have certain disadvantages as well. In the 1970s and 1980s, English cricket was seen as suffering from 'over-coaching.' Pakistan's flamboyance, vivacity, and haphazardness contrasted with the rigidity and the stolidity of English cricket where coaching had strangled any natural flair. This was typified by the great English opening batsman, Geoffrey Boycott, known for his practice regime, his technical correctness, his consistency as a batsman, and for being dropped from the team after scoring a painfully slow double-100 against India in 1967. Pakistan's cricketers took the opposite route, often depending on their minimally-coached, hyper-talented match winners who played a high-risk, low-percentage game which, while it produced spectacular wins, was, by definition, unpredictable. Mercurial. Waqar Younis, one of Pakistan's greatest fast bowlers, as quoted in Samiuddin, embodies the spirit perfectly:

> We've never given importance to coaching. We were never analytical or scientific. Actually, in the 1990s, we never did analyse anyone. 'He plays well here, don't put him there.' It's not how long do you bowl at him there, what kind of field, what lengths, what is the B plan, what is the C plan, after that goes wrong, what happens? We had one plan. Go out there, get a wicket. We had resources. We sensed it and said, okay, bring Waqar back. Not even the captain decided. Sometimes, I would go to the captain and say, give me two overs, let me do it. It was a kind of teamwork, within the team, but not like we'd have a plan from the beginning.[55]

But where instinctual responses failed, they were unable to fall back on a store of knowledge that might come from coaching. The result was inconsistency in performance. The lack of coaching was exacerbated by the fact that from the 1990s onwards in particular, Pakistan's cricketers often lacked even a basic education. Most developed countries have players with a basic educational background, and even developing countries have players who have completed a basic education. Sri Lanka draws its talent from a healthy, extensive school programme. India's cricketers have also been drawn from a more educated pool. In the long run, this lack of basic education is a negative factor in developing a cricketer's outlook and maturity.

For cricketers who have the benefit of consistent coaching, the advantage lies in the passing on of experience and the knowledge of just how particular situations may be dealt with. Pakistani youngsters, emerging from street or *maidan* cricket, usually receive their first genuine coaching when selected at the club or even first-class level. By that time, most are already 19 years old and set in their techniques. They have not received any coaching in the formative, 11–15 age bracket.

The nature of street and *maidan* cricket, as well as the mindset these forms engender, allows for an unfettered and exuberant type of player; but, along with the absence of coaching and, to a lesser extent, a basic level of education, this also leads to greater inconsistency, as bursts of instinctive brilliance are followed by periods of complete blankness. In fact, Heller quotes two former international cricketers—wicket keepers Rashid Latif and Moin Khan—who now run cricket academies in Karachi, on the need to introduce the basic skills of conventional cricket into the armoury of their teenage pupils who have only played tape-ball cricket, while trying to maintain the natural flair and élan of their own version of the game.[56]

Tape-ball cricket today dwarfs the amount of hard ball cricket that is played in Pakistan. But cricketers from poorer backgrounds learning their trade in the *maidan*s are given little opportunity or incentive to alter the playing skills of this informal urban and rural cricket. The risqué and flamboyant style of cricket played by the modern Pakistani cricketer is a hybrid of the 'informal' indigenous game and the formal international one, with more emphasis on the former. This is one of the reasons that the style of cricket exhibited by the Pakistan team on the international stage has been unpredictable and unconventional.

MODELS OF INCONSISTENCY

While characteristically inconsistent, the Pakistan cricket team has also been highly effective,[57] and the fact that this success has frequently been driven by the brilliantly inconsistent has prompted more players to follow this route. This has often resulted in Pakistan picking players from the wilderness, based simply on spotting their raw talent. Amongst the most famous examples include: one of Pakistan's greatest batsmen, Inzamam-ul-Haq; arguably the finest-ever left-arm fast bowler, Wasim Akram; and one of Pakistan's most explosive and popular all-rounders, Shahid Afridi. Inzamam and Wasim Akram were picked up after Javed Miandad and Imran Khan saw them at a practice session and found them to be far more talented than some of the players already in the national team. Shahid Afridi debuted at the age of 16 and in his first innings shattered the record for the fastest century in one-day cricket.

The team's success, driven by the type of players earlier mentioned, did mean a continued focus on talent and instinct, rather than coaching and method. This has been Pakistan's strength; and its weakness. But it did mean that the penchant for talent was reinforced, leading to a continuous replication of the system. Therefore, the continued emphasis on talent and the disparagement of the less flamboyant, coached player who might be less naturally talented but whose dedication in practice allows him to often surpass his more talented counterparts. Pakistan's most successful batsman— Younis Khan—is a typical example. Lacking the extravagance of his fellow Pashtun, Afridi, Younis Khan's work ethic and dedication saw him become Pakistan's leading run scorer. Similarly, Misbah-ul-Haq, Pakistan's most successful Test Match captain, put up, throughout his career, with taunts from local fans of '*tuk tuk*,' a derogatory reference to his sober and measured style of play.

This has led to a situation where talent is disproportionately valued over other aspects that together make for a successful cricketer. These would include fitness, mental strength, and the need for hours of practice. Yet, while young boys overwhelmingly want to be Shahid Afridi, few will say they want to be Misbah-ul-Haq or Younis Khan. In Pakistan, the spectacular match winner is in far greater demand than the solid, steady workhorse. The result is the continued emergence of players characterized by inconsistency—the ability to win matches with spectacular performances, but also the tendency to snatch defeat from the jaws of victory.

The late Bob Woolmer (d. 2007), who in 2004 became one of Pakistan's first foreign coaches, brought with him the newfound emphasis on modern coaching—fitness, biomechanics, mental conditioning—and these complemented the skill, talent, and passion of Pakistani cricketers. Under this regime, Pakistan gained a consistency that it had lacked in the past. It was also a period of relative stability, with few changes of captainship and management. Woolmer's first impressions of the team he was going to coach were that he had never supervised such a talented group of cricketers; but he was highly critical of the team's fitness levels. But, for Woolmer and other coaches who came after him, there was a recognition that this inconsistency would remain in place until the players and the administration themselves realized that consistent success in modern sport requires both talent and, increasingly, a commitment to structured practice sessions, fitness, and mental conditioning—areas that Pakistan has only fitfully addressed in the past and has, only recently and reluctantly, begun to institute on a more regular basis. The bureaucratization of sport using statistics galore has so far not been instituted in Pakistan.

This brings me to another important element in the unpredictable nature of Pakistani cricket, and which is alluded to earlier: Pakistan's inconsistency has always been exacerbated by the lack of stability in administration and leadership.

LEADERSHIP

Leading a team in a sport is always a key position to hold, but the captain in cricket has a particularly critical role. The length of the game—3 hours, at the least, and 5 days, at the most—means that on-field decisions are especially important, as strategy unfolds like a game of chess. A cricket captain is not only required to be a leader but must also be a man manager and be tactically adept at making bowling changes, deciding on the field, declarations, batting orders, and team selection. All this while also having to contribute as a player.

It is also true that Pakistan has historically been a difficult team to lead: rebellions against captains, tensions between Karachi and Lahore lobbies, and strong individualistic characters have seen a large number of players taking over captaincy. From the early 1950s, Pakistan's players were seen as eleven individuals unable to play as a team. In the mid-1970s, Mushtaq Mohammad became captain and his leadership revolutionized the way Pakistan approached the game. But after his removal as captain, the team disintegrated as senior players squabbled for the captaincy and it was not until the early 1980s under Imran Khan—an authoritarian, all-powerful captain who ruled on the basis of his charisma and character—that the Pakistani team played as a unit, bringing a degree of stability. As Samiuddin points out:

> Between 1995 and 1998, six different men captained Pakistan. Across 2009 and 2010, four different men captained the Test side. Sixteen different men have led Pakistan (in Tests) since Imran and Javed Miandad left. Between these sixteen, the leadership has changed a staggering twenty-six times.[58]

Imran Khan was able to groom a young team, inculcating qualities of professionalism and discipline that had been lacking in the past. However, since Imran's retirement in 1992, Pakistan has had seventeen captains—in contrast, Australia has had five, and England and India, eight.[59] Pakistan's seventeen captains also include two periods of six years at a stretch for Misbah-ul-Haq (46 Test Matches, between 2011 and 2017) and Inzamam-ul-Haq (31 Test Matches, between 2000 and 2006). But, for most of Pakistan's cricket history, captains, players, coaches, selectors, and administrators have changed repeatedly, and amidst this chaos any sense of order and consistency was lost.

Instability at the top leads to instability below, as each new regime change brings a new set of selectors, coaches, captains, and players. Stability, so that players can be identified and then given the confidence to become permanent members of the team, has been rare. The constant chopping and changing at all levels has meant that a great deal of inconsistency had been built into the system. One player that I spoke to had been dropped from the team five times in a career that had lasted only eleven matches!

Australian cricket's policies have been in stark contrast to Pakistan's. In the early 1980s, Australia went through a period of decline. Rebuilding began in 1984 when they appointed Allan Border as captain and Bob Simpson as coach. The two remained together at the helm of the Australian cricket team for an entire decade. Following Border's retirement in 1994, Mark Taylor captained for another five years, and his successors Steve Waugh and Ricky Ponting for six years and eight years, respectively. Individual players also benefited from the stability in leadership, as they found their respective niches in the team, each knowing his role intimately. It is therefore unsurprising that Australia have been the most consistently dominant team from the late 1980s onwards. In the case of Australia, a period of decline led to Australian cricket developing a plan and executing it meticulously. Structure and preparation brought consistency to their cricket.

As for Pakistan, during periods of stability—i.e. during the captaincies of Imran Khan, Inzamam-ul-Haq, and Misbah-ul-Haq—Pakistan produced more consistent results. They reached the number one Test ranking in 1988 under Imran Khan, and in 2016 under Misbah-ul-Haq. But every time an era of stability ended, it was replaced by a turbulent one where continuous change restored the conditions that bred inconsistency. Thus, instability stemmed not only from the players—their character and temperament—but also from the game's administrators who rarely promoted stability and sound leadership, and failed to implement long-term plans that would have put in place institutions and structures to strengthen Pakistani cricket.

The failure of cricket administrators is most obvious in the manner in which the domestic game in Pakistan has regressed. The importance of domestic cricket to the national team cannot be overstated as this is the arena where budding cricketers are incubated for international competition. Unfortunately, even here the seeds of inconsistency are nurtured rather than addressed. At the most basic level, even the format of domestic tournaments appears to constantly be in flux. The number of teams in the domestic game has varied from as little as 6 (in 2019) to 24 (in 2004) to 16 (in 2016 and 2017). It has been rare for the number to remain unchanged for more than a couple of years at a stretch.

In addition, most first-class teams do not have qualified staff in terms of coaches, trainers, physiotherapists, and analysts. In other cricketing countries, domestic teams have support staff that work all year round with their players and are often as competent as their international counterparts. Over the last decade, the quality of pitches and cricket balls in Pakistan has also declined, impacting the overall quality of both batsmen and bowlers. Part of this is related to Pakistan not being able to host foreign teams in Pakistan following the terrorist attack on the Sri Lankan cricket team in Lahore in 2009. This has placed an enormous financial strain on the Pakistan Cricket Board, as all international matches between 2009 and 2019 were played in the United Arab Emirates. It also meant that facilities and grounds in Pakistan have fallen into disrepair and ancillary staff is difficult to afford, thereby further weakening the domestic system.

The increasing mediocrity of the domestic game means that cricketers are unable to hone their skills at this level and are often ill-equipped to take on the challenge of international cricket. Some will survive through their talent and luck which are essential parts of any sport. But failure at the international level often leads to a return to domestic cricket where the player is meant to iron out shortcomings. However, the absence of an enabling environment usually means that remedial work is not possible as the domestic programme does not provide a competitive challenge to its players. Pakistan's famous opening batsman of the 1970s, Majid Khan, spoke to me about his experience of playing in Australia, stating that he felt that inter-state Sheffield Shield matches often had the intensity of a Test Match. Pakistan's Quaid-i-Azam matches, in contrast, hardly attract any spectators and are devoid of the challenge of competitive matches. Those trying to rectify their faults and inconsistencies then do not find the environment to make the required improvements, leading to players repeatedly making the same mistakes. At the same time, aspiring cricketers also do not have their physical or mental mettle tested. Inconsistencies remain endemic and are difficult to eradicate; as a result, players go in and out of the international team and are only rarely able to overcome their shortcomings. And when they do, it is usually through an atypical extended run at the international level.

I have spoken of the largely structural and social issues that have promoted inconsistency in Pakistani cricket. The background of aspiring cricketers in terms of their lack of coaching and their emergence into a culture that values flamboyance and exuberance over caution and structure are important factors that explain the ups and downs of Pakistani cricket. There is also an instability in the structure itself—in leadership and the composition of the team as well as in the leadership of the administration in the form of the Pakistan Cricket Board.

Having laid out the reasons for the mercurial nature of Pakistani cricket, I would nonetheless like to acknowledge that part of the unpredictable character of Pakistani cricket is, in fact, based on stereotype rather than reality. This is not to say that Pakistan is not a mercurial team; rather, the stereotype of it being unpredictable further strengthens what is already in existence.

The phrase 'that's cricket' or that 'cricket is a funny game' refers to its inherent unpredictability. Few games are as dependent on the vagaries of weather and the pitch besides the randomness of missed catches, run outs, and umpiring errors. Cricket, according to Ashis Nandy, is a game that permits anarchy, plurality, and randomness.

> It is a game of chance and skill which has to be played as if it is wholly a game of skill ... cricket is a game which is nearly impossible to predict, control and prognosticate. There are too many variables and many of the relationships among the variables are determined by chance.[60]

All countries have shown their share of inconsistency, driven by the unpredictability of the game itself. But, in the case of Pakistan, stereotypes came to define the team even when they did not apply.

Over the years, specific cricketing cultures have developed in all cricket-playing nations, partly through the way they played their cricket and partly through the Jamesian view that cricket reflects a nation's cultural heritage and character. As a result, the West Indians were 'Calypso Cricketers'—aggressive, colourful, and flamboyant. They reflected the huge talent and panache of the Caribbean people. The Australians were frank, truculent, and open-hearted, like most Australians. The English were cautious, low-key, and disciplined. India's image has changed along with its own global image. Once the epitome of the colonial gentleman—elegant, exotic, but genial—the team has changed along with India's rise as an economic powerhouse. From being a talented but almost timid team, the new generation is self-assured, aggressive, and untainted by its colonial baggage (see Chapter 6).

On the other hand, Pakistan was youthful, brash, and mercurial. Like the country itself, there was chaos and disorder as well as brilliance and exuberance. As typical of most polychronic cultures, Pakistanis may be lacking in organization and discipline but are unmatched in natural ability. However, stereotypes dominated reality. As Hall argues, *stereotyping is often employed to construct negative representations of people and groups*—such that even when the West Indies added an uncompromising professionalism to their natural flamboyance, they were still seen as carefree calypso cricketers.[61] (It must be noted that their punishing training and practice regimes, coupled with their natural ability, are what allowed them to dominate for decades, beginning in the 1970s.) Similarly, Pakistan has had periods of stability during which they were uncharacteristically consistent: under Misbah-ul-Haq they won eleven series and lost only five and, as mentioned earlier, Pakistan's overall win ratio would not have been possible without a degree of consistency. Yet, the mercurial tag would remain in place.

Despite all this, while Pakistan's mercurial nature may be a bit exaggerated, it is still a defining feature of their cricket. Attempts at trying to tame its volatile talent need to be carefully considered. The globalization and bureaucratization of sport and of cricket in particular has brought standard coaching techniques and training regimes to all countries. However, cricket would be much the poorer if teams began resembling one another, losing their indigenous and distinctive characteristics, and becoming standardized.

This chapter explains the changing nature of Pakistan cricket and in doing so it addresses the reasons for its characteristic inconsistency: from its haphazard domestic structure and frequent changes within the team, to a cricketing culture that has developed to value high-risk match winners rather than consistent performers. It is this ethos that has allowed Pakistan to produce some of the most exciting innovations in world cricket, including reverse swing and the *doosra*. In fact, the historian Richard Cashman has suggested that one of the secrets of Pakistan's success is the very anarchy of the country's cricketing structure.[62] Natural ability flourishes—and, thanks to individual patronage, quality players can be bloodied early. Pakistan has produced some of the world's most memorable cricketers. Their unpredictability produces the kind of roller coaster ride that makes for unforgettable sport, as has been demonstrated in some of Pakistan's most remarkable victories.

2

Politics, Organization, and Leadership

It is a central thesis of this book that cricket in Pakistan profoundly influences culture, politics, and society; simultaneously, cricket is in turn influenced by the wider social and political context within which it is embedded. Chapter 1 analysed the influence of these wider factors on the nature of Pakistani cricket, including the cricket team itself. This chapter looks more purposely at the appropriation of cricket by those in power for political ends. Not only does that provide us a unique insight into the political environment but it also allows an analysis of how political influences on cricket have affected its administration in the country. It also introduces the idea of cricket as a tool of diplomacy, a theme that is further developed in later chapters. At a more specific level, the chapter seeks to show how the Pakistan Cricket Board as an organization has been affected by state patronage and by the leaders that have been installed to run it. Bureaucracies, in this sense, are to be seen as living systems that do change and evolve internally through the informal system and externally through the peripheral environment which is made possible through each individual member's personal network of relationships to the wider society, including the countries in which they are located.

For Max Weber, bureaucracies as a type of social organization dominated modern life: 'the whole pattern of everyday life is cut to fit this framework.'[1] Sport is no exception to this rule. Invariably, today, sport is controlled by governing bodies, most of whom are themselves complex machineries of governance with a vast framework of departments, units, committees, and sub-committees. They are further structured into national, regional, and global levels. The Weberian model then is widely known:

> Bureaucracies achieve rational efficiency through well-defined formal structures. Each bureaucracy administers its official duties through an explicit hierarchical system. Specified roles and statuses divide necessary work into orderly spheres of professional competence. Bureaucracies are independent of personalities; their leaders and 'members' lives do not intrude in their work environment. In today's terminology, Weber's classical view of a bureaucracy is a closed system model.[2]

This model of a bureaucracy was recognized as an ideal type by Weber himself, though he chose to ignore a number of non-structural features which also influence an organization's performance. Thus, contra Weber, leaders' and members' lives and individual personalities do have an influence as does the wider cultural system that the bureaucracy is found in.

Building on Weber's seminal work, organizational theory[3] began to recognize that more goes on in a bureaucracy than is allowed by formal rules and structures. The anthropological studies of bureaucracy[4] recognized that the formal system is the 'map of the organizational structure, job descriptions, the hierarchy of decision making, the goals, rules and policies.'[5] In contrast, the informal system is the way individuals and groups and their lives outside the organization relate to one other. Both formal and informal organizational systems are affected by outside activities, persons, and groups. It is crucial to recognize that these living entities within formal systems have their emotions, affinities, identities, and interests. These will produce alliances, friendships, and alternative routes for promotion, advancement, and patronage, as well as factionalism, competition, and hostility.

> Bureaucrats aren't simply depersonalized cogs in an administrative machine; their personal lives unavoidably intrude on the work environment. Each bureaucrat's behaviour is influenced by his participation in multiple formal and informal outside groupings—his family, his union, his social club, his political party and so on.[6]

There is, therefore, a broader relationship between the ideology of the organization and that of other surrounding organizations and the society as a whole. The formal system is affected by the informal. Culture is seen to reside in the informal system and in the environment, but not in the supposedly neutral formal system; still, formal systems are not immune from culture, even if they are impacted indirectly.

In the next section I examine how, starting with the birth of Pakistan, the social, political, and economic environment influenced the emerging organizational structure of the Pakistan Cricket Board. This in turn put in place the foundations for subsequent developments.

AN EMERGING COUNTRY

> The tides of people flowing out of Pakistan and India were so fantastical, so vast and so thorough, that they unbalanced the entire substructure on which Pakistan had been built.[7]

Even before Partition occurred, the majority of investment in India had been concentrated in areas that fall outside Pakistan's present borders. Of the 924 major industrial units in pre-Partition India, only 34 were found in what came to constitute East and West Pakistan.[8] Some cities, like Dhaka, had no electricity. Literacy rates were below 20 per cent and the incidence of poverty ranged between 55 per cent and 60 per cent in West Pakistan.[9] Added to this was the enormous dislocations that occurred as an estimated 20 million people moved in both directions between the new nations of India and Pakistan. One in ten in Pakistan was a refugee and between half to a million had lost their lives.[10]

In the months following independence, Pakistan subsequently lost many of its Hindu[11] and Sikh bankers, merchants, shopkeepers, entrepreneurs, and clerks. According to Yasmin Khan, 'the wheels came off the machinery of the state. Those who came to Pakistan found that "entire government departments operated from tents and barracks in the new Pakistani capital" and as the *Dawn* newspaper reported "Cabinet ministers of Pakistan use packing cases as desks and crack jokes with painters who drop whitewash on them".'[12] Where infrastructure was in place—like the railway network—there were no trained personnel to run systems. The scenario was repeated in government offices, schools, hospitals, and other basic institutions.

Unsurprisingly, Gustav Papanek, the Harvard professor who became an advisor to the Pakistan Planning Commission from 1954 to 1960, and part of the Harvard Advisory Group that used Pakistan as a test case for early growth ideas, wrote that Pakistan was 'widely considered an economic monstrosity. The country was amongst the poorest in the world and had no industries to speak of, almost no industrial raw materials, no significant industrial or commercial groups.'[13]

At independence, then, the government was consumed with trying to put in place a basic survival framework: re-establishing law and order;

preventing epidemics; resettling refugees; and pulling together fragments of the government, transport, communication, and irrigation systems. Given its difficult birth and early infancy, the fact that Pakistan even survived is sometimes overlooked as a major achievement.[14]

The extreme overstretching of the government extended to most aspects of life. The Board of Control for Cricket in Pakistan (BCCP), as the organization that oversees the game in Pakistan, was forged in this difficult time and space and its embryonic development was influenced by the wider socio-political environment as well as by the key individuals that came to populate the organization. A structure that develops is a partially separate sociocultural system set into and articulated within a wider culturally entity. It therefore takes on some familiar bureaucratic features such as hierarchies and chains of command but also displays fewer universal features such as over-centralization, excessive dependence on top down leadership, and political appropriation. These in turn have both positive and negative impacts. I shall turn to those in the next few sections.

ESSENTIAL PATRONAGE: THE BIRTH OF THE BOARD OF CONTROL FOR CRICKET IN PAKISTAN

The Board of Control for Cricket in Pakistan (BCCP) was established in May 1948, less than a year after Pakistan gained independence. For a new nation with no funds to run its basic services, establishing a cricketing structure was an enormous challenge. Prior to independence, cricket patronage in the Subcontinent was through two indigenous bases.[15] The first of these sources was local businessmen, propertied magnates, and wealthy professionals. The ascendency of Bombay came initially from the support provided by the city's Parsi merchants and Hindu and Muslim businessmen. In Karachi, it was the sizeable number of Parsi, Hindu, and Bohra merchants that were responsible for setting up a number of well-endowed cricket clubs by the late 1880s.[16]

By the end of the 19th century, the Indian royal houses—the second indigenous source—also became an important avenue of patronage. The Indian princes' involvement in cricket was spurred on by their increasingly being educated in anglicized educational institutions[17] headed by English headmasters and teachers and by the princes seeing cricket as a means of forging connections with the highest levels of the imperial state in India and Britain. Appadurai states:

Whether it was by playing teams from England, which included men who had known each other at Eton and Harrow, Oxford and Cambridge, or during tours to England, a small segment of the Indian sporting population was initiated into the moral and social mysteries and rituals of Victorian cricket.[18]

While the financial support of these two groups was crucial in sustaining cricket at the grassroots, post-Partition, as mentioned previously, Pakistan lost much of its affluent Hindu and Sikh business community. Also, of the Princely states only Bahawalpur was significant in terms of cricketing support. But despite the much smaller pool, patronage for cricket in Pakistan continued to follow similar contours. Industrialists and businessmen were joined by feudal landowners[19] in providing financial support usually in the form of food, travel expenses, and cash and land handouts to the players. More importantly, they provided practice facilities to the earliest cricketers. This support was crucial considering that the board had few resources and scant existing cricketing infrastructure.

In recognition of the role played by these early benefactors, the first president of the board was Nawab Iftikhar Hussain Mamdot—a political heavyweight who prior to Partition was one of undivided Punjab's largest landholders, and who had thrown his weight behind Jinnah and the Muslim League. He was rewarded by being appointed the first chief minister of (west) Punjab. His appointment as president and chairman of the BCCP gave the board political and social clout. But while Mamdot was the figurehead president, the board was run by its vice-presidents, the most important of whom was Alvin Robert Cornelius. Cornelius had been appointed as vice-president of the inaugural board and the following year became chairman of the working committee and remained so until he relinquished his connection with the board in early 1953. The 'engine room' of the board during this period were Cornelius and a Parsi civil servant, Kaikhusroo Collector, and together they set about raising funds for basic cricket development through attracting private funds and official patronage. For Cornelius, this represented a delicate balancing act. On the one hand, he employed traditional patterns of patronage—he was the one who suggested Mamdot as president and, in the inaugural meeting of the board, Jinnah as head of state was requested to be patron. On the other hand, he oversaw the gradual introduction of newer, more sophisticated methods of sports management and development, such as sponsorship of cricket by commercial enterprises including the Pakistan International Airlines. At this point, the board did have other regional representatives. In a bid to maintain regional parity Cornelius represented Punjab but there were delegates from the NWFP and Sindh, as well as a few senior cricketers. Conspicuous by their absence were representatives from Balochistan and East Pakistan—Balochistan likely overlooked and East Pakistan receiving one of several snubs.

Prior to his first appointment in the inaugural board, Cornelius had been a leading activist in the Pakistan movement, closely collaborating with M.A. Jinnah. Post-independence he became the fourth Chief Justice of Pakistan (1960–68) and was known for his commitment to establishing a legal system of national repute for Pakistan. This organizational zeal translated into his work at the cricket board.

The direct involvement of patrons—be it Mamdot as president or Jinnah as patron—in the board was seen as a necessity as the game lacked funds and international recognition and Cornelius felt that these individual patrons were the only available sources of support. This political patronage created an early link between the board and the state and while Jinnah may not have done so, less scrupulous successors progressively began to treat the organization as a source of patronage, handing out key positions to eager clients. This was to become a source of considerable weakness further down the road.

However, the overt involvement of the state and politicians in cricket prior to the 1970s was muted. This is unsurprising as in the 1950s and 1960s governments were consumed with trying to tackle a critical shortage of funds, industry, skilled workers, a massive refugee and resettlement crisis, and a large-scale nation-building effort that sought to bring together diverse ethnic, cultural, and linguistic traditions. In this environment, thoughts of lending support to sporting and cultural activities was a luxury that could not be afforded. There was little political involvement or interference, but this also meant that these socio-cultural activities had to fend for themselves. Here the individual patrons of cricket were crucial through their political clout as well as their financial support. Despite obstacles, the cricket board achieved a significant amount. Three stadiums with capacities of over 20,000 were built in Chittagong, Dhaka, and Karachi. Three more were to follow in Hyderabad (1955), Multan (1956), and Lahore (1959). By 1952, Pakistan, sponsored by the Board of Control for Cricket in India (BCCI), had managed to gain entrance to the International Cricket Council (ICC) after two failed earlier attempts.

Much of this early progress was the result of the commitment and competence of a small group of individuals that comprised the board and who worked for it on an honorary basis. Cornelius's commitment to creating a system was unsurpassed. Collector, when not cobbling together essential funds, used his own personal funds in order to undertake board business.[20]

The leveraging of support of individual patrons and the government as well was important—even if the government was unable to provide financial support, they did provide land grants for grounds, human resources, and clout where required. The board, like the cricket team and the nation, overcame immense obstacles, not only to survive but to begin to thrive as well.

In overcoming these obstacles, the board officials showed the verve, excitement, and energy that drove the country and its early cricket. It is worth recalling that of all the nations that joined the ICC, Pakistan had the earliest success.[21] Pakistan's initial survival has much to do with the sense of purpose and zeal that its early architects had—of forging a nation and homeland out of chaos.

> Pakistan's first cricketers of the 1950s radiated the same integrity [as Cornelius]. Not charm—match fixers radiate charm—but decency and a quiet pride in what they had achieved. They had few resources yet they won a Test Match in the first series they played against every country.[22]

The early structure of the board already emphasized two important elements: firstly, an early connection with the state; and secondly, a tendency towards centralization, making the role of the leadership critical in the successful implementation of plans. Both these elements were crucial in the appropriation of cricket in the decades that followed. This in turn had a wide-ranging impact on the organizational structure of the cricket board.

PATRONAGE AND THE APPROPRIATION OF CRICKET

Initially, for a new and diverse nation seeking a sense of identity to bind it together, sport represented a civil or secular religion, and could be used as an important channel for strengthening social solidarity, particularly at the national level—'in this sense, sport may be viewed as one of many modern civil and secular occasions—such as national holidays, royal weddings, military parades, and remembrance gatherings—that function periodically to bind communities and nations.'[23] This Durkheimian functionalist approach has often been employed to explain how sports serves to bind social groups, particularly through its ability to provide its followers with an identity usually through attendance at highly charged sporting events in which they participate as audience members. Brett Hutchins, writing about the similar ability of cricket to draw together a disparate Australian nation,[24] refers to Anderson's concept of imagined community[25] in which he describes the 'national feeling of solidarity that accompany [sic] routine activities such as reading the daily newspapers, or in this instance playing a game with a bat and ball.'[26] He emphasizes that the meaning and significance of such mundane acts are increased exponentially by millions of other people, separated by large distances and who will remain unknown to one another, having the same interests and doing the same thing. The sport becomes a physical reality and maybe more importantly a collective cultural expression. According to Hutchins, cricket consistently announced Australia as an independent and successful country to the world. In the same way, in a developing country like Pakistan whose overt global achievements were limited, cricket could be the forum for creating the vision of a glorious and triumphant nation—a barometer of self-worth. The early involvement of patrons in the cricket board opened up the possibility of these individuals—if they were to become more involved—appropriating cricket in the Durkheimian sense as mentioned above. In return for their patronage they would be able to exert greater control, usually through the appointment of selected chairmen in the board.

Ayub Khan, Pakistan's first military dictator, had no real interest in cricket as a sport. But like his military successors Ziaul Haq and Pervez Musharraf, Ayub Khan did understand the impact that a successful, or unsuccessful team, may have on their legitimacy seeking regimes. All three tried to control and appropriate elements of popular culture in order to unify the nation under their rule and to boost their own and their regimes' validity. In fact, apart from Zulfikar Ali Bhutto's democratic government, military governments have used cricket much more effectively partly because they were more in need of validating their rule and partly through installing effective leadership that would give them the means to exert greater influence. Democratic governments, as I will explain later, were consumed by trying to survive their terms and subsequently had less of a focus on wider issues.

Ayub Khan, as patron of the board, began to exert greater control of the game and the board. He started by moving the BCCP to Rawalpindi where the military headquarters of the Pakistan Army were located, very visibly showing his intent to incorporate it within the realm of his regime. However, Ayub Khan had less to build on in the 1960s. Pakistan's fixtures were limited, and the game had not yet captured the imagination of the nation in the way it would in the following decades starting in the turbulent 1970s. Having said that, he did appoint Justice Cornelius as chairman of the board in 1960 for a three-year term.

But by the time we reach the 1970s, Pakistan is facing considerable change beginning with the loss of East Pakistan in 1971. A decade of military rule is brought to an end with Zulfikar Ali Bhutto heralding the first democratic transition in Pakistan's history. Backed by his manifesto of Islamic socialism, Bhutto was determined to radically transform Pakistan—its politics, economy, and society. A populist leader, Bhutto was keen on portraying himself as a man of the people. Twenty-five years into independence, the secession of East Pakistan and the creation of Bangladesh had dealt a blow to the idea of religion being the basis of Pakistan. But in cricket, and other aspects of popular culture, he saw cultural institutions that could be used to generate the support and approval of the masses.

Bhutto's appointment of Abdul Hafeez Kardar to the BCCP as well as that of another key minister as president of the Sports Control Board were primarily to take advantage of sport as a symbol of nationhood and unity. Kardar had a close association with cricket before his appointment as chairman of the board. In 1952, Cornelius had appointed him captain of the Pakistan national team. He had, prior to Partition, already represented India in 1946 and then Oxford University and Warwickshire county in England. Bhutto's appointment of Kardar had been a shrewd one. The appropriation of cricket required capable individuals to be installed in key positions.

Bhutto's foresight in appropriating the game for political gain coincided with cricket's growing international commercial appeal. In the mid to late 1970s, the Pakistan team began to meet with significant success and a number of the more successful cricketers took up positions in the English county system as well as in the breakaway Australian World Series Cricket (WSC) league. The larger international profile and success that Pakistan acquired as a result of changes that the game underwent in the turbulent 1970s left Bhutto's successor, Ziaul Haq, the military dictator who overthrew him, with a growing opportunity as well as an emerging challenge.

Having deposed Bhutto in a military coup and then having him controversially tried and executed by the Supreme Court of Pakistan in 1979 for authorizing the murder of a political opponent, Zia's military government needed to improve its standing by any and all means. The growing mass appeal of cricket provided Ziaul Haq the opportunity to garner greater public support at home and change his and his government's image, both nationally and internationally. But before that was possible, Zia would have to deal with an emerging threat to the cricket-as-nation-building project—Beckles refers to it as the 'cash before country'[27] issue and Appadurai points to it as being representative of a fundamental change in the ethos of the game.

Nothing marks this change in ethos as much as the arrival of the professionalized, strictly commercial phenomenon of World Series Cricket (WSC), a global, media centered cricket package created by an Australian by the name of Kerry Packer. Packer's WSC was the first major threat both to the colonial ecumene of amateur sportsmanship and the post-World War II ethic of cricket nationalism, centered as it was on the major innovation in the sport since the war—one-day cricket—in which a single day's play (as opposed to five or more days) settles the outcome. One-day cricket encourages risk taking, aggressiveness, and bravado while suiting perfectly the intense attention appropriate to high-powered television advertising and a higher turnover of events and settings. Packer's WSC bypassed national loyalty in the name of media entertainment and fast economic benefits for players. West Indian, English, Australian, and Pakistani cricketers were quick to see its appeals.[28]

For the cricketers, Kerry Packer's rival system—which ran in opposition to international cricket as administered by the International Cricket Council— offered salaries that dwarfed those being offered by national boards. Several Pakistan cricketers—by this time amongst the most high profile in international cricket—signed up and were promptly banned by the BCCP. A similar situation had occurred when Pakistani cricketers contracted to play for English counties in the 1970s had pressurized the board to raise salaries or face losing their services.[29] More than two decades later, the Indian Premier League and other franchise-based leagues, modelled along the lines of the American National Basketball Association or the English Premier League, would bring similar 'cash before country' conflicts to the modern game. This is somewhat ironic because in 1977, India was one of the few countries not to have any defections to the breakaway World Series Cricket. Mihir Bose states that it was largely due to India wanting to reaffirm its commitment to the values of the traditional five-day game.[30]

The emergence of conflicting loyalties with the nation seemingly relegated in favour of commercial interests meant that cricket's capacity to act as means of nation building and identity construction was threatened. Cricket in Pakistan was crucial to the identity of the new nation. The same was the case for the West Indies—myriad Caribbean islands with different cultures wedded together by a team that sought to bring a greater sense of self-worth in a post-colonial world. Cricket, then, served a greater purpose. But Packer's brazen enterprise signalled that cricket had moved into another, 'post-nationalist phase, in which entertainment value, media coverage and the commercialization of players would transcend the national loyalty of the early post-independence period and the Victorian amateur ethic of the colonial period.'[31]

The commercialization of the game meant that, far from being ambassadors for the nation and the state, in the eyes of the government the cricketers were increasingly becoming an embarrassment. Cricketing success, growing global coverage and viewership, and international exposure in England and Australia meant that these sporting spokesmen were offering global audiences an alternate view of Pakistan from what the state had hoped. The competing narrative became one about low salaries, non-existent benefits, inefficiencies in the system, and poor leadership in the day to day running of the game.

For a military dictator bent upon crushing dissent and portraying a view of a nation united under his leadership, the situation was uniquely disconcerting for Ziaul Haq. But Zia was a canny leader with an extraordinary ability to manipulate situations to his benefit. While certain areas of society were dealt with an iron hand—cinema and the performing arts were strictly censored, for example—cricket offered too much potential benefit not to be controlled to assist in legitimizing his political position and authority as a leader. A successful cricket team would allow Zia, as patron and as head of government, a way of conveying nationally and internationally the possibilities of similar successes in other fields under his command. While he consistently appointed chairmen from the armed forces to the board in an attempt to gain further control,[32] he also intervened personally to mediate a settlement between the players and the board over the banning that followed the WSC crisis. Zia recognized the political importance of the game and its growing power in terms of the public's consciousness. Once the disputes over pay were overcome through his direct involvement, cricket was restored to being a channel for nationhood and of national identity.

To take advantage of his power, Zia made it a point to make regular appearances at cricket matches in his role as patron of the board, increasing his visibility as a leader and identifying himself with occasions of national social solidarity. He would also make the government partly fund expensive treatment for a leg injury which threatened the career of Imran Khan—one of the greatest cricketers of Pakistan—and in 1987 he famously talked Khan out of retirement. In February of the same year, Ziaul Haq made an unexpected appearance in Jaipur, India, to watch the second test match between India and Pakistan. The visit was made at a time of heightened Indo-Pakistan tensions, arising out of the insurgencies in Indian Punjab and Kashmir. As troops massed on their respective borders, Zia's public relations coup managed to defuse the situation and within months thousands of troops had been withdrawn (see Chapters 5 and 6). This was perhaps the first instance of 'cricket diplomacy.' It would be repeated by another military leader, Pervez Musharraf, in 2005 as well as the democratically elected Prime Minister Syed Yousuf Raza Gilani in 2011. But Zia's Jaipur trip showed the importance that cricket had come to occupy in Pakistan by 1987 and how it could be used to influence bilateral relations. As Corrigan notes:

> The game itself was an important piece on the general's diplomatic chess board: he instructed the Board of Control for Cricket in Pakistan to reinstate the banned Packer players for a tour of India (against whom a loss could have unpredictably dangerous consequences for life, limb and social and political stability), and twice ensured that the team continued to play when they did not want to (because of violence at Colombo and a sub-standard pitch at Jaipur). Continuing to play kept available a means of continuing to maintain relations with Sri Lanka and India, while refusing to play could have endangered them. Cricket, then, was an instrument of foreign policy as well as a way of building domestic solidarity.[33]

In September 1999, General Pervez Musharraf brought military rule back to Pakistan after a decade of democracy. Like Zia, Musharraf's attachment to the cricket board was through his recognition of the importance of cricket to his regime—in terms of foreign relations as well as domestic popularity. Shaharyar M. Khan, a former foreign secretary who was appointed as chairman of the Pakistan Cricket Board in 2004, recalled his first meeting with Musharraf:

> I knew Musharraf cursorily when he visited Jordan when I was Ambassador there in the 1970s. When I first met him as Chairman of the board, he was warm and said he was not interested in the day to day running of the board but that it was important to work towards the 2007 World Cup as this would boost Pakistan's image. He was also keen on engaging with India and I felt that my appointment—as a civilian—was partly as a means of assuaging public criticism of the army taking so many key administrative positions and partly out of his seeing me as a conduit for improving relations with India. I had been appointed previously as manager for the 1999 tour that Pakistan made to India, which was a cricketing and foreign relations success, at what at the time had been a tense India–Pakistan relationship. Like Zia, Musharraf was keen on cricket diplomacy.[34]

Shaharyar Khan's diplomatic skills, contacts, and commitment did in fact do much to restore Pakistan's reputation in the ICC as well as bilaterally. There was a notable thaw in India–Pakistan cricketing relations. The two teams played a number of series in a short span of time. The cricket was often thrilling, played in a competitive but sporting atmosphere. In 2004, India toured Pakistan for the first time in fourteen years. The tour was an enormous success—logistically, in cricketing terms, and in terms of bilateral relations (see Chapters 5 and 6).

The warmth of the tour radiated beyond cricket. Bollywood film makers suggested that Indian films should stop pushing and Pakistan propaganda. About 15 Pakistani musical bands crossed the border between January and May. And the business sector brimmed with optimism at the potential for trade. The tour provided the highest possible profile for friendship and the strongest metaphorical way of saying 'peace over conflict.'[35]

Maybe what elevated it even further was the bonhomie between fans as they crossed borders for the cricket and for many a return to their roots for the first time since the bloody partition of 1947.

Accolades for the success of the series poured in from all quarters. Laurens International, the World's leading sports concern, nominated the India and Pakistan cricket teams as joint winners for their annual team sports prize. The UN recognized the impact of the series in peace-building by announcing a special tribute to both teams as ambassadors of peace. For Pakistan these international tributes were of special significance as they projected the moderate, peaceful and hospitable image of the country that had been tarnished by exaggerated accounts of events in the country.[36]

Musharraf revelled in these opportunities to cast himself as the man who would bring peace to the region. I recall being in the crowd at Gaddafi stadium in a stand packed full of Indian and Pakistani fans when Musharraf appeared in the balcony of the VIP box. He was loudly cheered by both sets of fans. He found time to partake in witty banter with the Indian cricket team famously urging a young Mahendra Singh Dhoni not to cut his hair as he too, like Samson, might lose his strength. In 2005, he was welcomed with much fanfare when he witnessed a match in Delhi. A raft of confidence building measures were announced. Musharraf's popularity as a leader reached its peak. Even President George W. Bush visited, albeit briefly, in 2006 and was immediately introduced to cricket and the cricket team. Musharraf understood the power of cricket just as Zia did before him. Now that the reach of the game had expanded exponentially, so had its importance as a leading identity marker for the nation.

It is clear that authoritarian leaders have appropriated the game in order to legitimize and popularize their regimes and build national unity and identity. This was most apparent with Zulfikar Ali Bhutto and with the two military regimes of Ziaul Haq and Pervez Musharraf. However, as that appropriation was implemented through the Board of Control for Cricket in Pakistan, it did have significant impacts on how the board's structure developed. In particular, it led to an overly centralized organization heavily dependent on good leadership.

LEADERSHIP AND CENTRALIZATION

The early linkage of the head of state as patron of the board and the acceptance of this involvement by heads of state from Ayub Khan onwards in the affairs of the board was an attempt to control the BCCP by the various governments. The first step in this exercise was the appointment of the chairman of the board with a brief to run the board for the sitting government.

There was already a tendency towards centralization inherent in the emerging institutions in Pakistan. Colonization had established systems where the colonial chief, deeply distrustful of the 'natives,' would insist on all decisions passing through him. The post-colonial state was built on this principle and added to it through traditional South Asian patterns of leadership and authoritarianism which often invest absolute authority in the hands of a few charismatic individuals giving them significant influence within an organization. Both predispositions strengthened a strongly top down decision-making structure. During military regimes there was an additional tendency to appoint senior retired generals to the chairmanship of the BCCP. This was part of a wider strategy whereby senior military officers were given control of key economic and cultural assets within the nation. Most held multiple roles, in charge of several organizations and institutions simultaneously, thereby consolidating military rule and reducing any chances of dissent and opposition to authoritarian decision making. Both Ziaul Haq and more so Pervez Musharraf appointed military personnel to administrative posts in large numbers.[37]

The non-democratic appointment of chairmen—even during democratic governments—invested a great deal of centralized power in the role of the chairman. Pervez Musharraf and Tauqir Zia, a serving lieutenant general whom Musharraf had appointed chairman of the board, both defended their top down approach as born out of necessity. Musharraf was determined to ensure that Pakistan's two biggest sports—hockey and cricket—were well run. Tauqir Zia was more blunt about taking control: 'I am unrepentant because personally I feel that Pakistan cannot be run as a democracy. In any case the PCB at the time could not be run as a democracy. With match-fixing and all the scandals coming in, I had to take centralizing command.'[38]

Undoubtedly, centralization has the ability to bring about rapid and positive change. Cornelius, Kardar, and later Nur Khan, Tauqir Zia, and Shaharyar Khan were all chairmen and leaders who oversaw considerable progress during their terms. Kardar took an organization that had no offices and barely any funds or staff and transformed it. By the time his chairmanship came to an end, the board had a fully functional office in the newly built Lahore stadium,[39] a set of international commitments for the national side, a thriving and fixed domestic structure involving Pakistan's banks and other major companies, and Rs. 5 million. Kardar also worked tirelessly to improve and refurbish facilities—new stadiums, practice facilities, and living wages and potential careers for players and coaches. Under Nur Khan's administration, the team and the board prospered. Within the International Cricket Council, Nur Khan, like Kardar, was a formidable presence. Khan succeeded in establishing an Asian bloc which ultimately led to the successful Indo-Pakistan bid for the 1987 World Cup and the start of a major power shift from England and Australia to India and Pakistan. Tauqir Zia expanded the game significantly within Pakistan while Shaharyar Khan's personal integrity and diplomatic experience won Pakistan many friends internationally after a long period of indifferent leadership.

The aforementioned individuals were also examples of large personalities and strong dedicated leaders who dominated headship in the board. In any organization, the influence of leaders is crucial. Organizational structure is affected by modelling—the extent to which the leader shows support for desired values. The centrality of these leaders is important as they provide employees with cues on what behaviours are desired and acceptable. In Cornelius, the board already had a personality whose personal example— he was known for his modesty, integrity, and humility, often cycling in to work and eschewing protocol and entourages—had laid down a culture of committed, hardworking individuals determined to succeed against the odds. Kardar would be another forceful personality whose impact would be widely influential for the board's early culture.

But authoritarian, centralized leadership can also prevent the formation of an organizational structure that can stand independent of the leader. It makes the organization strongly personality-driven. The strong personality-driven nature of the board developed early on in its evolution and appears to be characteristic of several South Asian institutions, maybe most evident in the area of politics with the influence of individuals such as Zulfikar Ali Bhutto and Benazir Bhutto, Nawaz Sharif and, maybe most evidently, Imran Khan. The respective political parties struggle without these leaders at the helm.

It is similar across the border in India with the likes of the Gandhi family and Congress and the personality cult that is Narendra Modi. Centralization works best given hardworking, competent, and organized leaders who can motivate subordinates to carry out necessary tasks. However, the system then places an enormous strain and responsibility on officials in top positions. It also produces a culture where individuals lower down the hierarchy are unlikely to take initiatives themselves and if anything is to be achieved it is only possible through accessing the top and bypassing the existing hierarchy.

This culture was germinating at the board where power was concentrated in the leadership position and there was little motivation to achieve anything lower down the hierarchy, making for a very top-heavy organization. Under a competent chairman the board would flourish. But just as benefits are magnified in a centralized system under a competent leader, disadvantages too are exaggerated where leaders are ineffectual. The organizational system itself remains undeveloped while the influence of the leader is disproportionately increased. I have mentioned before the fact that centralization can bring positive outcomes; however, these are vitally dependent on effective leadership. Under less competent leaders the system becomes significantly maladaptive. It is these negative impacts emanating from the now developed organization structure that I shall now examine.

Maladaptive Leadership

Our inquiry must begin with the question of why ineffectual leaders are appointed to important positions (such as the chairman of the cricket board), particularly in organizational systems that then invest them with considerable authority. Earlier sections of the chapter have described the appropriation of cricket through the office of the chairman of the board as important to successive governments. The success of that patronage required strong, competent leadership. Thus, the patron would appoint a suitable leader with an eye towards continued success in the game reaping rewards for the government. The coincidence of objectives brought dividends to both parties. Undoubtedly, there were some more successful than others but overall the recognition by governments of the benefit of having a successful cricket team meant that prior to 1988, leadership in the cricket board had not been maladaptive or deleterious. This changed quite significantly in the 'decade of democracy' that followed the mysterious death of President Ziaul Haq in a plane crash in 1988.

The decade of democracy between 1989 and 1999 is a deeply contradictory period for Pakistan. It saw the return to democracy after ten years of repressive military rule during which democratic institutions were summarily dismantled and destroyed. It was therefore a faltering democratic period during which the army was unwilling to surrender its authority. Christophe Jaffrelot describes this second transition to democracy as not being as substantial (or as democratic) as the first one.[40] This is a fair assessment, primarily because while the generals may have receded from direct governance, they maintained control over key policies—foreign policy regarding Afghanistan, Kashmir (effectively India), and matters of defence (including the nuclear programme). They also retained the power to oust democratically elected prime ministers, which they did regularly in the decade between 1988 and 1999. Twice Benazir Bhutto came to power and twice she was ousted before her term was completed. Twice Nawaz Sharif replaced her and twice he too was replaced before his term was completed. Rarely has democracy promised so much and delivered so little. This is unsurprising considering the constant instability that dogged the various democratic governments, and governments that are unsure of how long they will be allowed to stay in power tend to make more patronage appointments so they can gain more from their limited time in office.

Unsurprisingly, official positions of authority were increasingly made in return for political loyalty. Parliament became a 'fountainhead of patronage politics.'[41] The office of the chairman of the cricket board was no exception. That is not to say that this did not happen under military rule—retired generals with no background in cricket were appointed chairmen—but there was also an attempt by the army to try and appropriate cricket for their own ends and this required some degree of administrative competence. Under the democratic governments between 1988 and 1999, it appears that even the idea of appropriating the game had been forgotten in an attempt to shore up support through political patronage.

> Both PPP and Muslim League governments were corrupt, owing chiefly to the perennial need to reward kinsfolk and supporters. For example, the PPP Speaker of the National Assembly from 1993 to 1997 (and prime minister after 2008), Syed Yousuf Raza Gilani, created or freed no fewer than 500 jobs in various parliamentary services to give to his supporters. The PPP leadership under Benazir Bhutto (and her husband Asif Ali Zardari) went beyond patronage and limited corruption into outright kleptocracy.[42]

Initially, Benazir had left Ziaul Haq's nominee as chairman of the board in office.[43] By the time she was made Prime Minister a second time in 1993, though, she had appointed a PPP loyalist—Syed Zulfiqar Ali Shah Bokhari—as chairman of the PCB, a reward for his loyalty and a way of giving him some status (though no formal position in the government). Three years later, Nawaz Sharif would appoint Khalid Mehmood, a formal civil servant, in the chairman's role having in his earlier stint appointed Justice Nasim Hasan Shah. Both appointees were considered close to Nawaz Sharif. Arguably the most blatant of these political appointments was that of Mujeeb-ur-Rehman, a businessman with no cricketing background, but the brother of the minister heading the national accountability cell which at the time was hounding Nawaz Sharif's rivals. As Ali points out:

> During the 1990s, as the government changed hands between the PML-N and PPP, the bureaucracy was less a means of enhancing government performance, and more a means for the ruling party to cling to the few vestiges of power left behind by non-governmental forces. Each of the parties wanted to work with their loyalists and a change in government meant a re-shuffle to replace one set of favourites with another. In other words, politicians and bureaucrats were brought together by the precarity of Pakistan's political system.[44]

The one exception to the rule and a successful attempt at cricket diplomacy by Nawaz Sharif in his second term as Prime Minister was his appointment of former foreign secretary Shaharyar Khan as manager to the Pakistan team to India in 1998/99. This was prior to Khan being appointed chairman of the cricket board in 2004 by Musharraf. Nawaz Sharif and his Indian counterpart Atal Bihari Vajpayee had made significant progress in bilateral relations after the tensions that emanated from the tit for tat nuclear bomb tests that the countries had carried out in 1998. Keen to show their commitment to building momentum, Pakistan and India announced their first bilateral series in ten years to be held in India. Nawaz Sharif handed Khan the mandate to win hearts and minds on the cricket field. The tour was an enormous bridge-building success. The bonhomie lasted until Musharraf, then chief of army staff, engineered the Kargil conflict with India in May 1999.

However, the period of musical chairs between Nawaz Sharif and Benazir Bhutto led to a series of ineffectual chairmen and a growth of the patronage networks that came increasingly to be associated with the position of chairman of the board. While military leaders had appointed their fair share of poor administrators, their attempt to win over legitimacy tended to mitigate against outright ineffectiveness. Moreover, as authoritarian rulers they were not as dependent on handing out favours to remain in power as much as their undermined democratic counterparts were. This weakened the organization, losing the commitment and competence of earlier chairmen and all this at a time when the game itself was more visible and internationalized and would have benefitted immensely from sound leadership.

Pakistan's global image was also progressively under strain. Accounts of widespread corruption, frequent government dismissals, nuclear tests, and worsening relations with the US had increasingly isolated Pakistan. Cricket, now more able to convey Pakistan's identity than ever before, could have been the channel through which to portray a more positive view of the country. Instead, Pakistan cricket was engulfed by a match-fixing scandal that threatened its very existence. Like so much else in the country, it was a decade of missed opportunities as ineffectual leadership failed Pakistan and its cricket.

The situation changed under the military regime of Pervez Musharraf who with his emphasis on what he called 'enlightened moderation' was certainly focused on appropriating cricket for his own objectives and who appointed competent leaders to what had now been rechristened the Pakistan Cricket Board (PCB). His one misstep with regard to cricket occurred when growing popular unrest against a further term put him under increasing pressure to leave office. In an attempt to shore up his support, he installed his closest supporters to key positions including to the chairman of the cricket board where he appointed one of his closest advisors of the time, Dr Nasim Ashraf, a non-resident Pakistani doctor from the US. Musharraf had already inducted Ashraf as an advisor into the board in order to keep a closer eye on proceedings. Now he had moved to exert closer control while also 'rewarding' a loyalist who had helped organize his official meetings in the US.

Ashraf took the concentration of powers—and the subservience—to different, more formal levels. He inherited a constitution under review and proceeded to enshrine into it the role of (his) patron. Samiuddin refers to the new constitution as seeking to institutionalize not interference but a kind of political subservience.

Of the 15 members of the new PCB governing Board, 8 would be appointments by the chairman and requiring the Patron's approval. Effectively, along with the chairman himself, nine members would be appointed by the patron—at this point General Pervez Musharraf. Just in case that was not enough, the concluding clause stated that all 15 members elected or otherwise, would require the approval of the patron whose decision would be final. For all other decisions, the word of the chairman would be final and his word was only as his patrons. Where once the patron used to appoint three positions in the Board—chairman, secretary and treasurer—and this unwittingly enforce checks and balances on each position, he now only appointed one. That appointment had all the powers—the Board's and the game's fortunes, and every one of its players depended entirely on that man.[45]

In the years that followed Musharraf's resignation and the third coming of democracy in Pakistan, there has been a continuing politicization of the civil bureaucracy being staffed by party loyalists leading to more ineffectual and in some cases deeply maladaptive and damaging leadership. The role of the chairman, not associated particularly with corruption and financial gain, provided these individuals the opportunity for pursuing local, national, and transnational status and honour through association with and control of a prominent institution. With exceptions, the chairmen of the PCB have coveted this characteristic of the role and their political patrons have increasingly rewarded them by giving them the position. In some cases, far from being a vehicle to portray a positive image of Pakistan, cricket and the cricket board have threatened to isolate Pakistan further. This was highlighted by the reign of Chairman Ijaz Butt who was appointed by President Asif Ali Zardari immediately following the ouster of Pervez Musharraf.

Ijaz Butt had a long association with cricket administration in Lahore, but more importantly he was politically connected, being the brother-in-law of the defence minister in the incumbent government. Butt's tenure was a disaster. Under his chairmanship the PCB ignored warnings against holding a test match in Lahore, only for the terrorist attack to occur on the visiting Sri Lankan team, bringing an end to international cricket in Pakistan for several years thereafter. Osman Samiuddin, writing in the UAE newspaper *National*, summed up Butt's impact on Pakistan cricket: 'On and off the field, the reputation of a once proud cricketing nation had been shredded. It had become a paranoid wreck and Butt had steered that transformation.'[46]

Clearly, where effective leadership had been able to use cricket to portray a positive image of Pakistan, the deleterious impacts of poor leadership led to a shattering of Pakistan's cricketing and wider reputation. It appears that the practice of rewarding political loyalists has become an end in itself rather than a means to an end—the end being, for example, bureaucratic efficiency in order to achieve wider governance objectives. Longer term thinking is replaced by shorter and immediate concerns. Thus, in the past the appropriation of cricket by the government was done with an eye towards the benefits in terms of unity and image from having a successful team. Now, the appointment of the chairman was increasingly limited to appointing a loyalist. Even appropriation was too long term a goal.

In fact, today the appropriation of the game has again been taken up by the army. It is the army that helps prepare international cricketers for overseas tours by coaching and preparing them in gruelling training camps run by army trainers. Having won a test match in England in the 2016 tour that followed one of those training camps, Misbah-ul-Haq and Younis Khan, captain and vice-captain respectively, paid a very open tribute to their army trainers by doing push-ups and marching in celebration. Even when not in power, the army has clearly understood what the military dictators had earlier. Appropriating the cricket team has enormous promotional value for the army's image amongst the population. The army has continued to engage with cricket through building cricket grounds in North Waziristan (and most recently supervising the construction of one in Gwadar, a feat that was celebrated in a tweet by the ICC as the ground is stunning in its site and situation), through ensuring security for visiting teams to Pakistan, through training the cricketers, and through having individual cricketers tweet their unconditional support for the army in comparison to the divisive and tarnished political parties. As Pakistan becomes a more and more securitized state, cricket and the army are today more closely associated than ever before.

The chain of ineffectual leaders in a centralized system brought about a number of changes to the culture of the Pakistan Cricket Board. In this concluding section, I look at how the emergent structure of the board, influenced by its political, economic, and social environment and its leadership, affected the culture of the board.

CONSEQUENCES FOR THE ORGANIZATION

Instability breeds short termism and the frequent changing of chairmen in the board more recently[47] has weakened a structure that is heavily dependent on effective leadership. It has also led to the emergence of a strangely unchanging and conservative culture lower down in the bureaucratic hierarchy. Thus, while chairmen changed fairly frequently, some bringing a more coherent vision than others, the senior staff lower down the hierarchy entrenched themselves ever more strongly in order to guard against losing their own positions in the frequent changes on top. 'You can put Mickey Mouse in charge and it won't make a difference to the PCB'—this sentiment which was widespread amongst many who had interacted with the PCB was related to me by a former cricketer who had worked with the board in the 2000s.

Ordinarily, the ability to keep working regardless of changes in leadership need not be a negative trait and actually indicates a strong institution. However, the early centralization of the system meant that there was little initiative that came from anywhere but the top and the frequent changes bred a lack of scrutiny and accountability amongst staff lower down the hierarchy.

Instead, a conservative culture of mutual survival developed, a 'you scratch my back, I scratch yours' kind of attitude that became enshrined within the institution over time. A proactive chairman could shake up the structure to an extent, but as it became larger and more insulated, even bringing about small changes became more and more difficult. Senior management—in the tier below the chairman—have taken the organization hostage making every new chairman believe that the they—the senior management—are indispensable. As a result, no matter what changes occur at the top, the system replicates itself below. During interviews with staff I was told on the basis of anonymity of one of many initiatives that had been halted because of the lack of initiative from the staff.

> In 2007 we purchased equipment to establish a bio-mechanics lab. We would have been only the fifth such facility in the world. A few months later the Chairman was changed, and the equipment was put into cold storage. We spent 15 crores[48] on a lab building for biomechanics lab building and 8 crores on equipment purchased 10 years ago and since then has gathered dust. I joined the board in 2014 and inquired about the project. I literally found the equipment lying untouched in boxes. That was surprising enough but what was even worse was the resistance I faced from senior management when I tried to restart the project. The Chairman was supportive, but it seemed like the possible success of the project would be seen as showing up the incompetence of my colleagues. If they had not done it, it should not be done at all. At every step I had obstacles placed in my way by people within the PCB. Every attempt was made to sabotage the project. Fake news items were given to the media and to the government. It took us 4 years from 2015 to finally establish an internationally recognized centre and only the fifth of its kind in the world.

There was also a deepening lack of trust within employees in the board. Different chairmen brought in different people, some of them unprofessional. The biggest increase occurred under Nasim Ashraf who had been appointed by Pervez Musharraf as he tried desperately to shore up his own support. This influx of employees on dubious contracts with the main objective being patrons handing out favours to clients meant incompetence and an inability to deal with the demands of a rapidly changing game and a growing lack of trust within the organization. A senior staff member who had worked at the board for several years but who resigned recently told me:

> Many staff were on short term contracts—given jobs as favours and with no idea of how to do their work. Jobs were not advertised properly—we hired people and not as per the requirement of the job. Or jobs given as favours

as under Nasim Ashraf's tenure where the staffing levels increased to 800 though only 100 were doing the work. Cricket was being run much more efficiently before. The senior administration feel threatened by intelligent people. People who work here cannot find good jobs elsewhere because they are so incompetent and unqualified—only here because they were given a job in return for a favour. Such people will only recruit similarly mediocre people.

Many later chairmen continued in this vein. Speaking anonymously to me, a senior officer in the board spoke of a previous chairman who 'created networks of patronage where he had his trusted people and those he mistrusted. Those he trusted could do anything—others had their telephones tapped and were constantly harassed. This produces a toxic atmosphere. Changing this is going to be one of the major challenges.'

Patronage is so deeply entrenched in the system that basic organizational features are often missing—job descriptions and the criteria for promotions and for hiring and firing are poorly laid out if they are present at all. Their implementation is in the hands of individuals taking arbitrary decisions. Job requirements that are advertised are often bypassed. This has bred a culture of nepotism, non-accountability, incompetence, and corruption, which in turn will affect the game itself. No effort is made to socialize new inductees into a positive work culture; instead, the dominant mode of socialization was 'this is the way things are done here.' Initiatives such as the bio-mechanics lab are discouraged.

Where there is trust, different parties can enter into collaborative relationships more quickly, sustain coordinated action by making mutual adjustments, and learn from each other rather than be stagnating for days, weeks, or months in formulating cumbersome contracts or building elaborate hierarchies that enforce a limited form of cooperation. Distrust on the other hand actively inhibits cooperation and coordination. When distrust exists between work groups, social interactions between them tend to create, perpetuate, and reinforce boundaries that maintain social distance, either physical or symbolic. It is not uncommon to find senior administration sitting behind locked doors and further being 'guarded' by secretaries that make accessing them extremely difficult.

The PCB's inability to build a shared set of values or *communitas* inhibits generalized reciprocity which in turn enables teamwork and cooperation amongst members within an organization. Given nepotism, patron-client relations, entrenched venality, and other improper use of authority, it is surprising that any cooperation even takes place. Today the PCB lies frozen by its culture of negative reciprocity where individuals actively work against one another.

In its early years, Pakistan cricket was sustained by willing amateurs. Its administrators, notably A.R. Cornelius, Abdul Hafeez Kardar, and Nur Khan combined their work in cricket with other major responsibilities. In the formative days, the national team was an expression of the selflessness of the creators of Pakistan. In later decades, when appointed, competent leadership allowed the board to prosper in the same way that good leadership and stability in the cricket team allowed a similar prospering. But the centralization in board operations combined with the increasing effects of political patronage has meant that the ossified arrogance of an entrenched political elite has contributed to making the PCB into a dysfunctional organization. In great part it could hardly be expected to have avoided this fate given the deterioration of the broader environment it has been operating in.

This chapter has shown how political influences affected cricket in Pakistan, from the initial support provided to an impoverished board to the appropriation of an increasingly popular national pastime by successive governments. But the political involvement in cricket and some of the issues that resulted as a consequence of this are likely to be reflective of a general decline in other institutions in Pakistan for the reasons discussed in the chapter. This would include, for example: the civil bureaucracy which was seen as amongst the best in the world well into the 1970s;[49] and Pakistan International Airlines which helped establish Emirates Airline in the 1980s. Today Emirates is amongst the biggest airlines in the world while PIA struggles to survive on government handouts. Both these institutions have seen sharp declines in their quality and reputations over the decades. The chapter also shows how cricket influences politics and, in particular, international relations between countries—an issue that is looked at in detail in subsequent chapters.

3

Corruption, Match-Fixing, and Redemption

'Oh no, anybody but the kid'

– Nasser Hussain,
former England Cricket Captain, on hearing that Pakistani players
were accused of spot-fixing.[1]

But it was the kid. Mohammad Amir, Pakistan's 18-year-old prodigy, had been caught along with two teammates, Salman Butt and Mohammad Asif, in a spot-fixing scandal. The story had broken the night before while the fourth Test Match between Pakistan and England during the 2010 tour was still on going. The next morning, I sat in the crowd wondering, alongside others, whether the Pakistan team would even turn up at the ground. There was an increased police presence in the ground and, living a stone's throw from the hotel that the team was based at, I saw the massive media attendance from the night before when police had searched the rooms of team members. Just weeks before, Salman Butt had run across the street from the hotel to pay his respects to the former PCB chairman as I walked with him. He was courteous and polite, accompanied by another team member, Umar Akmal. Butt had just led his young team—there were only two senior players in the team at the time—to a memorable win against Australia. Now weeks later, the Pakistan batsmen entered the field to finish a game that had become incidental. Salman Butt, Mohammad Asif, and Mohammad Amir had been accused of manipulating the game for money. It was a surreal day as both teams went through the motions. The MCC members in the pavilion managed a polite but subdued applause for the Pakistan team but a sense of a 'loss of innocence,' betrayal, and sadness pervaded the ground. The final presentations happened inside the pavilion; the teams barely spoke to each other. This was as far from a sporting event as could have been imagined.

In the days that followed, there was disbelief from some England players on how anyone could stoop so low as to fix a match. 'How do people get involved in that type of thing,' said Jonathan Trott.[2] '*It was vile information to digest*,' remarked Graeme Swann.[3] In Pakistan, effigies were burnt of Salman Butt and the media spoke of the shame heaped on the country while family members denied any wrong doing. The Prime Minister of Pakistan, Yousuf Raza Gilani, stated: 'The latest fixing allegations have bowed our heads in shame.'[4] On 3 November 2011, over a year after the incident occurred, jail terms were handed down—thirty months for Butt, one year for Asif, and six months for Amir.[5] The International Cricket Council banned all three players—Butt for ten years, of which five were suspended, Asif for seven years, of which two were suspended, and Amir for five years.

All sporting, religious, and other communal events are marked with emotion. Therefore, it is unsurprising that reactions to such events are charged with strong feeling and the hues of colour become black and white rather than shades of grey. The condemnation of the tainted trio and the shame heaped on the noble game of cricket and on the Pakistani nation were repeated ad nauseum, and yet corruption in sport and match and spot-fixing in cricket is anything but a black and white matter. This becomes a story of greed, deception, loss of innocence, and some degree of redemption. Chapter 2 introduced the themes of corruption, patronage, and mismanagement. In this chapter, I will attempt to unpack what conditions led to the growth of corruption in cricket globally and Pakistan particularly. Why did players indulge in it, how did they get caught up in such activities, and what were some of the responses and reactions to corruption in cricket? Match-fixing, then, can be seen as a symptom, or a reflection, of wider global and local factors.

It's Not Cricket: The Ethics of Cricket

But as soon as we stepped on to the cricket or football field, more
particularly the cricket field, all was changed.[6]
– C.L.R. James

All sports are infused with an ethical code revolving around fair play but none
more so than cricket. C.L.R. James's quote above refers to the cheating and
lying that took place in the classrooms in the Caribbean only to be replaced
immediately when the children stepped on to the hallowed turf of the cricket
field. The moral imperative of the cricket field trumped that of even the
pulpit or the classroom.

Much of this early influence came in the game's infancy in England by way
of the 'gentlemen' infusing the game with a very particular moral sensibility
which, according to Birley, involved 'a holier than thou attitude,' which
included 'not waiting for the umpire's decision—not expressing dissent,
either orally or by body language, however disappointing or seemingly unfair
the umpire's decision.'[7] The practice of not waiting for the umpire's decision
emphasized the pre-eminence of the honour code over the authority of the
humble umpire. Birley goes on to quote the English journalist E.W. Swanton
that 'cricketers are apt to claim, with not too conspicuous modesty, that
especially noble virtues are inherent and derivable from cricket.'[8]

The 'gentlemen' alluded to above refers to amateur players, most of whom
were members of the middle and upper classes, usually products of the
English public school system. In opposition to the erstwhile gentlemen
were the professionals known as the 'players'—working-class wage-earners.
The difference, therefore, between the teams was defined by the prevalent
English class structure.

For the Victorians, cricket was not so much a game as it was a 'way of
life.' Victorian society glorified it as a system of ethics and morals which
embodied all that was most noble in the Anglo-Saxon character. They prized
it as a national symbol, something that they saw as purely an English creation
unsullied by oriental or European influences. All classes of Victorians were
encouraged to play cricket as it increasingly came to be seen as the perfect
recreative pursuit—as a guarantee against illness and a means of building
character and leadership amongst men. As Sandiford emphasizes:

It is difficult to exaggerate the importance of cricket in Victorian life. It was
a ritual as well as a recreation, a spiritual as well as a sporting experience. Its
values and its language came to be freely used by politicians, philosophers,
preachers and poets.[9]

Poets and writers of the 19th and early 20th century, including the likes of Byron, Tennyson, Dickens, Oscar Wilde, and Wordsworth,[10] wrote in praise of the virtues of cricket. Descriptions of the game are filled with the language of idealism revolving around cricket's nobility, its hallowed turf. Take for example the couplet from James Dance's *An Heroic Poem* written in 1744:

> *Hail, Cricket! Glorious, manly, British game!*
> *First of all Sports! Be first alike in Fame!*

Like other sports of the era, cricket expanded in popularity across the spectrum from the 1860s onwards. This was partially due to the gradual improvement of living standards even amongst labourers and the steady reduction of working hours. There was also the conviction amongst the upper classes and the church that organized sport was the most effective form of socialization. It was during the Victorian period that the term 'it is not cricket,' denoting something ungentlemanly or improper or morally unacceptable, was coined.[11] Cricket, then, embodied the English values of strength, persistence, courage, chivalry, and sportsmanship. Cricket was a gentleman's game.

As with most matters relating to Victorian culture, mores, and social attitudes, leadership in the cricketing cult came from the aristocracy, the church, and the crown. Moreover, the pre-eminence of the upper and middle classes in cricket grew when the public schools—Eton and Harrow—and universities—Oxford and Cambridge—took on the role of producing leaders and used cricket as a means of moulding the character of students. Both the church and academic institutions encouraged and popularized the game and gave it a respectability that other sports lacked. In time, the working class in England turned increasingly to football, and particularly after the Second World War football displaced cricket as the dominant national sport, its appeal concentrating in a narrow middle-class base. But cricket's early association with public schools and universities and its supposed influence on the development of leadership and spiritual qualities gave it an almost 'sacred' status to be looked at with reverence.

> Almost to a man, the Victorians viewed cricket as the game least tainted by human foibles. It became so closely identified in their minds with religion, morality and public health that it could loom large in every discussion from education to imperialism. It had to be encouraged in academic institutions because it was an indispensable aid to intellectual pursuits. It was equally a part of the white man's burden as it had become also an integral feature in the process of imperial assimilation.[12]

As cricket diffused to the colonies, some indigenization and syncretism occurred—however, it maintained its core ethical values. Cricket continued to be identified with fair play and the language for the game continued to draw on religious metaphors such as the 'sacrosanct game' or the 'sanctity of the sport.' Mike Brearley, former England captain, for example, writing on match-fixing asserts how prior to the 1980s cricketers had lived in a 'Garden of Eden.'[13] Cricket demanded adherence to what it viewed were its core virtues, summed up in Lord Harris's ode to the game:

> You do well to love cricket, for it is more free from anything sordid, anything dishonourable, than any game in the world. To play it keenly, honourably, generously, self-sacrificingly, is a moral lesson in itself and the classroom is God's air and sunshine. Foster it, my brothers, so that it may attract all who can find time to play it; protect it from anything that would sully it, so that it may grow in favour with all men.[14]

David Frith points out that for 100 years or more, ever since the mid-Victorians elevated it to something approaching holy devotion, the game of cricket stood principally for gentlemanly, and preferably heroic, conduct. Frith notes: 'So pure was cricket that it sometimes resembled a branch of Christianity.'[15]

> It remains the case, however, that only in cricket (though golf comes close in this respect) do the laws of the game contain a section which explicitly addresses the importance of sportsmanship and formally prescribes the required 'Spirit of the Game.'[16]

It is from these idealist notions of the virtues and values of cricket that we must then look at the fall from grace to the period of match-fixing representing the corruption and distortion of those very values that defined the sport.

THE BEGINNINGS OF MATCH-FIXING

On 7 April 2000, the cricket world was struck by one of the biggest crises in its 250-year existence. Following an undercover operation, the Delhi police revealed that they had evidence that South African captain, Hansie Cronje, and other international players were associated with bookmakers in manipulating the results of international cricket matches.[17] This event had a cascading effect with national cricket boards being forced into investigating the players named in the report. In June 2000, the International Cricket Council appointed a director of its newly formed Anti-Corruption Unit (ACU). The ACU released its first report in April 2001. The Qayyum Commission Report in Pakistan was circulated in May 2000, the Central Bureau of Investigation (CBI) in India released its report in November 2000, and the Judge El King Commission in South Africa published its final report in June 2001.

The Qayyum[18] Commission in Pakistan in fact pre-dated the CBI (India) investigation and was the consequence of a series of rumours that had enveloped Pakistan cricket soon after the World Cup win of 1992. There had been other fact-finding inquiries[19] prior to the Qayyum inquiry but no action had resulted from them. Qayyum's report was completed in September 1999 but was 'buried' until the Cronje scandal forced Pakistan to publicly address the concerns that had emerged and release the report. All these various inquiries disclosed that, since the early 1990s, cricket was riddled with match-fixing corruption which authorities—the various boards as well as the International Cricket Council—had failed to address for a variety of reasons.

Betting on the outcome of the game as well as on individual events within a game goes back to the start of cricket itself. The earliest reference to gambling on the sport is to a game in Kent, England in 1646.[20] Distinct from betting on a game, match-fixing relates to:

> deciding the outcome of a match before it is played and then playing oneself or having others play below one's/ their ability to influence the outcome to be in accordance with the pre-decided outcome. Match-fixing is done primarily for pecuniary gain.[21]

The CBI in India adds to this definition:

> besides losing a game deliberately, match-fixing involved betting on individual or collective underperformance by some players, insider information provision and player introductions to 'bookies,' and ground preparation to guarantee certain predetermined results.[22]

The second half of this definition refers to what is now termed 'spot-fixing,' and while both refer to illegal and dishonest activity in a sport, spot-fixing does not attempt to change the result of a game nor does it necessarily imply underperformance; however, it does refer to fixing a specific part of a game. Spot-fixing will include, for example, changing the order in which a player bowls or bats or bowling a wide ball or a no-ball at a particular time or scoring fewer than a certain number of runs in an over.

If the various inquiries do identify the 1990s as the decade when match-fixing became widespread, why was that the case? I believe there are a number of reasons for this, some of which find their roots in the decades before match-fixing actually began to proliferate. The most significant of these was the commercialization of cricket which greatly increased the opportunities for corruption and attracted the attention of corruptors in the form of criminal networks. Commercialization also led to a change in the ethical values associated with the 'noble' game. Money and greed are powerful forces that can become corrupting influences on people and their environments. Michael Sandel argues that money can erode values[23]: the joy of learning is reduced if children are paid to read; money may switch moral behaviour off by, for example, introducing fines which can undermine a parent's sense of ethical obligation to be on time for the teachers.[24] Lateness then becomes 'just another commodity' to purchase.

COMMERCIALIZATION

Up until the 1970s, cricket had changed very little. Apart from England and its former colonies—Australia, South Africa, West Indies, New Zealand, India, and Pakistan—no other country had been granted Test Match status.[25] The laws were remarkably stable, opposing teams both wore 'whites,' and the game was played out over five days, often not producing a win-lose result at the end. Cricket continued to be bound to what Appadurai termed the 'capability to mimic Victorian elite values'[26] of sportsmanship: the umpire is always right, sportsmanship trumps winning, and as in life you treat both triumph and disaster with Kiplingesque stoicism. More than any other sport, it retained vestiges of purity and innocence of its origins. Comparatively speaking, it remained unsullied by the commercial imperatives of the modern world. This was to change significantly with the introduction of one day cricket and the commercial possibilities it represented. The first Cricket World Cup held in 1975 introduced the one-day international variant of cricket on an international level but the most profound changes occurred when the Australian media tycoon Kerry Packer set up a breakaway World Series Cricket (WSC) League in Australia in 1977.

It is at this point that one-day cricket inherited many of its distinctive features including coloured clothing (accentuating the difference between teams who previously both wore white) and floodlit day-night matches. In sharp contrast to the five-day Test in the limited overs variety, one team wins at the end of every day and is rewarded for doing so. The pace of the game was no longer leisurely, and crowds became larger and more diverse, drawing an increasing number of 'non-specialist' supporters. Packer introduced commercialism to cricket, thereby increasing the number of cricket's 'consumers,' earning plenty of sponsorship dollars and offering the kind of salaries that saw the best players moving to the WSC as highly paid professionals.[27] WSC popularized the shorter version of the game. It changed cricket forever from simply a sport to media entertainment. In later decades, cricket would convulse again with the Twenty20 (T20) revolution—a further reduction in the time scale of a match so that in thirty years the sport has gone from a five-day spectacle to a movie length one. The change is significant, the extent of which few other sports have faced. With the hectic rate of transformation in the game and the commercial imperatives and the dictates of the mass market that have followed, it is unsurprising that the values associated with the game have also changed.

In India, which was soon to become the commercial hub for cricket, the first steps of the Kerry Packer revolution came, surprisingly, via Pakistan. Sataduru Sen argues that during Pakistan's tour to India in 1979–80[28] it became apparent how the images of the Pakistani players that had played in the WSC, most notably those of Imran Khan, had been transformed.

> The 'sex symbol' persona that Imran brought to India in 1979 was a product not of his looks alone, but of the media circus that surrounded Packer's enterprise. During the tour Imran, Zaheer Abbas and their team mates made a further transition that had been enabled by the 'memory' of WSC: they became the performative equivalents of Indian film stars, shadowed by the paparazzi off the field, sought out not only by 'serious' cricket journalists like Kishore Bhimani and Dicky Rutnagar but also by 'lifestyle columnists' and by women reporters such as Tavleen Singh (who did not usually write about sport), escorted to parties by assorted movie stars and starlets, and captured by the cover page editors of dedicated magazines such as *Sporstworld* as well as news magazines such as *Sunday*.[29]

The move from sport to media entertainment was evident in the parallel changing images of cricketers from simply sportsmen to celebrities. South Asian society with its tendency of deifying politicians and film stars now had a new set of individuals who could be the object of worship. Four years later, in 1983, India won the cricket World Cup and subsequently followed that by another major title in Australia in 1985.[30] The demand for one day cricket soared and the fortunes of the Asian cricket boards improved rapidly. Today the Board of Control for Cricket in India is the commercial powerhouse of the cricketing world and yet on the night of India's World Cup victory in 1983 the board was so financially constrained that it could not afford the winning team members a decent dinner and saw them instead celebrating at a fast food outlet in Piccadilly.[31]

Prior to 1983, India's cricket tradition had revolved around Test cricket and crowds had thronged to stadia to see their heroes. Ashis Nandy argues in his book *The Tao of Cricket* that while the British invented cricket, it was best suited to the Indian character and even caste identities within Hinduism.[32] Expanding on this claim, Sharda Ugra states that India's attachment to the traditional version of the game, Test cricket, was supposedly explained:

> by the very open endedness, the protracted nature and complexity of the game. That India, an ancient culture, loved the long, unfolding drama of a Test Match and had a greater tolerance even of the tedium that some matches brought, as it mirrored the rhythms of life as lived out in the East. Indians then were perceived to have a deep rooted and fundamental understanding of the idea of the draw because it's very ambiguity (no one won, yet no one lost) suited a country where society was based on joint families, compromise and cooperation, and not on competition of individualism. The essential purposelessness and timelessness of some of the cricket rituals perfectly matched a land where, in some languages, yesterday and tomorrow were the same word.[33]

While the above arguments by Nandy and Ugra are somewhat reductive and have a tone of cultural essentialism, they do highlight a conservatism in Indian cricket and society at the time. But India was changing too. The ancient culture was being replaced by the emergence of a combination of modern influences, alongside the resurgence of 'traditional' ones in the form of Hindutva. A young population was burgeoning, restrictions associated with decades of Nehruvian socialist rule were being eased, and the economy was beginning to grow rapidly. 'The dramatic expansion of Indian television after 1982 boosted the revolution further. By the end of the decade, over 80 per cent of the country was covered by Doordarshan (the national broadcaster) and this reach was exponentially supplemented by the arrival of satellite TV in the early 1990's.'[34] The commitment to the traditional values of the game mentioned in previous pages began to erode.

Administrators in India found that the one-day game—which they were excelling in—was a gold mine and that they could make more money from One Day Internationals (ODIs) than from the five-day Test Matches. The board began to schedule more and more one day fixtures. Matches sold out, grounds filled to capacity, and television rights sold for increasingly large amounts. Up until 1983, India had played 48 ODIs; in the decade that followed, they played 134.[35] And since 1991, they have played 357.[36] The number of Test Matches has increased only marginally (42 in the 1980s, 47 between 2000 and 2009). It is the boom in the shorter format of the game, and later in the even shorter T20 format, that made the BCCI, through its control of Indian cricket, spectacularly rich. Over 80 per cent of cricket's global revenues are now estimated to be generated in India,[37] giving India enormous clout on the international cricket stage.

In order to capitalize on the popularity of ODIs and to reinforce that even further through putting the Indo-Pakistan rivalry into the mix, the 1980s saw the emergence of cricket's first off shore venue—in the Gulf emirate of Sharjah. Keen to tap into the large South Asian expatriate population in the Gulf, Sharjah became the centre of the Indo-Pakistan rivalry and particularly between 1984 and 2000 teams from India and Pakistan played matches in this most unlikely of venues—a green oasis in the midst of a vast desert. The audience often included South Asian glitterati, including politicians, Bollywood stars, and, significantly, shady underworld gangsters based mainly out of Mumbai. The success of Sharjah led to the organizing of more off shore events in Singapore, Hong Kong, and Canada. Unfortunately, the surfeit of unimportant matches arranged mainly for profit by the boards were increasingly seen by the players as 'meaningless and as opportunities to maximize the receipt of gifts or indulge in under-performance for betting purposes.'[38]

In the four years between 1983 and 1987, world cricket had changed immeasurably with the most significant aspect being the flush new market for cricket in India. By 1987, the foundations of the commercial transformation were almost complete as India, Pakistan, and Sri Lanka won the bid to host the next World Cup on home soil, signifying a major shift in the game's epicentre from England which hosted the first three World Cups to now the Asian Subcontinent.[39] The event was a financial and organizational success, despite neither of the hosts reaching the final. By the time the 1996 World Cup came back to the Subcontinent there had been a huge expansion in the game in the Subcontinent and particularly in India. A further commercial revolution would occur with the launch of the enormously profitable T20 Indian Premier League (IPL)[40] which today ranks as amongst the richest events in the global sporting world.

If we accept that match-fixing became widespread in the mid-1990s, then the commercialization of the sport in the previous decade set the stage for subsequent corruption in cricket. The leisurely pace of the five-day Test Match which would often produce a no-result (or draw) at the conclusion of the five days had been replaced by a one day, result-oriented game replete with coloured clothing, floodlights, aggressive sponsorship, and media driven interest. The gentlemanly sport was no longer so gentlemanly. The change in the nature of the game and the values associated with the game led also to a common narrative—cricketers now played for money rather than their countries. World Series Cricket had seen several cricket boards ban players who chose the rebel league over their national commitments. Money had trumped patriotism. It was fearing the disruption of the nation building role of cricket, in the case of Pakistan, that led General Ziaul Haq to broker a compromise, allowing Pakistan's banned cricketers to return and represent the nation.

Since the arrival of the T20 leagues this cry has become even louder as cricketers retire from national duty in order to prolong their careers in the shorter, more lucrative forms of the game, often playing for leagues that are not based around national teams but clubs as in premier league football. Andy Bull, writing in *The Guardian*, quoted the former West Indian captain Clive Lloyd as saying that this T20 format has 'messed up' cricket in the West Indies. The players were interested only in the financial gains. 'It doesn't seem playing for our country is paramount,'[41] remarked the man who had been credited in his career with building an outstanding West Indian team that the disparate Caribbean Islands had enormous pride in. In the West Indies, the movement away from cricket as something that served a bigger purpose than itself—the struggle for social justice, identity, and political freedom into commercially driven entertainment—has been felt acutely. Where Vivian Richards had refused to play in the Apartheid period in South Africa, Brian Lara took his team on strike over a pay dispute on the eve of the historic tour to South Africa as Nelson Mandela waited to receive the team at the airport.[42] Similar statements have been made about Pakistani cricketers who have also prematurely retired from Test cricket[43] in favour of playing in the lucrative leagues.

The glitz, glamour, and money that increasingly became part of one day cricket also attracted the attention of criminal elements who were drawn by the large profits available through illegal betting networks. This was facilitated further through the spread of live television coverage of cricket which made it possible to watch and bet on cricket almost every day of the year, and mobile phone technology which enabled communication during matches between bookmakers and punters, and in match-fixing, between 'bookies' and corrupt players and journalists.[44]

MATCH-FIXING IN PAKISTAN

While the transformation that was occurring in cricket due to its commercialization was experienced across the cricketing world, there were local influences and happenings specific to Pakistan that defined the nature of match-fixing in Pakistan cricket.

Fame, Greed, Celebrity

The statement, 'My players are more interested in making money than playing the game,' was made by the World Cup winning Indian captain, Kapil Dev, a few months after India's surprise win over the West Indies in the 1983 World Cup final. In an interview with sports journalist Pradeep Magazine, Dev goes on to lament that the team had lost direction and that the lure of money was affecting the commitment of the team. They were more interested in accepting invitations to visit people and places in the hope of being showered with gifts.[45] Magazine sees this changing attitude within the team—who months earlier had celebrated the biggest moment in Indian cricket at the time with a fast food dinner—as indicative of the greed that preceded the match-fixing scandals that engulfed India in the mid-1990s. Under a decade later, the Pakistan team would face a similar scenario, in a time period which was even more ripe for match-fixing.

Pakistan's remarkable World Cup victory in 1992 was a seminal moment that brought the country the glory of cricket's biggest prize. Cricket had already established itself in the consciousness of the country as a marker of national identity. Pakistan's politicians were quick to exploit the win. Announcements of gold medals, plots of land, cash prizes, guaranteed tax-free shopping, and a fully paid religious pilgrimage to Makkah en route home were just the start of a windfall of gifts and adulation. Imran Khan, the triumphant, inspirational captain was by this time nearing the end of his career and was focussed on building a cancer hospital in memory of his mother who had died of the disease. Seeing that the World Cup win was an ideal opportunity to raise money for the hospital, Khan requested that the team attend a series of charity functions organized by rich businessmen who would put large sums of money into the players' pool in return for their attendance at their events. He requested that the proceeds be shared 50-50 between the players and the charity hospital.

While the team had agreed to the arrangement initially, they soon became reluctant to share the spoils that they increasingly felt were their right.[46] Following an event in Singapore, the majority of the players decided that the sharing formula was unacceptable and that they preferred keeping the money entirely for themselves. Khan writes in his autobiography that senior players began pushing plans for a tour to major cities in Pakistan 'so that an organized collection of gifts and prizes could be made from companies interested in rewarding them for winning the World Cup.'[47] These were to be purely for the players and not to be shared with the hospital fund. When I asked Mushtaq Ahmed, one of the rising stars of the winning world cup team, about the incident, 'Mushy,' now a born-again Muslim, was embarrassed. He referred to it as one of the most shameful moments of his career but something he only became fully aware of when he had his spiritual reawakening and turned to Islam after years of chasing materialistic pleasures.

> We were at the peak of our popularity after the World Cup. Everyone was giving us gifts and our potential earnings were huge. I remember landing in Lahore and leaving the plane. There were so many people … I couldn't see beyond them. We were put on top of a bus. It took us six hours to cover a 15-minute journey to the hotel. People were calling us *badshah* (king); they were throwing money at us. Everyone wanted to meet us. We would easily charge £50,000 per function. But we didn't want to share the money. The seniors were saying why should we pay for the hospital. The government should pay. We deserved to be rewarded. The youngsters agreed to go along with the more established players. Some of us were not well off. So, in the function in Lahore we decided that we would all leave the stage when Imran spoke. Now I look back and see that moment, when Imran was left alone on stage as we all left, as one of my most shameful. We were blinded by greed.

Disillusioned by what he saw as the new materialist ethic amongst the team, Khan retired from the game. One of the team's senior players subsequently stated that 'with no superstars in the side, we are happier.'[48] It was a dramatic twist as the team that had idolized Khan turned on him. It was also the start of a slide in team ethics and morals.

These two similar instances for India and Pakistan do indicate a focus on the material as it becomes more available. For many of these young men, several of whom came from modest economic backgrounds, the riches that were suddenly available would have been unimaginable a few years ago. With it came the fame and adulation of millions. There were also powerful justifications being used—a moral disengagement using the argument 'we deserved the riches, we brought laurels to the country'—and with little support or mentorship (if anything the senior players incited them on!) it is unsurprising that ambitious, driven individuals were caught in this slipstream. As the proceeds from the World Cup win began to fade, match-fixing came to provide a new avenue for enhanced income from cricket. But while greed may have driven the materialistic frenzy that occurred after the World Cup, explanations for match-fixing were more complex and varied and which may have included greed but were not confined to it. It is to these multiple influences that I now turn.

Insecurity, Inequality, Envy

The influx of money into the game and the multiplying effect that occurred after the success of the 1992 World Cup should be set against the changing 'demographics' of the Pakistan team. By the early 1990s, the team was being sourced from a much broader socio-economic base and several cricketers, unlike those prior to the 1980s, were from much more modest economic backgrounds. This has continued to be the case right up to the present day. Cricket offers these young men access to financial success and global recognition. Mohammad Amir and Mohammad Asif, for example, both of whom were caught in the spot-fixing scandal of 2010, came from poor families. Amir's father found employment plastering the walls in the houses of other villagers. Asif's father maintained a few buffaloes as a source of livelihood. For those who have known financial insecurity, the lure of wealth in order to banish the days of anxiety and chart a new future not only for the individuals but their families and future children is a powerful motivation.

This desire for financial security is exacerbated by characteristics of the sporting profession which is by nature insecure—injuries can end careers early, competition may lead to loss of team places, and the career span rarely extends past 40 years of age. In Pakistan, inconsistency in selection and perceived favouritism also adds to the uncertainty. Moreover, there are few avenues open once a playing career finishes. Therefore, the incentive to make money quickly and in large amounts—possibly through corrupt means while the opportunity presents itself—is another factor that may have encouraged players towards corruption.

But it is important to understand that this one factor is far from a defining cause. Many cricketers from poor backgrounds have resisted the lure of corrupt earnings. Some who were already extremely well off have succumbed. For every Mohammad Amir there was a Salman Butt, or a Hansie Cronje, or a Mohammad Azharuddin. Salman Butt was from a middle-class background and had studied at an elite English school. Mohammad Azharuddin, at the time he received his life ban from the Indian board,[49] had played in more one dayers than anyone in the game and his personal wealth was estimated to be greater than any other player's.[50] Hansie Cronje was captain of the South African national team and was extremely well compensated.[51]

> Despite being a very rich man by South African standards, with trust funds set up in his and his wife Bertha's names, a benefit three years ago which yielded R1.4-million, a handsome stipend from the United Cricket Board, income probably amounting to R4-million from endorsements over the past five years, lucrative speaking engagements and a R3.8-million house on the luxury golf estate at Fancourt, Cronje simply could not say no to offers of what seemed to be easy money.[52]

Moreover, what started with insecurity may also become greed in time. As we move away from insecurity as a motivation, in an ambitious and competitive environment, it is maybe unsurprising that envy appears as an additional factor. Interestingly, the point of comparison seems to be progressively focussed on 'non sporting' traits. Whereas in the past the success of a cricket player may have revolved primarily around his performance in the cricket field, increasingly the commercialization of cricket has meant that cricketing success includes several other factors—markers of wealth and signs of social mobility such as large houses in metropolitan centres, expensive cars, designer clothes and watches, lucrative sponsorships, as well as other trappings of fame including social circles that include glitterati from the entertainment world, beautiful wives, and the number of social media followers. Salman Butt, for example, complained to his agent and co-conspirator in the 2010 spot-fixing incident that he was unable to afford the plush houses that others in the team had bought through the proceeds of match-fixing.[53] Not only was he envious of what they had, but he also believed that these trappings of success had been achieved through corrupt means which he went on to emulate. But the globalization of cricket also means that competition occurs not only within national boundaries but across them as well—and while it is true that that cricketers representing Pakistan are well paid by local standards, they are compensated more poorly than the majority of their international counterparts. Recent reports[54] suggest that while the top cricketers in the world earn around $1 million from playing international cricket, the top Pakistani annual contract ($74,000) is worth less in monetary terms than the top Ireland one—Ireland being the newest entrant to world cricket having joined in 2017.

Apart from basic salary, Pakistani cricketers have also suffered because the terrorist attack in Pakistan on the Sri Lankan team in 2009 led to the loss of cricket being played in Pakistan, forcing a shift of 'home' games to the United Arab Emirates. This is significant additional expense on the

Pakistan Cricket Board. Moreover, political tensions between India and Pakistan and India's refusal to play Pakistan in bilateral series since 2007 has meant that earnings for the board through a share of commercial rights has reduced considerably. From 2008, following the attack on the Taj Mahal Palace hotel in Mumbai by ten gunmen believed to be trained in Pakistan, Pakistani cricketers have also been locked out of the cash rich IPL, opening a further gulf in earning potential between themselves and the rest of the international fraternity. Pakistan became the bottom feeders. The richer cricket has become, the more inequality it has bred—and, as Hughes, Mehtta, Bresciani, and Strange point out, 'ugly emotions', like envy and greed, proliferate in environments of inequality.[55]

For Pakistani cricketers, the lower gains from cricket created resentment and formed a justification for some to engage in corrupt practices. What they saw was their own proficiency on par with other cricketers but their inability to translate that into the kind of financial windfall that other, even lesser-talented cricketers, were being able to achieve. Salman Butt, in fact, used these arguments when he appealed in the Court for Arbitration for Sport in 2011 in an attempt to try and reduce his punishment:

> Pakistani players were uniquely exposed and vulnerable to spot-fixing (and the financial inducements which accompany it), because (1) their earnings were lower than certain other players, (2) they were not permitted to play in the Indian Premier League, and (3) Pakistan was unable to host home games due to the 2009 terrorist attacks in Lahore.

The argument therefore was that not only were Pakistani cricketers unable to play cricket at home following the terrorist attacks on the Sri Lankan cricket team in 2009, they were also unable to join the scramble for the millions available from the Indian Premier League and forced to watch others reap the rewards now available at the pinnacle of the game.

Bernardo Brown argues in his analysis of the changing aspirations of Sri Lankan youth as they migrate to Italy that the new imaginary of transnationalism was no longer characterized by a national subject that sought to succeed locally, but one that dreamt of being a global participant and a transnational player.[56] In the same vein, as cricket globalized more and more, Pakistani cricketers increasingly became aware of the conditions of their peers in other parts of the cricketing world. With the first commercialization of cricket through the World Series Cricket league, several prominent Pakistani cricketers had actually been at the centre of the windfall and had used this experience to push for better salaries and benefits with their own board. The re-centring of the financial centre of cricket to South Asia and primarily to India should have allowed Pakistan to benefit financially as well. Unfortunately, political tensions and the inability of Pakistani cricketers to argue for better compensation meant that Pakistani cricketers found that they were soon amongst the least well paid in the global cricketing world. Regardless, the rapid globalization of cricket at this stage led to the emergence of a new social imaginary which inspired new narratives of success and prosperity that came to be embraced in the context of globalization and transnationalism. New ideas of success and progress were inspired by a particular awareness of the global and a post-national understanding of what the role of the local should be. Like their counterparts, Pakistani cricketers aspired to the same imaginary.

Mike Brearley argues that greed itself does not capture the complexity of factors that may influence an individual's decision to indulge in match-fixing any more than sexual desire captures sexual adventurism and dishonesties.[57] In some cases, greed may be the driving force. For Hansie Cronje, his fatal character flaw was his love of money—'I do like money. I'm not trying to get away from that,' he said when questioned by the King Commission set up to investigate his case.[58] But inequality and the envy that ensues, changing values, and financial insecurity may all have also had a part to play in tempting players into corruption. Moreover, justifications for corrupt behaviour—such as poorer pay and the inability to avail of better opportunities—act as facilitators to corrupt acts as they allow for moral disengagement in the minds of the individuals.

It is also worth remembering that sportsmen are ambitious. Risk takers, by nature. Ugra points out that eminent sports psychoanalysts like Mike Brearley, Rudi Webster, Maqbool Babri, and Sandy Gordon have expressed their views on the impulses that have led sportsmen on the threshold of fame to risk their careers through corruption and betting.[59] For these psychoanalysts, greed is too simplistic an explanation for errant behaviour. Brearley refers to the 'doomed fatality' of the first step for a sportsman when he gives casual assistance on the wrong side. Once in, it is very hard to get out. Sandy Gordon, an eminent Australian sports psychologist, has referred to 'derailers' that have induced great athletes like Mike Tyson, George Best, Diego Maradona, or Tiger Woods to stray into gambling, drugs, and violence against women. Gordon states that it is about 'character meeting opportunity.' Temptations come in many disguises. What stays constant is the powerful lure. Gordon states that individuals over-estimate themselves and their ability to get away with ill-advised risks. Elite sport contains characters Gordon calls 'narcissistic personality disordered,' who believe that their 'exalted status, based on personal performances' makes them 'entitled to do and say whatever they please.' The consequences of their behaviour are rarely considered until someone else brings it to their attention. Or when they get caught. In South Asia, the adulation bestowed upon cricketers makes many believe that they can get away with anything. Brearley lists other facets that, when pieced together, lead to a succumbing theme: 'the excitement of risk-taking, the omnipotence of believing one can get away with anything, and the filling of the sense of emptiness in one's life.'[60]

With opportunities, temptations, social change, and volatile personality types occupying the centrality of sport, the role of the mentor becomes a crucial element in encouraging positive character development and discouraging corrupt behaviour. Equally, poor mentorship can have a significantly negative impact with the same group of individuals. The following section examines the role of both positive and negative mentorship.

LEADERSHIP AND 'GROOMING'

Good leadership brings with it stability, security, and long term vision. Pakistan has rarely been able to find good leaders, and this has meant that mentorship has been sorely lacking. Teams require role models who subsequently influence the culture of the group and because culture is a critical part of ensuring integrity in groups it is important to shape it. Role modelling is how leaders demonstrate and show support for the desired values. The value of having good leaders allows both for the articulation of the value of integrity and a manifestation of it through actions. This suggests that visibility of leaders is important as they provide group members with cues on what behaviours are desired and acceptable. In order to show the contrasting effects of positive and negative leadership, I will refer to a few examples of both and the impact they had on the cricket team culture.

Transformational Leadership: The Case of Imran Khan

No captain had as big an influence on team culture and performance as Imran Khan who led the team through the 1980s until retirement after the 1992 World Cup win. Eschewing the age hierarchies that dominate South Asian society, Khan invested in youth and built a new team in his own image. Almost thirty years later, he would use the same youth-focussed strategy to come to power as Prime Minister of Pakistan. Khan was a charismatic and inspirational leader. An exceptional cricketer with an unwavering belief in his own abilities, he was able to make his young team believe that they were world beaters. Instilling in them a competitive spirit and self-belief, he brought unity, discipline, and professionalism that had previously been lacking. Significantly, he mentored each and every one of the younger players, passing on his knowledge freely in stark contrast to other senior players who hoarded their skills and remained aloof from younger team members, insecure that the new generation may surpass and displace them. Khan did not know the word insecurity and even when Pakistan faced near elimination from the 1992 World Cup he continued espousing the belief that Pakistan would win. Ramiz Raja, who was a member of the winning team, informed me that throughout that tournament, 'even when we were losing matches, Imran was 100% sure we would win the tournament. It was a mission for him. It was destiny in his eyes.'

Imran's leadership style and impact are captured by Samiuddin in his retrospective of the 1992 victory and the legendary talk he gave his players as they faced elimination having lost four of their first five matches:

> Imran spoke to each player and told them to look inside themselves, to understand that they were the best players in the world. 'You,' he asked one, 'is there a more talented player in the world than you?' Is there a better fielder than you, he asked another, a better batsman than you? Having roused each player, he ended twenty minutes later with the image on his t-shirt, the image that resonated most to him and how he saw himself; a tiger, a Pathan tiger, hunting, warring, surviving. Now he invoked a twist, one that had seen him through his toughest professional years when a shin injury threatened to finish his career. Fight like cornered tigers he told them, because nothing is more dangerous than a cornered tiger. Imran told them that he knew, not just thought, but that he knew and believed that Pakistan will win the World Cup. 'I know we will win it.' What he did was transmit his self-belief onto the rest of the squad, a monumental feat which doesn't just happen. This transplantation was the accumulation of a career, of a life, of every single day of success, of unchallenged authority, of every time he returned to the captaincy automatically, of every time he refused to play when it was too hot, or against too weak a side. It was the cumulative effect of a decade of Imran as captain, hero and icon, distilled in one talk.[61]

The effect was greatest on the younger players. They played for him, they idolized him. They were in awe of him. When I spoke with one of them, Aaqib Javed, who in 1988 was a 17-year-old inducted into the team by Khan, he recalled the devotion of the team to their captain: 'there was a match against India, I think in Sharjah. Imran got hit by Manoj Prabhakar while batting. I was in the dressing room with Wasim and Waqar. For us the match became Pakistan versus Prabhakar. When he came out to bat, we gave him a rough time. He must have had a lot of bruises on his body from balls that hit him. At the end of the match he apologized. But looking back...I felt we were playing for Imran and not for Pakistan. As a 17-year-old from a small town in Punjab he made me believe that I could bowl to the best batsman in the world and get him out. And we all went in with that attitude. Imran had that unique quality that a good leader must have: to make people believe in what he was saying and to believe in themselves.'

Imran Khan was also a scrupulously honest sportsman who brought an adamantine integrity and patriotism to his cricket. John Crace, writing on Imran Khan's honesty, relates an incident in which Khan as captain was approached by the home umpires for 'instructions.' Khan told them: 'you do your job, we'll do ours'[62]—and it was Imran Khan who would subsequently push Pakistan to become the first country to implement the use of neutral umpires.

Ramiz Raja, who like Aaqib Javed played under Imran for several years, states that Imran would never have tolerated any hint of dissent or corruption under his watch. 'No one would have the guts to try and fix a match when Imran was captain. Imran would have killed the guy...even if the board didn't do anything, Imran would never let that man play another game of cricket for Pakistan.' There had already been examples of players who had 'crossed' Imran Khan. Qasim Omar who played for Pakistan between 1983 and 1987 accused Imran Khan and other teammates of debauchery and carrying drugs in their cricket kit.[63] Omar was banned and never played for Pakistan again.

Khan displayed the characteristics of what Bass and Avolio state are core features of a 'transformational leader': charisma, inspiration, intellectual stimulation, and individual consideration.[64] Charisma included gaining the respect and trust of team members, winning the confidence of others, and having a strong sense of mission. Inspiration was operationalized as communicating the vision with fluency, enthusiasm, high optimism, instilling confidence, and giving pep talks. Individual consideration was operationalized as personal attention, each person feeling valued and recognizing each individual's contribution as important to the wider purpose of the team. Intellectual stimulation included developing mental toughness and preparedness.[65] Imran Khan was the case book transformational leader.

As a dominant and autocratic leader, Khan was an unusual though not completely unencountered Pakistani leader—eloquent and educated, worldly and aloof. Pakistan's first captain, A.H. Kardar, was similar, but looking more broadly, so too were Pakistan's founder M.A. Jinnah, and Zulfikar Ali Bhutto, Prime Minister and founder of the Pakistan Peoples Party. All the aforementioned were individuals who led others but were set apart from them and not representative of them. The contrast between the impacts of positive and negative mentorship are best illustrated through reference to the events that followed Imran Khan's retirement as captain and his replacement by leadership that was more flawed and adverse.

When Imran Khan retired in 1992, disillusioned at the team having turned against him, a dangerous leadership vacuum was created. It also occurred at a crucial time when guidance was required. The team had won the World Cup and had gained the kind of stardom and adulation that none had previously seen. Money had entered the game and with it came the interest of the underworld; match-fixing networks began making overtures to the Asian teams. At this critical juncture when leadership was most required, Salim Malik, who was later found guilty of match-fixing by Justice Qayyum, became captain. The means and the opportunity were both present. What allegedly followed was the start of years of match-fixing in which a culture of corruption made home in the Pakistan national team.

> I was sitting in the Taj Hotel in Colombo; the young cricketer seemed a little upset and came to sit on a bench where my colleague and I were seated waiting for some other journalists to join us. In those days the relationship between players and journalists was quite close. We would often interact, and I knew many members of the team. I asked the cricketer, who was clearly disturbed by something, if there was a problem. He said, fairly openly, that he was under pressure from senior team members to help ensure Pakistan lost whichever game was coming up. I forget if it was a Test or One-Day. He said he did not want to do this and hinted that the captain was among those pressurizing him and he felt that unless he cooperated he would be thrown out of the team. At least three other young players had been pressurised by a clique of senior players to assist in fixing matches. All these senior players had connections with bookmakers. The bookmakers openly socialized with the players, calling them to parties, showering them with gifts, showing them the high life. On the next tour to South Africa things got so bad that the team split into three groups—two groups working for different bookies and a third group being the whistle blowers. They spied on one another; they tapped each other's phones. Everything fell apart.[66]

The account above was provided by a journalist I interviewed and who had covered Pakistan cricket in some detail through the 1990s. It illustrates how rapidly the team culture changed following the 1992 World Cup. From having an inspirational and incorruptible team leader to an environment where the captain himself was the corrupting influence along with other senior team members, the role and the function of mentorship had been completely reversed. Having the captain on board makes match-fixing much easier and, as a result, individuals who have captained their respective teams have often been targeted by bookies. The captain can then exert influence on other team members. This was the case with Hansie Cronje (South Africa), Mohammad Azharuddin (India), and Salim Malik and Salman Butt (Pakistan), all of whom were banned for match- or spot-fixing and all of whom inveigled other members of their teams to become part of the corruption.

The damaging effects of negative leadership are well illustrated by the spot-fixing scandal that occurred in 2010. The ring leader of the scandal was the then captain of the Pakistan team Salman Butt. The case highlights many of the issues that have been covered above—leadership, mentorship, greed, insecurity, and envy. In the section below, I highlight these motivations through reference to the case of Salman Butt and his co-conspirators.

Flawed Leadership: The Case of Salman Butt

Salman Butt had all the makings of a transformational leader. For a short period, he was a charismatic and inspirational leader and could have been more. I interviewed him on several occasions. He showed bitterness at his treatment following his ban, as well as some remorse over his actions albeit with justifications, but I was struck most by his intelligence and broad vision. He spoke softly, always obliged fans wanting pictures with him, and made time for lengthy interviews. In these conversations he spoke with alacrity about issues across the cricketing world—new coaching techniques and managerial practices and the progress of the domestic game in India and how new cricketers were afforded opportunities and clear career progression there. And in all of these he felt Pakistan compared poorly internationally and even regionally and had made little progress. When he was appointed captain in 2010, he brought the kind of leadership that Pakistan has lacked since Imran Khan leading the team to an excellent win over Australia in his first Test Match as captain. Now, as he spoke with some feeling and passion, the overwhelming sense I had was of a tragic waste of potential.

> We don't have mentors in Pakistan cricket. I tried my best to help the younger players. I sat with each of them to make them feel included and to build that self-belief in them. I backed my players. We had a team full of young players. I even asked one of the Australian senior players to come and speak to my players so that they could benefit from his experience. They spent an hour and

a half with him. I did have problems with a senior cricketer though who I just felt was threatened by me. He was always hostile and would loudly complain that the manager had made *kal ke larkay* (boys from yesterday) too big for their boots and that they did not respect their seniors.

The hierarchical nature of the Pakistani society—with age hierarchy being amongst the most rigid—would always cause tensions within the team setup. Pakistan cricket has tended to follow societal hierarchical norms—the more senior you become, the more chance of taking over captaincy. A young captain has always been a gamble. Even when the value of central contracts was first being formulated, performance was not the sole criteria for what salary band the player was put in. Seniority was factored in as well. This is not the case in other cricket playing countries nor across the border in India where performance has been the sole criterion. Nevertheless, Butt, as a young captain, navigated the terrain well despite the occasional retort and again showed the qualities of a transformational leader: charisma, inspiration, individual consideration, and intellectual stimulation. But what happens when these qualities are used to achieve undesirable ends? It is ironic that he spoke forcefully about mentorship and yet failed to see the damage that his own 'adverse' mentorship had had on his team members. It is in this setting that we place the power dynamic between the captain Salman Butt and his 18-year-old team mate and later co-conspirator, Mohammad Amir.

Amir was born in Gujar Khan, a small town close to the capital city of Islamabad. He was the second youngest of seven children. His father plastered houses in his village to make ends meet. At 13, an academy in the nearby city of Rawalpindi took Amir on for his cricket. Four years later, he was playing for Pakistan and being touted as the brightest young star in world cricket. It was when he joined the Pakistan team at the age of 17 that he met Salman Butt, who at the time was 25 and had been playing for Pakistan for five years and had established a position for himself in the team. In an interview with Michael Atherton shortly after his release from jail for spot-fixing, Amir mentions how impressed he was with Salman Butt—his manners and his friendliness to newcomers which was so different to other senior players in the team.

> When we turned up for practice, he'd give gloves to anyone who needed them, or a bat to others. He was educated, well behaved, and most of the time the seniors did not mingle with the juniors the way he did. Because of that and because he treated the juniors differently to the others, I thought he was a nice man ... He treated me like an elder brother treats his younger brother.[67]

Butt had a rapport and trust with the younger team members, most of whom looked up to him. But all the while Amir was looking up to Salman Butt, Butt himself was being influenced by another individual, the conduit to the world of fixing—in this case his agent, Mazhar Majeed.

Majeed had been involved with the Pakistan cricket team for several years prior to 2010 and had become an agent for Salman Butt, trying to arrange sponsorships and county contracts. It is to Mazhar Majeed that Salman Butt complained that he was unable to buy the houses that some of his peers had bought through their match-fixing exploits. Majeed subsequently lured Salman Butt and a number of other Pakistan team players into a web of corruption. The 'grooming' of the cricketers highlights an interesting role reversal in terms of the dynamics between agent/fan and sportsman.

The Pakistan team of the 1990s and 2000s consisted of individuals that were from more modest backgrounds than their counterparts of the past. There was less international exposure and lower levels of education, as highlighted in Amir's case. When coming into contact with an individual like Mazhar Majeed, there is an immediate social and economic gulf that overturns the normal power dynamic where the sportsman is the dominant partner. Majeed was an ostensibly successful businessman. He had a £1.8 million house in London and a sports car worth hundreds of thousands of pounds alongside a host of companies and a football club.[68] His parents had immigrated from Pakistan, and for the young, impressionable, and aspirational cricketers he represented a successful, rich individual who enjoyed a millionaire's lifestyle—parties, celebrities, expensive cars, and houses. Majeed had it all. This is what a modern lifestyle was, and it could be attained through money.

Majeed 'groomed' the cricketers—there are photographs of Salman Butt and another cricketer driving Majeed's sports car in the driveway of his London mansion. Mazhar is seated in the back. In an interview with Vivek Chaudhry[69] while he was in jail for spot-fixing, Majeed spoke of how he held the Pakistani players he represented 'in the palm of his hand' to the point that he would order them to move out of their hotel rooms so he could have their bed for the night, how he would get them to run errands for him, and how senior Pakistani administrators sucked up to him.

Butt was overawed by Majeed and he introduced him to Amir. Amir's subsequent impression highlights the extent to which Majeed had a hold over his targets.

I was introduced to Mazhar Majeed by Salman. Mazhar also made a very good impression on me. He came across as a very good guy, who made jokes, the way a well-educated man and a well-mannered man would behave. He looked like a family man because I also met his wife. She wears a hijab and is religious. She says her prayers and he did too.[70]

Majeed represented modernity and success—material wealth but also religiosity and a link to Pakistan through his parents. If anyone was to be admired and emulated, Majeed was the one. Naïve and under the control of his captain, Amir had little opportunity of escape. He was set up and then threatened with being caught for corruption. Majeed preyed on the players' youth, inexperience, and desire for wealth and glamour. Justice Cooke, in his Determination of the ICC case against Butt, Asif, and Amir,[71] referred to Majeed as:

> Breezy, confident, someone used to getting things done; friendly, engaging, the man who promised in his capacity as their agent, actual or putative, formal or informal to open endless doors to wealth and fame for them, the three players were simply no match for him. The evidence strongly suggests that he consciously preyed on their youth and inexperience to lure them into a world, half real, half fantasy, of constantly increasing wealth and glamour.

This is the most common route of seduction of a player into corrupt behaviour. The relationship often starts innocently with admiration of players being used as the reason for invitations to mix socially. Gifts without obligation follow and eventually the true motivation for the relationship emerges. It is a subtle, ambiguous, and patient process. And in the event that gentle persuasion does not work, there are reports of intimidation[72] and the use of blackmail. At least two current cricketers that I spoke to mentioned in guarded terms the fact that they had received veiled threats about their own and the families' safety ('I was told that my family had been seen wandering in Mall of Dubai. I locked myself in my room and didn't come out for two days from fear').

Individuals like Mazhar Majeed and Salman Butt act as conduits for match-fixing but much of the serious intimidation comes from underworld criminals who became involved in cricket when they realized that the proceeds of corruption in cricket were sufficiently large and provided an opportunity for easy profit and simple money laundering. It was Sharjah that came under particular scrutiny and according to a senior journalist who covered matches in the emirate in the 1990s:

> almost everyone involved in cricket knew that games at Sharjah were almost always scripted in advance and to the advantage of criminal mafias led, it is

said, by extremely influential persons including prominent politicians and the underworld don Dawood Ibrahim whose D-Group have been implicated in almost all fixing scams since the 1990s. In the 1990s, these criminal elements had access to individual team members and even wielded undue influence over team selection and performance. It is also alleged that a murder in South Africa—that of the bookmaker Hanif Cadbury—was a contract killing as a result of a dispute between rival corruptors from other countries. Cadbury was apparently cut up into 'Cadbury' sized pieces and left in a body bag.

The motivations for match-fixing then are multifold and include greed, insecurity, envy, and the effect of negative mentorship which can lead individuals down the path of corruption. Once on that path, persuasion and intimidation make it difficult to step off. Junior players find themselves under threat of being pushed out if they do not cooperate. An honest captain can be undermined and removed. In fact, Mazhar Majeed and Salman Butt plotted to remove the previous captain Shahid Afridi from his position by having team members underperform.[73] This had happened previously as well. Ramiz Raja said he felt this acutely when he was brought in as captain following the rumours of widespread match-fixing in the mid-1990s. Younis Khan, known to be an honest and upright cricketer, resigned from captaincy claiming a lack of support from senior players. In this case Afridi was an obstacle to control over the team and Butt and Majeed had already decided to concentrate on the younger players. In an undercover interview of Majeed,[74] he is heard boasting of seven players out of eleven as part of the match-fixing plan. 'Getting the younger boys' was 'long term planning. These boys will be here for years.' Afridi did abruptly resign from captaincy and mentions in his autobiography *Game Changer* (2019) that this was because he had informed the team management about his doubts over Salman Butt and had been told, '*beta kya kar sakte hain ab*' (son, what we can do now). Disillusioned, he resigned from captaincy and from Test Cricket, leaving the door open for Salman Butt and Mazhar Majeed to engage in spot-fixing.

Mike Brearley, former England captain and later a practicing psychoanalyst and psychotherapist, states that when Amir was threatened by a corrupt figure, Mazhar Majeed, his fatal mistake was to ask that person on whom he should most have been able to rely—his captain—for help. This only led to Amir becoming further embroiled and being told that his only exit was to bowl the intentional no-balls.[75] Brearley goes on to point out other instances where younger players have been inveigled into corrupt acts including one where the two most senior Australian players including their captain were caught for illegally changing the condition of the cricket ball but 'the fingerprints on the ball were those of the most junior player in the side, a feature which suggested a lack of leadership responsibility.'[76]

It is apparent that Pakistan—in its cricket and more widely in the national arena—has thrown up few mentors and its more recent heroes have been deeply flawed. Pakistan's demographic structure—a large and young population—will produce talented young people and without responsible leadership or mentoring this group of young people will almost always end up behaving badly. Rock stars, film stars, and the like are prime examples. Keep in mind also that according to psychologists the pre-frontal cortex (PFC) of the brain, an area that deals with planning, forethought, motivation, impulse control, and the modulation of emotions, is also not fully developed until the youth reach their mid 20s. Professional sport has strong visible and invisible institutions for mentoring, but despite that sportsmen have often been those who have been hauled up for misconduct. Since Imran Khan retired, Pakistan have had 18 Test Match captains. In the same period Australia have had 5, England 8, and India 6. Pakistan's struggles with leadership are apparent.

But corruption does not occur in a vacuum and must be located in a much broader framework if it is to be fully understood. The renowned sports psychologist and former cricketer Rudi Webster, who worked on performance enhancement in Australia and with many of that country's best athletes and sports teams, stated that a 'player's behaviour is an interaction between him and the environment. The conduct of players found guilty of wrongdoing should therefore be judged not just in the context of their own environment but also in that of broader society.'[77]

If corruption is tolerated in the wider society, why should the cricketing world be different? Match-fixing in Pakistan has been roundly condemned in public from the Prime Minister's 'bowing its head in shame' statement when the spot-fixing charges were revealed in 2010 to the press and the wider society. But does the example of the wider society encourage or discourage corruption in cricket? It is to this question that I now turn to.

A CORRUPT SOCIETY

That corruption in Pakistan is pervasive and endemic is without doubt.

> Corruption manifests itself in various forms in Pakistan including widespread financial and political corruption, nepotism and misuse of power. Both petty and grand corruptions are prevalent in the country.[78]

There are few areas of society where corruption has not entrenched itself from the private sector to civil bureaucracy to politicians and the military junta.[79] Khan states that monumental levels of corruption are the norm in all government departments.[80] Since first being included in 1995, Pakistan has consistently performed poorly on the Transparency International's Corruption Perception Index (CPI) and is amongst the countries with the highest perceived corruption each year. In 2018, the CPI ranked the country 117th out of 180 countries.[81] Other reports such as the World Bank's World Governance Indicators[82] also indicate Pakistan as amongst the worst performers on controlling corruption. The most recent reports[83] indicate that Pakistan's latest corruption indicators have worsened further between 2019 and 2020.[84]

While it is difficult to ascertain definitively whether corruption has increased since Pakistan was created, it certainly appears that the perception of corruption multiplying has increased over the years. Jaffrelot states that the ruling elite had a marked propensity for corruption.[85] Almost every government—civil or military—has come to power with the promise of rooting out corruption; yet several of these very governments have subsequently been dismissed for corruption themselves.

Alongside political corruption there have been several prominent commercial scandals in Pakistan that have gained international coverage—most recently the Axact scheme which saw a Karachi-based software company secretly running an internet driven fake diploma business. Reports[87] state that Axact was, on a global scale, easily the biggest internet scam ever. It is still, however, considered small fry when compared to the scandal of the Bank of Credit and Commerce International (BCCI).

The BCCI was an international bank founded in 1972 by Agha Hasan Abedi, a Pakistani financier. At the height of its success, in the early 1980s, the bank had over 400 branches in 78 countries and assets in excess of $20 billion, making it the seventh largest private bank in the world.[88] However, this wealth and influence were achieved not only by defrauding ordinary citizens but also by laundering massive amounts of money for notorious dictators including Panama's Manuel Noriega and Iraq's Saddam Hussein. Years after the bank's collapse, the CIA found the BCCI had financed a number of terrorist organizations.[89] And while the Bank claimed to be global, it was essentially a Pakistani Bank. Founded by a Pakistani, many in the upper and middle management were Pakistani as well.'[90]

These instances of corruption on a massive global scale damaged the international reputation of the country and reinforced the widespread belief of the pervasiveness of corrupt practices. But beyond the political elite, government, and commerce, it appears that corruption has spread to such an extent that it is part of the everyday life of citizens—part of the culture itself. Syed Akbar Zaidi states:

> Pakistan society has a darbar culture, where ostentatiousness is the norm and privilege is misused and flaunted; patronage from those in power is the norm; corruption, from the thana [police station] and kutchery (judicial court) level to the highest public office in the country, is a standard and even accepted practice.[91]

Using data from the Pakistan National Corruption Perception Surveys of 2002 and 2006, Transparency International found widespread corruption across a spectrum of sectors. The surveys, which covered all major Pakistani cities, asked if respondents had any dealings in the past year with the Pakistani judicial, police, electricity, taxation, health, education, or land administration departments, and if corruption had been involved. Almost every single respondent reported having to pay a bribe or carry out some other corrupt act in order to complete their transaction. The police force was seen as the most corrupt institution followed closely by the judiciary, power, and taxation authorities.

There is also corruption in health and education sectors. Transparency International Pakistan reported that almost a quarter of those surveyed received admission in educational institutions through non-normal and alternate procedures. In the health sector, nearly half of those surveyed individuals reported gaining access to hospital services by a method other than standard admission, and 48 per cent reported either having to pay additional costs for essential services or being forced to utilize the services of a designated affiliate.[92] Pakistan's desultory social indicators in health and education are testament to mismanagement and corruption in these areas of basic service delivery. Hundreds of thousands of ghost schools exist on paper. Teachers are paid for working at these non-existent schools and contractors paid for buildings never constructed. Pakistan remains one of only two countries, along with Afghanistan, where polio has not been eradicated. As Khan points out, 'corruption has weakened the state so much that it is incapable of providing for its people's needs.'[93]

The widespread nature of corruption means that the average Pakistani citizen encounters corruption on a daily basis—paying bills, registering births, enrolling children at school, getting medical treatment, reporting a crime, getting an electricity or gas connection, or recording the sale of a house. So endemic is the practice that as Javaid points out, over time the acceptability of corruption has increased in society and there is little evidence that people feel guilty about their own role in it.[94] Indicative of this 'normalization' of corruption, Transparency International reports that bribery or palm greasing has become such a central part of the system that in all the ten surveyed sectors, the demand is directly made by the officer or person involved, without needing a negotiator or middle man.[95] As in the case of match-fixing, the justification is: 'if everyone is partaking, then why not us too?'

This was exactly what I encountered in multiple interviews. A journalist who covered several Pakistan tours in the 1990s stated that the players quite openly told 'trusted' journalists that the match they were playing the next day was on the books. 'They didn't seem at all regretful and while they didn't say they were involved themselves, it was almost as if since everyone was doing it, it was fine to follow suit.' And if caught, sportspersons often use what Boardley and Kuvassanu call 'moral disengagement,' which similarly includes the most common justification: 'everybody does it.'[96] Salman Butt used that explanation whenever I asked him why he had indulged in match-fixing—'everyone was doing it. Am I the only corrupt one in a sea of *farishta*s [angels]?' Thus, both the local environment and the broader one reinforce each other in diluting the social sanction against corrupt practices.

Organizational Corruption

The pervasiveness of corruption would lead us to conclude that cricket in Pakistan would not be immune to the influence of wider societal trends. And while we have examined the influences that at an international level led to the growth of match-fixing, it starts at a more local level with the domestic cricket system administered through the Pakistan Cricket Board (PCB). For Aizad Sayid who was General Manager at the PCB for two years, the initiation into corruption for players starts early. Sayid pointed out that in the last decade the PCB has seen a massive increase in staffing as successive chairmen have sought to extend their patronage by handing out jobs as favours. 'There are 800 people doing the job of 100. And while recent chairmen have tried to reduce staffing levels, staff are so entrenched that change is very difficult.' As a result, from the start, people interacting with the PCB confront the patronage networks that facilitate corruption.

Then we move to initiating the youngest of our budding cricketers into further corruption. When we began finalizing the squad for the under 19 World Cup squad, I realized that more than half the Under 19 players were overaged. Most were over 24. There were 20-year olds in the Under 16s. Parents and families pay for their kids to play at younger levels so that they have an advantage. We waste tens of millions of rupees every year on boys who have no future even in first class cricket, let alone international cricket. Most of these overage boys perform well in age-barred activities only due to their huge illegal advantage in age. The strength advantage that they gain is many times greater than what a sportsman can gain through steroid use. Unfortunately, when they graduate to first class cricket, many of them cannot compete at any level, since their performances in Under 16 and Under 19 cricket are largely due to superior physical development. I got hold of software on age verification that analysed X-rays to verify age. Winning Under 16 and Under 19 tournaments through cheating is unacceptable and must be discouraged at all levels. The Chairman supported this initiative but forces within the organization argued against it and within a month I found myself sidelined from the preparations. Players who had been removed as being overage were put back into the team. Those responsible for my removal argued that physical verification would be done as there was insufficient time to carry out the far more rigorous and accurate biometric testing. Moreover, the domestic U-19 tournament had already happened, and it would be wrong to bar players at this stage, especially after so much money had been spent on the tournament. When you tell kids to lie about their age, and then support it as acceptable, it starts there. And that is just the beginning. Managers appointed for domestic tournaments have been found pocketing half the budget provided for the meal and accommodation requirements of players. For a teenager taking his initial steps in a profession, there is no possibility of reporting such corruption. Instead, it becomes an initiation *into* corruption. As you graduate you are seeped into this culture.

There are multiple other examples of corruption within the organization— club cricket, once the pool for international cricket in Pakistan, is now riddled with corruption. Sayid estimates that of the 2,800 clubs in Pakistan, an astonishing 2,200 are 'fake' or ghost clubs that are present on paper to provide the owners with enough votes to be part of the regional cricket governance structure. Even when caught red handed, it appears that accountability is rarely pursued. The alleged mastermind behind a scam involving the construction of a biomechanics laboratory was caught red handed but the case was swept under the carpet as it would have pulled in several other employees and damaged the reputation of the board.

The same attitude is visible amongst not only the PCB but by several other cricketing boards as well, as they follow what the ICC Anti-Corruption Unit (ACU) report terms a 'nexus of silence.' The ACU inquiry report disclosed that, 'since the early 1990s, cricket was riddled with match-fixing corruption about which authorities had failed to act effectively.' The anti-corruption authorities felt that the allegations being made were simply the tip of the iceberg and that many people had significant information about corruption within the game but were not willing to divulge this information. Paul Condon, Head of the ACU, identified that loyalty norms prevented players from reporting colleagues who often not only have professional but personal relationships.[97] There were also concerns over players not wanting to be branded as informants and risk being ostracized from the team as was illustrated in examples above.

When I spoke to a senior member of the Pakistan Cricket Board and to Salman Butt on match-fixing, both stated that in many cases the boards are complicit in match-fixing. 'We caught two senior board officials on tape discussing fixing matches in the Indian Cricket League.'[98] The names of high-profile international players have allegedly been kept out of investigations through the involvement of board officials and politicians in Pakistan, India, Bangladesh, and Sri Lanka. Clearly, the damage to the game through a string of high-profile outings would be catastrophic. And while the rumours continue amongst the players and the administrators, the 'nexus of silence' ends up prevailing and only a few cases are pursued every so often.

Justice Qayyum who compiled the most extensive report on match-fixing[99] in Pakistan was clear on what had transpired.

> These cricketers were greedy and ran after money, the amounts of which they would not have dreamt of previously. All of them were evasive and none of them truthful. Some pretended that they didn't even know what match-fixing was but no one admitted to it though they were clear that match-fixing was widespread elsewhere. I was convinced that they were involved in match-fixing but finding the smoking gun is very difficult. They all supported each other.

Qayyum was also pressurized by the civilian government of Nawaz Sharif which had indicated that it did not want too bleak a picture to be painted in front of a global audience. Saving face and protecting the reputation of the country, the board, and the players overrode full exposure. Moreover, Qayyum mentioned to me that the ICC had already told him that if the cricketers under investigation were found guilty, they would consider banning Pakistan outright.

> I did not want this to happen. Cricket would be poorer without Pakistan and some of these cricketers. I also did not have clear evidence and felt the burden of proof needed to be high. So, I cautioned them and fined them for non-cooperation rather than ban them, except in the case of Salim Malik,

against whom there was material evidence and Ata-ur-Rehman who was guilty of perjury.

More than half the team's names were noted in the report.

Qayyum's report was completed in September 1999. Two weeks later it was with the board and the government. It took a further seven months for it to be made public; within those seven months, rumours of the contents being watered down damaged its credibility. In fact, it became clear that the board, with few exceptions, attempted to protect the named players and it was only in April 2000, after the Indian police released audio tapes of Hansie Cronje arranging a fix, that the Qayyum report was unearthed and finally released in May 2000. In the press conference that accompanied the release of the report, Chairman of the board, General Tauqir Zia, announced that Justice Qayyum's long-awaited judicial report had found no planned match-fixing and that Pakistan cricket has emerged from the match-fixing crisis without a stain on its character—'Pakistan's image will not be stained over this: we are giving a lesson to others.'[100] Apart from Salim Malik and Ata-ur-Rehman, all the other named players were criticized but exonerated of match-fixing. But what was clearly acknowledged was that the report was a devastating condemnation of the culture of Pakistan cricket in the 1990s—'It was morally sick, and many of the greatest players were criticized.'[101]

The failure to take strict action against alleged match fixers at this point and subsequent accommodation of tainted players by the board sent a further reinforcing message that corruption would not be punished. Few boards, in fact, have such a poor record in terms of implementing accountability as the PCB does. In 2009–10, a disastrous tour to Australia, which was also under suspicion of match-fixing, saw the PCB launch an inquiry into the conduct of players accused of match-fixing, indiscipline, and player power. Seven players were found guilty and penalized. Nearly all of them were let off through political graft and eventually reinstated. The moral of the story was that you may be caught and penalized but you can get off through using personal affiliations with influential politicians and business tycoons or because the team requires your skills. Mohammad Amir was fast tracked back into the team after his spot-fixing ban and others who had been banned for doping had their bans overturned. Even today, the Qayyum report continues to be disregarded. Several of those named in the report have been given key positions in the PCB.

In fact, following the 2010 spot-fixing scandal, the ICC stated that it had noted the continuing decline in the governance of cricket in Pakistan and would monitor closely the running of the game in Pakistan. In effect,

Pakistan had been told: 'it must act and be seen to be acting to uphold the zero-tolerance attitude to corruption in sport.'[102] Samiuddin points out that 'in effect, the PCB has been asked to take measures which should've been taken ten years ago after the Qayyum commission report, a decade in which the clouds of corruption have hovered consistently over Pakistan cricket.'

And yet, while progress has been made in some cases (it was after all the board that caught players involved in the Pakistan Super League spot-fixing case in 2017), its fast tracking of the return of Mohammad Amir led to considerable opposition. Ramiz Raja, a former captain and someone who played alongside match fixers, spoke out strongly against Amir's return stating that he had forever damaged the reputation of the game and the nation. Similarly, Mohammad Hafeez and Azhar Ali, senior players in the Pakistan team, were also opposed to playing with Mohammad Amir and protested by refusing to attend a training camp with Amir. When I spoke to Hafeez, who is known as a thinking, principled, and vocal cricketer, he stated firmly that Pakistani cricketers had suffered hugely as a result of the corruption of some players.

> We were abused by fans when these three were banned because they had damaged the integrity of Pakistan. After that, every time we lost there was suspicion on us and we wore the brunt of their anger. It took a long time to restore the image of the team and the nation in the eyes of the fans. I didn't want that to be repeated. But we were persuaded to accept Amir back.

Therefore, the wider social milieu that players find themselves increasingly caught up in is one where corruption, if not condoned, is not condemned either. It occurs on a daily basis in many areas of society, cricket being only one of them. We find corruption endemic in the wider society. We find it endemic in the organization that runs the game in Pakistan. We find it in club and age grade cricket and in the national team. In such an environment, it is almost as if the individual has little chance but to be caught up in the fix. The weak social sanction against corrupt behaviour and the lack of accountability have become features of the Pakistani society.

In conclusion, I want to analyse one of the most fascinating responses to the era of match-fixing—the redemption from immorality. We have established that throughout the mid to late 1990s, the whiff of match-fixing pervaded Pakistani cricket. The Qayyum report allegedly cleared the majority of players of further wrongdoing but the stain would not go—that is, until religion washed away the sins.

MATCH-FIXING, TABLIGHI JAMA'AT, AND REDEMPTION

The 20th century has witnessed the emergence of a number of movements for religious revival, revitalization, and reform amongst Muslims all over the world.[103] One such revitalization movement is the Tablighi Jama'at, literally, 'Society for Spreading Faith.' It was the Deobandi tradition in South Asia that gave birth to the Tablighi Jama'at, by far the greatest preaching organization in the Muslim world (indeed in the whole world), which each year draws millions of people to its great rallies at its headquarters in Raiwind near Lahore. The Tabligh was founded in India in the 1920s as a revivalist movement dedicated to strengthening scriptural Islamic practice among Muslims and resisting the efforts of Hindu preachers to draw them back into the Hindu fold. In recent decades, the Tablighi leadership has strongly emphasized its apolitical character and has firmly distanced itself from extremism and terrorism; but its networks and gatherings have been used by radicals as a cover for meetings and planning.[104]

The Tablighi Jama'at has made significant gains in Pakistan over the decades. Initially seen, because of its apolitical nature, as a counter to the main Islamist political party of Pakistan, the Jamaat-i-Islami, it had the support of the authorities. Ziaul Haq allowed Islamic preaching within the army, particularly by the Tablighi Jama'at.[105] Prime Minister Nawaz Sharif, whose father was a prominent Tablighi Jama'at member and financier, helped Tablighi members take on prominent government positions. For example, in 1998, Mohammad Rafiq Tarar, a senior Tablighi Jama'at activist, served as President of Pakistan till he was deposed in June 2001. During his time as President, Tarar is believed to have played a key role in the introduction in the Pakistani Senate of the Shariat Bill that sought to impose Islamic law in the country.

The Tablighi Jama'at has, undoubtedly, penetrated deep into Pakistani society and counts among its activists members of the civil and military bureaucracy, businessmen, university lecturers, celebrities from the entertainment industry, and, as we shall see, sportsmen. These members play an important role in furthering the aims of the movement and promoting an Islamization of state structures and civil society institutions as well as of wider society. Today the Tablighi Jama'at are the largest group of religious proselytizers of any faith, and are part of the reason for the explosive growth of Islamic religious fervour and conversion.

In the Pakistan cricket team, religiosity made its first real presence felt through the arrival of Saeed Ahmed. Ahmed played for Pakistan in the 1960s and early 1970s and was known then for his fondness for alcohol and nightclubs. After exiting the team in 1973, Ahmed settled in England, disappearing from the scene until 1998, when he resurfaced at a match in Sharjah where Pakistan was playing a tournament. Unrecognizable, the newly-bearded Saeed Ahmed revealed in an interview that he had joined the Islamic religious group, the Tablighi Jama'at, in 1978, following an 'extended mystical experience,'[106] and that he was keen on spreading the faith to other team members. Ahmed visited the dressing room often in the late 1990s, leaving behind cassettes and leaflets of the movement's leading preachers including Maulana Tariq Jamil who would go on to play a pivotal role in the 'Islamization' of the cricket team.

Tariq Jamil had already risen quickly through the Tablighi Jama'at ranks. Known as a brilliant orator whose 'motivational' lectures are replete with theatre, humour, religious parables, and personal accounts of his own religious journey, he has regularly been invited by the civil bureaucracy to 'enlighten and inspire.' Amongst the talks he has given was one at the request of the then Prime Minister Nawaz Sharif to address members of his cabinet on 'the responsibilities of rulers in the light of Islamic teachings.' More recent audiences include the Federal Board of Revenue's customs officials, universities in Lahore and Faisalabad, and the Khyber Pakhtunkhwa government.

The Tablighi Jama'at had already had considerable success through the 1980s in attracting politicians and academics to their fold. Jamil added a new dimension to their recruitment policy by focusing attention on celebrities— singers, actors, cricketers, and even including stage dancers, and prostitutes. Every successful 'reformation,' or even attempted reformation, is highlighted, bringing with it greater fame for Jamil and for the Tablighi Jama'at. A shrewd media strategy ensures a steady stream of information and photographs of Jamil with high profile personalities including the British Pakistani boxer Amir Khan, former cricketer turned Prime Minister Imran Khan, and the Bollywood superstar Aamir Khan.

One of Jamil's earliest successes was Saeed Anwar who, in August 2001, tragically lost a young daughter to a protracted illness. Saeed had been one of the few graduates in the Pakistan cricket team in the 1990s. Hailing from Karachi, he was known for his stylish batting as well as his love of Western music. Saeed Anwar's 'conversion' was initiated by a former cricketer by the name of Zulqarnain who had earlier joined the Tablighi Jama'at. Throughout the 1990s, Zulqarnain would pursue Saeed Anwar, pushing him to reform his way of life. I had met and interviewed Zulqarnain at his stationery shop in *andaroon shehr*—the old walled city area of Lahore and today a maze of historic gates and alleyways. Amidst piles of notebooks, Zulqarnain spoke of how Saeed Anwar had been resistant to the Tablighi Jama'at's initial overtures and it was only after the death of his daughter and through the influence of the charismatic Tariq Jamil that a disconsolate Anwar had sought solace and support with the Tablighi Jama'at. A confidante of Saeed Anwar whom I interviewed in confidence actually told me that while his daughter was unwell Anwar would say that his involvement in one fixed match was what had caused the illness. In fact, this strategy of approaching potential recruits at times of crisis appears to be a common strategy. In an interview with Ramiz Raja, a former Pakistan captain, Raja spoke of how three former colleagues who had joined the Tablighi Jama'at approached him at his father's funeral and how he angrily told them: 'don't come to me at my time of weakness!'

But within a year of his daughter's death, Saeed Anwar was sporting a long beard. A year later in 2003, he was back in the team for the World Cup in South Africa. As I sat with Chairman of the Pakistan Cricket Board, Shaharyar Khan, in his office overlooking the picturesque Gaddafi stadium cricket ground, he recalled with amusement how when, he was manager of the team during the World Cup, en route one of the opening matches, Saeed suddenly got up in the team coach, grabbed the microphone next to the bus driver, and triumphantly announced: '*Is baar Pakistan World Cup jeetay ga kyun keh Allah apnay farsihtay bhejen gay hamari madad kay liyay. Lakhon logon ki du'aen hamaray saath hain*' (This time Pakistan will win the World Cup because Allah will send His angels to help us. The prayers of hundreds of thousands of believers are with us). Shaharyar Khan states that Anwar spoke without an iota of doubt about his prediction and when the prophesied triumph failed to materialize, the response to why came without hesitation: 'we were not good Muslims, we need to improve our morals and habits.'

It was during this tour of South Africa, where the Tablighi Jama'at has a strong network, that Shaharyar Khan emphasized that he noticed an increasing number of players being influenced by the Tablighi message: 'Saeed was always an intelligent and perceptive individual. I noticed that by now he was clearly more devoted to spreading the faith than prolonging his playing career. In every city the team visited, Saeed would contact the local Tablighi Jama'at and take willing listeners with him to their meetings.' Within months, Mushtaq Ahmed, Saqlain Mushtaq, Shahid Afridi, and Inzamam-ul-Haq had also joined the movement—won over by Saeed Anwar and his mentor, Maulana Tariq Jamil.

Significantly, three of the Tablighi converts in the cricket team, including Saeed Anwar, had been named in a match-fixing report on Pakistan cricket. Suspicion fell on others as well who were part of the team at the time. All of them had risen to become internationally recognized celebrities. Mushtaq Ahmed and Saqlain Mushtaq had spent years playing cricket in England and during my interviews with them they often spoke about 'an emptiness' that was enveloping their lives. When Saeed Anwar came to see me to inquire whether I would be interested in joining the Tablighi movement, his opening remark was: 'Why is it that so many Hollywood stars and pop icons who are rich and famous, why do they commit suicide? It is because they have no religion and therefore no peace of mind. Money and fame are temporary. We have to prepare for the afterlife from now.' He had spoken in the same vein to his team mates.

Mushtaq Ahmed spoke at length about lifestyle excesses when he lived in England playing county cricket. The allegations of match-fixing encircled them; lurid stories of prostitutes being sent home in rickshaws and liaisons with dancing girls from Lollywood added to the taint of immorality. As Saeed Anwar had cautioned, peace of mind appeared to have deserted them. So much had been achieved—fame, money, adulation; was guilt beginning to gnaw at the souls of these cricketers? Had they been ungrateful for all that they had achieved? And despite this success, had they gone even further and fixed matches for additional financial reward sullying their own reputations along with those of the country and of the noble sport? Here began the search for redemption.

Saqlain, now settled in England but back in Pakistan for a coaching assignment, spoke of 'fate' and, in a moment of deep introspection, he reflected on how success and fame could easily have passed him by. He spoke with genuine feeling on how so many cricketers never achieve what he had, despite possibly being more talented and more deserving than he was. He then went on to relate the story of a cricketer who played one Test Match for Pakistan and had tremendous potential but ended up working in a take away:

> After a training camp, he fell off his motorbike and broke his bowling arm. After 12 months he came back, took a lot of wickets and got back into the Pakistan squad again. But he couldn't afford to buy a car, so while he was going to camp again, he had another accident and broke his bowling arm again. He was finished with cricket—even club cricket. Anyway, after a few years I was playing for Surrey and was going from the Oval to Tooting. I stopped at Balham station for a kebab roll, and that guy, Ashfaq Ahmed, was there, making kebabs. I said, 'What are you doing here?' He told me he was studying and working part-time, making kebab rolls. I just started crying and crying, thinking how unlucky he was.

Saqlain went on to speak of how a rare knee injury finished his career early, just as he was at his peak. These unforeseen instances that can change the course of a career are difficult to explain and sportsmen are constantly plagued with trying to make sense of the uncertainty that is inherent in sport.[107]

Inzamam-ul-Haq was one of those who was named in the report on match-fixing and who subsequently joined the Tablighi Jama'at in the wake of Saeed Anwar's 'conversion.' Already from a religious background and the son of a muezzin, Inzamam's joining of the Tablighi Jama'at was particularly significant because he had recently taken on the team's captaincy. One of the Tablighi Jama'at's most successful recruitment strategies is to focus attention not only on celebrities but also on those in positions of power and authority. Saeed Anwar's conversation with me had revolved around the importance of someone who had an influence on young minds becoming part of the Tablighi Jama'at. The singer Cat Stevens and the National Basketball Association player Kareem Abdul-Jabbar were high profile international converts. Inzamam-ul-Haq represented not only a star international cricketer but one who had just assumed charge of an entire team of high-profile sportsmen. The strong Tablighi network that he was now part of meant that Saeed Anwar and other senior Tablighi members were regularly invited into the team dressing room and even accompanied the team on foreign tours.

It is also true that Pakistan has not been an easy team to lead. Throughout the 1970s, a team of superstars failed to gel as a team and it was only under Imran Khan—a charismatic, all-powerful captain—that the team played as a unit. Inzamam-ul-Haq, lacking the same authoritative personality, inherited a team that had seen declining results, factional fighting, and a succession of short-term captains and regimes at the cricket board.

Inzamam turned to religion to bind the team together, maintain the discipline that the team had lacked since Imran Khan's departure, and to bring about a moral rebirth. Here, for the first time, religion became a major public influence on the Pakistan cricket team. For a while, this new ethos brought about a positive change with even Pakistan's English coach Bob Woolmer saying that religion had brought unity and discipline to the new team.[108] Demographically, too, as explained in Chapter 1, the composition of the team was different. Many of the new cricketers were formally uneducated and came from modest backgrounds and smaller cities and towns and it could be argued that for these individuals religion had a more central position in their lives as compared to the cricketers of the 1970s. Moreover, born and brought up in a different time, religious metaphors and language came much more naturally to the new generation.

It was during this period that overt displays of religiosity in the team spiked. The team was seen praying together after practices and often frequented Tablighi Jama'at gatherings at home and abroad. By 2006, rumours of forced wakings for the morning prayers, designated prayer and religious discussion rooms in hotels, and more attention being paid to

Tablighi activities as compared to cricket were common. A current player I spoke to stated that at that time (in 2006), Inzamam and his network had managed to convert almost the entire team to the Tablighi cause and players were spending lunch and tea breaks in prayer and even calling substitutes on to the ground during play so they could go off and say their prayers. 'Some threw away their earrings and grew beards to try and ensure they stayed in the team. Others were kept out because of their "incompatible" lifestyle. I think it also affected our cricket as we became more fatalistic, accepting defeat easily which is not good for a sportsman.' A team that never had a religious character now had a strong Islamic identity which it wore on its sleeve.

The pinnacle of this 'religiosity' was the conversion of Yousuf Youhana, the sole Christian in the team, to Islam, after which he took on the name Mohammad Yousuf. Youhana was helped along to his conversion through the persistence of Saeed Anwar who would secretly take Youhana along with him to Tablighi Jama'at sessions. Eventually, Youhana converted and soon he too had grown a beard and, as if touched by divinity, the very good player Yousuf Youhana became the great Mohammad Yousuf, who immediately after conversion found a peace of mind and focus that saw him break decades-old records.

By the time Youhana converted, the team's culture had changed unrecognizably from the teams of the 1970s and 1980s—it was unimaginable now that the captain of the team would drink a beer after a victory or even fraternize with the opposition if they were enjoying an alcoholic beverage. In its place was the now ubiquitous framing statement (whether a game had been won or lost): 'First of all, thanks be to Almighty Allah.'

Why the Spike in Religiosity?

The increased religiosity that became evident in the cricket team in the early part of the first decade of the 2000s was the result of a combination of factors that came together at a particular point in time.

The Islamization that started under Zia had taken root and religion and religious morality had seeped into every aspect of public life. To be good was to be religious. People 'swelled' with pride every time a TV channel showed the team praying together after practice—the epitome of discipline and piety. That the players were religious was important to the public now. In the 1970s, it mattered little in terms of their moral behaviour and attempts at bringing up the issue of immorality in the team were given no importance. The greater importance given to religion was a reflection of the changing socio-political environment of the country as a whole. Pakistan was more overtly religious and unsurprisingly the team reflected this. However, the rapidity of the transformation and its deep penetration into the culture of the team was something that was the outcome of a series of factors that were specific to the case of the cricket team.

Significantly, in this more religious environment, an additional impetus was provided by the spectre of match-fixing. Tainted by a decade of corruption, indiscipline, and moral degradation, several players sought redemption and answers to the uncertainties that they faced. The team needed 'cleansing.' The Tablighi Jama'at filled that desire for redemption— from match-fixing and from the excesses that some of the players had indulged in. '*Allah sab ko muaf kar deta hai*' (Allah forgives everyone), Mushtaq Ahmed said when I asked him about match-fixers being allowed back into the team. 'But you have to have faith.'

In fact, the Tablighi Jama'at was ideally positioned to 'convert' the cricketers at this point, having made the initial inroads that gave them an important foothold. Their message of trying to bring Muslims back on what they perceive to be the right path of Islam resonated perfectly with a group that was looking for redemption. Furthermore, the simplicity that the Tablighi Jama'at lifestyle promises may have acted as an antithesis of the materialistic and high-pressure environment that the cricketers had experienced for several years prior to their 'conversion.'

It is also the case that Tablighis are, by definition, trained as missionaries and their dedicated and persistent efforts have yielded enormous success throughout the world. Their emphasis on the unity of Muslims and its ability to transcend sects[109] is an additional strength. For some, the fact that they are avowedly apolitical is also important as it is for the also very successful women's Al Huda movement.[110] In the context of the cricket team, this may have been an additional attraction as few cricketers have publicly shown support for any particular political party.

I believe that demographics were not as important as initially thought. Undoubtedly, the team's culture changed with its composition, but the fact that cricketers in the late 1990s and early 2000s were generally from more modest backgrounds, less educated, and from smaller towns and cities did not make them more liable to religiosity or match-fixing. The elitist view that match-fixing and greater religiosity were problems brought about because of the changed composition of the cricket team was echoed by the chief of security of PCB when he told me during an interview that the spread of match-fixing was due largely to the influx of 'uneducated and impressionable' cricketers from smaller towns. The evidence, as we have seen, in fact shows that those accused of match-fixing were from a variety of backgrounds in terms of socio-economics, education and 'domicile.' Those who turned increasingly to religion also did not fit a pattern.

The changing demographic did, though, lead to an increased insularity as these individuals lacked the social and language skills to build up a rapport with players from opposing teams. Therefore, in stark contrast to their colleagues of the 1970s, 1980s, and 1990s, the players of 2000s were more isolated from the international cricketing community. Not only did they not play much county cricket in England, they were also barred from the cash rich Indian Premier League which drew cricketing stars from all other nations except Pakistan. This bred resentment and further isolation. In addition, the far greater surveillance and media exposure brought about by match-fixing scandals meant that players touring foreign countries were dissuaded from interacting with the public. Many took to going to the ground and then returning to their hotels where they spent time in their rooms. The days of frequenting movie halls and nightclubs were no longer a possibility. Particularly under a religiously inclined leader such as Inzamam, this promoted more focus on religiosity.

In fact, the influence of leadership which has been discussed in detail earlier represents a third specific stressor that explains the spread of religiosity in the cricket team. It is generally accepted that the role of the captain in cricket is crucial, giving the individual far greater influence than in other sports. The captain in cricket is a role model, a tactician, a mentor, and, in the case of Pakistan, one of the highest profile individuals in the country. Imran Khan's influence as an authoritarian leader through the 1980s—during the period of Zia's Islamization—meant that the cricket team was insulated from the wider trends sweeping Pakistan at the time. Imran Khan was yet to find religion and it remained conspicuous through its absence from the dressing room environment throughout his reign. He created a particular culture in the team he led. In contrast, Inzamam-ul-Haq's religiosity, aided by that of several senior team members, accelerated the influence of religion within the team. Here the Tablighi Jama'at's co-opting of the captain of the national team was a very significant advantage to their recruitment within the team. This was aided by a series of 'conversions' of senior team members, the most high profile of which was that of Yousuf Youhana who converted from Christianity. Again, the leader set the tone for the culture of the group.

Overarching trends in Pakistan had already created a socio-cultural environment where the importance of religion in the public sphere had increased significantly. But the factors referred to above—the need for redemption following a period of match-fixing, the influence of leadership, the conversion of high-profile players, and the changing composition of the team—were factors specific to the cricket team and which led to a sudden and deep penetration of religion in the team's ethos. And then the overt religiosity disappeared almost as soon as it had appeared. The reasons for this lie in the dissolution of the local factors that had earlier promoted the emergence of overt religiosity.

Firstly, there was a negation of the 'leadership' that acted as a conduit for the change. Following increasing media reports of manifest religiosity and how it was negatively affecting team performance, there was also concern by the Pakistan government over the blatant displays of religiosity by the cricket team. Inzamam-ul-Haq was told to tone down these demonstrations by the Pakistan Cricket Board. As the team's results began to falter, criticism mounted. Previously, religion had been seen as a binding force and reasons for poor performance were blamed on lack of skill or faulty team selection. Religion as a negative factor in the team's performance gained momentum when the government, its appointed cricket board chairman, and the team's manager, following the disastrous 2007 World Cup campaign, all stated publicly that the team's performance had suffered because the focus of several of the cricketers had been on preaching and not cricket. When I spoke to a former captain of the Pakistan team, Ramiz Raja, he related a story that had been told to him by Inzamam himself. According to Ramiz:

> General Pervez Musharraf had called Inzamam and Yousuf to President House soon after 2007 and proceeded to give them the class of their lives ... Yousuf and I did not know where to look as he told us that this constant show of religion was giving Pakistan a bad name and that it had to stop immediately.

Inzamam retired soon after and the en bloc prayers and involvement with the Tablighi Jama'at halted.

Religion continued to be important as can be expected of players who were born during and after the Zia years when Islamization had taken firm root. Celebrations still involve falling into *sajda* (prostration) and interviews are preceded with acknowledgements being given to Allah. But a new crop had become part of the team. The Tablighis of the early 2000s were no longer part of the set up and with that authority removed, one of the stressors had faded.

Secondly, the need for redemption has also disappeared. The sins of the decade of match-fixing and immorality have been washed and the players and the Pakistan team have emerged with a revitalized reputation. In that sense, religion has played its part and it will remain an important part of the identity of the cricket team as it is for the Pakistani nation. But the impetus provided by the 'immorality' of the decade of match-fixing has disappeared.

Thirdly, a significant change in leadership further reduced the influence of religiosity in the team culture just as it had increased it in the past. In 2010, after Salman Butt was convicted and jailed in Britain for match-fixing, he was replaced with Misbah-ul-Haq. A modest, educated, and upright man, Misbah brought dignity and gravity to the leadership of the team. A deeply religious Pashtun, Misbah differed from Inzamam in not being a Tablighi and kept his religion an intensely private affair. The team took on a similar characteristic. Instead of displays of religiosity, Misbah-ul-Haq and a number of senior members brought their impeccable character to direct the moral compass of the team. Without the alignment of factors that occurred in the past, there has been no return to overt religiosity since.

Match-fixing has hung over Pakistani cricket since the mid-1990s and the reasons for the spread of corruption in cricket and more specifically match-fixing in Pakistan are both complex and holistic. Undoubtedly, commercialization laid the foundations for corruption and the subsequent growth in match-fixing has been fuelled by the vast amount wagered on sport—around $2 trillion a year, according to the International Centre for Sport Security (ICSS), a think-tank.[111] It estimates that criminal groups launder $140 billion by match-fixing and illegal betting each year. But far from greed and avarice being the only impulses, there are more subtle and hidden influences such as the wider socio-economic environment, mentorship, intimidation, and the desire for modernity and financial security in a globalized world. Roads to redemption are limited—however, in Pakistan, religion provided one such avenue.

Sport and religion both create emotional responses and demand emotional attachment. Gods and sportsmen are worshipped. The worshippers enter into communion with the players to produce moments of heightened emotion in a display of what Émile Durkheim coined 'collective effervescence.' It is this passion for sport that allows the audience to believe that a sporting contest is anything but a trivial pursuit. Like religion, sport demands belief. The audience have to believe that all those involved in the contest are trying their best in the pursuit of excellence, in the pursuit of besting one another. Match-fixing—like doping in athletics or cycling—destroys that belief and without belief there is no religion nor is there sport. The achievements of opposing teams are diminished if it is found that their opponents purposely underperformed. The unpredictability of sport—what keeps viewers engaged—is put in doubt if it is revealed that a match's outcome was in fact fixed. If sport loses its unpredictability because of fixed results, the passion for sport is reduced, ultimately leading to indifference and a tarnished reputation which is difficult to redeem. Suspicions remain, leading to deep cynicism.

This chapter examined a number of alleged instances of match-fixing in detail in an effort to study what players, administrators, and the wider public felt was the truth behind match-fixing. It has also addressed questions such as why and how match-fixing began and how it 'progressed,' looking at a variety of both global and local influences. The wider influences include the commercialization of cricket, particularly in South Asia. This in turn created far greater opportunities for corruption and the involvement of international criminal networks. Commercialization also changed the values that were associated with cricket, including the balance between playing for cash or country. Moreover, the influx of money and media attention in cricket created new hierarchies and inequalities between the cricket-playing nations and their players leading to enhanced feelings of envy and greed and new parameters of what modernity and success entail. Specific local factors such as the impact of leadership—negative and positive—play important mitigating or facilitating roles.

But while global influences such as commercialization may have facilitated the emergence of modern-day match-fixing, at a more local level the chapter locates match-fixing in a broader national environment of corruption—within society, within club and first-class cricket, and within the institutions that govern the game of cricket in Pakistan. One of the questions that the chapter asks is that in a society where corruption is endemic and where accountability is routinely avoided by politicians and other public figures, why is it that cricketers are expected to be any different?

4

Pakistan in the Global Cricketing Order: England and the Colonial Legacy

Sport does not exist in isolation. Throughout the book so far, cricket has been used as a reflection of wider political, social, and cultural processes. Today, Pakistan is a significant geo-political country. Born as a result of the partition of the Subcontinent, it is inextricably linked to its former colonial master (Britain) and to the country it separated from (India). As a result, any study of cricket in Pakistan is intricately connected to both the aforementioned countries and must take into account Pakistan's bilateral relations with them, both in the past and currently. As we will see, this affects cricket and international relations.

Pakistan was admitted to the cricketing community on 28 July 1952, five years after it had initially lobbied to join the Imperial Cricket Conference (ICC). Earlier attempts had failed with the ICC rejecting its submission for membership in 1948 and 1950 on the grounds that there were 'insurmountable difficulties for the nation to overcome.' However, on the third attempt, the ICC, on the recommendation of Anthony de Mello (the President of the BCCI), awarded Pakistan full membership.[1] Abdul Hafeez Kardar, who had earlier captained Pakistan to victory over a touring MCC[2] team, referencing the struggles that the country had faced, dispatched a letter to the *Times* (13 February 1952) in which he stated: 'some had birth right to the membership. We have won it.'

Since joining the 'elite' club, Pakistan has established relations with all eleven of the other Test playing nations. Some of these are based solely on cricketing ties and are not complex or multifaceted. The countries this pertains to are South Africa, West Indies, New Zealand, Zimbabwe, Ireland, and to an extent Australia. It is with countries that Pakistan has wider global relations where the ties have been dynamic and multifarious. These include England and India in particular but also Bangladesh, Sri Lanka, and Afghanistan.

This chapter concentrates on Pakistan's relations with England, its former colonial master, examining the overarching historical and political relations, cultural misunderstandings, and the influence of particular individuals, whether cricketers on the field or administrators off it, that have affected the England-Pakistan relationship. In chapters 5 and 6, I will analyse Pakistan's relations with India—its uneasy neighbour with whom Partition occurred and who has been a traditional rival (cricketing and otherwise) ever since. The rivalry has also drawn in the other South Asian countries—Bangladesh, Sri Lanka, and Afghanistan.

THE COLONIAL LEGACY

'Quite honestly, when I look back on the Peshawar incident, I think
it was about the funniest thing I have ever seen in my life.'
– Donald Carr[3]

Carr was referring to an incident in 1956 when several of the touring MCC team members, including Carr who was then captain, abducted the Pakistani umpire Idris Baig from his hotel in Peshawar and proceeded to douse him with water. Baig found it anything but amusing and threatened to sue the MCC for injury to person. The prank was not considered to be funny either by the Pakistani press or the British High Commission in Pakistan who viewed it as a setback to years of repairing relations between Britain and Pakistan. The tour was saved amidst mounting protests when the MCC President, Field Marshal Harold Alexander of Tunis, made a sincere apology to his counterpart at the Pakistani board, Iskander Mirza, an old colleague of his from the campaigns on the North-West Frontier Province in Pakistan.[4]

Throughout the tour there had been a series of cultural missteps—what the English saw as harmless school boy fun the Pakistanis saw as public humiliations; an affront to the nation as much as to the individual. The English team and the press continued—even after the tour ended—to insist that the incident with Idris Baig was nothing more than a storm in a teacup by the humourless hosts, though the British High Commission blamed the players for poor behaviour. The Wisden, considered the bible for cricket writing and statistics, noted: 'Unfortunately, some of the players did not realise that the type of humour generally accepted by most people in Britain might not be understood in other parts of the world.'[5] But the cultural misunderstandings also revealed an underlying and unquestioned contempt for the hosts—a condescension that was borne of a historically unequal relationship which involved the domination of an indigenous population by a foreign invader; in which one side came to be seen as the master and the other the subject. The reversal of roles—Pakistan defeated the MCC 2-1 in the series—was not easily accepted.

The England-Pakistan cricketing relationship came to be defined by a tension between colonial arrogance on the one side and a desire for decolonization on the other—'from a game played and controlled by white English and colonial elites, to a sport carrying the aspirations of national independence and democratic ownership.'[6] Moreover, unlike India, which took twenty years to register a first Test win against the old colonial power, Pakistan won a Test match in their very first series against England in 1954. Mihir Bose points out that 'the audacity of a former colony, brown at that, to achieve a test victory was too much for the white sahib. Ever since... Pakistanis have always felt that whatever they do will never be able to win the unqualified approval of the English.'[7] The subaltern had found its voice early on and would be seen as an upstart from then on.

England's relations with Pakistan, however, would be mediated not only bilaterally but also through the ICC which remained a firmly colonial institution as indicated by its name, the 'Imperial' Cricket Conference—and England's historical supremacy to the game of cricket needs to be recognized. As shown in earlier chapters, international cricket grew out of the British Empire where initially the British played amongst themselves before allowing the 'natives' to join in. 'Many colonial subjects were taught to play this game, often as part of the frequently invoked "civilizing mission".'[8] Cricket was very much a vehicle for instituting and instilling Empire, and thereby reinforcing existing power structures.

The Imperial Cricket Conference as it was initially known was created in 1909 and consisted of three members—England, Australia, and South Africa. The idea for the body was proposed by South Africa and was seen as a way of consolidating the empire in the African colony.[9] In 1926, three further countries joined the ICC—the West Indies,[10] New Zealand, and India. The connection to the British Empire was laid out specifically in the ICC's meeting of 1926 where it was agreed that membership should comprise, 'governing bodies of cricket in countries within the Empire to which cricket teams are sent, or which send teams to England.'[11] This statement, while encompassing the British Empire, meant that the United States which had regularly received teams from England since 1859 and had dispatched several teams to England was effectively locked out. Cricket's spread remained confined to societies under the direct rule of the British Empire and relations were shaped by pre-existing imperial hierarchies. After Partition, India, which had initially attempted to incorporate Pakistan cricket under the umbrella of India, sponsored Pakistan's admission to the Test club, despite England's scepticism.

The Imperial Cricket Conference's transition to a post-colonial order was remarkably slow. The 'Imperial' in the name was not changed to 'International' until 1965 and it was not until 1989 that the practice of the MCC president automatically being the chairman of the ICC was terminated. In 1993, the first non-British chairman was elected, and in the same year England and Australia lost their power of veto, signalling a definitive shift away from the traditional power centres of the game. Thus, as Mike Marqusee points out, long before cricket was a global game, it was an imperial game. 'At least, that was how it was seen by the rulers of the British Empire, in Whitehall and at Lord's.'[12]

British subjects, though, viewed the game differently. Initially cricket was a means of establishing relations with the upper echelons of the British Empire. The empowering of the colonized through the game, as Subhash Jaireth states, came much later when it was 'acquired, appropriated and assimilated by them.'[13] Yet, when colonialism collapsed taking with it many of the structures that supported colonial rule, cricket not only remained but gained popularity in South Asia. The newly independent nations saw it as a space for defeating their previous colonial rulers at their own game. For these new nations, cricket had become, as C.L.R. James argues in *Beyond a Boundary*, a vehicle for popular struggle; a site for anti-imperialism and anti-racism and an enemy of colonialism.

For the British, their dominance was built on military, economic, political, and racial (including moral) superiority and this ascendency extended to all aspects of life including sport. The domination of the administration of cricket by England and Australia as founding members for decades[14] further intensified feelings of superiority that were strengthened by colonial and racial discourses that had been used in constructing the 'other' as inherently inferior. Moreover, England and Australia were rich, developed countries amidst poor, developing nations. As a result, as Jaireth in his article 'Tracing Orientalism in Cricket' claims, all third world cricket nations are poorly represented by

Western journalists and players largely because of the orientalist tendency of essentializing and constructing realities.[15] For Edward Said, orientalism constructs notions of an absolute and systematic difference between the East and the West on the basis of cultural generalizations or stereotypes that depict the Orient as irrational, backward, corrupt, undisciplined, chaotic and 'excitable.' In contrast, the West is rational, disciplined, scientific, fair. In fact, when cricket first came to India, it was seen as not being immediately suitable to the 'natives.' Lord George Harris, governor of Bombay between 1890 and 1895 and a keen patron and promoter of the game in colonial India, was convinced that this peculiarly English game required the 'doggedness of the English temperament.'[16] The 'excitable Asiatics' would need to be taught the disciplined and the scientific manner[17] that came inherently to the Anglo-Saxon. Not only did this attitude justify the 'civilizing' mission of cricket but it would embed in cricket the idea of the oriental stereotype long after colonialism had been dismantled.

It is this context that moulded the attitudes of the cricketing nations, England and Pakistan, towards one another. The perceptions that developed about Pakistan were mediated through the discourses of colonialism, race, and underdevelopment and it was this perceived reality that dominated how English cricket viewed their Pakistani counterparts. Perceptions are reality, Clifford Geertz stated in his book *The Interpretation of Cultures*.[18] When these perceptions are firmly held, they express and give rise to deep, powerful, and lasting beliefs, attitudes, and behaviours. Pakistan came to be seen through stereotypes which are themselves based on the collapsing of complex differences into simple cardboard cut outs.[19] In Pakistan's case, these simplistic Western representations overwhelmingly focussed on negative features.

Unsurprisingly, then, media portrayals and the accounts of returning English (and Australian) cricketers concentrated on images of widespread poverty, extreme heat, disease, unruly crowds, and unsanitary accommodation and living conditions. Infamously, Ian Botham, one of England's greatest cricketers, described Pakistan in 1984 as the 'kind of place to send your mother-in-law for a month, all expenses paid.'[20] The Australian fast bowler, Dennis Lillee, prior to touring Pakistan in 1980—against 'his better judgment'—had been warned that living conditions were terrible and that it was likely he could pick up a disease that could affect him for the rest of his life. When he did decide on touring, he described Faisalabad 'as the worst place I've ever seen…filth, mud, flies, the lot.'[21] Ian Healy, who toured Pakistan with the Australian team in 1988, summing up the general feeling amongst Australian and England cricketers touring Pakistan, wrote that:

a Pakistan tour was always seen by Australian cricketers of the 80s as the worst to go on—little beer, no social life, poor hotels, dodgy food and dubious umpiring. Talk among the Australian team from the very beginning of the 1988 tour revolved around horror tales from previous trips.[22]

In fact, these tales that cricketers who had travelled to Pakistan earlier narrated were instrumental in creating a kind of inhibiting paranoia for many who toured later. Umpires and players in a land where corruption was rife were viewed with suspicion and often accused of cheating. The wider culture (including food)—inferior to their own—was to be insulated from. Bob Willis, the England captain on tour to Pakistan in 1984, wrote in his diary prior to setting off for Pakistan:

> We bought tinned ham and turkey, smoked oysters, seafood pate, crackers and crispbreads and then, satisfied with the haul, we indulged ourselves with a hamburger at McDonald's. None of us can be sure what food will be available in Pakistan. We hear hotels in Karachi and Lahore are new and well equipped, but it is better to be safe than starving.[23]

It was not uncommon well into the 1990s for Australian and English teams touring the Subcontinent to routinely survive on tinned food shipped over from home.

> We lived on cuppa soup and baked beans…I volunteered myself to be in charge of the team microwave which I kept in my room for safety. I can still do a great Peshawar hotpot; microwave tinned stew and baked beans. Heaven![24]

The Yorkshireman Brian Close touring with the MCC during the notorious Idris Baig tour showed a complete disinterest in the country:

> They showed us their new dams and their monuments to local heroes like Jinnah and Liaquat Ali Khan. They took us hunting. But their hotels were not yet up to Western standards and the food was strange in the extreme to most of us.[25]

In later years, several cricketers would recognize the development of a siege mentality while on tour whereby pre-conceived notions and a reluctance to challenge dominant stereotypes simply strengthened a specific view of the country and led to a self-fulfilling prophecy. Ian Healy—quoted earlier and who spoke of the negative perceptions of the country even prior to leaving for the tour—wrote of the way dominant negative views were reinforced:

the moment our pessimistic expectations came to fruition in the slightest way we cocooned ourselves from the voice of reason. Instead we preferred to indulge in a siege mentality and let the negativity snowball out of control.[26]

Derek Pringle, another former England cricketer, commented:

the attitude of most England players on recent tours has done little to break down these barriers. Few players ever attempted to embrace or understand a culture they were plonked in the middle of, preferring instead to cocoon themselves with videotapes and an array of familiar comestibles.[27]

The lack of interaction meant that any challenging of stereotypes was unlikely to occur and routinely unflattering portrayals of Pakistan continued to be reinforced. When individuals showed more of an inclination to step out of the cocoon that had spun around them, a far less negative picture of the country emerged. Jack Russell, who was unable to eat the local food, was still enamoured with the history and culture of Peshawar: 'The venue was memorable for a start. Peshawar, just nine miles from the Khyber Pass on the North West Frontier, is a town full of the old colonial atmosphere, reminiscent of the days of the Raj. You could almost feel the history.'[28] A talented artist, Russell spent a considerable amount of his free time sketching the surrounds, finding it enervating. He completed forty sketches which incidentally sold out in two days when he exhibited them on return to England. Vic Marks, who toured in 1984, also wrote of preconceived notions and the fact that they did not always fit the reality:

We had heard horror stories. Either they were exaggerated, or conditions have improved considerably. The hotels in the main cities of Karachi and Lahore were excellent and eager to meet any special needs such as supplying lunch to the ground or even transporting an evening meal 120 miles from Lahore to Faisalabad.[29]

Mike Coward, in his account of the 1988 Australian tour to Pakistan, wrote that with 'few exceptions the behaviour of the team was so irrational and the prejudices so deep that it became impossible for journalists to distinguish between events just and unjust.' Coward added that the Australians were at least 'guilty of elitism, behaving as they would not have behaved elsewhere in the cricket world and condoning behaviour that they would not have condoned elsewhere in the cricket world.'[30] But Steve Waugh, who later captained Australia, was part of that tour and was one of the more inquisitive of the tourists making his way to the markets of Faisalabad and the beaches of Karachi.

When he toured again in 1998, he was adamant about maintaining a positive mindset and spoke of some of the brighter aspects of touring the country:

> The best thing about touring Pakistan is the unexpected random incidents, such as having the opportunity to take the team bus up the fabled Khyber Pass, fire a few rounds from an AK47 with the Khyber Rifles and mingle with the locals in this territory ruled by the tribal owners and not by the government.[31]

In 1995, Nasser Hussain toured with an England A team and spoke of Pakistan as being an 'eye opener, the people being so warm and friendly.'[32] Even Bob Willis, who had stocked up on tinned food prior to arriving in Pakistan, admitted that in fact the food and accommodation had been superb and that Ian Botham's disparaging remarks on Pakistan's poor food and accommodation were completely uncalled for and had in fact been based on a very limited[33] stay in Pakistan during which he spent all his time in five-star hotels in Karachi and Lahore.[34]

However, these accounts remained marginal, being unable to challenge the dominant narratives on Pakistan. Moreover, as Valiotis and Jaireth both point out, what distinguishes Pakistan further from all the others—and more particularly India, and makes it the least preferred destination of all—is Islam.[35] Few other writers have highlighted the fact that until Bangladesh became a full member of the ICC in 2000, Pakistan was the only Muslim country playing international cricket, and touring an Islamic country had specific challenges and perils.

> It is interesting that both India and Pakistan are scripted similarly: the metaphors and the visual images are the same. The portrayal, however, becomes different as soon as the focus shifts from these immediately visible features to Islam. Added to the image of dirt, dust and dysentery—physical discomfort— Islam represents the elements of suspicion and threat so that Pakistan becomes a land of danger. The discourse about Islamic fundamentalism penetrates the discourse about economic "backwardness" of the "third world" countries. Islam represents the elements of suspicion and threat so that Pakistan becomes a land of danger.[36]

The stigma against Islam in the West—from Australia to Europe to the United States—has grown rapidly since the 9/11 attacks in 2001. The coming to power of Donald Trump and other right wing leaders in the West has mainstreamed Islamophobia in the respective countries. But even well before 2001, Islam has a long history as the collective 'Other' of the West. Islam, as Lutfi Sunar points out, always represents the closest other and the most active enemy for the West.[37] Otherizing it, therefore, is not only a cultural but also a strategic matter.

The association with Islam meant that perceptions about Pakistan were even more negative than for other South Asian countries—India and Sri Lanka—which were seen as more welcoming and less austere and hostile to the West. Pakistan, with its religious component, was coloured with a more severe discourse than orientalism, leaving it, as Valiotis states, in an untenable position with little sympathy and even less support from the community of cricket nations, let alone the Western press.[38] Pakistan with strict restrictions on alcohol, public entertainment, and social behaviour left touring teams even more quarantined. Bob Willis touring in 1984 referred to it as the most boring tour he had ever experienced, 'partly because there is so little to occupy the mind.'[39] He also highlighted the English bafflement with Islam, complaining about the 'wailing' of the *azaan* in the morning and referring to a recital from the Quran before a dinner. He commented, 'what we had not expected was that before the dinner began, we had to stand for a recital from the Quran, the Muslim Bible, read in Urdu. It might have baffled us in English, but in Urdu was incomprehensible.'[40]

Nearly all accounts[41] of Pakistan, even more positive ones in later years, which often praised the standard of food, accommodation, cricketing facilities, and the efforts of the hosts to go out of their way to meet the needs of touring teams, point out the difficulty of touring a 'dry country,' mainly because of the loss of the 'bar' acting as a point of relaxation and socializing after a day's cricket. This also translated into a lack of entertainment opportunities such as nightclubs though with a culture tracing its roots back 4000 years there were certainly opportunities for alternative forms of distraction. John Etheridge, writing the tour report in the Wisden,[42] actually complains that in 2005 the majority of cricketers touring Pakistan made little or no attempt to fathom out where they were. 'They apparently preferred to play computer games in their bedrooms, saying there was "nothing to do". Only five chose to go on an organized trip to the fascinating Wagah [border] gate where Pakistan meets India, a 30-minute drive from their hotel in Lahore.'

Up until the 1990s, England and Australian teams touring Pakistan were mired in the powerful stereotypes that surrounded Pakistan and its cricket. Such stereotypes can facilitate intergroup hostility and give rise to deep and long-lasting prejudices about groups. However, this does not mean that all stereotypes are false but that they tend to highlight certain traits unduly. Prior to the 1980s, accommodation outside the major cities was 'basic,' often lacking showers and hot water—and opportunities for off-field entertainment were limited. The crowds were often unruly, partisan, and aggressive. England had faced crowd disturbances on almost all their tours up to the late 1980s. While the majority of these were not aimed at the tourists themselves but were motivated by internal political issues, they led to rioting, the use of tear gas, and the abandoning of cricket. In comparison, Indian crowds were more welcoming. These factors contributed to the negative experiences of those touring Pakistan.

But possibly the point of greatest conflict and angst for visiting teams, particularly keeping in mind their mindset as described above, was the standard of local umpiring.[43] Here the hosts did not always contribute to disproving negative stereotypes of their own countries through a series of poor strategies which I shall now turn to. Umpiring also became one of the main factors in defining the nature of the relationship between England and Pakistan.

Umpire vs. Empire

The way that English cricket viewed Pakistan cricket, the continued impact of the 'colonial attitude' and the effect of conflicts over umpiring are epitomized in an incident that occurred between the England captain Mike Gatting and the Pakistani umpire Shakoor Rana during England's 1987 tour of Pakistan. The altercation was the outcome of an evolving dynamic between England and Pakistan cricket and went on to define this relationship for several years.

Umpiring has been a flash point for England-Pakistan cricketing relations since the infamous dousing of Idris Baig described earlier. As mentioned, even if cultural differences in humour were accounted for, it is difficult to deny the contempt that was shown by the England team for their hosts. The incident and the attitude of the English team in the aftermath personified an outlook of arrogance and superiority that came with their colonial heritage. The altercation between Shakoor Rana and Mike Gatting in which the two abused one another, pointing fingers and gesticulating wildly, had never before been seen on the cricket field. The third day's play in the second test was lost as Rana refused to resume umpiring duties without an apology. The incident, however, was the outcome of a series of earlier provocations, starting with Idris Baig, that had come to dominate the relationship between England and Pakistan.

The 1987 series, which Wisden describes as one of the most acrimonious ever played,[44] had come after the just concluded World Cup jointly hosted by India and Pakistan (won by Australia who defeated their arch-rivals England by seven runs). Pakistan had been highly fancied to win but a semi-final loss to Australia had been a deep disappointment to the Pakistani public and had seen Pakistan's talismanic captain Imran Khan retire from international cricket.[45] He was replaced by Javed Miandad, a man whose reputation as an agent provocateur was unsurpassed. It is fairly widely alleged[46] that General Zia, who was facing an election the following year and who had used cricketing success to prop up his own popularity, had made clear to the Pakistan players and the cricket administration that a further loss following the World Cup disappointment would be unacceptable. These 'dictates' were likely handed down to the umpires by a compliant Board of Control for Cricket in Pakistan (BCCP). Mickey Stewart, the England coach at the time, wrote in his tour diary of being warned about poor umpiring by a local Pakistani contact.[47] The pressure placed on Pakistani umpires is also highlighted in other accounts. John Crace, while tracing the careers of the Pakistani fast bowlers Wasim Akram and Waqar Younis, states that all Pakistan umpires unofficially admit that Imran Khan was the one captain who never asked them to help out[48]—and, as mentioned in the previous chapter, Khan had dismissed their voluntary attempts to assist. A similar incident is related about another umpire—Idris Baig!—approaching the Pakistan captain A.H. Kardar for similar instructions when India toured in 1954–55.[49] In the 1987 England series, with Miandad at the helm, it is likely that the umpires would have played their part.

The BCCP also saw the tour as an opportunity to even the scores with their English counterparts. Three months earlier, Pakistan had won a series in England for the first time with Imran Khan leading a young Pakistan team out of the shadow of colonial domination. I recall speaking to Imran Khan before the series started. He was excited because he felt he finally had a team that was not intimidated by the old colonial masters. Khan had overseen a generational shift in Pakistan cricket, starting with the dropping of his own cousin and childhood hero Majid Khan whom he felt was past his best. The two did not speak again for two decades. Pakistan arrived in England with a new aggressive mindset, shedding the timidity of the past. The BCCP took an equally assertive stance, requesting that a particular English umpire not stand in the series. A similar request by India had been agreed to earlier the same summer. But in a strong rebuke, the English board appointed umpire David Constant to not one but two Tests. The message was clear—how dare Pakistan cast aspersions on English umpires, long established as the best in the world. The refusal and the further decision to give the umpire not one but two Test matches was to drive home the message that Pakistan should know its place in the hierarchy and not challenge it.

On the 1987 England return tour to Pakistan, Pakistani officials—still piqued at what they saw was English heavy handedness—were bent upon returning the compliment with interest against an England team that had already spent weeks in the Subcontinent for the World Cup and now faced six more weeks away from home in Pakistan. There was also the added disappointment for England of having lost the World Cup final ten days earlier. For English players, the mindset was epitomized by Bill Athey, the English batsman who allegedly stated early on in the tour: 'the sooner we get out of this f****ing country the better.'[50]

In such an environment, a confrontation was almost inevitable. Unfortunately, once the incident occurred, it spiralled further out of control. The England team rallied behind Gatting who had refused to apologize to Rana without a reciprocal apology. Javed Miandad, Pakistan's captain, later admitted in his autobiography that he had insisted that Rana demand an unconditional apology, 'not because I was the opposing captain, but as a Pakistani. Gatting's audacity in yelling at umpire Rana was an insult to Pakistan. Can you imagine what the English would have demanded had I berated an English umpire the way Gatting had Shakoor Rana.'[51] In a similar vein, a telegram was sent to Rana from his employers at the Pakistan Railways: 'Do not supervise the match unless Mike Gatting apologises in writing. He has abused the whole Pakistani nation and I cannot bear it. I think he is not the son of a man. That is why his face is from a white monkey.'[52]

In England, there were several former cricketers who felt that their team had been wronged. Tom Graveney who toured Pakistan in 1968–69 stated: 'they (Pakistan) have been cheating us for 37 years, and it is just getting worse and worse. The TCCB [Test and County Cricket Board] should bring England home.'[53] The use of the word 'cheat,' reinforcing the age-old construct of Orientals as 'cheats,' compared with the fair play that was inherent to the game played by 'us.' Ian Botham added: 'You wouldn't see those sorts of decisions given in village cricket, let alone Test cricket. The England players have my sympathy.'[54]

But there were also voices of opposition seeing Gatting as responsible for bringing the game into disrepute and that far more was expected of a captain. Possibly the strongest retort came from the former West Indian cricket captain Clive Lloyd who said: 'just a few days ago a British boxer—and I am British now—threw a punch at the referee. I did not think British sport could sink any lower. How I bitterly regret what Mike Gatting has done.'[55] Lloyd, who had led the West Indies through a period when his team had faced racial abuse both in England and Australia,[56] and whose team's rise in the late 1970s to being one of the greatest ever was so closely linked to the ideology of Third World liberation, may well have understood the imperial and racial undertones to the confrontation that clearly had eluded others.

Gatting was ultimately forced to apologize by the TCCB and he did so 'minimally and gracelessly.'[57] The team made public their unequivocal support for their captain and that they were playing on under protest.[58] It appears likely also that in this case British diplomats pressurized the TCCB and the cricketers to make the apology. The British ambassador in Pakistan at the time, Nicholas Barrington, had been less than sympathetic to the English team stating in a communiqué to the Foreign Office that the possible cancellation of the tour 'would create a great deal of ill-will in Pakistan towards Britain and could have damaging financial and legal consequences.'[59] Barrington believed that Gatting had behaved 'disgracefully.'[60] Neil Robinson points out that that in April 1987 the Pakistani Prime Minister Muhammad Khan Junejo had visited the United Kingdom and discussions had included the sale of British-built frigates to Pakistan.[61] Pakistan was also a major export market for British industry and it seems likely that the Foreign and Commonwealth Office pressed for this relationship not to be jeopardized. Had the tour been cancelled, it is likely that the TCCB would also have had to financially compensate the BCCP.

However, the brevity of Gatting's apology, 'Dear Shakoor Rana, I apologise for the bad language used during the second day of the Test match,' scrawled on a torn piece of paper indicated what the tour management and the players thought of the directive to apologize. The Chairman of the TCCB, Raman Subba Row, flew out to Pakistan to ensure that the tour did proceed and, as a sweetener, each England player was given £1,000 as 'hardship allowance.' A request to remove Shakoor Rana from umpiring in the final match was agreed to by Pakistan but only after English officials were pointedly reminded that when Pakistan had made a similar request, not only was it turned down, but two Tests were given to the umpire who had been protested against. *The Guardian*'s editorial[62] would sum up the issue and the acrimonious tour succinctly:

> National prestige, cultural tradition, class and racial prejudices play their irrepressible parts. They affect this Test match as they affect every match between black and white cricketers, and perhaps also every match involving either the world's only Islamic cricketing nation or the representatives of the most snobbish and hypocritical sports administration.

The feelings of national prestige (*izzat*), class, and racial prejudices were themes that had been highlighted in the Idris Baig case as well as in the

Gatting-Rana altercation and which would come up again when the Pakistan captain Inzamam-ul-Haq would forfeit a match in 2006 in response to umpire Darrell Hair's accusation that Pakistan had tampered with the ball.[63] For Inzamam, as for Miandad, quoted earlier, and Idris Baig, the issue became not so much one of personal insult but calling into question the *izzat* or honour of Pakistan. The disrespect shown to the Pakistani umpires was equated with disrespect towards Pakistan whom they were representing. An insult to the nation was unacceptable. This attitude does indicate how closely Pakistan cricket had come to being identified with the Pakistani nation, its prestige, and its aspirations.

The Gatting-Rana incident highlights a number of issues that came to define the relationship between English and Pakistan cricket at the time. The colonial mindset of the England team and its management and of former English cricketers remained deeply ingrained. This included the preconceived notions that the touring cricketers had about Pakistan. In the 1970s and 1980s, the narrative from English teams touring Pakistan was similar—poor food and accommodation, hostile environments, poverty, biased umpiring, and players who pushed the boundaries of acceptable behaviour. For Pakistan, cricketing success was one of its first expressions of national identity and prestige. The early success in international cricket, a general insecurity borne of a new nation with precious little else to celebrate on the international stage, political dictates, and the fact that cricket is seen as so much more than simply a game did mean that umpires were routinely pressurized to favour the home team. This is not to say that favouring the home team did not happen elsewhere—it did, though probably not because of political pressures. Almost every tour was blighted by complaints by the visiting team. The West Indies complained in Australia, Pakistan complained in England, England complained in India, Australia complained in Pakistan. Yet Pakistan's push for neutral umpires was resisted by England in particular. But the record of Pakistan's umpires was not enviable at this point and as someone who watched the series it was clear that the umpiring was substandard and biased throughout the tour. The two boards involved also did little to improve relations, straitjacketed by their own prejudices about each other.

Throughout the early decades of Pakistan's entry into international cricket, relations with England had been defined by a patronizing contempt rather than outright hostility—the restraint largely based on the premise that Pakistan did not assert itself either on or off the pitch. But increasingly Pakistan had become more assertive. On-field victories for Pakistan from the 1980s had certainly contributed to more hostility between England

and Pakistan but there was also a similar change at the administrative level. Jack Williams points out that England's role at the ICC seems to have been interpreted as a hangover of an 'English sense of innate superiority that had helped uphold the Raj, and created an impression that countries whose cricket had become as strong or stronger than England's were not treated as equals.'[64] He adds that not only Pakistan but the representatives of India and the West Indies too assumed that the TCCB representatives imagined that they continued to have the right to control cricket as they had for much of the twentieth century.

Between 1972 and 1977, A.H. Kardar as Pakistan's representative to the ICC often took up positions opposing England. Kardar, fiercely nationalistic and a champion of anti-apartheid, strongly resisted any softening over the isolation of South Africa during the apartheid years. There was a feeling amongst the non-white nations that the predominantly white countries in the ICC would have resumed Test Cricket with South Africa had it not been for the resistance from within the ICC from Pakistan, India, and the West Indies and, more importantly, if the politicians in the white countries had allowed them. Kardar was also the first person to question England and Australia's veto power at the ICC,[65] even though it was not abolished during his tenure as Pakistan's representative to the ICC. However, in 1992, Pakistan again brought up the veto and the ensuing discussion ultimately led to it being abolished the following year. England and Pakistan also clashed in the 1980s and 1990s over Pakistan's support for neutral umpires and England's opposition, which was based on England's conviction that their umpires were the best and the implementation of neutral umpires would mean England would never be supervised by the best, in other words their own umpires, and they may end up playing against 'Australia at Lord's with an Indian at one end and a Pakistani at the other and that would hardly be satisfactory.'[66]

How England's ICC representatives viewed these changing dynamics is uncertain, but it seems likely that Kardar's principled belligerence was resented by the English cricket establishment.[67] Moreover, other prominent personalities from English cricket were more open with their views indicating their discomfort with the growing power of the Asian bloc with fears of the predominantly white members being outvoted. Writing in the aftermath of the Gatting-Rana confrontation, former England captain Raymond Illingworth summed up the growing resentment that was developing at the time. Illingworth saw the altercation as part of:

> an international plot to deprive this country of its influence in world cricket—a political power game. Cricket wise, Pakistan has always been iffy, and

Pakistanis, in the main difficult. Now they are becoming downright Bolshie. Given a chance they would trample all over us ... Out there I heard and read repeatedly of campaigns to take the International Cricket Council permanently to the sub-continent and to blazes with England ... We have spread the game and made allowances for eccentricities in other countries. But we have been weak ... It's time we showed we won't tolerate being messed about.[68]

Illingworth would repeat the sentiment against the Asian bloc when he showed his support for the rebel England tour of South Africa and his criticism of the opposition voiced by the West Indies, Pakistan, and India against the tour which was in breach of international sanctions against apartheid—'We have been dictated to for too long by these countries overseas for too long.'[69] The fear of the Asian bloc was realized further when India, Pakistan, and Sri Lanka won the bid for the 1996 World Cup amidst much rancour[70] and allegations of bribes and unethical backroom deals. The English board had believed it was England's turn to stage the event and that the Asian bloc had swung the vote by 'bribing' the ICC non-Test playing Associate Members, thereby managing to overturn the 5-4 vote by Test playing nations in favour of England.

Thus, both on and off the field England's receding influence and power, contrasted with the rise of Pakistan and India, seemed to culminate in the disdain and condescension of the past being replaced by outright hostility in 1992 and following this a relationship that was less inimical and more supportive. There are multiple reasons for these changing dynamics which I now turn to.

'PAK OFF THE CHEATS'[71]

The growing animosity between Pakistan and English cricket does coincide with Pakistan's rise as one of the best teams in the world in the late 1980s and early 1990s. Apart from a sole win in their first series in England in 1954, Pakistan did not beat England again until 1982. This included heavy defeats in the 1960s and a series of draws in the 1970s. From 1983 onwards, Pakistan reversed the pattern and gained ascendency over England, winning every series until 2001. This change in fortunes starting in the 1980s led to a growing hostility against the Pakistani upstarts.

The 1987 tour to Pakistan had been the most acrimonious in decades, fuelled by the events described earlier and the fact that Pakistan was now an ascendant team while England was in steep decline. Another series between the two teams did not occur for five years in the hope that the break would allow relations to heal. Unfortunately, if the 1980s had signalled tensions resulting from the start of changing power relations between English and Pakistani cricket, the 1992 Pakistan tour to England signalled a chauvinistic, almost xenophobic, retaliation from a nation that had lost its political and cricketing dominance. Much of this was evidenced by the attitude of the English press during the tour. As Chris Searle points out: 'If popular sport can become the mirror of the attitudes within a society, the reporting of it in a press which itself poses and parades as "popular" can make that reflection even more lucid.'[72] Before analysing what happened during the tour itself, there are important contextual factors that need to be accounted for.

Firstly, the tour came soon after Pakistan had defeated England in the final of the 1992 World Cup in Australia. It was England's second consecutive loss in a World Cup final and the memory of the loss was still fresh. Secondly, Pakistan's captain Imran Khan had retired. Many in English cricket admired Khan and on the last tour to England in 1987, he had kept his youthful charges in check, even admonishing them publicly on the field for unsportsmanlike behaviour. Khan was also Oxford educated, English speaking, tall, fair, and good looking. He socialized easily and often amongst British high society and was seen as part of the English elite circle. In contrast, in both the subsequent 1987 England tour to Pakistan and the Pakistan tour to England in 1992, captaincy was in the hands of Javed Miandad, seen as the antithesis of Imran Khan, and a man reviled by the English team, not only for his on-field ability to get under the opponents' skin but also because of his alleged role in the Gatting-Rana episode. Miandad was a confrontational opponent, more likely to fan the flames than to douse them. In a series that required calmer heads, Miandad was not best suited for such a diplomatic role. Just as Gatting had been a factor in 1987, Miandad was a factor in 1992. Individuals and personal animosities continued to impact wider relations between the cricketing nations and would do so again in subsequent decades.

But Miandad also represented *the* caricatured villain—the negative stereotype—that the English press so sought:

> Of course I am a fighter. I adore to fight all the time … it doesn't worry me that I've been branded the wild man of cricket. I'll tell your Test stars Ian Botham and David Gower they're lousy cricketers if it helps Pakistan grind England's noses in the dirt. Cricket is a game of psychological warfare and there is a lot of bad mouthing out there. I admit I am one of the worst. I hate people getting runs against Pakistan and I'll do anything—yes anything to stop them.[73]

Mike Langely, writing in the tabloid newspaper *The Mirror*, described Miandad as a 'wild man with a face you might spot crouched behind a rock in ambush along the Khyber.'[74] The insinuations were clear—here was Kipling's wily Pathan;[75] not an honourable opponent but one who would ambush you; not a gentleman but a wild man. It would not stop there. Colin Milburn, a former England cricketer, called him the Colonel Gaddafi of cricket.[76] Tony Lewis, former England captain, felt that Miandad would take Pakistan cricket to further depths: 'they will certainly shake your hand but that is all part of their duplicity. I think Miandad is a terrible ringleader. If people think Mike Gatting is cheating, then Miandad is unbelievable. He gets up to every trick in the book.'[77] However, Miandad was certainly not alone in displaying these traits. But, while the Australians were admired for their toughness and competitiveness, and for having pioneered the 'art of mental disintegration,'[78] Miandad, instead, was coloured by racial undertones and branded a 'cheat.'

If it was thought that the memories of the 1987 tour to Pakistan would have faded, this proved untrue. Clearly, even before the tour began it was evident that English cricket saw its Pakistani equivalent as riddled with corruption, cheating, and duplicity. While the TCCB may have forced Mike Gatting to apologize in Pakistan, they had provided each player a hardship bonus of £1,000 suggesting a tacit admission of the 'cheating' that the players had endured. Williams quotes the TCCB chairman in 1990 saying: 'the cheating was aided and abetted by the Pakistani officials ... oh absolutely, absolutely. There is no doubt. It was a carefully conceived plan.'[79]

The English management and press had felt that the England team had been poorly treated in Pakistan. Alongside this, Pakistan's increasingly aggressive and abrasive demeanour, both on and off the field, meant that there was a seething resentment against them which would be vented through the press's representation of Pakistan cricket. The tour in 1992 would show the depth of the feeling that Pakistanis were habitual cheats—cricketers, administrators, and the nation. Years of English cricket's resentment came to focus on the 'uppity, ungentlemanly Pakistanis.' 'In 1992, this elite impatience with black self-assertion merged with raving tabloid racism, which had singled out Pakistanis for its own reasons. The combination proved highly combustible.'[80]

The major flashpoint during the tour revolved around allegations of ball tampering—and thereby cheating—against two of Pakistan's greatest fast bowlers, Wasim Akram and Waqar Younis. The two had repeatedly destroyed England's batting line up during the tour and had been the major reason for Pakistan registering a third consecutive series victory over England. Initially, innuendos and press leakages were made by the England team management.[81] However, towards the end of the tour an interview with the England player Allan Lamb was published by the *Daily Mirror*[82] under the title, 'How Pakistan Cheat at Cricket.' Despite lack of evidence, many in English cricket saw Lamb's accusations as confirmation of the Pakistani/Oriental tendency to cheat. It was also the start of what Searle states was a 'scurrilous, vicious and subliminally racist campaign' that sought to completely 'otherize' the Pakistan team and nation.[83] Allan Lamb, the whistle blower, was lionized as the talisman of English cricket and its historically derived values of 'fair play,' despite the fact that he was actually a South African-born batsman who had qualified to play for England. In contrast, Pakistani players, even beyond the named bowlers, were branded scoundrels, cheats, and liars.

The stereotyping extended to English and Pakistani umpires as well, respectively. English umpiring was seen to have been relatively poor in the series with a number of critical decisions going in favour of the home team. Marqusee states that non-English observers found much of the English umpiring during the series to be 'inconsistent.' He quotes a former Anglophile Indian as saying, 'It seems your umpires are now no better than ours.'[84] Williams argues more strongly that even some English observers felt that 'mistakes' by English umpires had helped England win the fourth Test and keep the series alive.[85] Mike Selvy, *The Guardian*'s premier cricket correspondent, pondered what the reaction would have been had similar mistakes been made in Karachi.[86] Scyld Berry was scathing in his appraisal:

> There was a smell during the fourth test that I had never detected before in a Test in England. There was something in addition to the inevitable, unconscious, bias which umpires have towards home teams and in particular home captains. Tight-lipped and highly formal, the umpiring at Headingly generated the impression that, come what may, judgements were not going to be delivered in Pakistan's favour until England were safely established in both their innings.[87]

Despite these observations, the stereotype remained: English umpires were the best in the world and made mistakes; Pakistani umpires were biased and were unequivocally cheats. Questioning a foreign umpire—like Shakoor Rana—would be treated differently from Pakistani cricketers questioning an English umpire where their appeals were often dismissed as hysterical attempts to put unacceptable pressure on the umpire. During the 1992 tour, an altercation between a group of Pakistani players and the English umpire Roy Palmer was poorly handled by Miandad who inflamed the situation rather than diffuse it. While it reflected poorly on the Pakistan team, it was not in the same order as the Gatting-Rana quarrel. Yet the Pakistani action was described by Richard Hutton, the editor of *The Cricketer* magazine, as the 'monstrous behaviour of these anarchists.' In contrast, Gatting's argument with Rana was 'regrettable.'[88] However, the altercation provided the press with further ammunition to criticize the Pakistan team.

The press representation of Pakistan also constantly emphasized how culturally different they were to the English—in religion, dress, diet, and in adherence to the rule of law and fair play. It was an irreconcilably alien way of life and calls were made to have them 'removed' from England and world cricket. Pakistan were branded the 'Pariahs of Cricket.'[89] *The Mirror's* cricket correspondent thundered, 'Pakistan's cheating cricketers fly out of England today—as free as birds', implying that they should have been detained like criminals. An editorial in the same paper stated that there should be some kind of deportation against them and that the team should be 'drummed out of England in disgrace.'[90]

While the tabloids continued with their racist tropes, the ill feeling spread to the broadsheets as well, albeit with the use of more restrained language. Regardless, the Pakistani cricketers were often described as 'capricious, hot-headed, volatile, excitable, undisciplined, petulant and aggressive'— stereotypical white prejudices that have been used about people of colour and the same that Lord Harris had thought would make the 'excitable Asiatics' unsuitable for cricket. Moreover, the 'otherness' of the Pakistani cricketers based on these stereotypes and caricatures was somehow also seen to be part of the 'national character' and was used to establish the moral inferiority of Pakistan and Pakistanis more generally.

For the Pakistanis, ball tampering accusations represented another example of bias and racial prejudice—an attempt to undermine the outstanding achievements of the team by labelling them cheats and covert rule breakers, thereby maintaining English superiority. It strengthened the view that whenever England lost it was because Pakistan cheated. Wasim Akram and Waqar Younis—the accused ball tamperers—in fact issued a statement in which they alluded to the accusations being motivated by racial prejudice: 'We can only guess at Allan Lamb's motives…but we hope they are nothing so base as money, or even worse, our nationality.'[91]

Eventually, some newspapers and a number of former international cricketers began to report how common ball tampering really was, both internationally and in English county cricket. Simon Barnes, writing in *Times*, stated that 'everybody knows that ball doctoring is as much part of English cricket as the tea interval,'[92] and when the ICC chairman, the former England captain Colin Cowdrey, finally commented on the 1992 affair, his remark to the tabloid that started the vilification campaign was 'they're all tampering with the ball.'[93] In fact, one of the earliest reported incidents of ball tampering involved England during their tour of India in 1976–77, when the bowler Peter Lever was accused of smearing Vaseline on the ball to help it swing. In 1991, England were cautioned for ball tampering in a little reported incident against West Indies.[94] In 1994, the England captain Michael Atherton would be caught on camera tampering with the ball. In 2018, the Australian captain Steve Smith and two other colleagues were involved in a ball tampering controversy. There have been several other instances of ball tampering,[95] but none have merited the kind of wide-ranging campaign that the 1992 Pakistan tour managed.

Ball tampering, like poor umpiring, was not a Pakistan-specific trait. Since 1992, the 'skill' of reverse swing used so devastatingly by Wasim Akram and Waqar Younis has spread all over the world. Several English bowlers have used it to great effect without any of the taint that their Pakistani counterparts faced. There is now a belated acceptance that this Pakistani invention was one of the genuine innovations that occurred in cricket and that it required enormous skill and not illicit means of ball tampering.

All this is not to obscure the fact that Pakistani umpires may have cheated and that their bowlers roughed up the ball illicitly. In fact, there is reasonably strong evidence that ball tampering was widespread particularly in the 1990s. Certainly, in domestic cricket in Pakistan, ball tampering was occurring and there appeared little sanction against it. Chris Pringle, the New Zealand fast bowler who toured Pakistan in 1990, wrote in his autobiography of his tampering with the ball in a Test match and the fact that the umpires appeared unconcerned.[96] Throughout the tour, the New Zealanders had been suspicious of ball tampering by the Pakistan bowlers. In later years, several Pakistani players were penalized for ball tampering having been caught on camera[97] and one of those penalized, Shoaib Akhtar, stated in his autobiography that all the Pakistani bowlers did indulge in ball tampering but that this was no different to any other international cricket team.[98] Similarly, there is fairly convincing indication from the accounts of umpires asking for instructions from captains that Pakistani umpires did favour their own team on occasion.

But what is important to recognize is that the fact that umpires and players may have been involved in these objectionable activities does not mean that they did so exclusively or on the scale imagined by their critics. Even if it is accepted that Pakistani players had practiced ball tampering during and before the 1992 tour of England, or that umpires had been biased, the fact that Pakistan were singled out and made out to be the sole purveyors of this deceit and cheating meant that there were strong grounds for seeing the accusations as prejudice and the application of double standards against them. The condemnation of Pakistani players and umpires as cheats was linked to the way that Pakistan and Pakistanis were 'otherized' and the fact that this otherness implied the moral inferiority of all Pakistanis.

The 1992 tour deepened the animosity between English and Pakistan cricket and had an impact beyond the cricket field. Tension in the crowds spiked. During the Test match in Leeds, located in the north eastern county of Yorkshire, a severed pig head was thrown into part of the seating where Pakistani supporters had congregated.[99] Racist chants were not uncommon in the stands. The stereotyping of the Pakistani team also spilled over into the British Asian community where aspersions made against the touring Pakistanis were repeated on playing fields and school grounds, in pubs, and on buses throughout the country. Tragically, within six weeks of the press campaign, three Asian men were killed as a result of racist violence. Popular sentiment had been galvanized to believe that an entire immigrant community, and indeed Pakistanis everywhere, were false, dangerous, and violent.[100] Marqusee summarized the effect that the series had:

> the clash between "England" and "Pakistan" became not only a battle between nations, but part of a larger war between "the West" (embodied in fair play, honest umpires, and decorum on the field) and Islam (embodied in extravagant appealing, disrespect for umpires, and cheating).[101]

The perceptions that defined Pakistan in England in 1992—a legacy of past interactions as described in the previous section—represented a low point in the relations between Pakistan and English cricket. But it also signified a watershed. Relations would improve with Pakistan's tour in 1996 and with the tours thereafter. There were important socio-political transformations in the United Kingdom and Pakistan that aided this but there were also more cricket-specific changes that assisted in bringing about better relations.

IMPROVING RELATIONS

When Pakistan next toured England in 1996, a convulsing world order was beginning to settle somewhat. Pakistan had emerged from a decade of military dictatorship with Benazir Bhutto becoming Prime Minister in 1988. The same year the Soviet Union had begun withdrawing from Afghanistan following Mikhail Gorbachev's new vision of perestroika and glasnost. The fall of the Berlin Wall in 1991 had been followed by a historic expansion of democracies and open markets. The European Union was formed in 1993 and expanded steadily. India opened up its markets and began a process of economic liberalization in 1991.

In 1992, the United Kingdom had re-elected a Conservative government (lead by Prime Minister John Major), without apparent enthusiasm. Margaret Thatcher's long reign had come to an end but with a deepening economic recession the government was already unpopular. In this setting, it is unsurprising that nationalism as evidenced by the press reaction to the series against Pakistan took a racist turn. Black people and those of Asian descent in the United Kingdom were a reminder both of a bygone empire and a global market that did not respect traditional national boundaries. Their success in cricket hurt precisely because cricket summed up all that was precious and all that had been lost in the national heritage. In fact, Pakistan's 1992 tour was preceded in 1991 by a tour by the West Indies which had also elicited extremely racist press coverage.[102]

By 1996, the insularity had been replaced by a more open, inclusive attitude as the economy was beginning to recover and new labour began to take hold of society. The United Kingdom would be more multicultural in itself and more open to embracing—on an equal footing—the economies and cultures of its former South Asian colonies. In India's case, the rapid expansion of its economy and its rise as a global power from the 1990s onwards firmly established a relationship of parity with the United Kingdom. If anything, the balance of power had shifted significantly to the former colony.

This changing attitude had an impact on cricketing relations as well. The colonial attitude of superiority so apparent in dealings with Pakistan earlier was receding. The rise of India as cricket's superpower had seen an inexorable shift of power from the traditional England-Australia nexus to the 'Asian bloc' epitomized by the way in which India, Pakistan, and Sri Lanka had won the bid for the 1996 World Cup. The democratization of the ICC saw the abolition of the president of the MCC automatically assuming the chairmanship of the ICC (1989), the veto for England and Australia (1993), and the election of the Barbadian Sir Clyde Walcott as the first non-British Chairman (1993). There was more acceptance now of the influence and position of the Asian members, including Pakistan, as equal partners.

It mattered also that the England team of 1996 had witnessed a generational change. Several of the older players who had detested touring the Subcontinent had retired. A new generation were born into an increasingly globalizing and multicultural world unfettered by colonial baggage. The atmosphere around tours to Pakistan improved significantly—partially as hotel accommodation improved considerably and partially as touring

England cricketers approached the country without the trepidations of the past. Darren Gough (2001), Kevin Pietersen (2006), Nasser Hussain (2004), Duncan Fletcher (2008), and Andrew Strauss (2013), all of whom toured Pakistan in the early 2000s, spoke of the excellent facilities and accommodation. Hussain and Gough along with Fletcher as coach were part of the first England tour to Pakistan since the infamous Gatting-Rana showdown. Nasser Hussain as captain was very aware of the need to build bridges and repair the damage caused by various squabbles over umpiring and ball tampering from the past series.

Gough wrote in his autobiography:

> the hosts could not do enough for us off the field. A few of the tour journalists had also been on Gatt's [Gatting's] tour, but it was hard to understand how relationships could have deteriorated so badly that we had stayed away for so long.[103]

Nasser Hussain wrote:

> People talk about Pakistan being a difficult place to tour, but apart from the obvious things, like social interaction and stuff like that it's actually fine. You notice things like the lack of bars in hotels. Not that we're a bunch of pissheads, but it's not quite the same as meeting up in a coffee shop at the end of long day's play. The cities are interesting. Lahore is a beautiful city, really, with a lot of open spaces, and the temperatures can be quite pleasant. Then you have the supposed dangerous places like Peshawar, from where we always go up the Khyber Pass and Karachi, which is hot and busy.[104]

During the 2000 tour, the team even managed to get out, 'We used to enjoy going out, mixing with the locals and that sort of mentality led to the series success in 2000.'[105]

The closed mindset of the past had been replaced by a more open one. It helped that thirteen years had elapsed, and the horror stories of the past were less relevant now. There was also a better relationship between the players of the two teams. Wasim Akram, Pakistan's captain on the tour in 1996, commented about a much better rapport with England team members who were now closer in age to their Pakistani counterparts.[106] In contrast, Akram had stated that on earlier tours to England, with a few exceptions, senior England players never made the effort to interact with the Pakistan players. Now Akram and England captain Michael Atherton who played together for Lancashire were committed to putting the recriminations of past years behind them.[107] England's defeat was accepted sportingly and there were no accusations of ball tampering. During the 2000 tour to Pakistan, Andrew Flintoff writes of spending a lot of time off the field with the Pakistan captain Wasim Akram.[108] 2000 even saw an unexpected guest tour Pakistan. Jan Waller, Ian Botham's mother-in-law, accompanied him to Lahore where he was commentating on the series and she ended up loving her visit to the country: 'The country and its people have absolutely blown me away,' said the 68-year-old grandmother. After a trip round Lahore's old town she said: 'I could not have imagined seeing some of the sights I have seen today. They were indefinable and left me feeling totally humbled and totally privileged.' She concluded: 'All I would say is: '''Mothers-in-law of the world, unite and go to Pakistan. Because you'll love it''. Honestly!'[109]

It is unfortunate that by the time England returned to Pakistan in 2005, the security situation had become such a concern that players were much more confined in their movements, this time more out of necessity than choice. The other point of contention—umpiring—had also been addressed. By 1994, the ICC had adopted the practice of having one neutral umpire stand alongside a home umpire in all Test matches. Far fewer complaints resulted.

In addition, the 'globalization' of cricket began to break down barriers, blurring the lines between the 'us' and 'them' that had been made so prominent in the early 1990s. Two deeply religious British Asian Muslims—Moeen Ali and Adil Rashid—became part of the England team. Rashid made his debut in 2009; Ali in 2014. Both have since played regularly for England and were part of the 2019 World Cup-winning England squad; both trace their roots back to Pakistan. Following England's dramatic win in the World Cup final, their Irish captain Eoin Morgan said the team won because 'Allah was definitely with us.' It was a very different England team to those of the decades gone by. Two former Pakistan cricketers—Saqlain Mushtaq and Mushtaq Ahmed—would also act as spin bowling coaches to the England team and the Englishman Bob Woolmer would become arguably Pakistan's best and most loved coach. Moeen Ali would comment in his autobiography that the 2016 series with Pakistan was 'played in the best of spirits' and, much to his delight and at the request of the Pakistani players, he would lead them in prayer when the tour ended.[110] The Pakistan team was well received by crowds; press coverage was positive and particularly sympathetic of Pakistan's inability to play cricket at home following the terrorist attack on the Sri Lankan team in 2009. There was much praise for the mild, dignified captain Misbah-ul-Haq who had been instrumental in restoring Pakistan's image following the spot-fixing scandal of 2010.

Even a major confrontation during a 2006 Pakistan tour to England, in fact, serves to show how a stronger and more stable relationship provided a more supportive response in comparison to the recriminations of the past. The incident itself refers to an episode when the Australian umpire, Darrell Hair, standing in the fourth Test match between England and Pakistan, ruled that the Pakistan team had been involved in ball tampering. The accusation of cheating by the umpire—without evidence being provided—led to the Pakistan captain Inzamam-ul-Haq refusing to take the field in protest and then forfeiting the match, the first ever forfeiture in the history of the game.[111] But in sharp contrast to the earlier decades when the press and general public opinion were sharply aligned against Pakistan, on this occasion there was widespread support for Pakistan's position from the English press, former cricketers, and the ECB management.[112] Even Ian Botham, one of Pakistan's fiercest critics—writing for *The Mirror*, the newspaper that launched the 1992 campaign against Pakistan—wrote: 'to accuse an individual, or a team, of cheating, you need conclusive evidence—not just to look at a few scuff-marks and make assumptions about how they got there.'[113] Botham, commentating on the Test match, stated that no footage which suggests any ball tampering malpractice by Pakistan had been found. Instead, it was Hair—with his stand offish, officious attitude—who was seen as the architect of the crisis.

I believe that the incident highlighted Pakistan's improved standing in world cricket and particularly its relations with English cricket. The ICC did, in fact, clear Inzamam-ul-Haq of the ball tampering charge following an investigation and Darrell Hair never umpired an international game again.

PEAKS AND TROUGHS

When looking at wider social issues and organizations, there is a tendency to concentrate on structural influences as being responsible for change. Yet, throughout this book, I have also brought up the influence of individuals. Two episodes in the 2000s highlight the importance of individuals in the making or breaking of relations between England and Pakistan. Just as Javed Miandad and Imran Khan had contrasting influences on the teams that they captained, so too did two cricket board chairmen.

In 2005, Pakistan were determined to oversee a successful home tour following a string of cancelled tours by visiting teams because of the perceived security threat after the 9/11 attacks. It was significant that former foreign secretary and former high commissioner to the United Kingdom,

Shaharyar M. Khan, was chairman of the Pakistan Cricket Board in 2005. Khan brought all his diplomatic experience to the table. He was assisted by Pakistan's English coach Bob Woolmer and an equally committed England Cricket Board keen on building on improved relations and banishing the antipathy of the past. On arrival in Pakistan, the England team was afforded a warm reception and immediately made a favourable impact in its public relations when two of their leading players visited the earthquake zone in Pakistan's northern areas, contributing to relief operations. Both teams agreed to dedicate the entire income from the Lahore ODI to the relief fund. The tour proceeded smoothly even though security was restrictively high.

The tour also saw about a hundred of English cricket's boisterous (and occasionally bawdy) supporters, the 'Barmy Army,' make a foray into Pakistan. They were warmly received by local fans not only in the larger cities but also in smaller cities such as Multan and Faisalabad. Shaharyar Khan recalls a bittersweet memory from the tour that epitomized the success of the tour as well as the new relationship.

> The animosity of the past had receded, and I felt this was epitomized in the way that the Barmy Army was treated in Pakistan. The Barmy Army travels in much larger numbers to other countries—Australia, South Africa, West Indies—they sometimes outnumber the local supporters. Increasingly they have become prominent in India and Sri Lanka as well. This was their first major foray into Pakistan. They enjoyed the cultural hotspots of Lahore, but in Multan, for example, I saw locals offering them rides back to their hotels from the ground. The atmosphere was wonderful, and they embraced Pakistan like few other tourists have, eating at local eateries, staying in small guest houses. In Faisalabad, one of the Barmy Army had a heart attack and died at his hotel.[114] When I came to know of the tragic incident, I went personally to his hotel and organized a proper funeral with the help of the local church. His parents decided to fly out to Faisalabad. I had them received at Lahore and driven to Faisalabad. We had a small commemorative function which was attended by his colleagues and his parents. A plaque was put up in his memory in the Sandal Bar Hotel. I know that this gesture was appreciated not only by the parents but by the entire Barmy Army and the British High Commission who had sent a representative. The following year when Pakistan played England, the parents came to the Oval from the Midlands to meet me and to thank the Board again.

The goodwill generated by the 2005 tour saw England push to break Pakistan's increasing cricketing isolation. Australia, the West Indies, and New Zealand had all cancelled tours on security grounds. Australia and the West Indies had not toured since 1998/99. Following the tour, the England Cricket

Board offered to host Pakistan's forthcoming matches against Australia on English grounds and to repeat the process in the following years.

In sharp contrast, the 2010 Pakistan tour to England saw Pakistan's spot-fixing saga (described in Chapter 3) bring deep tensions to the relations between England and Pakistan again. While the press remained far more restrained than what was witnessed in the 1980s and early 1990s, the nature of the episode left Pakistan cricket's reputation in tatters. Much of the criticism was justified and, unsurprisingly, the revelation that Pakistani cricketers had been involved in taking money to manipulate the game was going to cause tension between the teams. However, the handling of the crisis by the chairman of the Pakistan Cricket Board, Ijaz Butt, somehow managed to make a dreadful situation even worse. Butt first maintained that the players were innocent[115] and then proceeded to accuse the English players of match-fixing.[116] The accusation prompted a strong retort from the English captain Andrew Strauss:

> We would like to express our surprise, dismay and outrage at the comments made by Mr Butt yesterday. We are deeply concerned and disappointed that our integrity as cricketers has been brought into question. We refute these allegations completely and will be working closely with the ECB to explore all legal options open to us. Under the circumstances, we have strong misgivings about continuing to play the last two games of the current series and urge the Pakistani team and management to distance themselves from Mr Butt's allegations.[117]

Ijaz Butt then proceeded to accuse the England Cricket Board of being biased and stated that the ICC's handling of the investigation was 'terrible' and Haroon Lorgat, the chief executive, should be sacked. Ten days later, Butt was forced to make a humiliating climbdown and apologize to the England players and the England and Wales Cricket Board.[118]

Unsurprisingly, this was a time when relations between England and Pakistan suffered significantly—where Shaharyar Khan had managed to improve relations, Butt had inflamed them not only with England but with almost every other Test playing nation's administration (see Chapter 2). Butt was removed from his post soon after and relations began to return to normal. On this occasion, it was clearly Pakistan's house that had to be put in order and subsequent chairmen did manage to do this alongside Pakistan's cricketers who, under captain Misbah-ul-Haq, saw their battered image improve immeasurably. Relations have continued to improve with Pakistan touring England in 2020 in the midst of the Covid pandemic, thereby protecting the England Cricket Board from substantial revenue losses due to a cancelled series. England did cancel a scheduled visit to Pakistan in October 2021 eliciting a furious response from the Pakistan Cricket Board. The PCB felt that while Pakistan had gone out of their way to assist the England Cricket Board at their time of need, this was not reciprocated by England. Instead, the cancellation was seen as an ungrateful slap in the face of Pakistan. The seriousness of the incident led to the British Foreign Office expressing their displeasure at the impact this would have on UK–Pakistan relations. However, a month after cancellation the chairman of the England Cricket Board travelled to Pakistan in order to repair relations and subsequently announced an extended tour to Pakistan in October 2022.

'Woolmergate'

Before concluding the chapter on Pakistan and England's cricketing relations, I draw attention to 2007 when there was a brief resurgence of hostility by the English press against Pakistan. The incident that caused this reiterates some of the themes that had been so evident in 1992, in particular Pakistan's vulnerability to being classified as the 'other' when compared to all the rest of the international cricket teams. It is important to recognize this as a period when the Pakistan cricket team was showing a strong and very public Islamic identity that set it apart from other international teams. It is also a time when there was a growing hostility towards Islam following the events of 9/11 in 2001 and the London bombings of 2005.

The incident itself was the death of Pakistan's English coach Bob Woolmer following Pakistan's shock defeat to Ireland in the 2007 World Cup held in the Caribbean. The loss meant that Pakistan crashed out of the tournament and Bob Woolmer was dead a few hours after Pakistan's unexpected elimination. At the time of Bob Woolmer's tragic and controversial death, a plethora of controversies were unleashed by the British tabloids, sensationalizing the forensic experts' initial verdict that Woolmer had died under suspicious circumstances. The fact that he was Pakistan's coach appeared to spur the most outlandish theories with suspicions falling on Muslim fanatics, an angry Pakistani fan, the match-fixing mafia, or even members of the Pakistan team itself. When the team were quarantined in a Jamaican hotel for weeks during which they were fingerprinted, questioned, and cross-questioned by the Jamaican police, it only confirmed the tabloid impression that the players were the prime suspects. The fact that the team could be considered capable of committing a criminal act—a murder at that—without any evidence, testifies to the strength of the negative stereotypes that surrounded Pakistan.

In their article 'Woolmergate,' Malcolm, Bairner, and Curry state that, with one exception in which Mike Marqusee objected to the clichéd use of the word 'volatile' and argued that media reactions to Woolmer's death had 'more to do with stereotyping and hyperbole than the facts,'[119] the remaining 767 articles that they reviewed followed the same narrative with the particular attributes to which writers drew attention revealing a broader set of underlying assumptions about the defining characteristics and thus inherent 'superiority' of the West.[120] Woolmer is described as 'humane, rational, calm, committed, benevolent, tolerant.' Malcolm, Bairner, and Curry emphasize that articles by David Gower, Allan Donald,[121] and Colin Crompton[122] all explicitly linked Woolmer's character to his *Englishness*.[123] Woolmer thus was the embodiment of the positive characteristics that the English attribute to themselves.

The contrast between 'us' and 'them' though is made starker when the 'them' are concurrently depicted as the complete opposite. Malcolm, Bairner, and Curry's review of the press again reveals the use of the caricatures that were previously used to define Pakistan—irrationality, chaos, intrigue, turbulence, lack of discipline, corruption, violence. The divergence between the cultural representation of the West (via Woolmer) and the depiction of the irrationality, violence, and premodern character of Pakistan culminated in a narrative[124] that asserted that the differences between the two cultures were unbridgeable and this divide could have led to Woolmer being murdered by religious fanatics (including the Pakistan captain Inzamam-ul-Haq) who were upset by the loss and by rumours of Woolmer's opposition to the team's overt religiosity. The 'truth' was far removed from the typecast version that was being put forward. Ultimately, after foreign experts reviewed the evidence in his untimely death, the coroner decided that Woolmer had died of natural causes.[125] The team was then allowed to return home, but his death left a shadow over Pakistan cricket.

Bob Woolmer was greatly admired by the Pakistan team. He had replaced Javed Miandad, a Pakistan cricket icon, as coach; but his rapport with players far exceeded his predecessor's. Many of those who played under Woolmer continue to credit him today for their success. Woolmer had recognized the religiosity of the team as a positive, binding factor and had supported it. His death devastated several members of the team who had come to see Woolmer as a father figure. Woolmer's passing was a sad chapter that highlighted how quickly stereotypes and caricatures of Pakistan cricket that have been examined in this chapter as lying at the heart of its relations with England could re-emerge.

Relations between Pakistan and England have evolved since Pakistan joined the Imperial Cricket Conference in 1952. They have been affected by the legacy of history and a changing economic and political environment. Globalization and multiculturalism have also made the exotic a little less so, with later generations being more accepting of cultural differences. But relations have also been influenced by umpiring and individuals (cricketers and administrators).

5

Pakistan in the Global Cricketing
Order – South Asia I

Relations with England were defined by a number of factors, the most important of them being the historical colonial link. A second, more complex relationship is also the product of colonialism and involves the two nations that were created in 1947 when Britain oversaw the bloody partition of the Subcontinent into India and Pakistan. The relationship that emerged between the two new nations is extraordinary in many ways and this includes the cricketing ties that emerged soon after Partition.

Lala Amarnath of Lahore and India

Until 1947, the cricketing legacy of the Subcontinent is shared—as it was for all other aspects of culture and society prior to Partition. The shared heritage as well as the separate paths that were taken subsequently is epitomized by the story of a young Hindu boy playing cricket on the streets of Lahore.

It must have been in the 1920s that Tawakkul Majid, a senior official in one of Lahore's largest and oldest cricket clubs—Crescent Club—saw a group of youths playing cricket on the street. One boy—the batsman—caught his attention as a phenomenal talent. He asked the youngster to take him to his family who turned out to be his grandparents. Their house was located in the Hindu quarter of old Lahore. The boy was born in Kapurthala in East

Punjab but sent to live with his grandparents in Lahore when his mother died.[1] Majid noted that the family were poor and appeared delighted when he offered to take the youth in to his house to learn to play cricket. He would be raised in a Muslim household in Lahore's Mochi gate—a five-minute walk from his own grandparent's house. The boy was Lala Amarnath who would go on to become one of Lahore's finest cricketers. On his Test debut in 1933, aged 22, he scored the first ever century for India in Test cricket and later became independent India's first captain. In subsequent years, he managed the Indian team and was also father to two further Indian cricketers—Mohinder and Surinder Amarnath.[2]

But it was in Lahore, the centre of North Indian cricket, that Lala Amarnath learnt his cricket. He played for Tawakkul Majid's club where he interacted with many of the cricketers who would go on to become the first generation of Pakistani Test players. Prominent amongst them were A.H. Kardar who would become Pakistan's first Test captain and Fazal Mahmood, one of Pakistan's finest fast bowlers. In an interview given to Peter Oborne, Tawakkal Majid's son, Jamil Rana, spoke of how proud his father had been of Amarnath's achievements and the many trophies that he had decorated his room with, within his adopted family's house.[3] Today Amarnath's grandparents' house no longer stands. Like many houses in the densely populated Hindu quarter, it was burnt down during the violence that accompanied Partition. Amarnath was not in Lahore at the time. Today the sprawling wholesale Shah Alam market encompasses the area.

Amarnath's biography—*Lala Amarnath Life and Times: The Making of a Legend*—written by his third son Rajendra, does not dwell on his connection with his Muslim patrons. In India, he is instead seen as a Hindu who escaped Muslim prejudice and hostility to make a name for himself as a great Indian cricketer. Lahore, however, did not give up its claim to Amarnath. There is also anecdotal evidence that Amarnath himself maintained a deep connection to the place where he learnt his cricket. Jamil Rana in his interview recalled an incident narrated to him by his father Tawakkul Majid which appears to confirm Amarnath's deep affection for Lahore and for the family that had adopted him. Majid, standing outside the light blue front door of his old family home, recounts:

> Whenever he [Amarnath] came to Pakistan after Partition, he used to call on my family. Once he brought two sons. He bowed down in reverence at the threshold of this house. He ordered his sons to do the same. One of them got some dirt from the floor on his forehead, and brought out a handkerchief to remove it. Amarnath told him. 'Put that handkerchief away and spread the

dirt on your face. If this house hadn't been here, you two would have been playing in the street.'[4]

Amarnath would visit Pakistan several times. He came as manager of the first Indian tour to Pakistan in 1954; in 1978 and 1983 he would be invited by Pakistan Television to commentate on India's tour to Pakistan.[5] He was always received with warmth and a feeling of 'ownership'—what in Urdu is termed *apnapan* which roughly translates to 'being one of us' or 'kinship.' In 1983, on a taxi journey back to his hotel in Lahore, the driver would refuse payment, stating: '*tussi te Lahore di shaan ho* (you are the pride of Lahore).'[6] On the earlier tour of 1978, thousands thronged Lahore airport. Many had come to get a glimpse of Amarnath's sons, who by this time were representing India as well. Surinder and Mohinder recall: 'People asked us if our father was also coming. When we replied in the affirmative, they were excited. It was amazing to see these people still remembering dad and holding him in such high esteem, even after a gap of almost two decades.'[7] When Lalaji disembarked himself, he was given a tumultuous welcome befitting his association with Lahore. According to his biography, thousands had come to get a glimpse of their returning son. For an emotional Amarnath, it was reminiscent of the reception he had received at the train station in Lahore when he returned after scoring India's first ever Test century in 1933, 'The reception at the airport touched Amarnath and he was unable to express his happiness in words to his friends and well wishers.'[8] During the tour, Amarnath would strike up a warm friendship with President Ziaul Haq. On reaching Lahore for their tour in 1983, the Indian team moved to the terminal building in a coach while the team manager Fatehsinghrao Gaekwad and Amarnath discussed something on the tarmac. As a black limousine pulled up near the aircraft, Gaekwad, assuming it was for him, bid Amarnath goodbye and moved towards it. He was intercepted by a tall Pathan who stopped him and said: 'Sir, this is not for you. The car has been sent specially for Lala saheb.'[9] In later years, Amarnath would himself comment, 'If I ever fought an election in Pakistan, I'd win! I'm really proud of the great regard and respect the people there have for me.'[10] The genuine warmth that Pakistan, and particularly Lahore, had for Lala Amarnath indicates that Jamil Rana's story may have been at least partially accurate. When the colourful, larger-than-life Amarnath died in 2000, he was deeply mourned in Pakistan[11] by those who had played with him in Lahore as well as those who had played against him when he represented India against Pakistan.

In 1952, when India became the first country to play a Test match with Pakistan, the two captains—Lala Amarnath and A.H. Kardar—had a common heritage and would have understood each other very well. They had lived a stone's throw from each other in Lahore. Both had learnt their cricket in Lahore and had played on the fields of Minto Park. Both had played for the Crescent Club. They spoke the same language and shared the same culture. Prior to Partition, both had in fact been part of the Indian team that toured England in 1946.[12] Now, despite their common origins, they were playing against each other representing two new nations. In fact, prior to Partition, Muslims had formed a sizeable proportion of the Indian Test team. Nearly all of them were from the Punjab, and with Lahore going to Pakistan, India was to lose many of these cricketers to Pakistan including Fazal Mahmood.[13] Fazal, like Kardar and Amarnath, learnt his cricket in Lahore and for the 1947 tour to Australia, Amarnath as the Indian captain sent a telegram to Fazal asking him to join the touring party. Fazal declined, saying that he had opted for Pakistan.[14] During the violence that engulfed the communities at the time of Partition, Amarnath's house in Lahore was burnt down and he narrowly avoided being butchered on a train journey. On another train journey, Fazal was saved from extremists by the Indian cricketer C.K. Nayadu brandishing his bat at the assailants.[15] All four cricketers would face each other in the first India–Pakistan Test match. When the teams would line up against each other there were Indians that had fled from Pakistan and Pakistanis who were refugees from India. Several had played together prior to Partition. Such was the intertwining of the two countries and their cricket; such is 'our' story, as Rahul Bhattacharya says.[16]

EARLY RELATIONS

There is an important preface to the first India–Pakistan cricketing encounter. Pakistan made its first submission to join the Imperial Cricket Conference (ICC) in 1948 and then again in 1950. On both occasions, the ICC rejected membership citing 'insurmountable difficulties' for the new nation to overcome.[17] But while undoubtedly the challenges to the nation were overwhelming, Pakistan was determined to 'go it alone.'

Just prior to independence there had been consternation in the Board of Control for Cricket in India (BCCI) at the prospect that a newly-independent Pakistan would want to seek Test match status. On 11 August 1947, four days before independence, Anthony de Mello, the BCCI president, argued strongly against separate cricket teams, 'I call upon sportsmen in all parts of the land to rally round the idea of unity in Indian sport. The other nations will always refer to us as Indians, irrespective of whether some of us belong to India or Pakistan.'[18]

Following independence, India, having joined the ICC in 1926,[19] remained part of the organization. Pakistan, as a newly-formed nation, had no status. A number of options were put forward at this time, the most prominent being the idea of a kind of regional team which would draw on cricketers from India, Pakistan, and Ceylon (now Sri Lanka), as it had prior to Partition. The MCC also sent out signals that it would prefer India to remain, for cricketing purposes, a single country. Reiterating its view that Pakistan lacked the resources, infrastructure, and organization required to support a cricketing structure, the ICC were unwilling to grant Test match status to Pakistan. The proposal of having first class and Test cricket only as part of India was rejected outright by the newly-formed Board of Control for Cricket in Pakistan (BCCP) which argued that Pakistan was an independent state and could accept nothing less than the international recognition of its cricket team.[20] During the impasse, the BCCI attempted to draw some of the best Pakistan cricketers back to their own domestic structure, in the hopes of strengthening its own domestic competition which had also suffered losses as a result of Partition. This was seen as a hostile move by the BCCP which, following two rejections by the ICC, felt that it was being undermined by the other cricketing nations and denied its rights.[21] While Oborne argues that the BCCI was holding Pakistan hostage—either you play cricket as India or no cricket at all—the minutes of the ICC meetings show that the BCCI actually supported each of Pakistan's submissions to the ICC.

India's initial reluctance to support independent status for Pakistan as a cricketing nation parallels its reluctance to accept the communal division of the Subcontinent into two nations. Not only did Hindu nationalists dream of *Akhand Bharat* (undivided India), but statements made by senior Congress leaders also lent themselves to a similar interpretation. Jaffrelot writes that the then Congress party president, Acharya Kripalani, for instance, declared in 1947: 'Neither the Congress nor the nation has given up its claim of a united India.'[22] Vallabhbhai Patel, the Deputy Prime Minister, reiterated: 'Sooner than later, we shall again be united in common allegiance to our country.' From before Partition, the Indian National Congress, led by Nehru and Gandhi, had sought a unified country[23] and even after Partition many Pakistanis feared that Indians continued to reject the two-nation theory that led to Partition and sought to reabsorb Pakistan into India.[24] But far from unification it was war over Kashmir that broke out almost immediately after independence that brought about the first crisis for the newly-formed nations.

As the anxiety-filled weeks passed, Mohammad Ali Jinnah, Pakistan's founder and first Governor General, became convinced that the Congress leadership wanted to strangle Pakistan at birth.[25] Nehru was reluctant to give

Pakistan its share of the Raj's assets and only Gandhi's hunger strike ensured that some of Pakistan's rightful inheritance was transferred.[26] Moreover, on 1 April 1948, India stopped water flowing in two canals irrigating West Punjab [Pakistan] from tributaries of the Indus River.[27]

But while tension over Kashmir remained, some of the other areas of conflict gradually eased, indicating a reluctant acceptance of the creation of two separate nations. Waterflow to West Punjab was restored on 19 May 1948.[28] The initial opposition to Pakistan fielding an independent cricket team also eased and by the summer of 1948 the BCCI supported Pakistan's applications including the successful one in 1952 where the BCCI actually sponsored Pakistan's entry.[29] It was therefore befitting that Pakistan played its first ever test match against India in 1954.

And yet the support given by the BCCI to the BCCP throws up a question that is asked throughout this chapter. Partition brought some of the worst inter-communal violence that has ever been witnessed. 'Violence must sit at the core of any history of Partition. It is the phenomenal extent of the killing during Partition which distinguishes it as an event. It affected women, children and the elderly as well as well-armed young men.'[30] A million people died. Ten to twenty million moved across the newly-established borders.[31] The carnage was astounding—children watched as parents were dismembered, women were raped and disfigured, entire villages were exterminated, and trains arrived at their destinations full of dead bodies.[32] Partition and the resultant turmoil triggered off hatred, distrust, and prejudice in almost every sphere of activity in the Subcontinent. Why then did the BCCI lend its support to its Pakistani counterpart having been so opposed to Pakistan? How was it then that only five years later a team from Pakistan would travel to India to play cricket? How is it that fans on both sides of the border would welcome the opposing team? And yet, as we will see later, there is also a history of cricketing relations contrasting with the wider, more hostile political atmosphere between the two nations. I shall return to this paradox even though a definitive answer will be difficult.

Against the Grain

The first meaningful bilateral exchange between the newly-independent nations would in fact be Pakistan's cricket tour to India in 1952 and India's return tour to Pakistan in 1954. Both tours led to what Bandyopadhyay terms a 'spontaneous albeit tense response.'[33] Only five years had passed since Partition and the violence that accompanied it. In contrast, for example, England and Germany would not play football against one another for nine years after the end of the Second World War and sixteen years in total if the War is taken into account. Following Partition, India and Pakistan had already fought a war over Kashmir and even though hostilities had ended, Indian and Pakistani soldiers were now face to face along an increasingly militarized border.[34] But as mentioned previously, some points of conflict had eased—water was flowing down river to Pakistan again after India had choked it off, trade which had been disrupted in 1949 had resumed, defence and financial quotas due to Pakistan had been adjusted,[35] and an official ceasefire over Kashmir had been negotiated.[36]

It was against this backdrop that the Indian board invited Pakistan for its first Test series and in the winter of 1952 the Pakistan team was making the 50 km journey by road from Lahore to Amritsar. At the time, land routes were still accessible. All the way to the Wagah border, the Pakistan team was accompanied by a convoy of supporters in taxis, rickshaws, and tongas, all hooting and cheering.[37] The cricket trip was meant to contrast sharply with the political rhetoric and hostility, as it would in several subsequent tours. The barometer of relations between the people of the new states would fall on the way that the Pakistan team was received. There was both expectation and apprehension from the travelling cricketers. Fazal Mahmood, Pakistan's legendary fast bowler, stated:

We were joyful and excited at the prospect of facing the Indians in cricket. India was not new for us. Many of us had already played together ... [However] the wounds of large-scale carnage on both sides of the Wagah border that followed soon after the announcement of the partition plan, had not yet healed. The political relations were not normal. Amid these fears we crossed the border and were warmly received.[38]

At an official level, no stone was left unturned by the hosts. On arrival on the Indian side of the Wagah border, Waqar Hasan, one of the Pakistani touring party, wrote in his autobiography that the Pakistan team were warmly greeted and profusely garlanded before being taken to Amritsar.[39] Once in Amritsar, Pakistan would play a warm up game in surroundings that were familiar to several Pakistani players who had previously lived in Amritsar. In Delhi for the first Test match the reception was similarly generous despite the fact that the same day the Muslim League in Karachi announced the launching of an all-out struggle for the liberation of occupied Kashmir.[40] The Pakistanis were received at the train station by a delegation that included the Indian captain Lala Amarnath. During the Test match, the Pakistan cricketers were introduced to the Indian President Rajendra Prasad and the Indian Prime Minister Jawaharlal Nehru and his daughter Indira Gandhi.[41] For the third

Test match in Bombay, affluent Pakistanis took the boat down from Karachi to watch, as they would have been able to more routinely in the pre-Partition days. The warmth of the Indian public's welcome to the Pakistan cricketers was commented upon by the visiting captain himself.[42] The autobiographies of three of the Pakistani team members from the tour—Hanif Mohammed,[43] Fazal Mahmood,[44] and Waqar Hasan[45]—all comment on the cordiality of the Indian reception during that first tour.

It was not a trouble-free tour, though, and Pakistan's first win in the second Test at Lucknow saw crowd disturbances. Ramachandra Guha remarks that the 'pain and bloodshed of Partition was still fresh in the minds of all and there was some trouble between supporters.'[46] Whether these supporters were Pakistani visitors or Indian Muslims is unclear, though Fazal Mahmood in his autobiography states that in Lucknow:

> as the Pakistan team emerged from the bus that carried us to the Gomti ground on the first day of the match, some college students, of both sexes, told us not to worry as they would wholeheartedly support us during the course of the play. They were all Muslims, and I must admit that whenever our bowlers appealed against any batsman, these students supported them with loud voices from the boundary.[47]

Guha was right in suggesting that the memories of Partition were still fresh and for India the 'affiliation' of Indian Muslims—fans and players—would go on to become a point of debate. The ire of the majority of the crowd though was aimed at the Indian team for their loss rather than at Pakistan and Lala Amarnath had to resort to a lathicharge himself in order to save his teammates from an angry group of supporters.[48] There were very few demonstrations by Hindu extremist groups against the Pakistan team—and where there were protests by the Mahasabha party, A.H. Kardar, Pakistan's captain, would write that following the protests 'when we left the ground that evening to the cheering of hundreds of people I felt the inner urge of humanity for peace and cooperation.'[49] Guha describes these disturbances as being met by wider society with contempt and indifference at a time when Hindu extremism was at the fringe of the political spectrum. Overwhelmingly, the crowds had turned out in huge numbers to welcome and cheer the Pakistani tourists throughout the country.[50] Kardar, an inveterate diary writer, would pen in his notes of the long train journey from Lucknow to Nagpur:

> The monotony of the 36 hour[s] in the train was broken by the hearty welcome we were accorded by the Indian cricket fans at almost all our halts. These fans would knock at our doors in the middle of the night requesting us

for autographs, asking for Hanif, his age, wanting to get as near as possible to see Fazal Mahmood and Nazar Mohammad, the heroes of the Lucknow Test.[51]

Fazal Mahmood would recount similar incidents in his autobiography adding how their hosts spared nothing to make their stay happy and comfortable. He would go on to add that 'in Lucknow, our singing was very popular. The cricket fans, in their typical Lucknow style, would request us to sing a song with every autograph. We thoroughly enjoyed this.'[52]

Waqar Hasan, another of the touring Pakistanis, stated that 'the hospitality and the care for the visiting team was such that it seemed to us all the enmity that existed during the partition of India and in the creation of Pakistan between the two nations had fizzled out in the air.'[53] Lala Amarnath's biography notes that for a majority of the Pakistanis, the tour was an opportunity to meet their old friends, cricketers, and relatives who had stayed back in India—a kind of homecoming, 'I could empathise with them and felt sad watching them become nostalgic when they embraced their dear ones.'[54] It was remarkable that the first tour produced such warmth between the players and the crowds.

The return tour to Pakistan in 1954 was a little more tense. The political atmosphere had deteriorated not only because of the continuing tension over Kashmir but also because the two countries took divergent paths in the emerging Cold War alliances. Pakistan had joined the US sponsored Defence Pacts that included Iran and Turkey while India became one of the main sponsors of the Non-Aligned Movement and moved closer to the Soviet Union.[55] However, despite the political temperature, the Wagah border crossing was left open *and* '10,000 Indian fans travelled to watch the Lahore Test match; those that lived in Amritsar were allowed to cross back each night to their homes.'[56] The borders remained porous and the home crowds welcomed their Indian counterparts and the team, 'The Lahorites received them with open arms and not a single anti-India slogan was raised.'[57] The Indian captain Vinoo Mankad took this literally to heart and allegedly fell in love with a Pakistani singer[58] and, according to Fazal Mahmood, played with 'divided attention.'[59] Guha quotes a journalist from Madras (now Chennai) remarking on the great fraternization that was witnessed among the Pakistanis and Indians during the Test match days[60] and at the end of the tour the Maharaja of Vizianagaram, speaking for the Indian board, would state proudly that 'where politicians had failed, we [cricketers] succeeded by coming nearer to each other.'[61]

However, as early as this second tour, one of the defining features of early Pakistan–India encounters was emerging. All five Test matches in Pakistan produced dull, defensive cricket resulting in a 0-0 series scoreline. Despite having a raft of exciting cricketers on both sides the weight of political tensions and the cricket teams acting as a proxy for hostile nation states meant that the cricketers felt their primary duty was to avoid defeat and humiliation at the hands of the other. The crowds, though, continued to patronize the matches in large numbers and in generally good spirit. Oborne states: 'While the cricketers were paralysed by history, the humanity of the spectators demonstrated the belief among Sikh, Muslim and Hindu alike that cricket could somehow show the way to reconciliation and the end of hatred and war.'[62] According to Oborne, it was this attitude that explained the contradiction between the 'humourless, unforgiving cricket played out in the middle, and the joyful attitude of the crowds.' The aggressive rhetoric of the nation states had not yet filtered down to the common people who remained largely willing to embrace a process of reconciliation after the horrors of Partition.

But the turgid cricket and declining political relations meant that neither country was keen to have another visit and when the next encounter did occur, relations had been further strained by the coming to power in Pakistan of Ayub Khan—the first of several military strongmen. Ayub had spearheaded Pakistan's close alignment with the United States from the 1950s and while the signing of the Indus Water Treaty was an outcome of Pakistan's constructive diplomacy with India, tensions over Kashmir remained as Pakistan's hopes for a plebiscite receded.[63] Despite these continuing frictions, Pakistan's second tour to India took place in 1960–61. In fact, Qamaruddin Butt argues that Pakistan's second tour of the neighbouring country was sought to ease the tension between the two countries[64]—the success of the earlier tours had opened up cricket as an early possible ice-breaker in terms of political relations, decades before General Ziaul Haq would use it further as a form of cricket diplomacy.

While the two boards maintained good relations and the Pakistan team was welcomed by former and current Test players and administrators in receptions and social events, the cricket remained burdened by the political tension and an increasing nationalistic expectation. Again, all five Test matches were drawn—there had now been a run of 12 where no result had been produced and the cricket by both teams had been defensive and tedious.

The Question of Indian Muslims and the Rise of Hindutva

This second tour to India did bring into focus the third element in the India–Pakistan relationship—Indian Muslims and their relations with Pakistan.

I have already mentioned Fazal Mahmood's reference to the support that the team received from Indian Muslim supporters in Lucknow during the 1952 tour. In India, there remained a suspicion that their minority Muslim population harboured a soft spot for Pakistan because of their religious affinity.[65] Mihir Bose, analysing the issue of conflicting loyalties in India–Pakistan matches, recollects an incident on the first day of the Test match in Bombay (now Mumbai) during the 1960 tour. As he walked past the Brabourne stadium where the Test was being staged, he recalls seeing a whole crowd of:

> very Muslim-looking people entering the stands. One passer-by observed the rush of the Muslims and commented, 'No wonder these Meibhais [as some Muslims are called] come crawling out now. It is their team that is playing. No prizes for guessing who they are supporting.' This bitter remark reflected the feeling of many Hindu Indians during the series – that Muslims in India were all supporting Pakistan.[66]

The suspicion around the allegiance of Indian Muslim fans would continue through the decades and, in the 1990s, Bal Thackeray, leader of the Hindu nationalist political party the Shiv Sena, devised his own Indian version of the 'Tebbit Test.'[67] He argued that Indian Muslims must prove that they were not Pakistani sympathizers and not anti-national by supporting India in cricket rather than Pakistan: 'I want them with tears in their eyes every time India loses to Pakistan.'[68]

But the *supposed* support for Pakistan was not confined to fans; it sometimes extended to questioning the motives of Indian Muslim cricketers who represented India. During the 1960s series between India and Pakistan, India's rising star Abbas Ali Baig, a Muslim, performed poorly following his excellent performances against Australia earlier. A failure by a Hindu may well have been overlooked but for a Muslim to perform poorly against Pakistan led some to contend that he had purposely underperformed so as to help Pakistan triumph.[69] The accusations and insinuations[70] led to Baig withdrawing from the following Test match. He played only two more test matches seven years later. The Indian Muslim issue would come up frequently when India played Pakistan. In 1982, the promising batsman Mohammad Azharuddin, who went on to captain India through the 1990s, was omitted from the Indian touring party to Pakistan. Raj Singh Dungarpur, the chairman of selectors at the time, admitted years later that the decision was made because the selectors 'felt it might be a handicap for him to make his debut in a country where the culture so matched his own.'[71] In later years, however, the excellent performances of a string of Muslim players meant that even Bal Thackeray, the Shiv Sena leader, had to declare that his Shiv Sena was not against 'patriotic' Muslims.[72]

In my experiences of visiting India between the late 1980s and 2000s, I found attitudes changed noticeably over the years. Initially, many Indian Muslims would privately profess admiration and support for Pakistani cricket teams. Emily Crick states that there have been many occasions when Muslims have supported Pakistan rather than India in matches 'and conversations that I have had with Indian Kashmiri Muslims support this view.'[73] Fazal Mahmood's conversation with Indian Muslim fans also shows that there was support for Pakistan amongst the Muslim community. Even more recently there have been reports of Indian Muslims supporting Pakistan against India. Crick reveals that during the 2003 World Cup clash between India and Pakistan in South Africa, a discussion was held within the police force in Calcutta (now Kolkata) in which it was proposed that Muslims should be prevented from supporting Pakistan during the match.[74] Whilst this proposal was not carried out, the discussion suggests that the authorities still believed that there was a possibility of support for Pakistan. In 2014, a group of Indian Kashmiri students were expelled from a university in North India for allegedly cheering Pakistan's victory over India and, in 2017, fifteen Muslim men were arrested in central India for celebrating Pakistan's win against India in the final of the Champions Trophy.[75]

But while Kashmiri resentment against Indian excesses may be a particular case, the support of Indian Muslims for Pakistan appears to have waned from the 1990s onwards. There are several possible reasons for this. Firstly, a new generation born after Partition grew up with the nationalist project of both countries influencing attitudes more strongly. Secondly, prior to the 1990s, Indian Muslims looked at Pakistan with a certain admiration. Here was a country that Muslims had created and not only had it survived at birth against all odds, it also appeared to be progressing faster than India. For example, its economy had performed better than that of India's in terms of GDP and per capita income up until the 1990s.[76] Untainted by terrorism and extremism, Pakistan appeared to be a success story. Its cricket team was brim-full of exciting and charismatic players that routinely dominated India in bilateral encounters. Pakistan's declining fortunes from the turn of the millennium—particularly vis-à-vis India's economic and political ascent and its struggle with extremism, corruption, and human rights—tarnished its reputation and replaced it with the much more downbeat 'dream that had turned sour' scenario.[77] From wondering if it may have been better to have migrated at Partition, increasingly many Indian Muslims stated that they were in fact better off having stayed in India. Thirdly, the rise of prominent

Indian Muslim players particularly in the 2000s made it easier for Indian Muslims to support India.

Dasgupta and Crick both emphasize that during the 2003 World Cup encounter, Indian Muslims firmly supported India in the match against Pakistan.[78]

> For instance, students of Madrase-e-Fazeelath-e-Quran, a coeducational madrasa of Bangalore's Hidayath Nagar, even took leave on the day of the match. In Kolkata and Mumbai Muslims pledged their allegiance to India very publicly. It seems commonsensical that all these would be examples of a growing feeling of national identity among the minority community.[79]

And certainly, a growing sense of national identity for the reasons I have stated above would have meant greater support for India from Indian Muslims.

There is a fourth reason as well that may further explain the 'perceived' as well as actual decline in support for Pakistan amongst Indian Muslims. The changing international system between 1989 and 1991 caused reverberations across the world. In India the transition was all the more challenging because it came at a time when the country was going through its own social, economic, and political revolutions. The 1990s was the decade when the 'so-called Nehruvian consensus, based on secularism, socialism, and nonalignment,' was put to rest.[80] In its place, along with liberalization, came the rise of the Hindutva—the idea that the essence of Indianness is Hinduism, and therefore to be a true Indian is to be a Hindu.[81] Liberalization and economic change fed extremism as the emergence of a newly affluent middle class—which had earlier felt stymied, resentful, and disconnected by the Nehruvian 'third path' between communism and capitalism—aligned perfectly with the pent up desire of this class to express its wealth and power in extreme Hindu politics. McDonald further argues that Hindutva arose out of a sense of deprivation among Hindus—that the country was suffering because of a supposed favouring by the state of minority groups in particular.[82] Reinforcing this point, Hansen writes that Hindutva portrayed the Hindu community as the silent majority whose patience had finally run out.[83] There is therefore a simmering anti-Muslim hostility within the Hindutva ideology which is deepened by the fact that Muslims ruled over parts of the Subcontinent for centuries. In addition, as Aloysius points out, Hindutva, in its attempt to protect upper caste privilege and prevent class solidarity, pits the mass of lower caste Hindus against the Muslim population, many of whom are drawn from the lower castes themselves.[84]

The Hindutva ideology grew in strength alongside the spectacular rise of the Bharatiya Janata Party (BJP), the two feeding off each other's success. Jaffrelot states that the Hindu nationalist movement started to monopolize the front pages of Indian newspapers in the 1990s when the BJP rose to power. From two seats in the Lok Sabha (the lower house of the Indian parliament) in 1984, the BJP increased its tally to 161 in 1996 when it became the largest party in that assembly. Two years later they formed a coalition government, an achievement it repeated after the 1999 mid-term elections. For the first time in Indian history, Hindu nationalism had managed to assume power.[85] Nationalism and national identity were remoulded from an identity based on the Nehruvian Consensus—a political project contoured by the values of socialism, democracy, secularism, inclusiveness of all ethno-religious and language groups—to a right-wing, chauvinistic, anti-Pakistan/Muslim ideology.

During the 1990s, India witnessed the destruction of the Babri Mosque in Ayodhya (1992) and the communal riots that followed. In Maharashtra, in 1995, Congress lost power for the first time ever to the BJP and its ally the Shiv Sena. The year 2002 saw more communal riots in Godhra, Gujarat. The rising communal tensions continued to put the spotlight on Indian Muslims, calling into question their loyalty to India. India–Pakistan matches progressively became occasions to show nationalistic sentiment. Indian Muslims appeared increasingly under pressure to publicly show their allegiance to their homeland. Furthermore, the terrorist attacks of 2001 in the United States had made displaying a Muslim identity more problematic as well. Crick argues that several scholars felt that while support for Pakistan remained, it was now kept hidden for fear of reprisals.[86] Thus, Indian Muslim support for Pakistan has been suppressed for the reasons discussed above but also from the not unfounded fear of being labelled anti-national or 'Pakistani agents.' Since the BJP's return to power in 2014 and the appointment of Narendra Modi as Prime Minister, this fear of reprisals has risen exponentially as militant Hindu groups are increasingly legitimized and made more powerful. According to Filkins:

> ever since Modi was first elected Prime Minister, in 2014, he has been recasting the story of India, from that of a secular democracy accommodating a uniquely diverse population to that of a Hindu nation that dominates its minorities, especially the country's two hundred million Muslims. Modi and his allies have squeezed, bullied, and smothered the press into endorsing what they call the "New India."[87]

In an environment that is increasingly hostile and dangerous for Muslims, supporting Pakistan, even if the preferred option, would be a threat to life and limb. Therefore, whatever latent support may have existed in the past cannot now be demonstrated.

But after Pakistan's second tour to India in 1960–61 came a period when relations between the countries—including sporting relations—were severed as a result of a second war over Kashmir in 1965. The 1971 war which saw the secession of East Pakistan confirmed this breach in relations. Pakistan and India would not play cricket against each other again for seventeen years.

Cautious Resumption

During the long break in ties (1960–1978), the nation states' new narratives meant that the nationalist project in both countries and the demonization of the 'other' sowed the seeds of greater suspicion between the nations and their people. Travel restrictions were imposed and most road and railway links shut off. Visa regimes became stricter and the previously porous borders were increasingly difficult to navigate.[88] Migration to Pakistan from India, which had continued at a steady pace between 1947 and 1971, slowed to a trickle.[89]

Zulfikar Ali Bhutto—Pakistan's President from 1971 to 1973 and Prime Minister between 1973 and 1977—had been too closely related with the events that led to East Pakistan's secession to rebuild relations with India. Surprisingly, it was General Ziaul Haq, who had led the military coup against Bhutto in 1977, who began the process of re-establishing relations with India. He was pushed by the United States and aided by the fact that in India too a new party, the Janata Party led by Morarji Desai which was not associated with the 1971 war, had come to power by defeating Indira Gandhi and her Congress Party in the 1977 elections.[90]

While relations between the states had been severed, a sporting amity remained between the players of both sides as they continued to meet on neutral ground. In 1965, when the two countries went to war for the second time, Mansur Ali Khan Pataudi, the Indian captain and Hanif Mohammed, the Pakistani captain, were both playing for a Rest of the World side against England at Scarborough. They sent a joint telegram to their respective governments:

> We wish to express deep regrets at the war between India and Pakistan. We find unity on the cricket field by reaching for a common objective. We fervently hope both countries can meet and find an amicable solution.

By a strange coincidence, when the 1971 war broke out, Sunil Gavaskar and Zaheer Abbas were playing again for a Rest of the World team in Australia and would share a room, 'they shared the tension while consoling each other.'[91]

In 1996, when Marqusee quoted the Hanif Mohammed–Mansur Ali Khan Pataudi telegram,[92] he also commented that it was a measure of how much the climate in both countries had deteriorated since 1965 that it was hard to imagine today's Indian or Pakistani cricketers issuing a similar appeal in times of war. In 2021, it is not only hard to imagine, it is unthinkable. There was still space for contrary views that may have opposed the nationalistic rhetoric of wartime and that too by an Indian Muslim. Today, such space has almost disappeared. I shall return to this point later in Chapter 6.

The push by Ziaul Haq and Morarji Desai for renewed relations between India and Pakistan meant that the 1978 Indian tour to Pakistan took on a renewed diplomatic importance and both sides made it a point to brief their teams of the sensitivities involved in the first meeting for almost two decades. This was helped by the fact that unlike the larger populations of the two nations some prominent cricketers were able to meet and interact while playing in the English county season. For example, the two captains Bishan Singh Bedi and Mushtaq Mohammad were friends and colleagues who had played together for years for the English county Glamorgan. Pakistan Television invited Lala Amarnath, Lahore's 'home-town' boy, back to Pakistan to join its commentary team for the tour.

The Indian players were received at the Karachi airport with surprising warmth and enthusiasm. Despite the prolonged break in relations, two wars in the interim, and a further partition of Pakistan, there still appeared a bank of cultural commonality for fans to signal their happiness at the resumption of cricket relations and perhaps the desire for peaceful relations with India, something that the *Wisden Cricketer's Almanack* commented on: 'The warmth and enthusiasm with which the Indians were received, plus the cordial relations between the players, made it plain enough that the renewal of cricketing rivalry between the two neighbouring countries was long overdue.'[93] There was less traffic from across the border but Bhattacharya states that as many as two thousand Indians still crossed over for the series.[94] Imran Khan, who was a member of the Pakistan team at the time, also remarked on the warmth and hospitality with which the Indian team were received wherever they went in Pakistan.[95]

Pakistan's return tour in 1979–1980 followed a similar script except that the result was reversed with Pakistan losing 2-0 in India. The public interest in both tours though had been massive. Imran Khan wrote in his autobiography of the yearning amongst his Pakistani teammates for a resumption of cricket between India and Pakistan because of the passion and intensity involved in the contest.[96] He would go on to describe remarkable scenes at the airport when Pakistan arrived, 'the whole country seemed to be on the verge of cricketing hysteria. Wherever we went, cricket was the sole subject of conversation.' In keeping with the previous tours, the Pakistani team would strike up strong relations with their hosts so much so that the Wisden notes that the players were 'distracted by commercial and social interests.'[97] The Pakistani and Indian boards, eager to build on the rivalry following the resumption of cricketing ties and encouraged by the generally warm reception given to the tourists on either side of the border, decided to start an annual exchange of cricketing visits which lasted throughout the 1980s.

During the 1980s, the BCCI and the BCCP forged a strong working relationship. Together, they formed the first Asian Cricket Council in 1983, a key moment in the rise of the Asian bloc to dominance a decade later. The spur for the Asian bloc had been India and Pakistan's joint bid to host the 1987 World Cup. The idea for this came the day after India's World Cup victory in 1983 at Lord's itself. At the official lunch, N.K.P. Salve, the BCCI president, had wondered out loud to his Pakistani counterpart Nur Khan how it would have been had the World Cup been held in India. The two presidents had already established a warm relationship and Nur Khan, who had experience of similar events being held in hockey, jumped at the idea. The Indo-Pak bid for the 1987 World Cup far outstripped England's and despite misgivings—mainly from the English press—the World Cup was successfully held for the first time in the Subcontinent.[98]

The two boards would cooperate closely again to win the rights to hold the 1996 and 2011 World Cups. In 1996, they were joined by Sri Lanka in what turned out to be an illustration of the close partnership forged by its cricket administrators. The crucial meeting to decide where the World Cup would be held was at Lord's in 1993, in what is widely seen as the most unpleasant meeting ever of the ICC.[99] Alan Smith, the chief executive of the TCCB, described the 14-hour meeting as 'by a long way the worst meeting I have ever attended ... fractious and unpleasant ... beset by procedural wrangling.'[100] The English board had come to the meeting convinced and maybe complacent over hosting the 1996 World Cup. The Test playing nations in fact voted 5-4 in favour of England but with the votes of the associate countries, South Asia prevailed. There were accusations of 'bribing' as well as threats that the ICC would break into two camps—the Asian countries in one and the independent founder members England and Australia and the dependent Anglophile New Zealand and the West Indies with them. There were also remarks—probably that rung true—that where no solidarity appeared to exist amongst South Asian countries in any other field, here they were firmly in support of one another.[101]

The 1996 World Cup would throw up further instances of Asian solidarity. When Australia and the West Indies refused to play in Sri Lanka following a suicide bombing in Colombo, the Indian-Pakistani-Sri Lankan organizing committee declined to change the schedule and to reaffirm their confidence in their Sri Lankan counterparts India and Pakistan sent a joint team to play an exhibition match in Colombo prior to the start of the tournament. The Pakistani coach for the team, Intikhab Alam, flanked by the Indian captain Mohammad Azharuddin and the Pakistan captain Wasim Akram, jubilantly stated, 'This is history ... it is the first time Indians and Pakistanis have played together on the same side. It's a tremendous sight—everybody mixing like old friends. Let's hope it's a turning point in relations.'[102] The gesture was never forgotten by a grateful Sri Lankan nation who went on to win the title in the final in Lahore. Cricket was a shining example of what South Asian cooperation could achieve if the countries worked together.

Throughout the 1980s, political tensions remained high between India and Pakistan. Pakistan lent covert support to the Sikh insurgency that was raging in the Indian Punjab and Pakistan accused India of fomenting violence in the province of Sindh. In 1984, the two countries posted troops on the Siachen glacier creating a new point of confrontation. Across the decade there was also a progression of the nuclear capabilities of both India and Pakistan.[103] In August 1986, a series of Indian military exercises, dubbed Brasstacks, began a spiral of competitive troop mobilization which, by January 1987, led to both countries' military forces being on alert, with Indian and Pakistani armoured formations poised along the international frontier.

> Just as quickly as it began, though, the crisis abated. By the end of January, Islamabad and New Delhi began negotiating over withdrawal of troops from border areas, and in early February the two sides agreed to a phased demobilization of forces that was implemented over the next few months.[104]

What Hagerty and Hagerty do not mention was President Ziaul Haq's trip to Delhi at the height of the tension in 1987 in the first of what came to be termed 'cricket diplomacy.'[105] Zia watched the third Test match in Jaipur with Prime Minister Rajiv Gandhi, and what followed was a dramatic reduction in hostilities. The occasion of the Test match provided an opportunity to communicate between the two heads of state which subsequently facilitated a lessening in tensions.

In fact, throughout the tension-filled 1980s, cricket continued, aided by the close cooperation between the boards and amicable relations amongst players.[106] The crowds were generally favourable as well though the nationalist fervour fanned by the two wars had worked to crystallize unanimous support for the respective national teams. Cricket, as Bandyopadhyay argues, had become the ultimate test of patriotic zeal and loyalty.[107] Fans were increasingly partisan and in 1987, for example, political tensions seeped into play with crowds sometimes pelting the touring Pakistani players with stones.[108]

Up until the early 1990s, despite the ongoing political tensions, the wars and the break in playing one another, the boards, players, and fans showed surprising amity summed up in the way that the Pakistani bowler Abdul Qadir referred to India's great batsman Sachin Tendulkar who made his debut against Pakistan in 1989. Bhattacharya describes Qadir breaking into a glow of affection when asked about Tendulkar,

> Darling boy, *bilkul!* Real darling. I treated him like my little brother. I took him everywhere. I took him shopping. I encouraged him to hit my bowling. He is still a darling. *Badhiya insaan, badhiya batsman* [wonderful person, wonderful batsman].[109]

The collective histories and cultures remained at odds with the political relations between the nation states. The two countries share similar languages, music, dress, customs, and cuisines, and when their citizens meet abroad they slip easily into camaraderie. Indian films remain part of culture across the border and Pakistani television serials and musicians have been popular in India. A citizen of either country visiting the other is soon overwhelmed with the hospitality showered upon them by anyone discovering where they are from.[110] The apparent popular perception of an ever-rising enmity between the two nations thus stood in striking contrast to the friendly ties between the two cricket boards at the international level almost from the time of Partition.

But 1989 marked another interruption in cricketing relations. Politics did impinge on cricket relations and Pakistan and India would not play another Test for a decade, meeting only in World Cups and One Day Internationals (ODIs). There were significant and wide-ranging changes occurring in the 1990s that changed the India–Pakistan relationship. This in fact makes the Pakistan tour of India in 1999 and the tours to Pakistan and India between 2004 and 2006 particularly striking.

RISING NATIONALISM

Guha argues that up until the late 1970s, 'win or lose sporting exchanges could be understood in a spirit of brotherliness, bhai bhai-ism.'[111] I have mentioned the growing partisanship of fans but even up to 1992, Asian fans celebrated one another's successes. Many Pakistanis supported India in their 1983 World Cup win and in 1992 Indians did the same for Pakistan's win.[112] The scenario began to change in the 1990s with the start of the Kashmir insurgency. So serious was the situation that Hagerty and Hagerty state that some analysts believed that in 1990 Pakistan had readied its nuclear weapons for deployment,[113] though others discount this view. Relations continued to deteriorate with the destruction of the Babri Mosque in Ayodhya in 1992 and the Mumbai riots described by Metcalf as an anti-Muslim pogrom and the retaliatory bombings that followed.[114] These communal incidents exacerbated tensions between Muslims and Hindus in India and further strained India–Pakistan relations.

As mentioned earlier, this period also coincided with the rise of the BJP and their Hindutva project. Iain McDonald, in his article 'Between Saleem and Shiva,' argues that the collapse of the Indian National Congress and the concomitant rise of the BJP meant that there was a significant ideological shift in the battle for the soul of Indian nationalism.[115] McDonald links the changing identities in India to the social and economic changes of the 1990s, pointing in particular to the emergence of a newly affluent middle class that sought to express its wealth and power in extreme Hindu politics. Sengupta argues that the one aspect of politics that has been singularly affected by sport is nationalism (and national identities); sport has the ability above all to tell us about who we are and who we want to be, while promoting a sense of national identity.[116] Cricket, because of its central position in civil society and as a significant element of popular culture, became one of the most effective forums for articulating Hindu chauvinist and communal ideologies.[117] An emerging and altered nationalism and cricket would thus increasingly influence one another as well as the relations between India and Pakistan.

By the mid-1990s, the Indian team began to develop a more aggressive posture, reflecting the changes occurring in the wider society. This was in stark contrast to earlier encounters, particularly with Pakistan and especially in the 1980s. Not only had Imran Khan's fast bowling prowess shattered the famed Indian batting in 1982–83, but on 18 April 1986, Pakistan won the Austral-Asia Cup final at Sharjah, defeating India by two runs. Needing four runs off the final ball to win, Javed Miandad hit the last ball of the match for a six. The winning hit became legend on both sides of the border and gave Pakistan a massive psychological advantage which was to last for more than a decade—Pakistan won 21 of their next 26 encounters against India. The Indians buckled under pressure again and again and many Indian fans felt that their team lacked the aggression to defeat the more belligerent and fervent Pakistanis who appeared to find the extra motivation for the clash against their great rivals.

In keeping with the stereotypes promoted by the advocates of Hindutva, they perceived the Pakistanis as aggressive and unashamedly nationalistic, in contrast to the docile and apologetic Indians. Some even claimed that Pakistan's religious identity gave them an advantage on the cricket field. To match the enemy, India would have to emulate them; it would have to rediscover itself as a Hindu nation. One of the major themes of Hindutva has been the need for Hindu aggression to compensate for centuries of deprivation, insult, and injury at the hands of Muslims.[118] Christophe Jaffrelot in fact argues that there was a noticeable 'inferiority complex' among the Hindu majority of India vis-à-vis not only India's Muslim 'other' but also other players in the international arena.[119] The rise of India economically and politically and its association with a strong Hindutva-inspired identity began to resolve the issue of the 'inferiority complex.' It was also assisted significantly by the emergence of a number of outstanding players and an intelligent and ambitious leader in Saurav Ganguly in the year 2000. But India have always produced outstanding cricketers. Now, though, they had self-belief and were no longer intimidated. In fact, from the middle of the first decade of the 2000s, the roles have reversed with India now holding a significant psychological advantage over Pakistan. In the last ten years the two teams have met in twenty ODIs and T20 internationals. India has won fifteen of these. Overall Pakistan still leads the rivalry 74–61, highlighting the extent of their earlier dominance.

The changing economic, political, and social environment from the 1990s in India and Pakistan affected their cricketing relations. Pakistan had entered a decade of democracy, but democratization did not lead to improved relations. Benazir Bhutto and Nawaz Sharif, Pakistan's two democratic leaders during the 1990s, vied with each other for power by using more and more hostile language against India.[120] The two countries engaged in an arms race involving the deployment of medium and short range missiles[121] and, in 1990, nearly went to war over Kashmir. By 1994, even talks at foreign secretary level were in abeyance.

Beginning with the escalation of militancy in Kashmir in the early 1990s, and culminating during the Kargil war in 1999, a semi-consensus emerged in India that since people were dying due to Pakistan's subversive activities, India should not play with Pakistan on either Indian or Pakistani soil.[122] Bilateral cricketing ties were therefore severed after 1989, affected by the growing state hostility, the Kashmir insurgency, and opposition in India from hard-line groups. However, it should be noted that whilst government level relations were frozen, both the Indian and Pakistani cricket boards maintained cordial relations and attempted to restore cricketing ties.[123] Unfortunately, the threat from Hindu extremists led to Pakistan cancelling tours to India in 1991, 1993, and 1994. Between 1991 and 1994, India also boycotted the offshore venue of Sharjah in protest to alleged anti-India bias among (Muslim) officials.[124] But the fact that tours were still contemplated and planned suggests that there was still some form of South Asian 'solidarity,' even though political relations between India and Pakistan had been severely damaged by the events of the early 1990s.

A glimpse of changing relations could be seen in the quarterfinal of the 1996 World Cup between India and Pakistan in Bangalore [Bengaluru]. The encounter would be their first meeting in India or Pakistan in seven years. Massive public support for the rivalry to resume led to the Shiv Sena 'allowing' the match to proceed as it was an international event.[125] Marqusee observed that despite political tensions the Indian media took a positive approach to the renewal of Indo-Pak cricketing ties and urged fans to welcome the visitors. On the morning of the match, the newspapers were full of stories about players from the two countries mixing freely and of Hindustani-Pakistani *bhai bhai* (brotherhood). Cricket was still somewhat insulated from the wider political environment so that while many of the same papers in their news coverage and editorial comments struck anti-Pakistani poses, backed nuclear weapons and high defence spending, and took a tough line on 'Pakistani terrorism' and Kashmir, on this cricketing occasion they urged readers to celebrate the India–Pakistan contest in a friendly, if decidedly, partisan spirit. They did not however challenge the underpinning logic of India–Pakistan hostility.[126] There was also the positive impact of the South Asian rivals jointly holding the world cup and of the solidarity they showed in their support of Sri Lanka when a joint Indo-Pak team played in Colombo following the suicide bombing that had threatened Sri Lanka as a venue for the tournament.

But by the time the match was underway, the crowd grew increasingly hostile. McDonald speaks of the Hindu nationalist influence in cricket being increasingly evident through the partisan nature of crowds.[127] Marqusee added weight to this finding when he referred to the atmosphere during the match as being characterized by 'hate-filled chauvinism with communal overtones.'[128] India's 'victory precipitated an orgy of national celebrations, which seemed less about progressing to the semi-final, and more about victory over a nation considered a political, military, social and economic inferior.'[129] McDonald goes on to refer to an incident that the historian Ramchandra Guha witnessed when he stood to applaud the exit from international cricket of one of Pakistan's great batsmen Javed Miandad after his dismissal, which effectively secured the match for India:

> 'What are you clapping him for' yelled a man behind me. Through a long evening I had stood the crowd's shameful partisanship, now I responded. 'You too should clap him too. He is truly a great player, and we shall never see him again.' The short definitive reply—'Thank God I'll never see the bastard again.'[130]

Guha and Sengupta both suggest that the rise of cricket nationalism in India during the 1990s can be linked to the rise of Hindu chauvinism seen at the same time.[131] The Indian 'self' was thus increasingly equated with the Hindu 'self' which contrasted with Pakistan as India's 'Muslim other.' The hardening of identities and their distinctive opposition coupled with the political tensions between the neighbours strengthened the view that the Islamic nation of Pakistan was an inveterate enemy of Hindu India and no longer merely an arch-rival. We had reached a point where India–Pakistan matches were 'war minus the shooting' as the Bangalore match had been dubbed by the Indian media.[132] In time this narrative would begin to filter down to the larger population with the more damaging impression that the Pakistani nation or the people as a whole were inimically disposed towards India, and that India too should resort to similar comprehensive hostility in order to bring Pakistani hostility to heel. Accordingly, any triumph over Pakistan in any sphere of life is taken as a cause of celebration; any setback is seen as a national humiliation.[133]

A FALSE SPRING: THE 1999 PAKISTAN TOUR TO INDIA

By 1998, deteriorating Indo-Pak relations would be pushed to the brink. In May 1998, India and Pakistan conducted tit for tat nuclear tests all the while exchanging fire across the border. On 2 August 1998, Pakistan's Prime Minister Nawaz Sharif accused the Indian government of 'taking South Asia to the brink of war.'[134] In response, India's Prime Minister Atal Bihari Vajpayee warned Pakistan that 'India would use a firm hand to respond to any attack on its border' and that the Indian Army would 'repulse the nefarious designs of Pakistan.'[135] The escalation of violence across the Line of Control, claiming over one hundred lives in a week of shelling, and the belligerent rhetoric used by the two enemies led both the United States and China to urge restraint.[136]

The turnaround in relations occurred in September 1998 when the two Prime Ministers met over lunch in New York.[137] This third face to face meeting appears to have led to a strong personal bonding between the two premiers with the interpersonal rapport reversing a declining relationship and in fact replacing it with a surprising warmth which subsequently led to a raft of confidence-building measures. It was decided that foreign secretary-level talks would be held between India and Pakistan, and a direct bus service between Lahore and Delhi was proposed.[138] The sudden change in tenor mirrored the similar rapid escalation in tension and the equally rapid drop in temperatures that followed a meeting of the heads of states in 1987 when President Zia met Prime Minister Rajiv Gandhi as part of Zia's cricket diplomacy.

When Sharif returned to Pakistan, he pushed for the Pakistan cricket team to tour India in January and February of 1999—ten years after the last Test series that they had played.[139] The diplomatic importance that Sharif attached to the tour can be gauged by the fact that he requested former foreign secretary (later PCB chairman) Shaharyar Khan to be the manager for the tour. Khan records how in his meeting with Sharif prior to the start of the tour, the Prime Minister had stressed on 'achieving optimum public relations benefit.'[140] Khan also states that the decision to proceed with the tour, despite strong opposition from his close advisors, had been Sharif's alone and he wanted his decision to be vindicated both in a political and cricketing context. The Pakistani Prime Minister 'recognized the serious risks to the team and to Pakistan–India relations and left it to me to abort the tour if events turned sour and there was a danger of injury or a negative political fallout.'[141]

The possible cancellation of the tour was a response to the Shiv Sena announcing a hostile boycott of the tour—as they had throughout the 1990s. The Shiv Sena supremo, Bal Thackeray, had angrily stated that India should not play Pakistan because 'Pakistani terrorists are killing our people in Kashmir. Women and children are mercilessly slaughtered every day.' As part of a ruling coalition, he also threatened to withdraw parliamentary support if the series was not cancelled.[142] Prime Minister Vajpayee's Bharatiya Janata Party (BJP), the leading party in the governing coalition, refused to give in to the threats even after the Shiv Sena damaged the Delhi pitch, attacked the BCCI offices in Mumbai, mounted a noisy demonstration outside the Pakistan Embassy in New Delhi, and threatened to release venomous snakes at the grounds where Pakistan was supposed to play.[143] A tense Pakistan team therefore took the 30-minute flight to Delhi in the face of considerable risks ahead of them. But soon after landing they were to find that the threats had been withdrawn in the first of a set of remarkable incidents on the tour that demonstrated the contrary nature of India–Pakistan relations.

The first of these episodes involved Lal Krishna Advani, the hawkish BJP Home Minister at the time (in 1999). Shaharyar Khan, the manager on that tour, and someone who has spent his professional life as a diplomat committed to better Indo-Pak relations, recounted to me Advani's first encounter with the Pakistan team:

> Advani had come straight from the airport after persuading Shiv Sena to withdraw its threats to the tour. The Home Minister speaking in Hindi, then addressed us. He was warm in his choice of words and gave us the government's assurance of security and of welcoming crowds. He appreciated the decision to maintain the tour and hoped that it would lead to a better understanding between the two countries. He then became wistful about the past, referring to our common history, culture, and language. Advani wandered back to his childhood which he spent in Karachi attending St Patrick's School. As the conversation continued, I noticed Advani's eyes moisten and his lips quiver as he held back feelings. It was an extraordinarily emotional moment to see the most powerful man in India, the leader of the Bharatiya Janata Party, and the symbol of right wing Hindutva attitudes deeply moved when talking of his childhood to the Pakistan cricket team. As someone who had seen Partition and had moved to Pakistan, I could understand the sentiment. Some of the younger players were less aware of this connection but they still noticed Advani's emotional meeting.[144]

Advani was the man who had masterminded Hindu nationalism's rise to power in India by inflaming religious sentiments with a pilgrimage to the claimed birthplace of the Hindu god Ram in Ayodhya.[145] Yet, like Vajpayee, he was of the generation that had seen Partition and known that the peoples of the Subcontinent did share a common history, culture, and language. There was a connection that could not be denied. The ties that bind the two were deeply emotional and could still be felt.

Seven years later, Advani would travel to his birthplace Karachi. He was accorded a warm welcome, 'hundreds of people on their balconies cheered him and his family. They waved back … I spent a good deal of my childhood in these streets and today I feel myself extremely nostalgic but elated to return here,' he said as he stood in the street.[146] There were pictures of him dancing, arms aloft, to the strains of his native Sindhi music. He also visited

Islamabad and was particularly moved by the government's decision to restore the Katas Raj temples in Pakistani Punjab—one of the oldest Hindu religious sites in Pakistan. Advani would go on to praise Pakistan's founder Mohammad Ali Jinnah for his liberalism. He would also seemingly discard the Hindutva vision of *Akhand Bharat* by stating that 'Partition could not be undone' and that India and Pakistan were 'unalterable realities of history.'[147] Unsurprisingly, back in India L.K. Advani's pronouncements were seen as treasonous and, with no support from within his party, he resigned as BJP president to be replaced by a new generation of hardliners. In the twilight of his political career, Advani referred to the episode of the destruction of the Babri Mosque as the 'saddest of his life.' He appeared to believe that India and Pakistan should ease tensions through wide-ranging contacts and in doing so he showed himself to be open to changing his views and flexible in his approach. The emotional ties that were clearly present and their physical manifestation which followed through interaction with Pakistan must have played an important role in the softening of his views.

The second memorable incident also described by Shaharyar Khan in his diary but remembered by anyone who saw it occurred on the last day of the first Test match in Chennai.[148] Pakistan won an unforgettable Test match in front of a capacity crowd. Fortunes had ebbed and flowed throughout a tension-filled last day and finally when Pakistan triumphed a spontaneous victory lap led to a standing ovation from the Chennai crowd. Twenty years later, Siddhartha Vaidyanathan, writing for the cricket website *Cricinfo*, recalled the momentous event:

> Somewhere in the middle of the ovation—in a stand erected for TV cameramen—stood [Harsha] Bhogle, preparing himself for a 'little post-game show' leading up to the presentation ceremony. The noise around him made it hard to hear the instructions through the earpiece. 'I just heard the director say: "Don't go off, I'm going to give you some pictures, just talk over them." Then I saw this victory lap starting.' ... this is the best sight you will see anywhere in the world ... far away from their homeland ... I've never seen a stronger statement in favour of sport ... The crowd noise gets louder and louder. Bhogle is being drowned out. Which makes it that much more stirring: as if he is broadcasting a watershed event from a far-off continent, maybe even from a distant past. A spectacle is turning to something momentous. A match is turning into a milestone. News is turning into history.[149]

Shaharyar Khan, himself a veteran diplomat with years of experience in Indo-Pak relations, was moved enough to state that the positive waves of goodwill that the Chennai crowd emitted surpassed anything that had happened at the popular level in the fifty-year history of Pakistan–India relations.[150] It stunned all those who watched this extraordinary match.

The two incidents highlighted above and more generally the groundswell of public acclaim as the tour progressed provided the ideal stage in both countries for Vajpayee's historic bus journey to Lahore in February 1999. It also brings up the question posed at the beginning of the chapter. India and Pakistan had endured a bloody partition and in the subsequent five decades they had gone to war three times. Tensions remained over multiple issues and months before the tour both had tested nuclear devices. The rise of extremist ideologies had escalated in both nations and the states had more often than not continued to trade bellicose statements. And yet, whenever given even a small opportunity, people on both sides of the border appeared desperate to live in peace and amity. The 1999 tour:

> provided a unique opportunity to humanize, if not normalize the strained relations between the two nations. The cricketing skills on display, the emotions on the field, all draw people on one side towards the other side—and the appreciation can sometimes go beyond national pride.[151]

The standing ovation given to the victorious Pakistan team in Chennai, ordinary people lined deep in Gwalior to wave the team off, the remarkable warmth shown to Pakistani visitors in Mohali where Sikh girls painted both Indian and Pakistani flags on their cheeks, the spontaneous chants of 'Pakistan-Hindustan dosti Zindabad' by the Pakistani element of the crowd—these were images that seemed unbelievable when seen against the backdrop of the Shiv Sena threat to the team before the tour began and the daily vitriol exchanged between the two governments. The emotional power of sport appeared to rekindle the bonds that exist between Indians and Pakistanis and the parallel political rapprochement threw up the possibility of enduring peace.

Sadly, forces that were opposed to improved relations between India and Pakistan conspired to bring relations—both cricketing and otherwise—to an abrupt halt. In Spring 1999, Pakistan's army instigated a limited war in Kargil[152] and only after intense US diplomatic pressure was the conflict called off. But the damage had been done; and Pakistan and India endured yet another break in cricketing relations between 1999 and 2004.

CRICKET: A BRIDGE OF PEACE?

From the Kargil war in 1999 to late in 2002, Indo-Pak relations remained fraught. In October 2001, Islamic militants attacked the Kashmir Legislative Assembly in Srinagar killing thirty-eight people. Two months later, five Islamic militants, attacked the Indian parliament in New Delhi.[153] India blamed Pakistan-based Islamic groups Jaish-e-Mohammed and Lashkar-e-Taiba for the attacks. The audaciousness of the attack on India's capital struck a crushing psychological blow to Indian society and New Delhi responded by deploying half a million troops to border positions, severing road, rail, and air links with Pakistan, and recalling its High Commissioner from Islamabad. Pakistan's response was to send three hundred thousand of its own troops to the border areas of Punjab and Sindh.[154] Tensions continued to rise and, in May 2002, Islamic militants attacked an Indian military base in Jammu killing thirty-four people. The incident sparked a near nuclear showdown. Prime Minister Vajpayee warned the Indian Army to prepare for a 'decisive battle.' General Pervez Musharraf responded with a thinly-veiled threat that 'if India insists on launching all-out war to attack Pakistan's support for Kashmiri militants, Pakistan is prepared to go nuclear.'[155] The British and US governments issued warning to their citizens in India and Pakistan to depart immediately.[156]

Since the Kargil episode, the Government of India had reverted to the position that until Pakistan refrained from engaging in military adventures in Kashmir and promoting cross-border terrorism, India should stop playing Pakistan in one-on-one encounters. There were a few bilateral matches in international tournaments on 'neutral' venues. Sengupta, Chatterjee, and Bandyopadhyay, all refer to the India–Pakistan encounter in the 2003 World Cup played in South Africa as indicative of a changed relationship.[157] It was apparent that by 2003 the nuclear rivalry, the Kargil war, and the skirmishes that nearly led to a war in 2002 had further increased antagonisms between the two countries. The partisanship of the crowds made for an uglier, more confrontational atmosphere in the ground and when India defeated Pakistan it was followed by a:

> deluge of nationalistic triumphalism as top BJP leaders such as Prime Minister Atal Bihari Vajpayee, Deputy Prime Minister Lal Krishna Advani promptly sent their congratulations. The defeat sent Pakistan crashing out of the World Cup which appeared to make it all the sweeter.[158]

Chatterjee quotes a middle-aged Indian waving a tricolour following India's win, 'That's it. I don't care if India loses every single match from here on.

The World Cup is over for me. We have won. We have thrashed the Pakis.'[159] Whatever South Asian solidarity had existed up until the 1990s seemed to have been destroyed by Kargil and the continued bad blood that followed. Nawaz Sharif's ouster by Pervez Musharraf's military coup had left India without a partner for peace and it took hectic diplomatic efforts from the United States to prevent war in South Asia.[160] And then, in the kind of turnaround that had been seen in the past, relations unexpectedly took a turn for the better.

Vajpayee, encouraged by Musharraf's commitment to clamp down on cross-border infiltration, offered a raft of confidence-building measures in order to foster a conducive atmosphere for the resolution of outstanding issues. This led to significant subsequent steps such as: the restoration of relations at the level of High Commissioners and an increase in the strength of respective High Commissions; resumption of the Lahore-Delhi bus service and rail links; high level exchanges at the level of parliamentarians, businessmen, media, artists, writers, judges, peace activists, and others; permission to senior citizens (65 years and above) to cross at Wagah on foot; free medical treatment to twenty Pakistani children; release of prisoners and fishermen on both sides; and the commencement of bus service between Srinagar and Muzaffarabad, starting a bus or rail link between Munabao in India and Khokhrapar in Pakistan. Also included in these measures was the resumption of bilateral sporting encounters, including cricket.[161] Pakistan responded by ordering the armed forces to cease fire along the Line of Control during the month of Ramadan. Vajpayee further announced that Indian troops would stop all offensive actions against Kashmiri separatist groups in Jammu and Kashmir during Ramadan. The ceasefire was extended three times by the Indian government in order to facilitate negotiations with Kashmiri groups.[162]

> Even though it was a political decision, the ceasefire created an impact of cultural goodwill on the people on both the sides of the Line of Control. The decision of the Indian government to stop the military actions during the holy month of Ramadan had a great effect on the Muslim people in the both countries. The people of both countries welcomed the decisions with great hope that the ceasefire would solve the border issues even if it would take some time. Hence, the Ceasefire was a successful contribution both politically and culturally towards the normalization of the India–Pakistan relations.[163]

In this dramatically improved atmosphere, the resumption of cricketing relations was announced with the India tour of Pakistan scheduled for March 2004.

Shaharyar Khan, who had just taken over the chairmanship of the PCB, reveals that despite the political tensions, the two boards had maintained equable relations. Jagmohan Dalmiya, the president of the BCCI, and Shaharyar Khan already had an excellent rapport from Pakistan's 1999 tour to India. Now they prepared for India's first full tour to Pakistan since 1989. Dalmiya had informed Khan that the BCCI was supportive of the tour but that the government would have to greenlight it.[164] The BCCI was in fact keen on a resumption of ties. India's refusal to play Pakistan had caused losses of millions of dollars in television rights for both the Indian and Pakistani boards. The BCCI kept pushing the government gently for a resumption arguing that continued refusal to play Pakistan was isolating India. Seeing the potential financial windfall from an Indo-Pak series, Chatterjee argues that, by the end of April 2003, the BCCI was keen enough to propose to New Delhi that India and Pakistan should be allowed to play in third country venues.[165]

But the resumption of cricketing ties, despite the vastly improved bilateral relations, was complicated by security concerns and the impending elections in India. The media raised the spectre of the Munich Olympics in 1972 when Palestinian terrorists kidnapped and killed Israeli athletes—an event of this nature would destroy Indo-Pak relations forever.[166] Musharraf had also recently survived two assassination attempts and the wives of several Indian players had been reluctant to allow their husbands to travel to Pakistan.[167] There was trepidation amongst the BJP over how the tour may affect their re-election chances. A good tour could provide them with a feel-good boost. An unsuccessful tour could lead to a backlash. How would a loss to Pakistan be received? Could making further overtures to Pakistan on the eve of the elections be counter-productive?[168] Eventually, after a promise from General Musharraf that the Indian team would be provided with presidential-level security, Vajpayee, like Sharif in 1999, took the decision to clear the tour, despite objections from several quarters including his Home Minister L.K. Advani.[169] Famously, Vajpayee would urge the Indian team: '*Khel hi nahin, dil bhi jitiye*' ('Not only the game, win hearts as well'). The placards waved around while Vajpayee met the team, featuring messages such as 'Best of Luck' and '*Atal ne diya cricket ka uphaar, India–Pakistan sadbhavana ka prachar*' ('Atal's cricket gift spreads harmony in India and Pakistan').[170]

In fact, the tour was an unprecedented success in terms of bilateral relations, the consequences of which would be felt for years. It was also one of those rare occasions where all concerned parties contributed to the overall achievement. The two boards worked closely together. The PCB mounted a massive organizational and logistical operation that ensured visas were provided for thousands of Indian fans and a large contingent of journalists.

Global interest meant media from across the world were present as well. Shaharyar Khan's diplomatic network and his family linkages with India[171] meant that a series of high-profile Indian guests were set to 'accompany' the tour. Most prominent amongst them were Priyanka and Rahul Gandhi and Dina Wadia, Jinnah's daughter, who had not visited Pakistan since her father's death in 1948. For Khan, the tour was important both in terms of cricket (it had been fifteen years since India had toured Pakistan) as well as commercially, as there was no bigger financial bonanza than an India–Pakistan series. But it was also an opportunity for Pakistan to demonstrate to the rest of the world its willingness to shake off the increasingly negative image that had followed in the wake of Osama Bin Laden and the terrorist attack of 9/11. It was an opportunity to 'redress Pakistan's distorted image abroad, particularly in India.'[172]

The fifteen years that had passed had meant that a generation of Indians and Pakistanis had not interacted directly. Instead, the state narratives of both sides had fed sensationalized accounts of one another. Demonizing the 'other' intensifies distrust and dehumanizes the other party. 'Othering,' as Saskia Sassen states, 'undergirds territorial disputes, sectarian violence, military conflict, the spread of disease, hunger and food insecurity, and even climate change.'[173] Recent history has seen countless examples of the bloody consequences of demonizing the other, from Rwanda in 1994 to Myanmar in 2016. India and Pakistan were already polarizing their images as Hindu and Muslim opposites of each other. As walls went up, a new generation has grown up knowing each other only through media stereotypes and the propaganda that is spewed out by politicians. The Pakistani novelist Mohammed Hanif, writing of his first visit to India, sums it up:

> Like many Pakistanis I saw my first Indians in London and was surprised that they were a bit like us. Most Indians and Pakistanis have the same reaction when they meet. It seems as if they are brought up to believe that a community of ferals lives across the border.[174]

The previous generation of Indians and Pakistanis at least had the experience and interaction of having lived together. People traffic between the countries had also been more frequent in the past. Those linkages were now loosening and, as mentioned before, this has led to Pakistan and India viewing themselves as enemies that were ill-disposed towards each another rather than merely being arch-rivals.

Changing that mindset would be a major challenge and would require a targeted effort at moulding public opinion. The two boards briefed their respective teams. The captains, Inzamam-ul-Haq and Saurav Ganguly, were exemplary in their conduct, always stressing playing in a sporting spirit and carrying through on this on and off the field. Shaharyar Khan states:

> I discussed with him [Inzamam] how through cricket, we had the responsibility to project a civilised, moderate and peaceful image of Pakistan not only towards India but to the millions of cricket lovers in Australia, England, Africa and the West Indies who would be watching the series on television.[175]

Thus, the role of the captains and their teams was a crucial factor in the change from the rancorous, unpleasant, defensive contests of the past to building cricketing blocks for peace and better understanding between Pakistanis and Indians. It is in many ways unfair to expect sportsmen to be ambassadors for peace but the Indian team in 2004 were outstanding emissaries. From the polio eradication campaign in Pakistan that was launched by the Indian players, to the Indian cricket team appealing to doctors back home to treat a young Pakistani girl afflicted with cancer[176] to the Indian cricketers' visit to the Lahore University of Management Sciences where the students chanted for the Indian fast bowler Laxmipathy Balaji, the Indian cricketers forged a unique relationship with the Pakistani public.

While teams could be briefed and prepared, it was more difficult to engineer this with the larger populace. But the efforts of the PCB, the media, and an improved political environment paid dividends. The spirit of bonhomie and bridge building had been taken to heart and it was the response from the Pakistani public that set the optimistic tone for the tour. In the very first match in Karachi which India won narrowly, the crowd erupted in spontaneous applause for the Indian team. 'The mind went back to the beautiful occasion in Chennai in 1999, when Wasim Akram led his team for a victory lap to a standing ovation after a startling win in a stunning test ... Indeed, the applause at Karachi had been far more spontaneous than at Chennai.'[177] During the match, Rahul and Priyanka Gandhi had left the [PCB] chairman's box and mingled with fans in the public stands where they were warmly received.[178] The outstanding success of the Karachi ODI set the tenor for the remaining series. Everywhere the Indian team went, they were welcomed with immense enthusiasm.

The success in Karachi appeared to spur a rush of Indian fans to seek visas for the tour. It also settled the Indian players as security concerns eased to the extent that the teams were happy to socialize with one another. Rahul Bhattacharya, whose wonderful memoir of the tour is full of endearing anecdotes, writes of the ties between former and current Pakistani and Indian players:

The day before the Rawalpindi one day Javed Miandad, India's nemesis of the past hosted his old friend Dilip Vengsarkar, and his wife, at his Lahore home, as also Tendulkar, who took along a couple of younger team mates with him. Nehra joined Shoaib for an outing to a friend's farm. The Indian and Pakistani fan clubs organized a get together. Later Imran Khan would throw a party for players, officials and friends, but would controversially omit Miandad.[179]

In Peshawar, the Indian players appeared totally relaxed in the famous Qissa Khawani bazaar where they bought Peshawari chappals and inquired about the famous lamb tikkas made in the Namak Mandi.

But in an indication that the Indian psyche had changed since the 1980s and that years of 'inferiority' were being erased with a new, more confident India, Bhattacharya quotes a Pakistani cricketer saying that in the past 'the Indians were polite compared to us. Who was there to abuse? There was one Jadeja. And there was one Prabhakar. Sidhu was also a little like us. He's Punjabi after all! But this Indian team is very different. They are as aggressive.'[180] Contrast this with what the Pakistani captain Mushtaq Mohammad had stated about the Indian team when they toured Pakistan in 1978–79:

> The Indians were very mild in comparison. When they appealed against us they almost appeared apologetic while asking the umpire the question. Our appealing was hostile and aggressive and plenty of bad language was used in between. It definitely upset the more calmer-natured Indians, who were gentlemen and great cricketers but very, very soft.[181]

I had followed the tour closely, meeting with the teams on several occasions. As the action moved to Lahore for the final two ODIs, there was a surreal feel to the proceedings. The success of the tour thus far, the narrow winning margins of the matches, and the fact that the deciding two would be in Lahore, the city closest to India, saw an influx of Indian visitors.

> For the Indians poured in. They came in numbers that they had never been permitted to come in before; they came by air, they came by foot, they came by road, they came by rail using all the channels that had been opened up since Vajpayee's January visit. Larger flights, special flights, extra busses, thousands came on foot, with banners saying 'Friends Forever.'[182]

Well over 8,000 visas—more than the quota that was set aside for the series—were issued. Shaharyar Khan estimated that 20,000 Indians from India and the Indian diaspora came to Lahore.[183] Bhattacharya puts the figure closer to 11,000.[184] Lahore felt and looked different. As I drove around Liberty Roundabout, adjacent to the Gaddafi stadium and where some years later gunmen would fire at the Sri Lankan team, the markets and streets took on a familiar feel but with slight differences that a bystander could be forgiven for overlooking. Passers-by wore similar clothes, spoke similar languages, used similar gestures, had similar features, and revelled in similar cuisine. But a few wore turbans and visited the many sacred Sikh shrines in and around Lahore. Some of the younger Indian visitors spoke more often in English and had a slightly more Westernized dress sense. The shops were buzzing with activity. Shopkeepers and restaurants gave discounts, taxi drivers refused fares. Bhattacharya writes how his friends and family in India had advised before leaving that it would be better to be inconspicuous and try to pass of as Pakistani, 'by the end of it Pakistanis were seriously contemplating posing as Indians and reaping the rewards. I had not been made to feel so welcome anywhere in the world.'[185] In a car outside the Hot Spot ice cream joint, I sat with Dina Wadia, Jinnah's daughter, as she asked a waiter to bring her a scoop of ice cream—as the young man looked at her and saw the mirror image of the founder of the nation he drew back in awe, his eyes filled with tears and he put his hands together in supplication. Within minutes people had gathered around the car but kept a respectful distance. In the distance the floodlights of the Gaddafi stadium hummed to life as a test run and Lahore basked in the glow of bonhomie. New friendships were forged between the Indian spectators and the Pakistani public during the series. I recall sitting in the chairman's box when Shaharyar Khan told me his favourite story of the tour:

> My favourite story relates to the visit of a Sikh family from across the border. Two young fans had brought their elderly mother with them as she wanted to visit her former home that she had left in 1947 in Wazirabad—a township 15 miles outside Lahore. While the sons went to the Gaddafi stadium, they arranged for a taxi to take their mother to visit her former birthplace and home before she emigrated to India.
>
> Hesitantly, the elderly lady knocked at the door of her old home and when the housewife opened the door, the older woman explained with diffidence and many apologies that she only wanted to see her old birthplace from the outside. She would now return to Lahore having satisfied her wish and did not want to impose herself on the housewife's family. Having heard the visitor's story, the housewife insisted that the visitor share a cup of tea with her and look over her old home. Touched by the welcome the older woman entered the house and was shown around the building. The housewife then excused herself as she made tea in the kitchen while her young family made small-talk

with the visitor. After a while, the housewife produced a sumptuous meal for her guest from across the border, with traditional cakes, sweet dishes and of course tea. The Sikh visitor was overwhelmed by this welcome and thanked her hostess profusely. Before taking leave, the hostess asked her guest to wait a few more minutes and returned with six beautiful joras (dresses) which she asked the older woman to accept as a present for coming all the way from India to visit her birthplace. The traveller burst into tears at this gesture and the women hugged each other before making her way out to the waiting taxi.

There, outside the house, a large number of neighbours had gathered as word had quickly gone round about the old Indian lady's visit. The neighbours then presented the old lady with 64 joras that they had gathered as a mark of their affection for the family that had been obliged to leave home and hearth at the time of Partition. The woman wept and wept and asked how she could take back 70 joras to Lahore. 'We shall send them to you in another taxi. Tell us where you are staying,' said the women neighbours. Completely overwhelmed by her welcome the visitor got into the taxi and returned to Lahore with tears streaming down her cheeks throughout the 40-minute ride. When she arrived at her guesthouse, the taxi-driver refused to accept the fare.[186]

This is one of many such incidents that occurred during the tour. Many Indian fans came to see the matches. Many also came to visit places they—or their parents—had known and spoken about. In the stadiums, fans of both countries mingled happily, their faces painted with the flags of both countries; banners proclaiming 'Pak-India *dosti zindabad*' appeared all over the ground.

After the ODI series ended with a 3-2 victory for India, the Indian captain Saurav Ganguly wrote in his autobiography how he celebrated by sneaking past security and making his way to Lahore's famous food street for 'kebabs and tandoori dishes.' Ganguly reveals that when he had almost finished eating his cover was blown when an Indian journalist called out to him.[187]

> Soon chaos erupted and I got *gheraoed* (encircled). While I tried to pay the bill and escape, the shopkeeper refused to accept payment. He kept on saying 'Bahut acha. We need someone as aggressive as you to lead Pakistan.'

And on his way back to the hotel a speeding motorbike chased his car. When the biker asked Ganguly to roll down his window he obliged against the instructions of his co-passengers who feared the man may have a bomb. 'I, however, did not see any threat and echoed the shopkeeper in Food Street, "I am a big fan of yours. Pakistan needs a leader like you". Ganguly reached the hotel safely but was told off firmly by General Pervez Musharraf, 'Next time you want to go please inform the security and we will have an entourage with you. But please don't indulge in adventures.'[188]

Ganguly had travelled to Pakistan in 1997 as well to play a one-day series. Even then he relates an account of a shopkeeper refusing payment for clothes that he had bought for his wife:

> When the items were packed and I was about to pay, the man at the counter said 'We won't accept money from you. This is a small token of love from us.' I tried hard to convince him, but the shopkeeper remained unmoved. He kept on saying, 'Aap Indiawale hamare bhai hain' (you Indians are our brothers).[189]

The general public's attitude could not be ignored. An enabling environment had been provided by the governments, the boards, and the players, but the response from the general public was extraordinary. Decades of hostility, confrontations, and enmity had led only to suffering, poverty, and hardship for the populations of both countries.[190] As people from across the border interacted, they found a very different reality to what they had expected and a realization of commonalities rather than difference. Jaswant Singh in his book *Jinnah* says of Pakistan, India, and Bangladesh, 'we have all been born of Partition: we were one, India, Pakistan and Bangladesh, up till the third quarter of 1947, now we are three separated entities, but are we truly all that different?'[191] For people who shared a common history, culture, and language, here was a vision of what peace could bring. The public grabbed it with both hands.

Pakistanis, and Lahoris in particular, had opened their doors and hearts to their Indian guests. The Indian visitors returned home overwhelmed by Pakistani hospitality and many stereotypes shattered.[192] In a memorable phrase, the Indian High Commissioner Shiv Shankar Menon remarked to Shaharyar Khan in Lahore: 'Shaharyar Saheb, 20,000 Indian cricket fans visited Pakistan. You have sent back 20,000 Pakistan Ambassadors to India. Thank you for your hospitality.'[193]

Further accolades for the series poured in. Laurens International, the world's leading sports concern, nominated the India and Pakistan cricket teams as joint winners for their annual team sports prize. The UN recognized the impact of the series in peace building by announcing a special tribute to both teams as ambassadors of peace.[194] With the success of the 2004 tour fresh in people's minds, a decision was made to cash in on this positivity and the Pakistani team made a return tour to India in April 2005. While the heights of the first tour were never achieved again, the subsequent series of 2004, 2005, 2006, and 2007 continued to stimulate goodwill between the countries. According to Crick:

This indicates that the longer India and Pakistan play each other at cricket, the more the chances that the people-to-people contact instigated by such matches could have an impact on breaking down the stereotypes that reinforce the negative relationship. The more the two teams play each other, the less 'mythic' the differences become.[195]

There was a definite change in the way that Indians and Pakistanis viewed each other with cricket being used as an important vehicle for this change in perceptions. Bob Woolmer, Pakistan's English coach, would tell Emily Crick in a personal interview in 2005: 'The way you warm to the people, you warm to the society, you warm to the country because of their hospitality and that's all because of cricket really—it's all cricket related.'[196] This same sentiment was to be seen in the earliest tours as well. Guha states that spot interviews by a Lahore journalist during India's tour of Pakistan in 1960 revealed what the reporter dubbed was a 'distinct change in mental outlook.'

A young Sikh of a Western Punjab family told the reporter: I was a fool to imagine all these years that Pakistan is unsafe for Non-Muslims. I have been here four days now and wherever I went I have nothing but goodwill and friendship. A white-haired Hindu, who lived in Lahore before Partition said that he felt 'as I have returned to my old home. Lahore has not changed much. Nobody here asks whether you are a Hindu or a Muslim or Indian or Pakistani … it is so different from what many fanatics in East Punjab want us to imagine.[197]

Mike Marqusee, who watched the 1996 World Cup on the Subcontinent and returned to watch Pakistan's tour of India in 2005, also remarks on how the ambience had totally changed. Marqusee, who had castigated the Bangalore crowd of 1996 for its jingoistic nationalism,[198] found in Bangalore in 2005 handwritten signs welcoming the tourists, praising Indo-Pak friendship, and declaring that cricket is the path to peace.[199] On the same tour, Marqusee states that at Mohali the change in atmosphere was palpable. 'And it cannot be credited to either politicians or the media—they have merely followed the lead from below, from the bases of both societies, where the desire for South Asian peace has overcome decades of fearful mythologies.'[200] He also argues that South Asian cricket remains this kind of 'a reliable barometer of the society in which it is played. In the Indo-Pak series, it has provided a vehicle for the expression of a hunger for South Asian harmony that has been gestating for years.'[201] Cricket has thus provided for the most effective form of people-to-people contact touted so long through various types of track-two diplomacy, and in addition it has backed up the efforts at the state level. In short, the recent cricket tours between 2004 and 2007 exemplified the claim that sport bridges distances between people and nations by creating a shared cultural and emotional experience.

In 2007, there was a more significant diplomatic role to the tour as President Musharraf expressed his wish to travel to India, much like President Ziaul Haq had done in 1987, virtually inviting himself ostensibly to watch cricket in Delhi but mainly to discuss political issues. While this happened during ongoing peace talks, Musharraf felt this was an opportunity to hasten the peace process which he felt was stalling.[202] Musharraf and Indian Prime Minister Manmohan Singh watched the match in Delhi side by side, and pictures of the two leaders were broadcast throughout the world.[203] Furthermore, in a joint press conference after their talks, they announced that now 'the peace process was irreversible.'[204]

Cricket thus provided a multi-level tool for improving relations between India and Pakistan. It provided conversational space for Indian and Pakistani leaders to meet and discuss political conflict areas. It also provided the largest opportunity for people-to-people contact between 2004 and 2007. The improvement in relations led to a raft of cultural exchanges. In 2005, the first passengers from either side of the border crossed divided Kashmir as the landmark bus service across the ceasefire line dividing Indian- and Pakistani-controlled Kashmir got underway.[205] The ban on Indian films was lifted in 2008[206] in Pakistan after a period of over forty years and a number of Pakistani artists began working in Bollywood and some Indian actors appeared in Pakistani films.[207]

I return, at this point, to the question that has preoccupied me throughout this chapter and which I flagged earlier. How is it that after the horror of Partition, wars, political and religious tensions, and restrictions on people-to-people contacts, Indians and Pakistanis have so often been able to warm to each other like long lost siblings? I do not believe this is a riddle that can be definitively answered and while I am unable to profess a theory there are thoughts that struck me while analysing the undulating relations between India and Pakistan albeit through the lens of cricket. Gyanendra Pandey, whose in-depth investigation of the violence that marked Partition and how this is remembered, asks the same question.[208]

> Surprisingly, again, what all this has left behind is an extraordinary love–hate relationship: on the one hand, deep resentment and animosity, and the most militant of nationalisms—Pakistani against Indian, and Indian against Pakistani, now backed up by nuclear weapons; on the other, a considerable sense of nostalgia, frequently articulated in the view that this was a partition

of siblings that should never have occurred—or, again, in the call to imagine
what a united Indian-Pakistani cricket team might have achieved![209]

Some academics, such as Indian Marxist, political scientist, and political
activist Javeed Alam have ventured explanations that have looked at
Partition as a momentary loss of sanity provoked by the involvement of
large organizations which led to a frenzy of violence against communities
that had previously lived in relative harmony.[210] Gyanendra Pandey himself
disagrees with the view that the violence was 'an aberration, the handiwork
of "outsiders" and "criminals".'[211]

What is less disputed is that for thousands of years communities in South
Asia lived side by side. Islam made its way to the Subcontinent in the 7th
and 8th centuries and became part of a wider culture by the 12th and 13th
centuries.[212] Since then there have undoubtedly been conflicts between
Hindus and Muslims, but there have also been constructive exchanges.
As Varshney states: 'Indian culture is not Hindu; it is simply Indian.'[213]
Hinduism was a large part of that culture. Islam too was a component of
that mosaic; hence, the term that Nehru used to characterize Indian culture,
'Indo-Muslim.' This history has meant that local structures of cooperation
existed between communities and that these linkages transcended religion.

Partition succeeded in polarizing identities into Hindus, Muslims,
and Sikhs, thereby prioritizing the religious aspect over all others. But
those other parts of identities, those bonds that existed, are not so easily
forgotten. They have a resilience and emotional resonance that cannot
be denied. Indians and Pakistanis have a shared history, particularly if
we consider Pakistan and the large swathe of North India. They speak
similar languages—the national languages Hindi and Urdu have a common
vocabulary that makes them mutually understandable—giving further
shared poetry, songs, film, and literature. They eat similar foods and have
similar dress and customs. These elements can be supressed, but they can
also thrive when the opportunity arises.

Moreover, there is an emotional relationship that is evident and yet
easily overlooked because it is so obvious. Urvashi Butalia's wonderful
account of Partition stories illustrates this point clearly. Butalia speaks of an
'indescribable emotional pull' which she felt when she set out to meet her
long-lost maternal uncle in Pakistan even though she herself had no direct
experience of Partition. Her mother had migrated to India. Her uncle had
remained in Pakistan and converted to Islam. For forty years the two families
had no contact until Butalia turned up at her uncle's doorstep in Lahore.
It is a deeply moving story. There are several other such stories that involve

heart wrenching accounts of divided families and lost relatives finding each other after decades apart. There is talk of 'families' and 'home' in countries that have never been set foot in. These accounts have that indescribable emotional pull. Partition brought with it a terrible violence but there were also innumerable stories of how people had helped each other—stories of friendship and sharing. Ashis Nandy[214] in his research on Partition found that even in the terrible bloodbath that claimed the lives of millions, as many as one in four people among survivors said they were saved by the other community. Nandy also found that the first generation of victims, those that had been most directly affected by violence, had lesser rancour and prejudice against the other than later generations. In fact, this group had lived with the 'other' community and their fondest memories were still of the days when they lived with the ostensibly enemy community. Even many of those who engaged in the killings and escaped justice came later to suffer from a deep sense of regret. The enmity that we expect was mediated by these factors and in some cases these factors led to the re-emergence of positive bonds rather than negative ones as in the case of L.K. Advani. Let us also remember that there were 20 million people who moved between India and Pakistan—an unprecedented migration of people that has created a store of historical and familial histories of enormous emotional power. It is not possible to read or hear these accounts and not be moved by them. Those emotional bonds that are part of the Subcontinental imagination may provide a clue to this contradictory love-hate relationship that exists between Indians and Pakistanis.

This chapter has examined the contrary and undulating relationship between India and Pakistan through the lens of their cricketing encounters. It has highlighted how cricketing relations have often been at odds with the wider political relations and how these sporting ties have been used to improve bilateral relations. But the overarching environment does impact relations contained within it, including cricketing ties. Chapter 6 illustrates how a declining political environment has been reflected in the cricketing contacts between India and Pakistan.

6

Pakistan in the Global Cricketing Order – South Asia II

Pakistan's internal security situation began declining when Musharraf joined the US-led War on Terror in 2001. A collection of Islamist groups trained their guns on the Pakistani state and security agencies. The situation deteriorated further when Musharraf's government confronted Islamists in the siege of Lal Masjid in 2007.[1] From then onwards, Pakistan grappled with a virtual civil war[2]—multiple internal challenges from insurgencies in Balochistan and Khyber Pakhtunkhwa, a growing threat from the Taliban and Al Qaeda, and mounting sectarian killings. The number of fatalities due to terrorist violence increased rapidly from 2001 (38 fatalities)[3] and peaked in 2009 (11,704 fatalities) before declining gradually in the ensuing six years to 2015 (3,682 fatalities), from whence the decline has been more marked.[4]

Security concerns since the 9/11 attacks of 2001 had already meant that many cricketing countries had declined travelling to Pakistan. West Indies refused to tour in 2002, as did Australia. New Zealand declined in 2001, then toured in 2002 only for the tour to be cut short by a bomb explosion outside their hotel in Karachi.[5] Remarkably, the Asian bloc had continued to maintain a united front and when Australia refused to tour, the PCB Chairman Tauqir Zia stated: 'India, Pakistan, Sri Lanka and Bangladesh have signed a Memorandum of Understanding and if Australia don't tour Pakistan, then I don't think any Asian country will be visiting them.'[6]

New Zealand in fact returned in 2002 to Pakistan on the basis of the Indian board reiterating the threat of an Asian boycott if New Zealand did not tour Pakistan. Australia's cancelled tour to Pakistan was replaced by Bangladesh touring, again highlighting the solidarity amongst the Asian boards. This solidarity, it must be remembered, occurred at a time of heightened political tension between India and Pakistan.

The Pakistan Cricket Board lost an estimated £16 million in lost tours between 2001 and 2003 and it was in fact the Indian tour of 2004 that reversed their fortunes, bringing in a financial windfall.[7] England toured in 2005 and India toured again in 2006; but by 2008, tours by non-Asian countries were increasingly rare with South Africa being the last country to tour in 2007. Australia were due to tour in March 2008 when two suicide attacks left thirty-one dead in Pakistan's second largest city, Lahore.[8] The tour was 'postponed.' During this increasingly difficult security environment in Pakistan, support from India, Sri Lanka, and Bangladesh prevented the cricketing isolation of Pakistan. The four Asian boards had also collaborated closely in order to win the right to host the 2011 World Cup in the Subcontinent. Unfortunately, from 2008 a series of setbacks would send India–Pakistan relations into a potentially irreversible tailspin. Amongst other things, the damage to Indo-Pak relations would also cause repercussions for Pakistan's relations with the other Asian boards. There were a number of factors that led to this unfortunate turnaround, some political and some interpersonal.

ISOLATION IN SOUTH ASIA

On 26 November 2008, ten Islamic militants, carried out twelve coordinated shooting and bombing attacks lasting four days across Mumbai which took the lives of 165 people.[9] Indian authorities blamed members of Lashkar-e-Taiba, which had already been implicated in earlier attacks in India. The incident caused Indo-Pak relations to plunge and India's proposed tour to Pakistan, which was already under threat from security concerns, was immediately called off.[10] Four months later, twelve gunmen attacked a bus carrying the Sri Lankan cricket team to the Gaddafi stadium in Lahore. Seven cricketers and an assistant coach were injured. In another vehicle, a driver was killed. And a Pakistani umpire was shot twice. Eight Pakistanis lost their lives. Only the bravery of Meher Muhammad Khalil, the Sri Lankan team's bus driver, prevented further carnage as Khalil drove the bus to safety after it came under attack.[11]

If the attack was calamitous in itself, the response by the PCB and the government was nothing short of catastrophic even in a period when chaos reigned in Pakistan.[12] Political wrangling at the time of the attack had seen the provincial government dismissed and replaced by governor's rule in the Punjab. As Ishtiaq Ahmed emphasizes, with the chief minister sent home some days before the attack, the lapse that must have occurred in the Punjab's continual governance and administration played into the hands of the terrorists.[13] Chris Broad, the ICC official who was in one of the vehicles that came under fire, furiously stated: 'I am extremely angry that we were promised high-level security and in our hour of need that security vanished,' and that the security services had left them as 'sitting ducks.'[14]

This was an important point. Whereas in the past Musharraf acting on behalf of the state had been able to assuage the Indian government's security concerns, now not only had security deteriorated making persuasion more problematic, but the failure of the state to provide the promised security because of political wrangling meant that rebuilding trust at the state level was going to be extremely difficult. President Asif Ali Zardari's government was seen as incompetent, corrupt, and completely unreliable. Pakistan was teetering on the brink in 2009. David Kilcullen, a key advisor to US General David Petraeus, was alarmed enough to assert that 'within one to six months we could see the collapse of the Pakistani state.'[15] Given Pakistan's size, strategic location, and nuclear stockpile, it is no wonder that the Americans were concerned. Inept security provided by an inept government had contributed to the attack on the Sri Lankan cricket team.

Ijaz Butt, the chairman of the PCB at this difficult time, appointed by President Zardari, proceeded to dismantle whatever sympathy Pakistan may have had following the attack. Far from offering condolences to those who lost their lives or accepting the PCB's responsibility for not providing the fool proof security they had promised, he went ahead and proclaimed that there had been no security failure and that it was a 'big lie' that there was no police to protect the Sri Lankans and match officials and that he would report Chris Broad to the ICC for misreporting.[16] In the weeks that followed, Pakistan was stripped of its hosting rights for the 2011 World Cup, with the ICC resolving that all matches would be played in India, Sri Lanka, and Bangladesh.

Pakistan's offer of hosting their share of matches in a neutral venue such as the UAE was rejected by the co-hosts India, Sri Lanka, and Bangladesh, all of whom argued that a neutral country would dilute the concept of the event being held in the Subcontinent.[17] More damaging was the PCB's attempt to shift the entire tournament to 2015 through veiled allusions to poor security throughout South Asia. Ijaz Butt's statement included references to 'Sri Lanka's long running civil war, Bangladesh recently facing a mutiny by its armed forces and India's relocation of IPL due to the law and order situation.'[18] For obvious reasons, this angered India, Bangladesh, and Sri Lanka further.[19]

The Asian boards withdrew support for Pakistan. Ijaz Butt proceeded to take the ICC to court over the relocation and eventually reached an out-of-court settlement. But his leadership had damaged Pakistan cricket's relations with almost all the other cricketing nations. In particular, the Asian bloc—so supportive in the past—lay fractured. According to Mihir Bose, Butt felt that the Indians took advantage of the terrorist attack in Lahore and used the incident to isolate Pakistan, and he made public and private comments blaming the Indians for forcing Pakistan to play all its matches overseas.[20] The fact is that with such a breakdown in relations—, 'I am told the Indian cricket officials are not on speaking terms with Butt'[21]—it is unsurprising that a supportive relationship was transformed into a hostile one. Months later, a spat with Lalit Modi, the Indian board official who was responsible for the Indian Premier League (IPL) at the time, also led to Butt ordering Pakistani players be withdrawn from the cash-rich IPL on security grounds. Thus, while many of the world's best cricketers played alongside one another in the IPL, Pakistan's cricketers have not played since 2009. Pakistan was on an accelerated path to isolation from world cricket and while the overall security environment of the country was beyond the PCB's control, the board's policies at this difficult time hastened Pakistan's seclusion precisely at a time when they most needed Asian support.

In the past, despite seemingly intractable political problems, the Indian and Pakistani boards had maintained supportive relations. Three world cups being held on the Subcontinent was testament to their coordination. More recently, Tauqir Zia and Shaharyar Khan had ensured close cooperation. The antagonistic Ijaz Butt had so damaged relations that Indian board officials privately told the President of Pakistan Asif Zardari, who was also Patron of the cricket board, that the situation could only improve if he sacked Ijaz Butt.[22] Butt's inimical approach towards the Indian board meant that although in the past goodwill had led to support, now there was only hostility. This would become increasingly important as Pakistan's isolation grew with the prolonged loss of cricket being played at home. Ten years passed and only Zimbabwe visited for a short five-match tour in 2015. It was only in late 2019 and early 2020 that Sri Lanka and Bangladesh became the first teams to make the first steps back to Pakistan for full tours. South Africa followed in 2021 as the first non-Asian team.

Yet the fracture in relations with the Indian cricket board occurred at a time when political relations were still retrievable. India's response to the Mumbai attack had been restrained. Prime Minister Manmohan Singh who until the Mumbai attacks had overseen five years of the most promising peace process the two countries had experienced did not order any major military mobilization nor any retaliatory strikes against Pakistan.[23] The peace initiatives that had also seen the annual cricket tours by India and Pakistan between 2004 and 2007 had sparked hopes of the kind of peace forged between Germany and France after the Second World War. The negotiators hoped to develop a new regime of free trade and political cooperation in the region, from Central Asia to Bangladesh. In early 2007, at the height of this optimistic interval, Manmohan Singh had remarked in public, 'I dream of a day, while retaining our respective national identities, one can have breakfast in Amritsar, lunch in Lahore, and dinner in Kabul.'[24] The success of the peace process had left Singh—a committed peacenik—with the hope that the peace process could be revived and in fact dialogue was re-started in 2010 and saw considerable headway made despite the setback of Mumbai. Both countries focussed on increasing trade, energy, and connectivity and relations improved considerably.[25]

We had therefore reached a position that was contrary to those of the past where board relations remained warm despite political animosity. Now political relations, while damaged by Mumbai, were improving, but the boards were no longer on talking terms largely because of the personalities involved. It was despite the board's poor relations that cricket diplomacy again emerged when Manmohan Singh and his Pakistani counterpart, Yousuf Raza Gilani, met each other for the World Cup 2011 semi-final clash between India and Pakistan in Mohali, India. Gilani subsequently invited Singh to visit Pakistan. Peace talks started again and Pakistan toured India in December 2012 for three ODIs and a T20.

Personalities have always played an important role in the saga of South Asian relations, whether it was the personal bond that Vajpayee formed with Nawaz Sharif or Nur Khan and N.K.P. Salve. Manmohan Singh was known to have a personal commitment towards Indo-Pak peace.[26] The warmth of relations between Jagmohan Dalmiya and Shaharyar Khan was an important factor in the success of the Indo-Pak series between 2004 and 2007. In the past, political tensions had pulled India and Pakistan apart while the boards had maintained a back channel of communication that allowed wider relations to prosper as soon as the environment improved. In this instance, poor relations between the PCB and particularly the other Asian boards was an important factor in Pakistan's cricketing isolation. It was, however, one in a number of issues that led to a bigger breakdown in relations between Indian and Pakistani cricket.

THE POINT OF NO RETURN

In 2014, the BJP led by Narendra Modi, the hard-line Hindu leader, won the Indian national elections. A man who had ruled the state of Gujarat when more than a thousand people—mostly Muslims—were killed in religious riots in 2002 and whose political education was shaped by Hindu nationalists was now Prime Minister. Modi's new vision for India, the coming to fruition of the Hindutva project, the effect of the Mumbai attacks, a burgeoning and increasingly nationalistic media, and rampant commercialization, all combined to produce an environment that was not only not conducive for better India–Pakistan cricketing relations but was in fact progressively hostile to any improvements. Pakistan's own policies towards India during this period added to creating an antagonistic environment.

Modi's initial overtures to Pakistan—Prime Minister Nawaz Sharif was invited and ended up attending Modi's swearing in[27] and Modi made a surprise visit to meet Sharif in Lahore in December 2015 on his way back from Afghanistan[28]—led to a warming in relations. But almost immediately after the Sharif-Modi meeting at the end of 2015, a suspected Pakistan-based terrorist group attacked an Indian air base in Pathankot, Punjab, killing seven soldiers. The better relations to that point led to a decision by both countries to collaborate on a joint investigation of the attack.[29] The attack though was followed in July 2016 by the killing of the pro-separatist Kashmiri leader Burhan Wani[30] in a gunfight with the Indian Army, leading to days of deadly violence in Kashmir[31] and a sharp deterioration in Indo-Pak relations.[32] In September 2016, militants crossed the Line of Control and attacked an army base in Indian-administered Kashmir, killing seventeen soldiers. This triggered a crisis episode for India and Pakistan and eventually resulted in limited cross-border retaliatory strikes by India, which the Indian Army described as 'surgical strikes.'[33]

The September 2016 attack on the Indian Army base in Indian-Administered Kashmir signals a watershed in India's policy towards Pakistan. Departing from India's past strategic restraint, Modi ordered strikes across the Line of Control in response to the attack. There were other escalations as well, particularly along the Line of Control where a heavy Indian counter-bombardment policy was being implemented. Since the Ceasefire Agreement 2003, from 2016 onwards there has been a major increase in violations—152 incidents in 2015; 3,000 in 2017; and more than 1,000 in the first half of

2018.[34] Yusuf argues that these endemic but lower intensity skirmishes had a snowballing effect because of the newly burgeoning media, 'unlike the pre-2003 period, the mushrooming of news media in both countries has meant that today's incidents in Kashmir create media frenzies, forcing bellicose rhetoric and raising tensions.'[35] The Indian leadership was also increasingly aligned to loud public posturing, aimed at gaining domestic political mileage from these incidents.[36]

People-to-people contacts suffered as well. Following the uproar after the army base attack in Kashmir, the Indian Motion Picture Producers Association (IMPPA) decided to ban all Pakistani actors, actresses, and technicians working in India.[37] The Pakistani government responded with a blanket ban on all Indian television and radio programming in Pakistan. At the time there was some opposition to the breaking of cultural links;[38] however, as relations continued to deteriorate, attitudes hardened and the space for dissent against Modi's newly aggressive nationalist stance declined dramatically.

In cricketing terms, the BCCI ruled out the possibility of reviving bilateral cricket ties with Pakistan in the near future.[39] The BCCI also asked the ICC not to group Indian and Pakistan cricket teams together in international tournaments, keeping in mind border tensions between the two countries. Despite these setbacks the PCB continued to try for a resumption of bilateral cricketing relations. The inability to play at home because of security concerns and India's reluctance to play against Pakistan had caused immense financial strain on the PCB. A resumption in Indo-Pak matches would have reversed this. For Shaharyar Khan, who had been reappointed as chairman of the PCB in 2014, cricket was also a way to break the downward spiral in relations. But he found that in his second term the Indian board was far more reluctant to push the government for a resumption.

This is not unexpected. The attacks in Mumbai have often been described as India's 9/11[40] in terms of the effect they had on the psyche of the Indian public. The terrorist assault was a brazen attack on India's commer ial and entertainment hub in which 165 people were killed and over 300 injured. Moreover, there was no doubt in Indian society that the perpetrators were Pakistan-based militants and India blamed the Pakistani state for having directed the attacks.[41] The episode also represented a devastating failure of India's intelligence and security services. Public attitudes towards Pakistan changed dramatically following the Mumbai attack in 2008. The Indian media and public demanded a strong response. Yusuf argues that the potency of Mumbai in India dwarfed what Kargil managed in the years after that episode.[42] He is also right in highlighting that a whole generation of young Indians consider Pakistan as a nuisance. Pakistan equalled Mumbai in their minds. This was not the Partition generation that had known the 'other' and had experienced a shared history, culture, and legacy. This was a generation that saw each other as enemies, ill-disposed towards each another, different from each another. There would be little if any support for reaching out to Pakistan. All this while the Hindutva project was contributing to new aggressive nationalism which found its ideal home under Modi's new regime. Soon after the attack on the army camp in 2016, it appears that Narendra Modi's government, building on the growing anti-Pakistan sentiment, put in place a policy to isolate Pakistan in every possible sphere—political, economic, and cultural. In the immediate aftermath of the attack Modi stated at a rally in India: 'Let the terrorists make no mistake, India will never forget ... We will leave no stone unturned to isolate Pakistan in the world.'[43]

In fact, despite the initial warming of relations between Prime Ministers Nawaz Sharif and Narendra Modi, the signs for better relations were already unfavourable. Modi had appointed traditional hardliners on Pakistan to important positions in his cabinet and associated institutions in order to appease his right-wing constituency and his own ideological convictions. The historian Ramchandra Guha and Nobel Laureate Amartya Sen have both been critical of the BJP government for placing loyalists and Hindu hardliners at the head of major educational and cultural institutions.[44] Both have subsequently been pressurized out of positions in Indian educational institutions.[45] Sen was scathing in his criticism of what he calls 'extraordinarily large' interference of the government in academia. 'Nothing in this scale of interference has happened before. Every institution where the government has a formal role is being converted into where the government has a substantive role,' he alleged.[46] With hardliners dominating these institutions, there was little chance or interest of any compromise with Pakistan in political, economic, or cultural spheres. It was also the case that India did not need to compromise; such was the power disparity between the two countries—economically, politically, and militarily.[47]

The BCCI was no exception. McDonald writes, the Hindu nationalist influence was increasingly evident in cricket through, amongst other things, the occupying of key administrative posts by supporters of Hindutva ideology.[48] In 2016, Anurag Thakur was president of the board having earlier been the secretary. Thakur was a BJP MP and a serving member of the Indian Territorial Army[49] while heading the BCCI. An indication of the kind of views espoused by him can be gauged from his pronouncements at an election rally in 2020. In a widely circulated video of the rally, Thakur is seen leading the cheer by saying '*desh ke gaddaron ko*' after which the crowd adds a rejoinder '*goli maro salon ko*' (translated as shoot the traitors)—a slogan that has often been used in pro-BJP and anti-Citizenship Amendment Act (CAA) gatherings.[50]

Under new leadership the Indian board fell in line with Modi's policy. The BCCI had in 2014 already engineered a highly contentious and controversial change in the governance of the ICC by concentrating power and finances in the hands of the three richest boards—India, Australia, and England[51]— known as the 'Big 3.' The wildly profitable Indian Premier League had swelled the board's finances immeasurably. Alongside being the largest market for cricket in the world, the BCCI's economic heft has distorted cricket's finances to such an extent that the health of other boards is increasingly determined by how often their team played India. Opposition to the 'Big 3' initially came from South Africa, Sri Lanka, and Pakistan. But financial incentives broke down the resistance. Pakistan was the only country to resist, even turning down an offer of three series against India in eight years.[52] Eventually, a change in the PCB regime and a promise of six series against India between 2015 and 2023, four to be hosted by Pakistan, led to Pakistan dropping their opposition.[53] In reality, though, Pakistan and India did not play a single series, with India consistently arguing that bilateral series were dependent on governmental permission which was not forthcoming. Unlike in 2003, the Indian board, far from being fiscally less secure, was now the financial powerhouse of world cricket. Pakistan continued attempting to persuade the BCCI to honour its commitment with Shaharyar Khan holding several meetings with his Indian counterparts:

> I found the Indian board no longer interested in pushing their government to play Pakistan in bilateral matches. They had signed an MOU in 2014 to play Pakistan in six series in the 2015–2023 Future Tours Programme, but all were subject to clearance from New Delhi. We met on several occasions with our BCCI counterparts and on every occasion, the answer was the same 'we need government clearance.' Eventually, we travelled to Mumbai in 2017 to hammer home a series to be played in the UAE. The meeting never happened because the Shiv Sena stormed the venue of the meeting shouting slogans against Pakistan. We were left high and dry and only received a letter of apology from the BCCI when we had arrived back in Lahore. It was the last straw for many Pakistani's because they felt we should no longer plead with the Indians to play cricket if they were so unwilling to do so.

Ultimately, the Big 3 model itself was revoked[54] and Pakistan subsequently took the BCCI to court for not honouring the MOU; the case was settled in favour of India.[55]

While the decision to form the Big 3 may have been commercially driven, it allowed the BCCI to isolate Pakistan by demoting them from top-tier decision making. The 'exclusion' of Pakistani players from the IPL was another way of ensuring Pakistan's continued separation. While no ban was put in place officially, the IPL teams refrained themselves from buying any Pakistani cricket players during the 2009 auction. None of Pakistan's eleven players were picked up by any of the IPL teams despite Pakistan being the T20 world champions at the time.[56] The Pakistani players felt this to have been a deliberate and humiliating snub. There were strong rumours that the franchises were pressurized by the BCCI and the Government of India not to pick Pakistanis. At the time a few IPL team owners, most prominently the film star Shahrukh Khan, raised concerns about the 'ban' on Pakistani players. However, with Shahrukh Khan being a Muslim, his comments in favour of Pakistani players led to a strong backlash by Hindu fanatics who subsequently launched a boycott of his latest film.[57]

Pakistan had already become the pariah of international cricket following the attack on the Sri Lankan cricket team in 2009. They also lost World Cup hosting rights. This hit their finances dramatically. An Indo-Pak series would have revived the PCB's sinking financial position immeasurably. Not playing—as India ensured—became another method by which to sanction, punish, and isolate Pakistan. Moreover, this was a time when India increasingly began to try and downgrade the traditional Indo-Pak rivalry, pushing instead the importance of their encounters with Australia and England.

Ehsan Mani, a former chairman of the ICC and chairman of the PCB (4 September 2018–26 August 2021), spoke to me of problems with the politicization of the BCCI, 'in the past we were able to put aside our political differences; now the BCCI is deeply influenced by the political situation.' He also mentioned that ideological issues had become increasingly ingrained in the BCCI and that on one occasion a senior English board official had confided in Mani about the deep hatred of Muslims that an Indian board official had displayed in a private conversation. Mani believes that these factors have led to the BCCI attempting to isolate Pakistan and that has included India's attempts to influence Pakistan's relations with other South Asian countries, to which I shall now turn.

BANGLADESH, SRI LANKA, AND AFGHANISTAN

Pakistan's cricketing relations with the other South Asian nations have generally been mutually favourable. Pakistan supported both Sri Lanka's and

Bangladesh's applications for full member status to the ICC. However, more recently the erosion of the Asian bloc and political pressures have adversely influenced these relations.

– Sri Lanka –

Pakistan and Sri Lanka have had deep cricketing ties. A.H. Kardar, as the BCCP's representative to the ICC between 1972 and 1977, was well-known for his unstinting support of Sri Lanka's push for full status. In 1974, Kardar had 'thumped on the table' while making an impassioned plea for Sri Lanka's admittance only for England and Australia to use their veto and deny Sri Lanka.[58] Kardar nevertheless initiated a trophy between the two Under-19 teams and offered scholarships to Sri Lankan coaches to improve their knowledge by working with Pakistani counterparts. The good rapport continued when Pakistan became the first country to invite Sri Lanka for a bilateral series in 1981 after they were finally granted Test status. Nine of Sri Lanka's first twenty-one Tests were against Pakistan. By 1996, more than a quarter of their Tests and of their ODIs had been against Pakistan; no team had played them more often.[59]

Relations were helped by the fact that Pakistan's political rapport with the Sri Lankan government has always been strong. Pakistan provided military support to the Sri Lankan government during the government's fight with the Liberation Tigers of Tamil Eelam (LTTE):

> During a five day visit to Sri Lanka in December 1985, President Zia-ul-Haq was categoric about Pakistan's support for Sri Lanka's war against 'terrorism' and he called upon neighbours and friends of Sri Lanka to give maximum support to preserve its unity and integrity.[60]

In 2006, as the Sri Lankan government under President Mahinda Rajapaksa made its push against the LTTE, the Pakistan Air Force provided technical and strategic advice.[61] At the time they were being advised by Colonel Wali Mohammad, a former senior ISI officer who had been posted as Pakistan's High Commissioner to Colombo. In fact, he was thought to have been the target of a massive bomb blast in Colombo because of the support Pakistan was providing the Sri Lankan government.[62] In contrast, India's relations with Sri Lanka have frequently been uneasy considering that India has a sizeable Tamil population in South India and India's advocacy of the Tamils in Sri Lanka has often been perceived as interference in Sri Lanka's internal affairs. Pakistan's growing intelligence and military cooperation would undoubtedly have been a point of unease for India.

In 1986, when poor umpiring threatened to sour relations with the Pakistan players threatening to return home, General Zia ordered the team to complete the tour.[63] In 1996, the Indo-Pak goodwill match in Colombo, two weeks after the central bank had been bombed, put to rest security fears and led to Sri Lanka receiving points for the forfeited games. Subsequently, Sri Lanka received massive support when they won the World Cup in Lahore against Australia. The Sri Lankan board and press appear very cognizant of the support they received from Pakistan during their own troubled times.[64]

Since then relations have remained excellent, even after the crumbling of the strong Asian bloc and despite the attack on the Sri Lankan team in 2009. In May 2019, a month after the Easter bombings in Sri Lanka which left 250 dead, an Under-19 Pakistan team toured Sri Lanka to demonstrate their solidarity with the country. Sri Lanka returned the favour when they became the first international country to tour Pakistan for a Test series in ten years in September 2019. The thunderous welcome received by the Sri Lankans in Pakistan was testament to the appreciation of the Pakistani public for the immense support shown by Sri Lanka to Pakistan cricket. The fact that it was Sri Lanka that took the first step back to Pakistan, after its team was targeted in a terrorist attack ten years ago, was deeply symbolic.

The tour was not without drama though. Days before the Sri Lankan team was due to arrive in Pakistan, the tour was put into jeopardy by a security alert issued by the Sri Lankan Prime Minister's Office.[65] There were newspaper reports that the 'terror threat' was a fake that had been issued by India in order to sabotage the tour—when discovered, it was disregarded.[66] The tour went ahead backed by the newly elected Prime Minister Gotabaya Rajapaksa. Rajapaksa was Sri Lanka's all-powerful defence secretary when his brother Mahinda Rajapaksa was the country's president between 2005 to 2015. It was during this period that the Rajapaksa brothers worked closely with Pakistan against the Tamil insurgency. The strong backing of the government and the Sri Lankan board for the tour to Pakistan was likely made possible by the election of Rajapaksa. In contrast, his predecessor Ranil Wickremesinghe was considered close to India and had much less friendly relations with Pakistan and had, for example, joined India's boycott of the SAARC summit that was to be held in Pakistan in 2016.[67] There was however a recognition in the Sri Lankan press that Sri Lanka's tour to Pakistan may have repercussions. *The Daily News* in Sri Lanka noted that:

> There could also be a downside to Sri Lanka's tour to Pakistan as it may
> not have pleased India so much for if the tour is successful it could lead to
> breaking the ice and paving the way for future international tours to Pakistan.
> Sri Lanka Cricket must try to ensure that by sending a team to Pakistan, they
> have not antagonized India in any way for it is the tours that India makes to
> this country that are money-spinners not so much the others.[68]

The tour represented the historic return of Test cricket in Pakistan and was a
major public relations success for Pakistan. It was also marked by unwavering
Sri Lankan governmental and board support highlighting the strength of
cricketing ties between Pakistan and Sri Lanka.

– Bangladesh –

Bangladesh's cricketing relations with Pakistan—like its political relations—
are more complicated. After the secession of East Pakistan and the creation
of Bangladesh, Pakistan did not play in the former East Pakistan until 1979–
80 when a tour was abandoned midway because of crowd disturbances.[69]
The memories of the 'second Partition' remained high. However, the
BCCP supported Bangladesh's affiliate status in the 1970s[70] and then its
application for full membership which was granted in 2000.[71] By the mid-
1980s, relations between the countries had stabilized on the back of both
countries having military led governments—Ziaul Haq in Pakistan and
Hussein Mohammad Ershad in Bangladesh. In 1986, Pakistan played the
first ever ODI against Bangladesh in Colombo as part of the Asia Cup. In
the 2003–04 season, the Patron's Trophy—the premier four-day tournament
for departments—was expanded from 12 to 13 sides; the 13th team that
season was Bangladesh A.[72]

From the 1980s till the mid-1990s, Pakistani cricketers received
considerable support in Bangladesh. The Pakistan team had a number of
notable cricketers who had international appeal. The team itself was one of
the best in the world between the mid-1980s and the mid-1990s, often vying
with the West Indies for the top spot. A fledgling Bangladesh was no match
and India was routinely defeated. Pakistan was also the only 'Muslim' team
in the international game—and despite the 1971 war there were historical
and religious links between the two countries. Invariably in India–Pakistan
matches held in Bangladesh, crowd support would skew in favour of Pakistan:

> Pakistan team's charisma under Imran Khan's flamboyant personality, the
> team's high success rate against India, particularly in Sharjah, and their

subsequent World Cup victory played a major role in making the majority of Bangladeshis aggressive Pakistan fans.[73]

Things gradually changed in the mid-1990s when a post-1971 generation grew up and the national team began to meet with more success and Bangladeshi cricketers emerged as world class cricketers themselves. There was also an evening out of support for India and Pakistan.[74] This was related to a decline in the Pakistani team, a concomitant rise in India, and in particular the emergence and popularity of the Indian Bengali cricketer Saurav Ganguly as well as Sachin Tendulkar, considered by many to be one of the greatest batsmen of all time. There were also important political and economic reasons. While India and particularly Bangladesh have both seen considerable improvements in their social and economic conditions, Pakistan's instability and terrorism-related problems have halted growth and poverty reduction.[75] In the same way that Indian Muslims no longer saw Pakistan as a success, Bangladeshis now saw India and their own country as more advanced than Pakistan.

Politically, too, Bangladesh's relations with Pakistan have deteriorated over the last decade, and as with India this has also affected their cricketing relations. From 2008, Bangladesh has been governed by the Awami League. Hewitt points out that very few post-colonial states have disintegrated, and yet this is precisely what happened in the case of Pakistan which lost 32 per cent of its land and 56 per cent of its population in 1971.[76] According to Ahmed and Zahoor, this fact still shapes security and foreign policy approaches in Pakistan.[77] Given these deep fissures, Islamabad finds it difficult to establish good relations with the Awami League, a Bangladeshi political party that led the Liberation War of Bangladesh in 1971 with the support of Pakistan's traditional rival, India. As a result, tensions with Pakistan increase significantly when the Awami League holds office. From the early days of India's initial support to the Awami League-led freedom struggle in 1971, Islamabad has seen the party as hostile while New Delhi has viewed the party as its ally. Prime Minister Sheikh Hasina, the daughter of Sheikh Mujibur Rahman who was the driving force behind the independence of Bangladesh, has always maintained a fiercely anti-Pakistan, pro-India stance. In the decade since she has ruled starting in 2009, Pakistan-Bangladesh relations have deteriorated significantly. In 2010, Bangladesh re-established a war crimes tribunal for crimes committed during the 1971 war of independence. While criticized by Western and Muslim nations alike, the tribunal has faced no real hurdle to its operations because of wide backing in Bangladesh and from India. India has used the trials in Bangladesh to pursue its own strategic goal of isolating Pakistan in South Asia.[78] The Awami League's overt criticism of Pakistan and its closeness to New Delhi adds to the already aggravated relationship between Bangladesh and Pakistan.[79] There have followed attacks on the Pakistan High Commission, tit for tat withdrawal of diplomats, deportations, talk of severing ties, mistreatment of diplomats, suspension of academic exchanges, and political dialogue broken off at official and non-official levels. An informal meeting of diplomats occurred in 2006 and the last official visit by a head of state was in 2002. In 2016, Bangladesh followed India in pulling out of the SAARC summit that was to be held in Pakistan.

In such a poisoned atmosphere, it is surprising that the PCB has managed amicable relations with their Bangladeshi counterparts. Tours by Pakistan to Bangladesh have continued in 2011 and 2015 and Pakistan has hosted a tour by the women's team as well as the Under-19 team. But the Bangladesh Cricket Board (BCB), because of its political affiliation and financial dependence, allied themselves firmly with India since the collapse of the Asian bloc and there has been a reluctance to tour Pakistan. For Pakistan this has been problematic as the PCB had hoped that either Sri Lanka or Bangladesh would be the countries to break the international boycott of playing cricket in Pakistan.

The Bangladeshi board, having made commitments to tour in 2012 and in 2017, postponed both tours at the last minute. In 2012, a court order in Dhaka embargoed the tour over security issues.[80] The PCB reacted furiously, having made arrangements for the tour and over what it felt would have been a significant step towards the return of cricket to Pakistan. The chairman of the PCB, Zaka Ashraf, angrily stated that Pakistan would 'reconsider' its bilateral ties with Bangladesh after the BCB, once again, backed down from going ahead with the tour. Pakistan, he said, will not sacrifice their interests for those who do not honour their words.[81] Ashraf then petulantly proceeded, at the last minute, to pull Pakistani players out of the Bangladesh Premier League, causing more bad blood.[82] In 2017, in another bid to bring international cricket back to the country, the PCB had extended an invitation to their counterparts in the Bangladesh board after they had successfully hosted the Pakistan Super League final in Lahore. Again, the BCB vacillated, prompting the PCB chairman Shaharyar Khan to state: 'We want to host Bangladesh but its chances are not bright. Some of our friends think they may tour but I feel they will not because of political concerns more than security concerns.' They ultimately declined.[83]

Therefore, in contrast to Sri Lanka, relations with Bangladesh have been more fraught and less supportive of Pakistan. Historical political differences have been a constant hurdle and recent diplomatic skirmishes and India's influence have poisoned the atmosphere further. The BCB has been influenced and constrained by the government's overall anti-Pakistan stance and its lack of support for the return of cricket to Pakistan stands in stark contrast to Sri Lanka. Despite this, Pakistan cricketers remain popular in Bangladesh—many have returned to playing in the Bangladesh Premier League and their performances have made them popular with Bangladeshi fans. Indian players do not play in foreign leagues and therefore are in some ways more distant. The bond of religion remains, though a new generation of Bangladeshis have grown up with far fewer attachments with Pakistan, seeing it instead as an unfriendly nation.

There are signs of better cricketing ties as well as better political relations. In February 2020, Bangladesh, after weeks of hesitancy, agreed on a full tour of Pakistan. The tour came in the wake of the trouble-free Sri Lankan visit earlier in the year. The Bangladesh team were received warmly and again the tour proceeded without any untoward incidents. Both boards handled the situation tactfully, avoiding the flare ups of the past. Political relations between Pakistan and Bangladesh have also seen a recent uptick with quiet diplomacy being followed by Prime Minister Imran Khan phoning his Bangladeshi counterpart Sheikh Hasina and extending an invitation to visit Pakistan. There have been statements about a commitment to strengthening bilateral ties. The thaw in relations is likely driven by the fact that India's recent moves against its Muslim minority have caused friction in the India-Bangladesh relationship, thus allowing Pakistan a way to heal its own diplomatic bonds with Bangladesh.

– Afghanistan –

If cricketing relations with Bangladesh are reflective of the current state of its political relations with Pakistan, Afghanistan provides an even more glaring example of how changing foreign relations in South Asia have crept into changing cricketing ties.

Although religious, ethnic, economic, and cultural ties between Afghanistan and Pakistan run deep and wide, the two countries have frequently been at odds with one another. The Afghan government never accepted the 19th century Anglo-Afghan treaties which now demarcate its boundaries with Pakistan. This included the Durand Line which divided the Pashtun tribes between Afghanistan and what was then British India.[84] The division of the Pashtuns has prompted successive Afghan governments into supporting Pashtun autonomy across borders, causing separatist problems for

Pakistan. Afghanistan was the only country to vote against Pakistan's entry to the United Nations and in 1955 diplomatic ties were severed following the ransacking of the Pakistan Embassy in Kabul and again in 1961 when the Pakistan Army had to repel major Afghan incursions at Bajaur.[85] During the Cold War, Afghanistan became a battleground in the global conflict between the Soviet Union and United States, with Pakistan as a key US ally supporting the anti-Soviet Mujahideen. During the Afghan war, Pakistan hosted over 3 million refugees and over a million remain in Pakistan.[86]

Following the Soviet withdrawal, Pakistan's support for the Taliban further poisoned relations with Afghanistan. Since US forces removed the Taliban with Pakistan's reluctant assistance, Afghanistan adopted a strongly anti-Pakistan foreign policy while building on strong ties with India. Pakistan's continued concerns over a hostile western neighbour that is closely allied to India have continued to create an unreceptive environment between the two countries. Unsurprisingly, the two neighbours routinely accuse each other of cross-border infiltration and supporting and providing sanctuaries to militant groups. The Pakistan narrative is one of ungrateful Afghans. The Afghan one is of Pakistan using Afghanistan for its own ends. India has used the mistrust, strengthening its own relations with Afghanistan while working to isolate Pakistan. Afghan cricket has become a new arena of struggle—a pawn in the Indo-Pak conflict and nowhere do the changing political contours of South Asia make their presence felt as clearly as Afghanistan-Pakistan cricketing relations.

Afghanistan does not have the same history with cricket that India, Pakistan, Bangladesh, and Sri Lanka do, possibly because British maintained less of a presence in Afghanistan seeing it more as a 'buffer' state between the British and Russian empires. While cricket has been played in Afghanistan since the 19th century, its recent flourishing was really born of the Soviet occupation of Afghanistan (1979–1989). This saw up to 2 million Afghan refugees stream into Pakistan and it is in the refugee camps of Pakistan that Afghans had their first exposure to cricket.[87] In fact, many of the current Afghan players are a product of this route. The Afghan captain, Gulbadin Naib, stated prior to the Afghan-Pakistan match in the 2019 World Cup: 'If you look at our cricket, we learnt a lot of cricket in Pakistan and we also played cricket in Pakistan.'[88] Two of Afghanistan's best players—Mohammad Nabi and Rashid Khan—started playing in Peshawar. Some even played for domestic Pakistani teams. The Afghanistan Cricket Board's interim CEO Asadullah Khan is reported to have said in an interview: 'I played my initial cricket in Pakistan and acknowledge the overwhelming support of the neighbouring country.'[89] In the developmental phase of Afghanistan cricket, the PCB offered Afghan cricket considerable support by providing equipment and playing opportunities. Three former Pakistan cricketers—Kabir Khan, Rashid Latif, and Inzamam-ul-Haq—have played key roles in the development of cricket in Afghanistan as coaches over the past decade. Allah Dad Noori, one of the pioneers of Afghan cricket in the 1990s, said:

> The PCB invited us to Pakistan and organised matches and free stay for us in various cities. Later, we also applied on PCB's advice for ACC and ICC affiliation. In fact, the PCB provided us with reference for those applications.[90]

The PCB then accommodated them in their domestic tournament. Early training camps occurred in Karachi, Lahore, and Peshawar in 2008 prior to Afghanistan acquiring ODI status in 2010. In 2011, Afghanistan were invited to play in Pakistan's domestic T20 tournament. The Afghan players were allowed to use the national cricket academy training facilities in 2013, normally reserved for Pakistan national players and since 2014 Pakistan has been hosting young Afghans to be coached in Lahore. The Afghan Under-19 team prepared for the World Cup in Lahore.[91] In 2015, they shifted their home base from Sharjah to India.

From 2015, as India's influence in Afghanistan grew politically and economically, so too did its involvement and investment in Afghan cricket. India has contributed significantly, from financial assistance to Afghan players and funding the construction of a stadium in Kandahar to providing Afghanistan with a home stadium on the outskirts of New Delhi.[92] In June 2018, less than a year after they were awarded full member status, Afghanistan played their first Test match against India. But as Sidharth Monga points out, cricket co-operation from India came at the cost of culling of ties with Pakistan.[93] Afghan players were asked to stop living and playing in Pakistan;[94] they were stopped from giving Pakistan too much credit for their development as cricketers or talking about their time in Pakistan. They were even asked not to speak Urdu in press conferences anymore, even though some speak Urdu more fluently than Pushto, their mother tongue. Players were told to give credit to India or to speak well of India in interviews. From lavishly praising Pakistan for the support they had received over the course of more than a decade, there was a downplaying of Pakistan's contribution. On the eve of their first test match in India, Afghanistan Cricket Board (ACB) CEO Shafiq Stanikzai stated that Afghanistan owed a huge debt of gratitude to the BCCI and that India had played a bigger role in the rapid rise of the game in Afghanistan, 'BCCI's role has really been immense. Since we moved to India the team has done well. The conditions in India are suiting the team quite well. The support we receive from BCCI has been instrumental.'[95]

In fact, the PCB had hoped Afghanistan would play Pakistan in its debut Test but relations between the countries were so poor, especially in comparison to those between India and Afghanistan, that the plan fell through. Shaharyar Khan relates that in June 2017, the PCB had managed to repair relations with the ACB to the extent that the two boards had agreed to play Afghanistan's first Test against Pakistan. This would follow Pakistan travelling to Afghanistan for a first T20 match in Kabul. After a successful meeting in Lahore, the CEO of the ACB had stated that politics should be kept separate from sport and preparations for the tour would begin. Unfortunately, the following day a bomb blast occurred in Kabul. The Afghan government immediately blamed Pakistan. The ACB, which is closely connected with the ruling government, issued an unusually harsh statement:

> The ACB hereby cancel all kinds of cricket matches and initial mutual relationship agreement with the Pakistan Cricket Board. No agreement of friendly matches and mutual relationship agreement is possible with a country where terrorists are housed and provided safe havens.[96]

The favouring of India while downplaying Pakistan's contributions has infuriated Pakistan and played into the narrative of 'ungrateful Afghans who learnt the game from us but give credit to India.' Pakistanis and the PCB feel betrayed and it shows in the atmosphere of the Pakistan-Afghanistan matches which have an edgy, nasty feel to them. This has spread to the fans and the 2019 World Cup encounter in England was marred by fighting between rival fans.[97]

Both India and Pakistan have contributed immensely to the progress of cricket in Afghanistan, helping them to become the newest member of the ICC. Unfortunately, political issues have bedevilled cricketing relations as well and both Pakistan and India have sought to use Afghanistan for their own purposes. The Indian government's influence over Afghanistan, including the ACB, has meant that the ACB has been loath to support Pakistan cricket even at a time of isolation. Pakistan's own policies towards Afghanistan have created such opposition towards the country that a more favourable policy towards Pakistan has not been contemplated. There was some cause for optimism in 2020 when Prime Minister Imran Khan visited Kabul in 2020. His first visit since forming government in 2018 led to a meeting with the Afghan cricket team and an invitation to tour Pakistan. Until Khan's recent visit ties have been severed since the 2017 break in relations. Unfortunately, the withdrawal of US troops from Afghanistan and the rapid advance of the Taliban have again led to a significant spike in Afghanistan-Pakistan tensions.

THE FUTURE OF SOUTH ASIAN RELATIONS

The previous section lays out Pakistan's relations with other South Asian cricketing countries. India's position as the regional superpower—economically, militarily, and in cricketing terms—gives it enormous clout over its smaller counterparts in South Asia. While Sri Lanka's relations have remained strong and largely insulated from India's growing influence because of pre-existing positive political linkages, the same cannot be said of Afghanistan and Bangladesh. In the case of the latter two countries, poor political relations with Pakistan and better relations with India have prevented the Afghan and Bangladeshi boards playing a more supportive role vis-à-vis Pakistan. Bangladesh and Sri Lanka's recent tours to Pakistan may help Bangladesh, in particular, to adopt a more neutral stance in India's push to isolate Pakistan.

What would help most would be a normalization of Indo-Pak relations. Unfortunately, far from normalization, the deterioration in relations with India has not been stemmed. On 14 February 2019, a suicide bomber killed forty-six paramilitary police in Pulwama in Indian-administered Kashmir. The Pakistan-based militant group Jaish-e-Mohammed (JeM) claimed responsibility.[98] India undertook air strikes on an alleged JeM training camp in Balakot, the first time it has struck inside Pakistan since the 1971 war. Pakistan responded by downing an Indian fighter jet and capturing a pilot. Eventually, an unexpected chain of events that included the unconditional release of the Indian pilot by Pakistan as well as Prime Minister Imran Khan's emotional peace overture prevented the escalation and brought a quick-fix peace settlement in the world's most militarized flashpoint.[99]

Despite the uneasy peace that followed, the skirmish caused more bad blood and a reinforcement of negative attitudes. The day after the Pulwama attack, India revoked Pakistan's Most Favoured Nation (MFN) trading status, raised customs duties to 200 per cent, and reiterated its vow to isolate Pakistan in the international community.[100] There were more condemnations from Bollywood.[101] The Indian cricket team donned military caps in their match against Australia in solidarity with the armed forces and to pay homage to the 'martyrs of Pulwama.' The Indian cricketers would go on to donate their entire match fees to the National Defence Fund. The BCCI donated the entire budget of the IPL opening ceremony for the benefit of the families of those killed in the terrorist attack.[102] A media-inspired nationalistic frenzy took hold with anti-Pakistan sentiment being a focus.

In a continued push for Pakistan's isolation, the BCCI called on the 'cricketing community to sever ties with countries from which terrorism emanates' and to have Pakistan banned from the 2019 World Cup altogether.[103] Several former Indian cricketers called for India to forfeit the match rather than play Pakistan and some current players also allegedly stated that they did not want to play Pakistan.[104] Eventually, the match would go ahead with no untoward animosity or incident between players or fans. Earlier, an Indian event management company—IMG Reliance—pulled out of its deal as official producer of Pakistan T20 cricket league, putting the broadcasting of the tournament in doubt.[105] The official broadcaster of the PSL in India announced that it would not show the matches, and digital coverage of the tournament was also blocked in the country.[106] Pakistan responded by blocking the broadcast of the IPL in Pakistan[107] so that fans on either side of the border have even less chance of sharing experiences. The pettiness of the exchanges highlighted how far relations had deteriorated.

Nevertheless, the Pulwama attack and Modi's bellicose response helped him to a thumping electoral win in 2019. However, any thought that this may moderate Modi's policies ended when, in August 2019, following a deployment of tens of thousands of additional troops and paramilitary forces to the region, the Indian government revoked Article 370[108] of the Indian constitution, thereby removing the special status[109] of Indian-administered Kashmir. Since then, Kashmir remains under lockdown, with internet and phone services intermittently cut-off and thousands of people detained.[110] This has further inflamed relations with Pakistan, leading Pakistan to downgrade diplomatic ties, expel the Indian ambassador, and suspend bilateral trade.[111] In his 2019 address to the UN, Prime Minister Imran Khan expressed his fear of an uncontrolled escalation over Kashmir:

> I fear there will be a massacre and things will start to go out of control ... My main reason for coming here was to meet world leaders at the UN and speak about this. We are heading for a potential disaster of proportions that no one here realises ... It is the only time since the Cuban crisis that two nuclear-armed countries are coming face to face. We did come face to face in February.[112]

On the coattails of the Kashmir intervention was the passing of the Citizenship Amendment Act (CAA) by the Indian parliament. The CAA ensures that Hindus, Sikhs, Jains, Buddhists, Parsis, or Jains facing persecution in neighbouring countries will be eligible for citizenship in India and not treated as illegal migrants while Muslims will be excluded. Critics argue that the law violates the secular principles of citizenship in India. The CAA and the allied National Registration of Citizens (NRC) have triggered fears of marginalization and disenfranchisement among India's Muslim minority, who form nearly 15 per cent of the country's 1.3 billion population.[113] The ongoing siege in Kashmir is also a critical part of this equation. Many see the CAA and NRC as an unacceptable attempt by the Indian Prime Minister Narendra Modi and his BJP government to implement their Hindutva [Hindu nationalist] agenda and redefine India as a purely Hindu country.

In an environment of fear and intolerance, signs of dissent against the government's policies have become increasingly rare. The police have truncheoned, detained, and shot dead protesters. Many more are intimidated and threatened by BJP ministers and their extremist allies.[114] If we return to the telegram that was sent jointly by the Indian captain Mansur Ali Khan Pataudi and the Pakistani captain Hanif Mohammed at the outbreak of the 1965 war, we recall that the cricketers had 'deeply regretted' the war, that they had found 'unity on the cricket field', and they had 'fervently hoped for an amicable solution.' Even during wartime, the environment then had allowed the two to make such a statement. Today, a similar call would lead to severe repercussions against those making the plea. Sharda Ugra writes of the lack of opposition against the CAA amongst sporting celebrities in India but reminds the reader that while there is very little government influence in funding or operations of the BCCI, there is 'far too much of it in its centres of power.'[115]

In continuation of its policy of appointing proponents of Hindutva to key institutions, the BCCI 'elected' Jay Shah, the son of Home Minister Amit Shah, the man at the centre of the controversial citizenship laws and in public opposition to the protesters, to the post of secretary of the BCCI. This was followed by Arun Singh Dhumal, brother of finance minister and former BCCI secretary Anurag Thakur, being elected treasurer.[116] This makes it extremely unlikely that there would be any opposition from existing cricketers to the government's policies. In fact, in early December 2019, BCCI President Saurav Ganguly's teenage daughter excerpted a few lines from Khushwant Singh's writing on her Instagram post, including these words, 'Every fascist regime needs communities and groups it can demonise in order to thrive.'[117] The post was quickly deleted with Ganguly saying his daughter's account had been hacked and asked the public to 'keep Sana out of it' as she was 'too young a girl to know about anything in politics.'[118] Ugra and Haigh both point to the complete lack of opposition from former and current cricketers to any governmental-led policies—from the CAA to the farmers protests to the controversial resignation of a former Muslim Indian Test cricketer as coach of a regional side following allegations of 'communalism' from another BJP hardliner.[119] In such an environment where dissent is not tolerated,[120] where polarization between India and Pakistan continues unabated, unlike in the past, there can be little expectation of calls for a resumption in cricketing ties from Indian society, including its cricketers. This is unfortunate considering the influence of India's cricketing heroes on their public. India's current struggle with Hindutva-inspired hypernationalism lends itself to anti-Muslim and anti-Pakistan bias which is deepened by a frenzied media.

Despite the paucity of bilateral matches, Pakistan's lack of cricket at home has made crowds desperate for the return of international competition. The growth of coverage of cricket and the telecast of the IPL (until recently) have made Indian cricketers household names in Pakistan. Many current Pakistani cricketers profess their admiration of their Indian counterparts— some go further, barely disguising their awe of international cricket's superstars. Fans are equally effusive in their admiration of Indian cricketers. I recall an image of a young Pakistani fan of the Indian captain Virat Kohli riding his motorbike along the roads of Lahore wearing Kohli's 18 number shirt[121] with the name Kohli emblazoned on it. During the Pakistan Super League T20 competition held in March 2020, banners had been displayed asking the Indian team to visit. In 2020, when Sri Lanka made the first full tour to Pakistan in a decade, a Pakistan cricket fan in Lahore held up a sign, requesting the Indian captain Virat Kohli to come and play cricket in Pakistan.[122] There have been similar calls by former Pakistani cricketers as well.[123] While there were some positive responses on social media, it is unlikely that similar messages of support for the resumption of cricket would be possible in the current climate in India. In Pakistan, there is no societal backlash against calls for a resumption in cricketing relations. It is true that Pakistan needs the resumption much more than India, that Pakistan-based militant groups through activities inside India (Indian-Administered Kashmir, Mumbai, and New Delhi) have caused more chaos in India than India has caused in Pakistan, and that public opinion has not been inflamed against India in the way it has against Pakistan in India.

India's unwillingness to play Pakistan stems from a host of reasons that have been discussed in the chapter and which include the currently parlous state of political relations, the polarization of society (particularly more recently in India), and the magnifying of these differences through the media. India has also used the refusal to play cricket with Pakistan as a political tool in their wider policy to isolate Pakistan. An agreement to resume ties could be construed as a compromise, an act of support for a beleaguered and isolated enemy. A rekindling of the cricketing relationship, if we look at it historically and as this chapter has shown, opens up a potential path to better overall relations. It also creates opportunities for people-to-people contact and, as in the past, for the possibility of breaking down stereotypes that have hardened over the years. Cricket allowed President Ziaul Haq and Prime Minister Rajiv Gandhi the opportunity to meet at a time of high tension. Manmohan Singh and Yousuf Raza Gilani repeated the cricket diplomacy. More importantly, Indo-Pak tours brought the peoples of the two countries together, allowing them to see that they are not as different as their state and media narratives have made them out to be. The heightened emotions surrounding cricketing encounters have even facilitated the softening of hard-line views as in the case of L.K. Advani or when Indian fans in Lahore cheered the arrival of General Pervez Musharraf, the man responsible for the Kargil war. There is also enormous potential of better wider relations when, for example, fans on both sides see opposing players shaking hands before and sharing a light-hearted moment after, as was the case when Virat Kohli joked with a group of Pakistani players after the Champions Trophy which was held in England in 2017. Or when Mahendra Singh Dhoni was photographed holding Pakistan captain Sarfaraz Ahmed's son in his arms before the same match. It seems unlikely that Modi's hard-line government is in favour of a rapprochement with Pakistan and as a result cricketing ties are likely to remain in cold storage.

Chapters 5 and 6 have looked at the changing state of cricketing relations between Pakistan and India from the earliest days to the present. Much more so than in the case of England and Pakistan, India–Pakistan relations and Pakistan's wider relations with other South Asian nations have been affected by the overarching political relations between the countries. Up until the last decade, even when political relations were fraught, cricketing relations between the boards, or the desire for cricketing relations between the fans and players, were strong so that whenever the opportunity arose cricket provided the ice-breaking moment. Unfortunately, the environment has lately turned more hostile and it has affected relations at all levels.

Recently, the Indian cricketer Yuvraj Singh announced his retirement from the game. Tributes poured in from India but also from across the border where he was one of the last generation of Indian cricketers who played in the neighbouring country. An entire cohort of cricketers from India and Pakistan will complete their careers without playing each other in a Test series. The fissure has changed relations between the players. There is still a shared language, a shared cuisine, a shared culture—but the bonhomie of the past has not been allowed to prosper. The players are cordial, but the old ties, the friendships that comes with spending hours and days together during a tour, has gone. India and Pakistan now only play in the occasional international tournament. It has created a physical and emotional distance. This is also influenced by the fact that the Indian cricketers have become the biggest stars of the cricketing world, earning more than their counterparts in Australia and England. The cash-rich, glitzy, Bollywood-style Indian Premier League has made bigger stars of them than the superstars of Indian cinema.

While the Indian cricketers have breached the stratosphere of stardom, their Pakistani counterparts have struggled over the last decade to even, until recently, play in front of their own crowds. Pakistani cricketers, famed in the 1970s, 80s, and 90s for their charisma and panache, are now itinerant travellers. This distance is compounded by the exclusion of the Pakistanis from the Indian Premier League. While cricketers from all over the world—Bangladesh, Sri Lanka, and Afghanistan included—play alongside one another building new friendships, no Pakistani players are allowed to participate in the event. It has created a massive distance, reducing the rapport with their now much richer, much more successful, and much more savvy cousins. Even amongst the junior teams there was a distinct lack of camaraderie in the 2020 World Cup. Two years earlier the Pakistani team had spent a considerable amount of time speaking to the legendary former Indian batsman and now Under-19 coach Rahul Dravid. In the latest edition the teams avoided each other studiously.[124]

What does the future hold for Indo-Pak relations? The history of relations would indicate that a turnaround in relations is possible and can occur with surprising speed, like the flowering of a desert. In the past, India's and Pakistan's shared history and culture have made this possible. History is not easily forgotten, even though, unforgivably, both countries seek to redefine their past through changing their textbooks.[125] Unfortunately, recent history indicates that a resumption of ties is unlikely in the near future. This remains a tragedy for world cricket, and for Indian and Pakistani cricketers and fans all over the world.

I return to Pakistan's first tour of India five years after the ferocity and carnage of Partition wherein lies the cause for optimism and a plea for giving cricket a chance to spark a change. As the Pakistan team made its first trip across a new border to India, they were seen off by the government-run *Pakistan Times* stating:

> Pakistan expects her cricketers to play the game as it should be played, in a
> spirit of friendly competition, without rancour and without ill-will … we hope

... that on the cricket field will be forged new friendly ties that will help to bring the estranged neighbours closer together.[126]

This message of peace was reciprocated across the border in Amritsar where at a reception for the Pakistani cricketers the chairman of the Amritsar municipality spoke of:

the sense of fairplay and sportsmanship that transcend all barriers and helped to strengthen friendships between countries. Indeed, the extension of the spirit of comradeship on the ground to other fields as well would help solve many outstanding issues between the two countries.[127]

7

Conclusion—The Future

I was walking to work on a grey morning in March 2009 when I received a phone call from a friend in the PCB. The Sri Lankan cricket team had been attacked just outside Gaddafi stadium in Lahore. All the attackers had subsequently escaped. There were casualties and the Sri Lankans were being airlifted out. I was shocked though sadly not overly surprised.

Since 2007, militant attacks outside Pakistan's tribal areas had increased several fold. The trigger for an explosive growth had been the siege of the Red Mosque (Lal Masjid) in Islamabad, located in the heart of Islamabad and minutes from the Parliament and the Presidential Palace. The Lal Masjid complex had become a base for militants who began vigilante action against Chinese beauty parlours and CD shops in the locality. Ultimately, after repeated negotiations for surrender had failed, Musharraf ordered Pakistani troops to storm the complex. According to official figures, a total of 154 people, including 19 soldiers, were killed in the ensuing battle, during which militants retreated to the cellars of the building and fought to the death. The raid on the mosque inflamed public opinion and led to a wave of insurgency in the tribal areas, a huge increase in terrorism, and eventually the downfall of the Musharraf administration.[1]

In the years that followed, the Tehrik-i-Taliban Pakistan (TTP), an umbrella organization for militant groups operating in Pakistan's tribal areas, progressively targeted security and law enforcement agencies as well as 'soft targets' such as schools, mosques, universities, hotels, and crowded market places. As the TTP began increasing their influence and control beyond their strongholds in the tribal belt to the settled areas of what was then known as the North-West Frontier Province (NWFP; known as Khyber Pakhtunkhwa since 2010), the Pakistan government 'ceded' control to the militants. In 2009, the government signed a peace treaty with the local Taliban faction allowing them to enforce their interpretation of Islamic law in the district of Swat. In January 2009, there were 1,200 civilians killed and 170 schools destroyed and a vice squad along with its sharia courts went into operation: girls were prevented from attending school (their schools were the first to be demolished), women were no longer to appear in public, and men had to grow beards.[2] Soon, a video of a teenage girl being flogged by a Taliban commander emerged and sparked outrage within Pakistan and around the world as a symbol of a situation that had spiralled out of control. By April 2009, Taliban fighters had swept into the neighbouring Buner district and were portrayed by the international media, with some exaggeration, as being on the verge of a siege of Islamabad. The following month, Pakistan's military forces belatedly launched a campaign to regain control of Swat.[3] A few years later, in Swat in 2012, militants would shoot a 15-year-old school girl on her way to school—that girl was Malala Yousafzai. The year 2008 had seen a surge in violence and 2009 was to become the deadliest year in Pakistan with almost 4,000 attacks and over 12,000 killed and a similar number injured.[4]

For all these reasons, the terrible attack on the Sri Lankan cricket team was not entirely unexpected. But it was also made more possible by the political wrangling that was taking place at the time. Basim Usmani writes that the Supreme Court of Pakistan, widely seen as acting on President Asif Zardari's directions, had disqualified Punjab majority leader Nawaz Sharif and Chief Minister Shahbaz Sharif and declared governor's rule in the province[5] (the governor at the time was considered to be very close to President Zardari). The imposition of governor's rule in Punjab saw a massive reshuffling of the police force and a change of the inspector general. In the ensuing uncertainty the cricketers were left to the mercy of the gunmen. The ineptitude of the Zardari government was symptomatic of a general decline in Pakistan as the country slid towards a virtual civil war. The government's 'opportunism, patrimonialism and corruption' were highlighted by the spectacular unpopularity of those in power.[6] Yet the reaction on many television channels pointed the finger at 'external forces.' A presenter on a popular news channel discussed the incident, "'Which country didn't want the Sri Lankan team to come to Pakistan? Which country was very upset when Sri Lankans decided to come and play in Pakistan?" India, of course. "We don't even need to guess who is behind these attacks," he concluded his argument.'[7] The familiar narrative highlighted Pakistan's continued obsession with being the target of international conspiracies and the inability to consider the role of Muslims in an attack that was clearly aimed at Pakistan more so than on the Sri Lankan team who were 'collateral' damage.

At the time of hearing of the attack, my mind rushed to the fact that the touring team was meant to have been India. Had the Indian team been attacked, South Asia could have been looking at the outbreak of a war between two nuclear armed nations. The Sri Lankans were remarkably supportive. Not a single statement was made against Pakistan despite there having been a clear lapse in security.

The future consequences of the attack took longer to sink in. The Pakistani nation has always shown resilience in the face of adversity; however, an attack on cricket seemed to weigh the nation down immeasurably. In the midst of all the difficulties faced over the years, there was always cricket to take refuge in. Apart from the upsurge in militancy from 2007, Pakistan had seen a decline in several fields where it had once excelled. A once flourishing cinema industry ground to a halt in the 1980s under Zia's draconian censorship. Pakistan's reign in squash ended when the legendary Khans—Jahangir and Jansher—retired in 1993 and 2001, respectively. Pakistan's golden period in hockey had also ended by the mid-1990s. Pakistan's last Olympic medal was in 1992. Politically, the US abandoned Pakistan following the end of the Afghan war, imposing sanctions on its once close ally when it conducted nuclear tests in 1998. The Bank of Credit and Commerce International (BCCI), once a thriving international bank run largely by Pakistanis, was shut down in 1991 following investigations that revealed that it was involved in massive money laundering, financing of terrorist organizations, and other financial crimes.[8] Even the democratic period that followed the death of President Ziaul Haq in 1988 and which started as a period of optimism brought little in terms of peace and prosperity.

But throughout this period, cricket remained the one arena where Pakistan continued to compete globally. Throughout this book I have emphasized that cricket is far from just a sport—it is a shared passion, a force for unity, capable of transcending political, economic, and social differences. In a country with few 'heroes,' cricket consistently announced Pakistan as an independent and successful country to the world. Pakistan needed the likes of Fazal Mahmood, Imran Khan, Wasim Akram, Waqar Younis, Zaheer Abbas, and Javed Miandad to create a vision of a glorious history and a successful nation. In a developing country whose overt global triumphs are few and far between, cricket was the barometer of national self-worth. The attack on cricket and Pakistan's subsequent isolation through the loss of hosting games must be seen in light of the importance of the game to Pakistan's social fabric. The negative impacts occurred at multiple levels.

A Mirror to Society

Pakistan's recent cricketing woes and sequestration have mirrored its wider global isolation. Terrorist activity within the country has prevented investment and has bled the country of its resources. The Pakistan Economic Survey 2018–19 put total losses to the economy as a result of terrorism since 2001 as coming to an overwhelming $126.79 billion.[9] Furthermore, according to Crawford, over 23,000 Pakistani citizens and in excess of 8,000 members of the country's security forces were killed between 2001 and 2018 as a direct result of the 'War on Terror.'[10] Along with woeful governance and increasing corruption, Pakistan, once one of the better off South Asian nations, now finds itself the lowest ranked country in the UN Human Development Index. In 2019, Pakistan's ranking dropped one notch to stand at 152 out of 189 countries. In 2020, it dropped two places further to 154. All its social indicators from life expectancy, literacy, gender equality, and years at school rank below its South Asian counterparts.[11] Added to this is the fact that Pakistan saw a resurgence of polio cases in 2019, making it, along with Afghanistan, the only country yet to wipe out wild poliovirus transmission.[12]

Pakistan cricket has paralleled these wider difficulties. Between 2009 and 2019, for a decade, Pakistan's cricketers were forced to play all their international matches away from home. Most 'home' fixtures have been in the UAE. This has placed a crippling burden on the PCB's finances. Subhan Ahmad, the former COO of the PCB, told me that the board paid $50,000 per day to rent the stadiums in Dubai and Abu Dhabi. In Pakistan they paid only for the electricity. In the UAE, the cost of accommodating teams and officials in hotels (considered amongst the most expensive cities in the world) was prohibitive. In Pakistan, these costs are more than halved. There are also gate receipts. Subhan Ahmad would reveal that in 2017 gate receipts from one final at Gaddafi stadium were greater than all other games held in the UAE.

Pakistan cricket's finances have also been hit by India's refusal to play bilateral series. Not hosting India at all—even in the UAE—has cost Pakistan another $100 million, as broadcasting and other contracts are index-linked to playing them. Add it all up, and the total cost of terrorism and security fears for Pakistan cricket has been $200 million.[13] Dwindling finances and poor security have meant minimal investment in terms of new training facilities and academies, upgrading stadiums, hiring coaches and trainers, and even basic equipment such as quality cricket balls.

But more than the financial costs it is the psychological impact of the loss of cricket at home that has been the most damaging. A generation of cricketers has played their entire careers without a home crowd. Misbah-ul-Haq, Pakistan's most successful Test captain, led his team at home once in his seven-year career as captain. Cricketing achievements were played out in empty stadiums. Without a home season the cricketers were away from friends and family for all but a few months of the year. Mohammad Hafeez, who has been one of those international cricketers who has spent almost his entire career playing out of Pakistan, told me how stressful this was:

> We live out of suitcases almost all year and without our families and friends. Our homes are hotels and their lobbies. When we go out and play, we have no home support. In the UAE we play Test matches with no one watching. You never feel that surge of adrenalin that comes from home support. For a decade our players have not had the opportunity to use the experience of playing at home and as a result their confidence levels are often not great. We have lost self-belief. It has made some of us stronger and more determined to succeed. But it's been very difficult mentally.

Beyond the cricketers, it is the Pakistani public that has borne the brunt of the loss of cricket. Sam Morshead reports that 'former cricketing hotbeds have seen interest drop, much of the country has never had the chance to see their heroes play in the flesh, and Pakistan's status in the world has been left scarred.'[14] The loss of the chance to see your sporting icons perform at home or to be part of a global fraternity pushed the country into a kind of isolation that it had never previously faced. The danger was that disaffected youth, without sporting events and activities, would turn increasingly to drugs, militancy, and criminality. The suspended relations with India also led to a situation where a generation of Pakistani and Indian cricketers have played each other only intermittently in international tournaments. The exhilarating India–Pakistan rivalry with all its additional tensions was a vital part of international cricket. Its forced demise has left the cricketing world much the poorer financially and in terms of the kind of spectacle that sports thrive on.

And yet Pakistan—the mercurials—achieve the unachievable. They confound their supporters and their critics. In 2009, ravaged by terrorism and months after being stripped of the right to hold matches at home, Pakistan managed to win the World T20 Cup. Despite their continued isolation and financial difficulties, in 2016 they reached the number one spot in Test rankings and in 2017 they won the ICC Champions Trophy. That Pakistan was able to keep interest in cricket alive was admirable. That they were able to win international titles was a testament to the resilience and talent of the cricketers. The impact on the nation of these achievements cannot be understated in terms of morale and self-esteem.

But Pakistan's problem has never been confined to terrorism. I have spoken of political ineptitude and corruption above and more widely in the chapters leading to this conclusion. The terrorist attack on the Sri Lankan team was followed in 2010 by the spot-fixing scandal that involved the Pakistan captain Salman Butt and fast bowlers Mohammad Asif and Mohammad Amir. All three were jailed for their part in the episode. It was a particularly distressing occurrence seemingly representing all of Pakistan's mounting problems in the form of the 18-year-old Amir. Here was a young man—64 per cent of Pakistan's population is younger than 30 and a third are between the ages of 15 and 29[15]—with an abundance of untamed, natural talent. A glittering career lay ahead. Barely a year into his career his mentor led him down a path of corruption and crisis. Amir returned to cricket five years later but was never quite the same. A story of destructive leadership, corruption, and unfulfilled potential, Amir became one in a long line of flawed virtuosos.

But clearly these individuals were not born corrupt. Something in their immediate and wider environment allowed them to believe that what they did was acceptable. As Harsha Bhogle emphasizes:

> People often talk about the invincibility that power lulls you into believing in; on the subcontinent, young cricketers start believing that the adulation bestowed upon them will allow them to get away with anything. This is therefore as much the fault of Butt, Amir and Asif as it is of those who created the environment in which it was deemed acceptable to do the things these players did.[16]

The fact that Amir was condemned so strongly in Pakistan for tarnishing the reputation of the country is another indication of how much the nation identifies with cricket. A blot on a single cricketer is a blot on the reputation of every Pakistani. Similarly, an affront to Pakistan cricket is felt equally as a slight on the Pakistani nation as was evident when Inzamam-ul-Haq forfeited Pakistan's Test match against England after the umpires had accused Pakistan of tampering with the ball. Inzamam was celebrated at home as a hero for standing firm for his demand for an apology.

Cricket holds up a mirror to the rest of society. Corruption, instability, and lack of accountability have crippled the country preventing it from fulfilling its potential. Poor leadership has deepened the problems the country has faced. As a transformational leader, Imran Khan harnessed the potential of youth to win cricket's biggest prize when the team won the 1992 World Cup. Today as Prime Minister he is struggling to scale up to a country of 200 million. Wherever leadership has been good, cricket has flourished—either administratively or on the field. And the opposite of that has been true as well. In the absence of strong institutional structures in the cricket setup as well as in the country, leadership has a magnifying effect. Effective leadership can bring a positive windfall; at the same time, poor leaders have equally strong negative impact.

PAKISTAN'S REHABILITATION

Since peaking in 2010, the number of terrorist attacks in Pakistan, up to 2020, has fallen by 85 per cent. The decline has been most significant since 2014.[17] The improved security environment has allowed Pakistan cricket to start a gradual process of recovery. In 2015, Zimbabwe became the first international team to tour Pakistan since the 2009 attacks. Two years later, in 2017, a World XI toured. In the same year, the Pakistan Super League (PSL), Pakistan's T20 franchise-based league, held its final in Lahore with eight foreign players participating. In 2018, three matches of the PSL were played in Karachi and Lahore with a larger foreign contingent. In 2019, eight matches were played in Karachi over the space of a week. Thirty-nine foreign players from countries including England, New Zealand, Australia, and the West Indies participated. There were important milestones achieved in 2019. For example, Shane Watson (the Australian) had declined to travel to Pakistan twice previously, stating that his family were uncomfortable. In 2019, he spent a week in Karachi having heard from others that had come to Pakistan earlier that security had been excellent. Alex Hales, the Englishman, had pulled out of England's tour of Bangladesh in 2016 over security fears following a terrorist attack on a café in Dhaka.[18] In 2019, he made the trip to Pakistan and returned in 2020 along with Watson, indicating that perceptions of Pakistan were beginning to change. This was even more evident in the 2020 edition of the PSL which was held entirely in Pakistan.

With the phased return of the tournament to Pakistan, the PSL has been the ideal platform to bring international cricket back to the country on a more consistent basis. From two days to a week to several weeks over a period of four years, the gradual increase in the duration of time spent in Pakistan has increased the confidence of foreign players while also allowing the security framework to plan more meticulously for tours that are longer. The 2020 version of the tournament was by far the most challenging, covering four cities and a time span of over thirty days.[19] This was a far more complex operation than is required for a single international team tour and the fact that the tournament went off without a hitch until Covid-19 postponed the semi-finals and finals by eight months shows that Pakistan should be cautiously optimistic about a complete return of cricket to the country in the future. Credit for the success must be given to the PCB, the partnering team franchise owners, and the security establishment including the local security services and the army. But while security has played an enormous role in reassuring foreign players, the response of the Pakistani public has played the biggest role in changing the perception of Pakistan.

In the past, crowds in Pakistan have tended to be strongly partisan and not particularly welcoming of opposing teams. In 1980, the West Indian Sylvester Clarke had become enraged after being pelted by oranges and small pebbles on the boundary by a restive crowd in Multan. He responded by throwing a brick back at the offenders putting one of them in the hospital.[20] Tours to Pakistan had been seen as a hardship assignment and negative stereotypes built up about the country encapsulated in Ian Botham's 'mother-in-law' jibe. The prejudice had in fact been in place almost since Pakistan joined the cricketing world, driven initially by orientalism and later by growing Islamophobia.

But a decade without cricket has changed things significantly. Crowds have crammed into almost every match played in the PSL. The demographics have changed too. The shorter version of the game has attracted more families, younger women, and children. In the past, crowds were overwhelmingly male. Even for the Test match against Sri Lanka played in Rawalpindi where persistent rain had ruined any chance of a result, large crowds attended the days when play was possible. It did not matter that the game would not produce a result. The match represented the return of cricket to Pakistan and the crowd celebrated that return.

The overwhelming vibe from crowds has been a heartfelt appreciation that foreign cricketers would come to Pakistan and more importantly assist in bringing cricket back to the country. Sam Morshead, reporting on the PSL for *Cricketer*, the monthly journal for cricketing events worldwide, reported how widespread the gratefulness of Pakistanis towards the foreign players playing in Pakistan was:

from the construction company employees manning an abandoned clocktower in Multan, to the fans who flock around my interview with a TV local network, to teachers at a girls' school in rural South Punjab, the message is the same: Pakistan is not what you think it is. The people of Multan are genuinely grateful to the men and women from the Western world who have visited this week. It felt daft to shake the hands of so many in the crowd at the end of the match and hear them thank me for being sent on assignment to watch cricket in their hometown.[21]

The same Multan that threw oranges on Sylvester Clarke now roared its support for the South African Rilee Roussow as he raised his bat to acknowledge the deafening applause from 25,000 people for his hundred. It was also probably the first time that the crowd had ever seen Shahid Afridi, arguably Pakistan's most popular cricketer for generations, play live. It is a reminder of how much Pakistan has lost in the decade that has passed. How much the event has meant to Pakistan is summed up by Morshead:

> None of our songs echoes with the same depth of feeling as 25,000 voices screaming "Lala" upon what was quite probably their first sighting of Shahid Afridi in the flesh. None of our salaries could afford what this tournament means to the people of Multan, and more widely the people of Pakistan. This was not like any cricket experience I have ever had. Nor, I would hazard, will it be like anything I will experience again. ... This felt seismic. This felt seminal. This felt truly historic.[22]

When I spoke to Imran Ahmad Khan, head of player acquisition for the PSL, he commented on how overwhelmed the foreign players were by the crowd response to them: 'it was an experience that they had never previously encountered.' Of all the banners in the crowd in Multan—most of which reflected an unadulterated joy at being able to watch international cricket again—was the one that stated, 'This is not Sultan against Zalmi.[23] This is Pakistan against terrorism.'

In her book, *The New Pakistani Middle Class*, Ammara Maqsood argues that 'most Pakistanis are painfully aware of how they are viewed by the world outside; they are perceived as a country of terrorists or, at best, backward religious zealots.'[24] What became evident from the behaviour of crowds at the matches was that Pakistanis today are tired of being shunned, marginalized, and disconnected from the global. How they are perceived by the outside world is important and there is a genuine desire to correct the perception of being an unfriendly, unwelcoming country of terrorists. The global is important, as is the quest for modernity, another issue that Maqsood emphasizes in her analysis of the middle class in Pakistan. Cricket was how Pakistan has most visibly engaged with the outside world and the return of cricket, therefore, indicates a fervent desire to be back in the modern global world order and a desperate plea that the world needs to look at the country in a new light and recognize the recuperation of Pakistan from a very difficult decade and a half. In 2004, when India toured Pakistan, the chairman of the PCB had been adamant that one of the objectives of the tour was to show that Pakistanis were not what the outside world had made them out to be. Almost two decades later, cricket was being used again to tell the world what Pakistan is and not what it is made out to be.

For the first time ever, Pakistani crowds have cheered wildly for an Australian or a South African or a West Indian or an Englishman or a New Zealander. The multicultural nature of the event has helped reintegrate Pakistan with the wider cricketing fraternity. For Pakistanis, it shows Pakistan as part of a wider global community more so than at any other occasion or at any other setting. The PSL was one of Pakistan's most important cultural events of the 21st century, a long-awaited opportunity to open its doors internationally and show that it belongs on a global stage. It was a statement from Pakistan saying that we have our own tournament now and we can hold and run it at home. The PSL has also generated the few positive news stories coming out of Pakistan to an international audience. Cricket is once again providing the spark of optimism for Pakistan.

Even touring Pakistan—so often seen as a chore in the past (see Chapter 4)—has been made more comfortable for foreign players. Prior to the start of the PSL in 2020, I spoke to one of the organizers: 'These guys will be here for a month. We need to find something for them to do in their off days. It's not a three-day in and out visit.' In fact, the PCB, working with the individual franchises, has addressed this issue more than adequately. It helps that in the major cities of Lahore, Karachi, and Islamabad, the hotels are of an international standard and offer a choice of dining experiences, gyms, swimming pools, and shopping malls. There have been opportunities for dinners and excursions outside the confines of the hotels as well. In Multan, where facilities were more sparse, the franchise owners set up a recreation room with a ping-pong table, billiards/snooker table, and FIFA 2020 on a widescreen TV. The room has become the focus of unwinding and socializing after the cricket. In an interview with Moeen Ali, the England allrounder who was part of one of the franchises, he stated that he had been on international tours where he had been more hotel room bound than the current tour to Pakistan. The cricketers appreciated the efforts that had been made.

Successive governments have recognized the importance of the PSL as a means of reviving international cricket in Pakistan and as in the past they have looked to appropriate the game not only for political and economic gain but also for enhancing the nation's international image as a safe and welcoming destination for investors and tourists. For Pakistan, the PSL is not only a cricket tournament on home soil but a message to the world about the improved security situation in the country which became a no-go zone for international players after a terrorist attack on the Sri Lankan cricket team in 2009.

Sandwiched between the Sri Lankan tour that marked the return of international cricket to Pakistan and the start of the 2020 PSL, there was another international tour aimed at supporting the return of cricket to Pakistan. The MCC, consisting of a team of international cricketers, toured Pakistan in February 2020. The team was captained by the former Sri Lankan captain and current president of the MCC, Kumar Sangakkara. The tour was symbolically important as Sangakkara was part of the Sri Lankan team that was attacked in 2009. During the MCC tour Sangakkara returned to the site of the incident to play in front of a packed crowd at the Gaddafi stadium. Sangakkara would emphasize:

> Our job is to enjoy our experience here, play the best cricket, make the best connections and that will go a long way towards raising the confidence of teams to come here. International cricket does need to come to Pakistan. It's a cricketing powerhouse and to support that is a privilege for the MCC.[25]

Sangakkara would also comment on the brotherly relationship[26] between Sri Lanka and Pakistan referring back to when Australia and the West Indies refused to play their scheduled group games in Sri Lanka at the 1996 Cricket World Cup due to security reasons. In response, a combined XI of Pakistani and Indian players showed solidarity and support for the Sri Lankans by playing a one-off match prior to the start of the tournament in Colombo. Pakistan's strong backing for Sri Lanka joining the ICC and the unity shown in 1996 is often recalled by Sri Lankans and was a significant factor in Sri Lanka becoming the first country to return to Pakistan for a full tour in December 2019 prior to the PSL and MCC matches. After the MCC tour, a more circumspect Bangladesh followed suit.

But while cricket has taken the first steps back to Pakistan, there are potential pitfalls ahead. The most critical factor remains security. The security environment in Pakistan has inhibited its political, economic, and social development through creating a climate of instability and through the costs related to combating extremist violence. It is also the case that once the attack on the Sri Lankan team occurred in 2009, it became very difficult for Pakistan to overturn the perception that emerged. Subsequently, in the future even small incidents could have a severe impact. The memory of the attack cannot be exorcised. For that reason, arrangements for tours are as intense as they could possibly be. Teams are provided head-of-state protection costing hundreds of millions of rupees. This involves armed guards patrolling the hotels, stadiums being sealed off with military police bearing semi-automatic weapons, and snipers located on rooftops and motorcades accompanying every movement of the teams. Security is, by necessity, suffocating. But one false step and Pakistan may not get another chance for decades. While it is true to say that most high-profile sporting events now involve major security operations, tours to Pakistan require heightened awareness by those providing security and a recognition that the chain is only as strong as its weakest link. In the past, political disputes have been responsible for fatal security lapses. More recently, the chairman of the PCB, Ehsan Mani, hinted at the Punjab police demanding free passes for matches in return for cooperation.[27] In 2015, when the PSL final was played in Lahore, I witnessed police preventing food and water reaching the stadium in protest for not receiving free passes.

Match-fixing also remains a threat to the credibility of the game. Nasir Jamshed, a former Pakistan international cricketer, was recently sentenced to seventeen months in prison in England for his role in a fixing scandal involving T20 tournaments in Pakistan and Bangladesh. In a familiar story of greed, corruption, and ultimately wasted talent, Jamshed's British wife would tweet the following:

> Nasir could have had a bright future, had he worked hard and been committed to the sport that gave him so much, but he took a short cut and lost everything, his career, status, respect and freedom. He would have got UK nationality and played county cricket, and he threw his chance away. He would do anything to turn the clock back and not lose everything. I hope all cricketers look at his example as a deterrent against corruption.[28]

These 'derailers,' born of the endemic corruption that has been discussed in earlier chapters, continue to threaten Pakistan and Pakistan cricket.

DARK CLOUDS AND SILVER LININGS

There was certainly some cause for optimism in Pakistan cricket as 2020 saw the return of international cricket with the successful holding of the fifth edition of the Pakistan Super League entirely in Pakistan, followed by Bangladesh's tour to Pakistan. In early 2021, South Africa toured for the first time since 2007. New Zealand, England, West Indies, and Australia were all due to tour Pakistan in late 2021 and 2022 making for a busy home season and the hope that it would cement the full-fledged return of cricket in Pakistan. Unfortunately, the precarity of the situation was tragically highlighted in September 2021 when New Zealand, making their first visit to Pakistan in 18 years, aborted their tour only 6 days after landing and just minutes before the first ODI in Rawalpindi. Allegedly,[29] a security threat picked up by Western intelligence agencies and passed on to the New Zealand government caused the tour to be stopped at the eleventh hour. Despite reassurances from the Pakistan government and the army and a personal phone call from Prime Minister Imran Khan to his New Zealand counterpart, the tour could not be salvaged. Not only was this a devastating setback for millions of cricketing fans who were eager to see a complete rehabilitation of the nation in the cricketing sense, but also for the country as a whole as it tries to reassure the world that Pakistan is a responsible nation and safe for investment, tourism, and global integration. It may never be revealed how credible the threat to the New Zealand team was—however, it appears that the Taliban retaking power in Afghanistan has already changed the perception of threat within Pakistan. The last time the Taliban were in control of Afghanistan, the Tehrik-i-Taliban targeted Pakistan's security forces, its civilians, and its cricketers. A recent uptick in attacks since the Taliban takeover in Afghanistan is an ominous sign for the country and has likely already had an impact through the cancellation of the New Zealand series. Whether the threat becomes a reality is still to be seen. But if countries feel unable to tour at a time of relative stability and despite the highest level of security reassurances, it indicates that more difficulties lie ahead for cricket in Pakistan. The precedent set by New Zealand—cancelling their tour right before the series was supposed to commence—is a blow that Pakistan will struggle to recover from, following the enormous efforts that have been made to bring the game back to the country. As expected, days after the New Zealand cancellation, England too followed suit. There is, once again, deep concern in Pakistan over the prospect of a renewed period of isolation and whether the country and its cricket will be able to survive the storm again. There is also anger and a sense of betrayal at the fact that Pakistan agreed to travel to both England and New Zealand at the height of the Covid pandemic but were forsaken at their time of need. Deep imbalances in the game's finances threaten cricket's integrity.

Some remaining optimism springs from within. After a decade of quiet there is a sudden explosion of young potential superstars. A world class batsman from Lahore is Pakistan's young new leader. In keeping with the spread of cricket to areas previously not known for producing cricketers, two fast bowlers have emerged from Hyderabad and Larkana. In the meantime, Khyber Pakhtunkhwa—the province that was worst hit by extremist violence in the 2000s—has come to dominate the national team including emerging fast bowlers from the previously terrorist-ravaged tribal area of North Waziristan. A stunningly picturesque cricket ground has been carved out between jagged mountains and the Arabian coast in Gwadar—the port in the southwestern coast of Balochistan that is a focus of the Chinese-funded CPEC project.

While cricket continues to broaden its range to areas previously considered cricketing outposts, possibly the unlikeliest inroads it has made is in the women's game. The popularity of cricket through the decades meant that women always watched the game; there were women's enclosures in several stadiums including the Gaddafi stadium in Lahore and the National stadium in Karachi. In the 1980s and 1990s, Pakistan also had several prominent female sports journalists who were at the forefront of sports writing. But in a conservative society where female involvement in the very public sphere of sport is frowned upon, playing cricket was closed off to female involvement. The gradual change came only after Ziaul Haq's decade of Islamization was replaced by the coming to power of Benazir Bhutto. While Bhutto was unable to make much progress on women's issues in the parliament, the symbolism of a 35-year-old woman being elected Prime Minister of an Islamic country was significant. Inspired by this and in the space that opened up post-Zia's regime, two sisters from Karachi started up a women's cricket team. Sharmeen Said Khan (d. 2018) and Shaiza Said Khan are credited with being the pioneers of women's cricket in Pakistan and it was their untiring efforts that led to Pakistan fielding its first women's team in an international sporting arena.[30]

In the decades that followed, women's cricket in Pakistan faced opposition and hostility from officialdom and religious groups. A proposed match against retired men's cricketers was called off after death threats were received from religious groups.[31] At a more general level, women's cricket received no institutional support, severely limiting access to grounds, training centres, and even appropriate equipment. Despite these obstacles, the passion and commitment for the game amongst the players in particular has seen the women's game gain extraordinary strength to the point where Pakistan is today an established cricketing nation in the women's game. The Khan sisters' family funded the initial growth almost entirely from their own resources—building a dormitory for the cricketers, importing bowling machines, creating a cricket pitch and net facilities, and paying for tickets, accommodation, equipment, and food and drink while on tour. Gradually, support has grown—and in the last decade several cricketers have earned international reputations and today those making the national team have central contracts and a degree of financial security from playing cricket. Shaharyar Khan states that on becoming chairman of the PCB in 2004, he was committed to the promotion of the women's game in Pakistan but that he anticipated a backlash from the religious right. None came, except in the form of a polite letter from a representative of the Jamaat-i-Islami, saying that while the party recognized the importance of women's cricket as beneficial for the players' health, he hoped that their dress would respect Islamic traditions and that women would not play in front of men.[32] This was a far cry from the death threats of earlier times. And today, women's cricket matches are frequently broadcast live on television. Such is the passion for cricket that opposition from conservative and extremist elements appears to have been diffused. The considerable achievements of the team have also helped deflect criticism.

But as the women's game expands and becomes more visible in the public sphere, it brings new challenges and dangers which, in keeping with the central theme of this book, reflect the wider issues that women face in Pakistani society, particularly where they begin to enter into traditionally male-dominated spheres such as sport and the workplace. This is epitomized, for example, in the tragic 2014 case of a young female cricketer who alleged that the chairman of the Multan Cricket Club who was also a member of the provincial assembly, and another team selector, had demanded sexual favours in return for putting her and three other players on the regional teams or recommending them for the national team.[33] Haleema Rafique subsequently faced intimidation and threats by the 'harassers' who counter alleged that the women were indulging in 'immoral activities.' It led ultimately to the 17-year-old committing suicide. While women continue to make progress against the odds in all spheres of life in Pakistan—including cricket—major obstacles remain in place. The journey of women cricketers reflects these challenges.

Imran Khan's ascent to the office of the Prime Minister divides opinion at home. But internationally, Khan has the kind of profile that has advanced Pakistan's global image significantly. Even during his cricketing days, Imran Khan had a charismatic appeal that crossed national boundaries. His Oxford education, his image as a playboy socialite, and his long association with the Sussex County Cricket Club made Englishmen almost adopt him as one of their own. This feeling was increased further when he married Jemima Goldsmith, the daughter of the French-British financial tycoon James Goldsmith, in 1995.[34] As mentioned, Pakistanis appear to be increasingly aware of how they are perceived by the outside world and Imran Khan represents an opportunity for Pakistanis, particularly younger ones, to feel a certain pride through who represents them on the world stage. The modest hesitancy of Nawaz Sharif pales in front of the handsome, masculine presence of Khan.

For example, Pakistani social media was triumphant at the prospect of Imran Khan being voted as amongst the best-looking world leaders.[35] One of Imran Khan's successes has been the enhancing of Pakistan's image internationally, including in England. While Pakistan cannot claim to have initiated a 'reverse colonialism' with their old masters in the way India[36] can, its relationship with the United Kingdom has changed to one where the colonial hangover has been exorcised. But in cricketing terms, the international success and popularity of the Pakistan team, particularly amongst the British-Asian community in England, many of whom trace their origins back to Pakistan, has meant huge interest for cricket amongst the community. Unsurprisingly, a number of current and upcoming players are of Indian and Pakistani origin, highlighting a reverse of the spread of cricket during colonial times. Pakistan's relationship with the United Kingdom remains warm but is far less important than it was in the past as Pakistan turns increasingly to China and Saudi Arabia for economic and military support. Nevertheless, Pakistan and the United Kingdom will continue to share the bond of cricket and cricket continues to provide an important vehicle for portraying a positive image of Pakistan. In fact, during President George W. Bush's visit to Pakistan in 2006, his most featured photo opportunity was a 'practice session' with a group of children playing cricket and members of the Pakistan cricket team. Pakistan cricket has made enormous strides in rehabilitating its image since the spot-fixing disgrace in 2010. In 2016, Misbah-ul-Haq, who took over as captain soon after the scandal, spoke of his proudest moment as captain being Pakistan's triumphant return to England and the Lord's, the venue for the infamous match:

> The proudest moment, I always say, is the Lord's Test in 2016—scoring a century and winning the Test match. That was something special for us. From what happened to us in 2010, just regaining that dignity, the confidence, the support of our fans and performing like that—that was a massive thing for me.[37]

The crowd rose to Pakistan as the entire team famously, en masse, saluted their captain and performed coordinated push ups. Despite England having lost, the crowd reaction was genuinely warm.

Yet, despite the positive stories Pakistan cricket can generate, they cannot replace essential changes that Pakistan must make if it is to continue its rehabilitation in the comity of nations. Foremost in this must be the need to address the issue of home-grown extremism which is responsible for instability and violence within the country and for Pakistan's problematic relations with its neighbours. Imran Khan has a fanatical following in Pakistan and is admired abroad, even grudgingly in India. His commitment to Pakistan is unquestioned; however, if he is to address wider issues in society such as militancy, corruption, accountability, poverty, and firmer relations regionally and globally, it will require more than cricket's undoubted influence.

Sadly, the one area where little progress has been made recently and where relations continue to deteriorate is also one of the most important— Pakistan's relations with India. The tensions between India and Pakistan have held back both countries from fulfilling their potential, despite the myriad common challenges that they face. The animosity between the two large South Asian countries has also scuppered regional cooperation in the form of bodies such as SAARC which have been rendered moribund. Recent events from the militant attack on an Indian Army base in Pulwama blamed on Pakistan, India's retaliatory strike across the border, Pakistan's shooting down of an Indian jet, and India's revoking of Indian-held Kashmir's special status—all this has left the relationship at its lowest ebb. Cricket, so long the ice-breaker, has been suspended between the two nations for over a decade except in the occasional international event. As mentioned, this has major financial ramifications, not just for Pakistan in particular but also for world cricket. The suspension of the rivalry—often said to be more intense than the Australia-England Ashes series—robs the game and fans on both sides of the Indo-Pak border and across the world of one of its most thrilling spectacles. An idea of the popularity of the rivalry is provided by a worldwide TV audience reaching almost one billion for the last encounter between the two during the 2019 World Cup in England. The India–Pakistan match sold out faster than the final.[38] Unfortunately, politically, there seems little hope for the resumption of bilateral ties.

Yet in times of adversity even enmities can be set aside. As the world struggles in the face of the Covid-19 pandemic and South Asia faces a massive challenge in containing the impact of the virus on its population, there is some hope that the countries of South Asia, including India and Pakistan, will work together in order meet this enormous threat. It is possible that when the pandemic is overcome, regional relations may be looked at afresh. India and Pakistan have a history of both animosity and affection (see Chapters 5 and 6) but when given the opportunity affection has brought dividends of peace and goodwill to both nations. Appadurai points out that the peculiar tension between nationalism and decolonization was best seen in the cricket diplomacy between India and Pakistan, which involves multiple levels of competition and cooperation. According to Appadurai, perhaps the best example of cooperation in the spirit of decolonization was how 'politicians and bureaucrats at the highest levels of the antagonistic nations cooperated in the mid-1980s'[39] managed to move the venue of the 1987 World Cup to the Subcontinent signalling a seismic shift in the locus of power of cricket from England to South Asia.

Is it possible that India and Pakistan realize again the importance of cooperation rather than confrontation and will cricket lead the way as it has in the past? The importance of sport as a political instrument, cultural tool, or emotional bond in South Asian nations—such as Bangladesh, Pakistan, Afghanistan, and Sri Lanka—has not been given adequate attention in studies on society and culture of the region. It may take the ravages of a pandemic for many to realize the importance of sport in society. During the height of the pandemic, as cultural event after cultural event was cancelled, none garnered the kind of attention that sporting events did. Major sporting events were cancelled, postponed, or then played under very different circumstances.

In March 2020, the England and Wales Cricket Board recommended that all forms of recreational cricket be suspended indefinitely because of Covid-19.[40] All over the world, cricket came to a standstill. At the same time, in Pakistan, the majestic, Mughal-era Badshahi Mosque was closed off because of the pandemic. In its shadow, boys continued to play that beloved game of bat and ball. Once English in body and spirit—now, the lifeblood of Pakistan.

Epilogue: Cricket in the Time of Covid

It has been over eighteen months since the World Health Organization's official declaration of the Covid-19 pandemic. Life has been upended. And while vaccinations hold out hope, there is unlikely to be a return to what was 'normal' previously. Change is continuous and irreversible. The future will be different.

Across the length of this book, I have attempted to show how cricket in Pakistan reflects wider social and political trends. Throughout its history, Pakistan cricket has confounded its critics from winning a Test in its very first series to its unlikely World Cup triumphs in 1992 and 2009 to its continued, if inconsistent, excellence despite its decade long 'exile' from home following the terrorist attack on the Sri Lankan cricketers in Lahore in 2009. Like its cricket team, Pakistan's response to Covid too has confounded critics.

Initial projections by Imperial College had put deaths by January 2021 as peaking at 2.29 million unless urgent interventions were put in place.[1] In fact, fatalities have been several orders of magnitude less, with a total of just over 1 million cases and 23,000 deaths by July 2021.[2] The government's response has been—again like the Pakistan cricket team's performances described in Chapter 1—mercurial. Prime Minister Imran Khan initially compared the coronavirus to an 'ordinary flu,' claiming that 97 per cent of infected patients recover without requiring medical attention. With the unwavering confidence that he displayed on the field, the former cricketer turned Prime Minister stated that Pakistan's 'hot and dry' weather[3] would eliminate the virus. As the pandemic unfolded in the country, the highest number of Covid-19 cases and deaths were reported in its hottest months.

In June 2020, Pakistan was among the top-10 most affected countries.[4] Subsequently, in a televised address to the nation, Khan said that Pakistan could not afford a nationwide lockdown as one-fourth of its population lived below the poverty line. Instead, his government lifted many public restrictions before most other countries and imposed 'smart lockdowns' in an apparent attempt to revive the economy.

Since then, there have been a series of lockdowns followed by the easing of restrictions. But the government has struggled to get across the magnitude and the severity of the pandemic and has often been reluctant to put in place strict restrictions. Markets have remained largely open and many people continue to attend weddings, funerals, and political and religious protests. While Saudi Arabia and Iran banned group prayers in mosques, Pakistan continued to allow congregational prayers. Mosques in the Punjab remained open to the public as per routine, and citizens continued to participate indoors in close vicinities in religious congregations, religious activities, and shrine visits.[5] In fact, in March 2020, just as the pandemic was beginning to rage, the government allowed the Tablighi Jama'at—the organization that in the early 2000s had made inroads into the cricket team—to hold its annual congregation in Raiwind, albeit with a few restrictions. But the event became a 'super spreader,' causing spikes in the surrounding areas as the Tablighis flouted rules and continued to spread the pandemic as they met the wider public.[6]

The wearing of masks and social distancing has also been lax. During the course of writing this epilogue, Prime Minister Imran Khan tested positive for Covid-19. It was reported that Khan had addressed a security conference in Islamabad which was attended by a large number of people. He then inaugurated a housing project for disadvantaged people. On both occasions he did not wear a mask. Yet, cases remain low and, in July 2021, *The Economist*[7] ranked Pakistan third behind Hong Kong and New Zealand in its handling of the pandemic. The country continues to mystify and defy explanation.

Covid first hit Pakistan cricket in March 2020 when the last few games of the fifth edition of the PSL were postponed by eight months. I have already alluded to the significance of the PSL in bringing international cricket back to Pakistan and the 2020 edition was particularly important being the first time that the entire tournament was held in Pakistan. The event had seen packed stadiums and no security alarms. It had also generated a raft of positive stories on Pakistan paving the way for subsequent tours by international teams. It was therefore the desire to complete the last few matches that stretched the tournament until the surge in cases saw the PCB sensibly postpone the remaining matches to a later date. It was amongst the last sporting encounters to be cancelled in the wake of the pandemic.

But despite the fact that the tournament was not completed initially, the impact of holding the majority of it in Pakistan without any untoward incident was significant in generating positive word of mouth on Pakistan being a secure country for cricket. The former England captain Michael Atherton, who was in Lahore making a documentary on the return of cricket to Pakistan, stated that the perception regarding security in Pakistan was changing and more teams would come as foreign players who featured in the PSL would pass on the message of safety to their teammates back home. Atherton was quoted saying: 'You only have to look around—the crowds, enthusiasm and packed houses for every game. All these foreign players will now know that it is safe here, and they will be able to take that message to the players from their own countries.'[8]

Across the world, cricket returned to public viewing in July 2020 when West Indies and Pakistan agreed to tour England under new Covid protocols—these involved bio-security bubbles and the absence of crowds. The PCB announced that the touring party to England would go through three rounds of Covid-19 testing prior to leaving Pakistan and would be tested every five days once in England. Days before the departure of the 30-man squad, 3 cricketers were found to be Covid positive and asymptomatic. A few days later, a further 7 tested positive.[9] While government figures at this point were showing far lower rates of prevalence, the 30-man sample appeared to indicate much higher rates in the general population as well as the heightened danger of asymptomatic carriers. In fact, studies carried out by the Imperial College London and the University of Washington suggest that the actual number of cases in Pakistan could be anywhere between 3 to 10 times higher than those registered by the government.[10] Eventually, the tour went ahead—and the Covid positive players joined after returning two negative tests. But even before the series started, the PCB's official Twitter handle shared pictures of the cricketers celebrating Eid al-Adha in England. In the pictures that soon went viral on social media, neither players nor staff members were seen maintaining physical distance or wearing masks.[11] The photographs of cricket players, in which the entire team appears to be ignoring Covid guidelines, potentially influenced the attitudes and behaviour of millions of people back in Pakistan. When elite and high-profile sportspersons choose not to wear masks in public, it normalizes this behaviour and destroys trust in organizations and institutions recommending them.

In October 2020, Pakistan travelled to New Zealand for another bio-secure tour. Once in New Zealand, they faced some of the strictest Covid protocols in the world. Unsurprisingly, the members of the touring party breached these as well and were severely reprimanded for violations within the first 12 hours of their isolation. Subsequently, half a dozen players tested positive, putting the tour in jeopardy. While the tour did proceed following warnings from the PCB to its players of huge embarrassment to the country, the attitude of the players reflected the lax home environment vis-à-vis Covid protocols. Just as endemic corruption in society was reflected in the match-fixing scandals of the 1990s and 2000s, the cricket team continued to provide a mirror to wider societal trends and attitudes.

However, the most damaging fallout from the careless approach towards Covid occurred during the 2021 incarnation of the PSL. Scheduled, like the previous tournament, to be held entirely in Pakistan but restricted to Lahore and Karachi to try and ensure Covid compliance, the tournament became a litany of failings, epitomizing how what happens in the world of Pakistan cricket is so often reflective of what is happening in wider society.

Pakistan's rehabilitation in the cricketing community has been a success story, at least up until the cancellation of the New Zealand and England tours in September and October 2021. From the depths of 2009, when the attack on the Sri Lankan cricket team in Lahore led to the loss of international cricket to its return in 2019. The unfettered relief and joy amongst Pakistanis on the homecoming of cricket lifted the nation noticeably. The 2020 edition of the PSL and tours by Sri Lanka and Bangladesh marked a watershed in the return of international cricket. Covid dampened that elation somewhat, curtailing the PSL and taking away the crowds for the subsequent series against South Africa. In fact, it was a cruel irony that just as Pakistan was able to host teams at home, the fans that had waited for a decade to see live cricket were barred from attending. Players who endured empty stadiums when playing in their adopted home of UAE now again played in empty stadiums in Pakistan.

But the South African series still represented a significant step towards a full revival of Pakistan as a cricketing venue on the international circuit. It also represented the start of a full rehabilitation of the country back into a global network. England, New Zealand, and Australia promised tours in the near future. In light of this, the 2021 edition of the PSL was a key event which would showcase the gains made by Pakistan in the key areas of security and bio-security. A successful event would assuage any fears and confirm Pakistan's return as a safe and secure cricketing venue, building on the momentum of the previous PSL tournament.

Less than halfway into the tournament, seven players tested positive for Covid-19 and the sixth season of the PSL was suspended with immediate effect. When I interviewed a PCB official involved in the PSL, it became apparent that organizational mismanagement and incompetence within the board and a failure to recognize the threat of Covid-19 were responsible for the suspension of the tournament. The lack of seriousness over Covid-19 in Pakistan was already evidenced in the failure of the team in following protocols in England and New Zealand. Instead of sanctioning the team for their breaches, former fast bowler Shoaib Akhtar, for example, took the reprimand from New Zealand authorities as a national insult and had demanded the team return home. He berated New Zealand:

> We don't need you. Our cricket has not finished. You will get the broadcasting rights money. So, you should be indebted to us that we decided to tour your country in such difficult times. You are talking about Pakistan—the greatest country on the planet—so behave yourself and stop giving such statement. Be careful next time. Pakistan team now needs to smash them in T20 series.[12]

Even before the PSL started, there was a breach in the bio-secure bubble by a high-profile player and coach. Neither was placed in isolation and both were allowed back into the bubble after their team allegedly threatened to boycott their match if the two were quarantined. When I interviewed a member, who was inside the bubble, he was clear that the PCB was not in control of the situation nor were they in any way competent to deal with implementing a bio-secure environment:

> The teams were housed initially in different venues, and even when in a single venue they mixed freely with other guests at the hotels. No effort was made to implement protocols. We had decided 'Allah pe chor do' (leave it to Allah). Covid compliance 'officers' that were appointed to each of the six teams turned out to be PCB physiotherapists with no knowledge of what protocols were to be followed. And when the first case was reported, players came to know from the individual rather than through the doctors who, when questioned, responded lackadaisically with 'we forgot to inform the players' liaisons.

The organizational environment described in Chapter 2—the patronage leading to incompetence and the negative organizational culture that inhibits collaboration—has created a major setback for Pakistan cricket. In 2009, security was Pakistan's Achilles' heel; in 2021, bio-security was added as a second area of concern. Apart from the financial cost of cancelled broadcasting deals, gate receipts, and players' compensation, it is the reputational cost that will be most significant. Until this year, the word of mouth on Pakistan and the PSL had been very positive. The years of work in rebuilding trust has been damaged as foreign players speak of lies and mismanagement rather than excellent security, outstanding hospitality, and welcoming crowds. The PCB has lost social capital and credibility. While the Covid-delayed PSL was completed in June 2021, the venue for the tournament was shifted to Abu Dhabi. There was a pared down international presence of cricketers and Covid protocols were outsourced to an international firm. Completion was important for the tournament's reputation but subsequent tours to Pakistan will face increased scrutiny in the shadow of Covid. The process of rehabilitation will restart, and the resilience of the nation will again be tested. However, at some point, resilience alone will not be enough.

Along with Covid, recent events indicate that Pakistan will continue to face the challenge of instability and insecurity driven by regional relations that remain mired in mutual suspicions. India–Pakistan relations remain poor enough for them to even influence the fight against Covid-19. In January 2021, India donated millions of free vaccines to 'friendly neighbouring countries' as part of a diplomatic initiative; Pakistan was not one of them. Pakistan later did receive Indian manufactured vaccines, but the Indian government was quick to stress that these were part of the multinational vaccine alliance programme that sees their provision to countries in need rather than a bilateral arrangement.[13] The decline in relations between the two South Asian neighbours has clearly affected more than their cricketing relations.

However, in February 2021, there was an unexpected thaw in relations. Reports stated that back channel talks between the intelligence agencies of the two countries had begun to make some headway.[14] Pakistan and India recommitted themselves to the 2003 ceasefire arrangement at the Line of Control and agreed to address the 'core issues' that could undermine peace and stability.[15] In March 2021, talks on a water-sharing treaty were held for the first time in two years; days later Prime Minister Modi wished Imran Khan a swift recovery from Covid-19. This was followed by Narendra Modi writing to Imran Khan on the occasion of Pakistan Day, stating that 'India desired cordial relations with Pakistani people.' These were small but significant steps at a time when the momentum has been firmly backwards. An unnamed Pakistani official privy to the back-channel communication is quoted in a news item stating that 'the next steps might be a normalisation in the diplomatic relationship, and perhaps some sporting events.'[16] Unsurprisingly, amongst the first areas of conjecture by the media at this point was whether the warming of ties would lead to a resumption of cricketing ties.[17] Unfortunately, the precarity of relations has meant that these 'gains' have all but evaporated four months later. The US withdrawal and the Taliban's advance in Afghanistan has created new tensions which will have particular implications for Pakistan's relations with both India and Afghanistan but also beyond as was evident in the cancellation of tours by New Zealand and England.

The inability of Pakistan and India to address long standing issues has had an enormous impact on the region as a whole, breeding mistrust, instability, and poverty—and impeding development in both countries. Progress will require that the poisoned relations between the two are replaced by some degree of mutual trust and respect. India's policy of isolating Pakistan both in cricket and politically will leave an increasingly resentful and unstable neighbour. This will mire Pakistan in stagnation but will also threaten India's economic and social progress much more than a stable and prosperous Pakistan. From 2004 to 2008, India–Pakistan cricketing encounters had moved away from the communal undertones, hostility, and hate-filled chauvinism of the matches of the 1990s. The few encounters since then have been played in good spirit between the players though usually in neutral venues. The governments of both countries need to follow that example and commit to recreating an enabling environment that allows the flourishing of trade as well as cultural and sporting exchanges. As argued in earlier chapters, the ground is not yet barren and can still bear fruit but the longer that this does not happen the more unlikely it becomes as the walls of prejudice and mythmaking grow stronger. And undoubtedly any possible peace process between India and Pakistan will use the power of cricket to further its message.

In July 2021, the Pakistan cricket team toured England for a series of ODIs and T20s. Pakistan were both awful and brilliant. They were also, as always, exciting—and, where allowed by Covid protocols, the crowds packed into the grounds. The atmosphere was electric with the chants of *Pakistan Zindabad* echoing from one end to the other; and just for a while Pakistan's mercurial cricketers made us forget that we still faced a pandemic.

Notes

Introduction

1. C.L.R. James, *Beyond a Boundary* (Yellow Jersey Press, 2005 [1963]).
2. Andrei S. Markovits and Steven L. Hellerman, *Offside: Soccer and American Exceptionalism* (Princeton University Press, 2001), cited on p. 10, in Jason Kaufman and Orlando Patterson, 'Cross-National Cultural Diffusion: The Global Spread of Cricket,' *American Sociological Review*, 70/1 (2005), pp. 82–110.
3. Shaharyar M. Khan, *Cricket: A Bridge of Peace* (Oxford University Press, 2005), p. viii.
4. Stephen Wagg, 'Introduction: Following On,' in Stephen Wagg (ed.), *Cricket and National Identity in the Postcolonial Age: Following On* (Routledge, 2005), p. 3.
5. Boria Majumdar, *Twenty-two Yards to Freedom: A Social History of Indian Cricket* (Viking, 2004); Boria Majumdar, *The Illustrated History of Indian Cricket* (Roli Books, 2016); Boria Majumdar, *Eleven Gods and a Billion Indians: The On and Off the Field Story of Cricket in India and Beyond* (S&S Publications, 2018).
6. Mihir Bose, *A History of Indian Cricket* (Andre Deutsch Ltd., 2002); Mihir Bose, *The Nine Waves* (Rupa Publications, 2019).
7. Ramchandra Guha, *A Corner of a Foreign Field: The Indian History of a British Sport* (Picador, 2003).
8. Kausik Bandyopadhyay, *Sport, Culture and Nation* (Sage Publications, 2015).
9. Mike Marqusee, *War Minus the Shooting: Journey Through South Asia During Cricket's World Cup* (William Heinemann, 1996).
10. Chris Valiotis, *Sporting Nations of the Imagination: Pakistani Cricket and Identity in Pakistan and Anglo Pakistan*. PhD dissertation, University of New South Wales. Unpublished, 2006.
11. Peter Oborne, *Wounded Tiger: A History of Cricket in Pakistan* (Simon & Schuster, 2014).
12. Osman Samiuddin, *The Unquiet Ones: A History of Pakistan Cricket* (Harper Collins, 2015).
13. Peter Oborne and Richard Heller, *White on Green: A Portrait of Pakistan Cricket* (Simon & Schuster, 2016).
14. See for example: Ivo Tennant, *Imran Khan* (Gollancz/Witherby, 1995); Wasim Akram with Patrick Murphy, *Wasim: The Autobiography of Wasim Akram* (Piatkus Books, 1998); Mushtaq Mohammad, *Inside Out* (Uniprint, 2006); Shahid Afridi with Wajahat S. Khan, *Game Changer* (Harper Collins, 2019); Fazal Mahmood with Asif Sohail, *From Dusk to Dawn: Autobiography of a Pakistan Cricket Legend* (Oxford University Press, 2003).
15. See for example: Chris Searle, *Pitch of Life: Writings on Cricket* (The Parrs Wood Press, 2001); Jack Williams, *Cricket and Race* (Berg, 2001); Stephen Wagg, *Cricket: A Political History of the Global Game, 1945–2017* (Routledge, 2018); Wagg, 'Introduction'; Anthony Bateman and Jeffrey Hill, *The Cambridge Companion to Cricket* (Cambridge University Press, 2011); Boria Majumdar and J.A. Mangan (eds.), *Sport in South Asian Society: Past and Present* (Routledge, 2005); Jon Gemmell and Boria Majumdar (eds.), *Cricket, Race and the 2007 World Cup* (Routledge, 2008); Bandyopadhyay, *Sport, Culture and Nation*.

16. For example: Magnus Marsden, *Living Islam: Muslim Religious Experience in Pakistan's North-West Frontier* (Cambridge University Press, 2005); Humeira Iqtidar, *Secularising Islamists? Jama'at-e-Islami and Jam'at-ud-Da'wa in Urban Pakistan* (University of Chicago Press, 2012); Naveeda Khan, *Muslim Becoming: Aspiration and Scepticism in Pakistan* (Duke University Press, 2012); Anatol Lieven, *Pakistan: A Hard Country* (Allen Lane, 2011); Christophe Jaffrelot, *The Pakistan Paradox: Instability and Resilience* (Oxford University Press, 2015); Ammara Maqsood, *The New Pakistani Middle Class* (Harvard University Press, 2017); Marie Lall and Tania Saeed, *Youth and the National Narrative: Education, Terrorism and the Security State in Pakistan* (Bloomsbury, 2019).

17. Boria Majumdar, 'Prologue: Stepping Stones Across a Stream,' in B. Majumdar and J.A. Mangan (eds.), *Sport in South Asian Society* (Routledge, 2005), p. 8.

18. Anatol Lieven, *Pakistan*; Christophe Jaffrelot, *Pakistan Paradox*; Ahmed Rashid, *Pakistan On the Brink: The Future of America, Pakistan, and Afghanistan* (Penguin Random House, 2012); Ahmed Rashid, *Descent into Chaos: The United States and the Failure of Nation Building in Pakistan, Afghanistan, and Central Asia* (Penguin Random House, 2008).

19. Urvashi Butalia, *The Other Side of Silence: Voices from the Partition of India* (Penguin, 1998), p. 3.

20. Vazira Fazila-Yacoobali Zamindar, *The Long Partition and the Making of Modern South Asia: Refugees, Boundaries, Histories* (Columbia University Press, 2007), p. 6.

21. Arjun Appadurai, 'Playing with Modernity: The Decolonization of Indian Cricket,' *Altre Modernita* 14 (2015), pp. 1–24.

22. Vir Sanghvi, 'The Transformation of the Image of the Global Pakistani,' (2010), url: https://virsanghvi.com/Article-Details.aspx?key=540, accessed on 2 April 2021.

23. See Ali Khan, 'Cricket, Society and Religion: A Study of Increasing Religiosity in the National Cricket Team of Pakistan,' *Sport in Society* (online, 1 February 2019).

24. Richard Cashman, 'The Paradox that is Pakistani Cricket: Some Initial Reflections,' *The Sports Historian* 14/1 (1994), pp. 21–37.

25. Majumdar, 'Prologue,' p. 9.

26. Christopher R. Hill, *Olympic Politics* (Manchester University Press, 1992); Barrie Houlihan, *Sport and International Politics* (Harvester Wheatsheaf, 1994).

27. Arjun Appadurai, *Modernity at Large: Cultural Dimensions of Globalization* (University of Minnesota Press, 1996), p. 108.

28. Hilary McDonald Beckles, 'The Detachment of West Indies Cricket from the Nationalist Scaffold,' in Anthony Bateman and Jeffrey Hill (eds.), *The Cambridge Companion to Cricket* (Cambridge University Press, 2011).

29. Barbara Keys, 'International Relations,' in S.W. Pope and John Nauright (eds.), *The Routledge Companion to Sports History* (Routledge, 2009), p. 254.

30. Searle, *Pitch of Life*, p. vii.

31. Ibid., p. 4.

32. In terms of how this was reflected in cricket, Pakistan will always remember Ian Botham's retort that Pakistan was the kind of place you sent your mother-in-law on vacation all expenses paid. Having spent a few days in the country before flying home, one of England's sporting icons had condemned the entire Pakistan nation to derision and mockery.

33. Gyanendra Pandey, *Remembering Partition: Violence, Nationalism and History in India* (Cambridge University Press, 2003), p. 2.

34. Gyanesh Kudaisya, 'The Demographic Upheaval of Partition: Refugees and Agricultural Resettlement in India, 1947–67,' *South Asia: Journal of South Asian Studies*, 18/1 (1995), pp. 73–94; 73.

35. Jon Gemmell, 'Introduction: Cricket, Race and the 2007 World Cup,' in Jon Gemmell and Boria Majumdar (eds.), *Cricket, Race and the 2007 World Cup* (Routledge, 2008), p. xiii.

36. Mohammed Hanif, 'The Partition goes on: A Pakistani Perspective,' *AlJazeera* (15 August 2017), url: https://www.aljazeera.com/features/2017/8/15/the-partition-goes-on-a-pakistani-perspective, accessed on 2 April 2021.

Chapter 1: The Nature of Pakistan Cricket

1. J. Kaufman and O. Patterson, 'Cross-National Cultural Diffusion: The Global Spread of Cricket,' *American Sociological Review* 70/1 (2005), pp. 82–110.

2. Trobriand Cricket was a documentary directed by Jerry Leach and Gary Kildea in 1975. The film showed the transformation of the game of cricket introduced by British Missionaries to the Trobriand Islanders from its original form into a highly distinctive political ritual.

3. St Pierre (1995, 2008), p. 79, as cited in Richard Giulianotti, *Sport: A Critical Sociology* (Polity Press, 2016), p. 62.

4. The first International Cricket Match was in fact played in New York between Canada and the United States in 1844. For further details, see: Rowland Bowen, *Cricket: A History of its Growth and Development* (Eyre & Spottiswoode, 1970), and Kaufman and Patterson, 'Cross-National Cultural Diffusion.'

5. The 'gentlemen' referred to amateur players, usually members of the middle and upper classes, and products of the English public school system. The 'players' were professionals consisting of working-class wage-earners. See Derek Birley, *A Social History of English Cricket* (Aurum, 1999).

6. Simon Lister, *Fire in Babylon: How the West Indies Cricket Team Brought a People to its Feet* (Yellow Jersey, 2016), p. 264.

7. Ibid., p. 265.

8. Ibid.

9. Jackie Robinson became the first African-American to play in the major leagues in 1947.

10. For an account of Frank Worrell's journey to becoming captain of West Indies, see M. Malec and H. Beckles, 'Baseball, Cricket and Social Change: Jackie Robinson and Frank Worrell,' in *Anthropology, Sport and Culture* (Westport, 1999), pp. 137–144.

11. Boria Majumdar, *The Illustrated History of Indian Cricket* (Roli Books, 2006), p. 53.

12. Prashant Kidambi, *Cricket Country: An Indian Odyssey in the Age of Empire* (Oxford University Press, 2019).

13. Ibid., p. 65.

14. Ramachandra Guha, 'Cricket and Politics in Colonial India,' *Past & Present*, 161 (1998), p. 159.

15. Guha, 'Cricket and Politics in Colonial India,' p. 159.

16. Belkacem Belmekki, 'Sir Sayyid Ahmad Khan's Framework for the Educational Uplift of the Indian Muslims during British Raj,' *Anthropos* 104/1 (2009), pp. 165–172.

17. Kaufman and Patterson, 'Cross-National Cultural Diffusion.'

18. Arjun Appadurai, 'Playing with Modernity: The Decolonization of Indian Cricket,' *Altre Modernita*, 14 (2015), pp. 1–24.

19. Dominic Malcolm, '"It's Not Cricket": Colonial Legacies and Contemporary Inequalities,' *Journal of Historical Sociology*, 14 (2001), pp. 253–75, in Kaufman and Patterson, 'Cross-National Cultural Diffusion,' p. 99.

20. Guha, 'Cricket and Politics in Colonial India,' p. 160.
21. For a detailed account see Guha, 'Cricket and Politics in Colonial India'; and Shaharyar M. Khan and Ali Khan, *Cricket Cauldron: The Turbulent Politics of Sport in Pakistan* (Harper Sport, 2013).
22. Guha, 'Cricket and Politics in Colonial India,' p. 161.
23. Ibid., p. 163.
24. Charles Little and Chris Valiotis, 'Cricket in Pakistan,' in John Nauright and Charles Parrish (eds.), *Sports Around the World: History, Culture, and Practice*, vol. 1 (ABC-CLIO, 2012), p. 214.
25. Chris Valiotis, 'Cricket in a "Nation Imperfectly Imagined": Identity and Tradition in Postcolonial Pakistan,' in Stephen Wagg (ed.), *Cricket and National Identity in the Postcolonial Age* (Routledge, 2005), pp. 111–112.
26. Osman Samiuddin, *The Unquiet Ones: A History of Pakistan Cricket* (Harper Collins, 2015), p. 14.
27. Ibid., p. 47.
28. Ian Talbot, *Pakistan: A Modern History* (Hurst and Company, 2005), p. 126.
29. Samiuddin, *The Unquiet Ones*, p. 279.
30. Peter Oborne, *Wounded Tiger: The History of Cricket in Pakistan* (Simon & Schuster, 2014), p. 141; Valiotis, 'Cricket in a "Nation Imperfectly Imagined"…,' p. 116.
31. Valiotis, 'Cricket in a "Nation Imperfectly Imagined"…,' p. 117.
32. Peter Oborne and Richard Heller, *White on Green: Celebrating the Drama of Pakistan Cricket* (Simon & Schuster, 2016), p. 150.
33. Ibid., p. 150.
34. Oborne, *Wounded Tiger*, p. 312.
35. Little and Valiotis, 'Cricket in Pakistan,' p. 214.
36. Pakistan has managed to ensure that cricket remains available on terrestrial channels and this has ensured a continued wide coverage. In contrast, in England in 2005, cricket was shifted from terrestrial television to satellite at the behest of the England Cricket Board which sought to benefit from the highest bid for TV rights to cricket. This has further confined the reach of cricket to those who can afford satellite television and, more importantly, subscription costs for sports channels. Viewing figures are likely to have reduced considerably.
37. Ashis Nandy, *A Very Popular Exile:* [An Omnibus Comprising] *The Tao of Cricket; An Ambiguous Journey to the City; Traditions, Tyranny, and Utopias* (Oxford University Press, 2000), p. 1.
38. Nadeem F. Paracha, 'The 'Swinging Seventies' in Pakistan: An Urban History,' *Dawn* (22 August 2013), url: https://www.dawn.com/news/1037584, accessed on 25 June 2021.
39. Ibid.
40. Heller and Oborne, *White on Green*, p. 72.
41. Ian Talbot, *A History of Modern South Asia: Politics, States, Diasporas* (Oxford University Press, 2017), p. 217.
42. Shuchi Kothari, 'From Genre to Zanaana: Urdu Television Drama Serials and Women's Culture in Pakistan,' *Contemporary South Asia*, 14/3 (2005), pp. 289–305.
43. Marie Lall, 'Educate to Hate: The Use of Education in the Creation of Antagonistic National Identities in India and Pakistan,' *Compare*, 38/1 (2008), p. 104.
44. Talbot, *A History of Modern South Asia*, p. 216.

45. Imran Khan and Majid Khan represented Pakistan from the 1970s but were from Pashtun families settled in Mianwali, Punjab; Younis Khan and Shahid Afridi were from Pashtun families that had moved to Karachi.

46. Oborne, *Wounded Tiger*, p. 411.

47. Stephen Wagg, *Cricket: A Political History of the Global Game, 1945–2017* (Routledge, 2018), pp. 291–92.

48. Ibid.

49. Chris Rumford, 'More Than a Game: Globalization and the Post-Westernization of World Cricket,' *Global Networks*, 7/2 (2007), pp. 202–214.

50. Oborne, *Wounded Tiger*, p. 398.

51. See Samiuddin, *The Unquiet Ones*; Abid Hussain, 'Tape Ball Tales,' *The Cricket Monthly* (November 2015), url: http://www.thecricketmonthly.com/story/929545/tape-ball-tales, accessed on 5 December 2017; and Heller and Oborne, *White on Green*.

52. Hussain, 'Tape Ball Tales.'

53. Ibid.

54. Heller and Oborne, *White on Green*, p. 324.

55. Samiuddin, *The Unquiet Ones*, p. 467.

56. Heller and Oborne, *White on Green*.

57. Pakistan's Test Match record (percentage of wins) places them below Australia, South Africa, and England, but above India, Sri Lanka, New Zealand, West Indies, Bangladesh, and Zimbabwe. Their one-day record is even more impressive, with only Australia and South Africa having a better win percentage.

58. Samiuddin, *The Unquiet Ones*, p. 438.

59. This excludes stand-in captains.

60. Nandy, *A Very Popular Exile*, p. 25.

61. Stuart Hall (ed.), *Representation: Cultural Representations and Signifying Practices* (Sage Publications, 1997).

62. Richard Cashman, 'The Paradox that is Pakistani Cricket: Some Initial Reflections,' *The Sports Historian* (14 May 1994), pp. 21–37.

Chapter 2: Politics, Organization, and Leadership

1. Max Weber, *Economy and Society*, edited by Guenther Roth and Clauss Wittich (University of California Press, 1978), p. 223.

2. Gerald M. Britain and Ronald Cohen (eds.), *Hierarchy and Society: Anthropological Perspectives on Bureaucracy* (Institute for the Study of Human Issues, 1980), pp. 10–11.

3. See for example: William G. Scott, 'Organization Theory: An Overview and Appraisal,' *Journal of the Academy of Management* 4 (1961), pp. 7–26; James D. Thompson, *Organizations in Action: Social Science Bases of Administrative Theory* (McGraw Hill, 1967).

4. See Britain and Cohen, *Hierarchy and Society*.

5. Susan Wright (ed.), *Anthropology of Organizations* (Routledge, 1994), p. 17.

6. Britain and Cohen, *Hierarchy and Society*, p. 19.

7. Yasmin Khan, *The Great Partition: The Making of India and Pakistan* (Yale University Press, 2007), p. 156.

8. Figures from doi.punjab.gov.pk [weblink no longer active as of 25 June 2021].

9. Parvez Hasan, 'Learning from the Past: A Fifty-Year Perspective on Pakistan's Development,' *The Pakistan Development Review* 36/4 (1997), pp. 355–402; Parvez Hasan, 'Poverty and

Social Justice: Some Challenges for Islamization in Pakistan,' in R.M. Hathaway & Wilson Lee (eds.), *Islamization and the Pakistani Economy* (Woodrow Wilson International Centre for Scholars, 2004), p. 63.

10. Khan, *The Great Partition*, p. 156.

11. Karachi, for example, which was to become Pakistan's first capital, saw its Hindu population decline from 47.6 per cent in 1941 to half that number by the end of the decade—see William Dalrymple, 'The Great Divide,' *The New Yorker* (22 June 2015), url: https://www.newyorker.com/magazine/2015/06/29/the-great-divide-books-dalrymple (accessed on 8 September 2019).

12. Khan, *The Great Partition*, p. 120.

13. Gustav F. Papanek, *Pakistan's Development: Social Goals and Private Incentives* (Harvard University Press, 1967), p. 1.

14. According to Papanek, it was acknowledged by *The Times* of London though 'the survival and development of Pakistan is one of the most remarkable examples of state and nation building in the post war world' (*The Times* [London], 26 February 1966, quoted in Papanek, *Pakistan's Development*, p. 1.

15. See Richard Cashman, *Patrons, Players and the Crowd* (Orient Longman, 1980); P. Kidambi, *Cricket Country* (Oxford University Press, 2019).

16. Kidambi, *Cricket Country*, pp. 84–85.

17. These institutions included, amongst others, Aitchison College in Lahore, Mayo College in Ajmer, and Daly College in Indore.

18. Arjun Appadurai, 'Playing with Modernity: The Decolonization of Indian Cricket,' *Altre Modernita* 14 (2015), pp. 1–24.

19. See Samiuddin, *The Unquiet Ones*, chapter 4, for details of early patrons of cricket in Pakistan.

20. Collector travelled to the ICC at his own expense to make Pakistan's application for Test Status (Samiuddin, *The Unquiet Ones*, p. 62).

21. Pakistan won its second Test match the year it began playing Test cricket. In comparison, India took 24 Test matches and 26 years, Sri Lanka 14 Test matches and 3 years, Bangladesh 35 Test matches and 5 years, Zimbabwe 11 Test matches and 3 years, and New Zealand 45 Test matches and 26 years.

22. Scyld Berry, *Cricket: The Game of Life: Every reason to celebrate* (Hodder and Stoughton, 2015), p. 169.

23. Richard Giulianotti, *Sport: A Critical Sociology* (Polity Press, 2016), p. 6.

24. Brett Hutchins, 'Unity, Difference and the "National Game": Cricket and Australian National Identity,' in Stephen Wagg (ed.), *Cricket and National Identity in the Postcolonial Age: Following On* (Routledge, 2005).

25. Benedict Anderson, *Imagined Communities: Reflections on the Origin and Spread of Nationalism* (Verso, 1991).

26. Hutchins, 'Unity, Difference, and the "National Game",' p. 12.

27. Hilary Beckles, *Cricket without a Cause: Fall and Rise of the Mighty West Indian Cricketers* (Ian Randle, 2017).

28. Appadurai, 'Playing with Modernity.'

29. Mushtaq Mohammad, who captained Pakistan in the 1970s, did in fact spend two years in England between 1964 and 1966, 'qualifying' to play for his county during which he could not play for any other team. It meant a two-year hiatus from Pakistan at a time when he was at his peak.

30. Mihir Bose, *A History of Indian Cricket* (Andre Deutsch Ltd., 1980), pp. 291, 301.

31. Appadurai, 'Playing with Modernity.'
32. Ziaul Haq's first appointee was General K.M. Azhar whose credentials were his achievement in having conquered 1300 square miles of Rajasthan during the 1965 India–Pakistan war.
33. Peter Corrigan, 'Imran Khan: The Road from Cricket to Politics,' in David L. Andrews and Steven J. Jackson (eds.), *Sports Stars: The Cultural Politics of Sporting Celebrity* (Routledge, 2002), p. 237.
34. Shaharyar Khan has written extensively about this with reference to cricket being a 'bridge of peace.' See *Cricket: A Bridge of Peace* (Oxford University Press, 2005) and *Shadows Across the Playing Field: 60 Years of India–Pakistan Cricket* (Roli Books, 2009) which he co-authored with Shashi Tharoor.
35. Rahul Bhattacharya, 'Indians in Pakistan: Brothers, Not in Arms,' in John Stern and Marcus Williams (eds.), *The Essential Wisden: An Anthology of 150 Years of Wisden Cricketers' Almanack* (Bloomsbury, 2013), p. 523.
36. Shaharyar M. Khan and Ali Khan, *Cricket Cauldron: The Turbulent Politics of Sport in Pakistan* (Harper Sport, 2013), p. 63.
37. According to a *Dawn* report, 1027 civilian posts had been occupied by servicemen. See: Nasir Iqbal, '1,027 civilian posts occupied by servicemen,' *Dawn* (3 October 2003), url: https://www.dawn.com/news/118233, accessed on 25 June 2021.
38. Richard Heller and Peter Oborne, *White on Green: A Portrait of Pakistan Cricket* (Simon Schuster, 2016), pp. 222–23.
39. Later rechristened the Gaddafi stadium.
40. Under Zulfikar Ali Bhutto, from 1971 to 1977. See Christophe Jaffrelot, *The Pakistan Paradox: Instability and Resilience* (Penguin 2015), p. 4.
41. Ian Talbot, *Pakistan: A Modern History* (Hurst and Company, 2005), p. 287.
42. Anatol Lieven, *Pakistan: A Hard Country* (Penguin Books, 2011), p. 79.
43. Lt. Gen. Zahid Ali Akbar was later accused of corruption, fled the country, and was on the run until he was detained in Bosnia, by which time his British nationality allowed him to wriggle out of trouble. He was later extradited to the UK and took a plea bargain to return money he had gotten through illegal means. See: Syed Irfan Raza, 'Ex-chief of Wapda held in Bosnia on corruption charges,' *Dawn* (10 May 2013), url: https://www.dawn.com/news/1010570, accessed on 25 June 2021.
44. Sameen A. Mohsin Ali, 'Governance Amid Crisis: Delegation, Personal Gain, and Service Delivery in Pakistan,' in Mariam Mufti, Sahar Shafqat, and Niloufer Siddiqui (eds.), *Pakistan's Political Parties: Surviving Between Dictatorship and Democracy* (Georgetown University Press, 2020), pp. 181–82.
45. Samiuddin, *The Unquiet Ones*, p. 416.
46. Quoted in: Peter Oborne, *Wounded Tiger: A History of Cricket in Pakistan* (Simon & Schuster, 2014), p. 491.
47. Chairmanship changed eight times between 2011 and 2018.
48. About a million US dollars.
49. Albert Gorvine, 'The Civil Service under the Revolutionary Government in Pakistan,' *Middle East Journal* 19/3 (1965), p. 321; Stephen Cohen, *The Idea of Pakistan* (Vanguard Books, 2005), pp. 41, 316.

Chapter 3: Corruption, Match-Fixing, and Redemption

1. Huw Richards, 'After 5-Year Ban for Fixing, Player Returns to Pakistan,' *The New York Times* (13 January 2016), url: https://www.nytimes.com/2016/01/14/sports/cricket/after-5-year-ban-for-fixing-amir-returns-for-pakistan.html, accessed on 28 June 2021.

2. 'England's Jonathan Trott shocked by Pakistan spot-fixing allegations,' *The Telegraph* (4 September 2010), url: https://www.telegraph.co.uk/sport/cricket/international/england/7981536/Englands-Jonathan-Trott-shocked-by-Pakistan-spot-fixing-allegations.html, accessed on 28 June 2021.

3. 'Swann slams 'aloof and arrogant' Butt,' *ESPN* (2 November 2011), url: http://en.espn.co.uk/cricket/sport/story/119211.html, accessed on 28 June 2021.

4. Gary Payne, 'Pakistan refuse to suspend 'spot-fixing' players without proof,' *The Guardian* (31 August 2010), url: https://www.theguardian.com/sport/2010/aug/31/pakistan-england-spot-fixing, accessed on 28 June 2021.

5. Butt completed seven months, Asif six months, and Amir three months before being released early.

6. C.L.R. James, *Beyond a Boundary* (Yellow Jersey Press, 2005), p. 33.

7. Derek Birley, *A Social History of English Cricket* (Aurum Press, 2003), p. 273.

8. Ibid., p. 273.

9. Keith A.P. Sandiford, 'Cricket and the Victorian Society,' *Journal of Social History* 17/2 (1983), p. 303.

10. See Dickens's *David Copperfield, Pickwick Papers*; also, 'A Breathless Hush...': in David Allen and Hubert Doggart (eds.), *The MCC Anthology of Cricket Verse* (Methuen Publishing, 2007).

11. Sandiford, 'Cricket,' p. 303.

12. Ibid., p. 306.

13. Mike Brearley, *On Cricket* (Little, Brown Book Group, 2018).

14. Lord Harris, former English Test cricketer and Governor of Bombay, 1931. Letter to *The Times* (3 February 1931).

15. David Frith, 'Corruption in Cricket,' in Anthony Bateman and Jeffrey Hill (eds.), *The Cambridge Companion to Cricket* (Cambridge University Press, 2011), p. 40.

16. Dominic Malcolm, Jon Gemmell, and Nalin Mehta, 'Cricket and Modernity: International and Interdisciplinary Perspectives on the Study of the Imperial Game,' *Sport in Society* 12/4 (2009), p. 420.

17. Ed Hawkins, *Bookie Gambler Fixer Spy: A Journey to the Heart of Cricket's Underworld* (Bloomsbury, 2013); Simon Wilde, *Caught: The Full Story of Cricket's Match-Fixing Scandal* (Aurum Press, 2001).

18. Named after the judge who conducted the inquiry, Malik Muhammad Qayyum.

19. Justice Fakhruddin Ebrahim 1995, Justice Ejaz Yousuf 1998. For details, see Osman Samiuddin, *The Unquiet Ones: A History of Pakistan Cricket* (Harper Collins, 2014).

20. Hawkins, *Bookie Gambler Fixer Spy*, pp. 3–4.

21. The Qayyum Report, 1999, url: https://www.pcb.com.pk/downloads/Qayyum_report.pdf, accessed on 28 June 2021.

22. 'CBI Report on Cricket Match Fixing and Related Malpractices,' *Cricinfo India* (2000), url: http://www.aus.cricket.org/link_to_database/NATIONAL/IND/NEWS/CBI-REPORT.html, accessed on 9 July 2021.

23. Michael J. Sandel, *What Money Can't Buy: The Moral Limits of Markets* (Farrar, Straus and Giroux, 2012).

24. Uri Gneezy and Aldo Rustichini, 'A Fine is a Price,' *Journal of Legal Studies* 29 (2000); Steven Levitt and Stephen Dubner, *Freakonomics: A Rogue Economist Explores the Hidden Side of Everything* (William Morrow, 2005).

25. South Africa was banned from international competition between 1970 and 1991 due to its Apartheid policy and Sri Lanka became only the eight team to join in 1982 following a gap of thirty years. By 2019, four more teams had joined—Zimbabwe (1992), Bangladesh (2000), Ireland (2018), and Afghanistan (2018).

26. Arjun Appadurai, 'Playing with modernity: The decolonization of Indian Cricket,' *Altre Modernita* 14 (2015), p. 3.

27. For an in-depth account of World Series Cricket, see Gideon Haigh, *The Cricket War: The Story of Kerry Packer's World Series Cricket* (Wisden, 2017).

28. Sataduru Sen, 'History without a Past in Postcolonial Pakistan,' in Stephen Wagg (ed.), *Cricket and National Identity in the Postcolonial Age* (Routledge, 2005), p. 101.

29. Ibid., p. 101.

30. The Benson and Hedges World Championship of Cricket held in Australia.

31. James Astill, *The Great Tamasha: Cricket, Corruption and the Turbulent Rise of Modern India* (Wisden, 2013), p. 54.

32. Ashis Nandy, *A Very Popular Exile: An Omnibus, comprising The Tao of Cricket; An Ambiguous Journey to the City; Traditions, Tyranny, and Utopias* (Oxford University Press, 2020), pp. 1–7.

33. Sharda Ugra, 'Play Together, Live Apart: Religion, Politics and Markets in Indian Cricket since 1947,' in Stephen Wagg (ed.), *Cricket and National Identity in the Postcolonial Age* (Routledge, 2005), p. 82.

34. Sen, 'History,' p. 102.

35. Astill, *The Great Tamasha*, p. 53.

36. Ugra, 'Play Together, Live Apart,' p. 81.

37. Astill, *The Great Tamasha*, p. 79.

38. ACU report, 2001, para 92.

39. Mihir Bose, *A History of Indian Cricket* (Andre Deutsch Ltd., 2002); Ramachandra Guha, *A Corner of a Foreign Field: The Indian History of a British Sport* (Picador, 2002).

40. According to the data provided by the BCCI, the Indian Premier League (IPL) contributed Rs 11.5 billion ($182 million) to India's Gross Domestic Product (GDP) in 2015. The data were compiled by KPMG Sports Advisory Group through an economic survey which revealed that the economic output associated with the IPL in India stood at Rs 26.5 billion ($418 million)—see Manas Tiwari, 'IPL Economy: What the cash-rich league adds to India's GDP,' *Financial Express* (22 January 2018), url: https://www.financialexpress.com/sports/ipl/ipl-economy-what-the-cash-rich-league-adds-to-indias-gdp/1025063/, accessed on 28 June 2021.

41. Andy Bull, 'The tension between Test cricket and Twenty20,' *The Guardian* (6 January 2015), url: https://www.theguardian.com/sport/2015/jan/06/the-spin-cricket-big-bash-tensions-tests-twenty20, accessed on 28 June 2021.

42. Hilary McDonald Beckles, 'The Detachment of West Indi Cricket from the Nationalist Scaffold,' in Anthony Bateman and Jeffrey Hill (eds.), *the Cambridge Companion to Cricket* (Cambridge University Press, 2011), p. 166.

43. 'Wasim Akram, Shoaib Akhtar criticize Amir's decision to tire from Test cricket,' *The News* (27 July 2019), url: https://www.thenews.com.pk/la st/504478-wasim-akram-shoaib-akhtar-criticize-amirs-decision-to-retire-from-test-cricket, accessed on 28 June 2021.

44. Sir Paul Condon, *Report on Corruption in International Cricket* (Anti-Corruption Unit, 2001), para 69.
45. Pradeep Magazine, *Not Quite Cricket* (Penguin Books, 1999), p. 43.
46. Mushtaq Ahmed, *Twenty20 Vision: My Life and Inspiration* (Methuen Publishing Ltd., 2006); Wasim Akram with Patrick Murphy, *Wasim: The Autobiography of Wasim Akram* (Piatkus Books, 1998).
47. Ivo Tennant, *Imran Khan* (Gollancz/Witherby, 1995), p. 183.
48. Ibid., p. 184.
49. Simon Wilde, *England: The Biography: The Story of English Cricket 1877–2018* (Simon and Schuster, 2018).
50. Wilde, *Caught*, p. 92.
51. Peter Robinson, 'For the love of money, says Cronje,' *ESPN CricInfo* (21 June 2000), url: https://www.espncricinfo.com/story/_/id/23232893/for-love-money-says-cronje, accessed on 28 June 2021.
52. Robinson, 'For the love of money, says Cronje.'
53. Matt Scott, 'Cricket agent accuses Salman Butt of recruiting spot-fixing players,' *The Guardian* (2 November 2011), url: https://www.theguardian.com/sport/2011/nov/02/mazhar-majeed-accusations-salman-butt, accessed on 28 June 2021.
54. Osman Samiuddin et al., 'Who gets paid what in cricket,' *The Cricket Monthly* (17 October 2017), url: https://www.thecricketmonthly.com/story/1123792/who-gets-paid-what-in-cricket, accessed on 28 June 2021; Simon Lambert, 'How much do top cricketers learn?,' *This Is Money* (3 September 2010), url: https://www.thisismoney.co.uk/money/article-1702948/How-much-do-top-cricketers-earn.html, accessed on 28 June 2021.
55. Geoffrey Hughes, Chiara Bresciani, Megnaa Mehtta, and Stuart Strange, 'Introduction. Ugly Emotions and the Politics of Accusation.' In 'Envy and Greed: Ugly Emotions and the Politics of Accusation,' Special issue of the *Cambridge Journal of Anthropology* 37/2 (2019), pp. 1–20.
56. Bernardo E. Brown, 'From Guru Gama to Punchi Italia: Changing Dreams of Sri Lankan Transnational Youth,' *Contemporary South Asia* 22/4 (2014), pp. 335–349.
57. Sharda Ugra, 'What makes sportsmen go corrupt?,' *ESPN CricInfo* (4 November 2010), url: https://www.espncricinfo.com/story/_/id/21284459/makes-sportsmen-go-corrupt, accessed on 30, June 2021.
58. Robinson, 'For the love of money, says Cronje.'
59. Ugra, 'What makes sportsmen go corrupt?'
60. Ibid.
61. Osman Samiuddin, 'The Miracle of 1992,' *The Cricket Monthly* (November 2014), url: http://www.thecricketmonthly.com/story/793785/the-miracle-of--92, accessed on 28 June 2021.
62. John Crace, *Wasim and Waqar: Imran's Inheritors* (Boxtree Ltd., 1992), p. 15.
63. Osman Samiuddin, 'The Imran Khans I've Known,' *The Cricket Monthly* (10 August 2018), url: http://www.thecricketmonthly.com/story/1154531/the-imran-khans-i-ve-known, accessed on 28 June 2021; Brian Radford, 'Call girls to be questioned in cricket scandal,' *The Guardian* (21 January 2001), url: https://www.theguardian.com/uk/2001/jan/21/sport.theobserver, accessed on 28 June 2021.
64. B.M. Bass and B.J. Avolio, *MLQ Multifactor Leadership Questionnaire* (Mind Garden, 2000).

65. Eddie Corbin, 'Leadership Issues in West Indies Cricket: A Theoretical Analysis of Leadership Styles of a Purposive Group of Captains,' *Journal of Eastern Caribbean Studies* 30/1 (2005), p. 35.

66. There were taped conversations presented in front of the Qayyum Commission.

67. 'Full transcript of Mohammad Amir interview,' *ESPN CricInfo* (20 March 2012), url: https://www.espncricinfo.com/story/_/id/21284462/full-transcript-mohammad-amir-interview, accessed on 28 June 2021.

68. In fact, Majeed was deep in debt to the tune of £704,000 and 23 of his 26 companies had collapsed, making him an ideal conduit for corrupt dealings—Matt Scott, 'Cricket spot-fixing: How the Pakistan three fell into a trap,' *The Guardian* (1 November 2011), url: https://www.theguardian.com/sport/2011/nov/01/cricket-spot-fixing-pakistan-trial-guilty, accessed on 28 June 2021; Caroline Gammell, 'Pakistan's captain "raised concerns about Mazhar Majeed Two Months Ago",' *The Telegraph* (31 August 2010), url: https://www.telegraph.co.uk/news/uknews/7971839/Pakistans-captain-Shahid-Afridi-raised-concerns-about-Mazhar-Majeed-two-months-ago.html, accessed on 28 June 2021.

69. Vivek Chaudhary, 'Wide boy,' *The Cricket Monthly* (March 2015), url: http://www.thecricketmonthly.com/story/836893/wide-boy, accessed on 28 June 2021.

70. 'Mohammad Amir interview with Sky Sports in full,' *The Telegraph* (19 March 2012), url: https://www.telegraph.co.uk/sport/cricket/international/pakistan/9154012/Mohammad-Amir-interview-with-Sky-Sports-in-full.html, accessed on 28 June 2021.

71. Para 224, 'ICC vs Salman Butt, Mohammad Asif and Mohammad Amir.'

72. This is mentioned in the ACU (2001) report on corruption as well. My unit has met people who have made allegations about threats to their life as a result of exposing cricket corruption and I have met a number of people who were, in my opinion, genuinely frightened of the consequences if it became known they were cooperating with the Anti-Corruption Unit (para 90, 2001).

73. Matt Scott, 'Pakistan cricketers wanted to sabotage Afridi captaincy, agent claimed,' *The Guardian* (11 October 2011), url: https://www.theguardian.com/sport/2011/oct/11/pakistan-cricket-sabotage-captaincy-claim, accessed on 28 June 2021.

74. Original undercover video no longer available on this link: https://www.youtube.com/watch?v=eJ25OORslsk. The closest approximation of it can be found here: 'Top 3 Pakistani Cricketers Involved in Spot Fixing Scam,' *YouTube* (7 October 2011), url: https://www.youtube.com/watch?v=jWWCTni1oTM.

75. Brearley, *On Cricket*, p. 190.

76. Ibid., p. 193.

77. Rudi V. Webster, 'Would a code of honour help?,' *ESPN CricInfo* (14 November 2010), url: http://www.espncricinfo.com/magazine/content/story/486861.html, accessed 28 November 2010.

78. Marie Chêne, Overview of corruption in Pakistan (U4 Anti-Corruption Resource Center, Chr. Michelsen Institute, 2008).

79. Umbreen Javaid, 'Corruption and its Deep Impact on Good Governance in Pakistan,' *Pakistan Economic and Social Review* 48/1 (2010), pp. 123–134; Asad Sayeed, 'Contextualising Corruption in Pakistan,' *Social Science and Policy Bulletin* 2/1 (2010), pp. 10–18; Sadaf Ahmad, 'Pakistani Policewomen: Questioning the Role of Gender in Circumscribing Police Corruption,' *Policing and Society* 30/8 (2019), pp. 890–904.

80. Yasmin Khan, *The Great Partition: The Making of India and Pakistan* (Yale University Press, 2007).

81. CPI 2018.

82. World Bank, 'Worldwide Governance Indicators,' url: https://info.worldbank.org/governance/wgi/Home/Reports.

83. Ansar Abbasi, 'Is Pakistan More Corrupt Than Before?,' *Geo TV* (13 October 2019), url: https://www.geo.tv/latest/251054-v, accessed on 30 June 2021.

84. Transparency International, 'Corruption Perceptions Index,' url: https://www.transparency.org/en/cpi/2020/index/pak.

85. Christophe Jaffrelot, *The Pakistan Paradox: Instability and Resilience* (Random House, 2016), p. 199.

86. Jaffrelot, *The Pakistan Paradox*, p. 251.

87. Helen Clifton, Matthew Chapman and Simon Cox, '"Staggering" trade in fake degrees revealed,' BBC News (16 January 2018), url: https://www.bbc.com/news/uk-42579634, accessed on 30 June 2021; Michael Kugelman, 'Remembering Pakistan's Biggest and Baddest Fraud Scandal,' *Foreign Policy* (22 May 2015), url: https://foreignpolicy.com/2015/05/22/remembering-pakistans-biggest-and-baddest-fraud-scandal/, accessed on 30 June 2021.

88. Angelos Kanas, 'Pure Contagion Effects in International Banking: The Case of BCCI's Failure,' *Journal of Applied Economics* 8/1 (2005), pp. 101–123.

89. Kugelman, 'Remembering Pakistan's Biggest and Baddest Fraud Scandal.'

90. Ibid., According to Kugelman, 'the bank was close to Pakistan's political leadership, providing financial assistance to military leader Gen. Zia al-Haq and finding a job for his brother. According to Kerry's report, BCCI also helped finance Pakistan's nuclear weapons procurement.'

91. Quoted in: Jaffrelot, *The Pakistan Paradox*, p. 213.

92. 'National Corruption Perception Survey, 2010,' Transparency International (19 March 2013).

93. Khan, *The Great Partition*.

94. Ibid.

95. Pakistan National Corruption Survey, 2006.

96. Ian Boardley and Maria Kavussanu, 'Moral disengagement in sport,' *International Review of Sport and Exercise Psychology* 4/2 (2011), pp. 93–108; Ian D. Boardley and Maria Kavussanu, 'The moral disengagement in sport scale-short,' *Journal of Sports Sciences* 26/14 (2008), pp. 1507–1517.

97. ACU report, 2001, para 12.

98. The ICL was a private Indian-funded rebel league which was not sanctioned by the International Cricket Council. The League was riddled with match-fixing rumours and lasted two seasons (2007–2009) before collapsing.

99. The Qayyum Report was 150 pages long and was based on over 40 hearings, nearly 70 interviews with players, ex-players, former captains, administrators, ex-administrators, bookies, and police officers, and was spread out over 13 months (Samiuddin, *The Unquiet Ones*, p. 383).

100. Mike Selvey, 'Pakistan clears its players of match-fixing,' *The Guardian* (11 May 2000), url: https://www.theguardian.com/sport/2000/may/11/cricket2, accessed on 28 June 2021.

101. Oborne, *Wounded Tiger*, p. 395.

102. Osman Samiuddin, 'Clean up your act, ICC tells PCB,' *ESPN* (13 October 2010), url: https://www.espn.co.uk/cricket/story/_/id/22378298/clean-your-act-icc-tells-pcb, accessed on 30 June 2021.

103. Y.S. Sikand, 'The Tablighi Jama'at and Politics: A Critical Re-Appraisal,' *The Muslim World* 96/1 (2006), p. 175.

104. Anatol Lieven, *Pakistan: A Hard Country* (Penguin Books, 2012), p. 129.

105. Ibid., p. 184.

106. Heller and Oborne, *White on Green*, p. 74.

107. See George Gmelch, 'Baseball Magic' (1971), reproduced in Pamela A. Moro and James E. Myers (eds.), *Magic, Witchcraft and Religion: A Reader in the Anthropology of Religion* (McGraw Hill, 2008).

108. Shaharyar M. Khan and Ali Khan, *Cricket Cauldron: The Turbulent Politics of Sport in Pakistan* (Harper Sport, 2013), pp. 189–190.

109. Y.S. Sikand, *The Origins and Development of the Tablighi Jama'at (1920–2000): A Cross-country Comparative Study* (Orient Blackswan, 2002), p. 257.

110. Sadaf Ahmad, 'Al-Huda and Women's Religious Authority in Urban Pakistan,' *The Muslim World* 103/3 (2013), p. 369.

111. 'Match-fixing is more common than ever,' *The Economist* (23 September 2017), url: https://www.economist.com/international/2017/09/23/match-fixing-is-more-common-than-ever, accessed on 30 June 2021.

Chapter 4: Pakistan in the Global Cricketing Order: England and the Colonial Legacy

1. Chris Valiotis, 'Sporting Nations of the Imagination: Pakistani Cricket and Identity in Pakistan and Anglo Pakistan,' Unpublished PhD dissertation, University of New South Wales, 2006, p. 112.

2. MCC—the Marylebone Cricket Club—is the cricket club founded in 1787 and based at the Lord's Cricket Ground in London. The club was formerly the governing body of cricket in England and Wales and the game's legislator in terms of rules and regulations. The MCC would sponsor and organize cricket tours in which the England team would play Test matches. On unofficial tours—as in the 1955–56 tour to Pakistan—the team would be called the MCC.

3. 'Donald Carr: 'Few in cricket have been so close to so much for so long'—Almanack,' *Wisden* (12 July 2019), url: https://www.wisden.com/almanack/donald-carr-almanack-tribute, accessed on 8 July 2021.

4. Peter Oborne, *Wounded Tiger: A History of Cricket in Pakistan* (Simon and Schuster, 2014), p. 120.

5. John Stern and Marcus Williams (eds.), *The Essential Wisden: An Anthology of 150 Years of Wisden Cricketers' Almanack* (Bloomsbury, 2014), p. 509.

6. Chris Searle, *Pitch of Life: Writings on Cricket* (The Parrs Wood Press, 2001), p. 4.

7. Mihir Bose in: Jack Williams, *Cricket and Race* (Berg, 2001), p. 137.

8. Chris Wagg, 'Introduction: Following On,' in Stephen Wagg (ed.), *Postcolonial Pakistan in Cricket and National Identity in the Postcolonial Age* (Routledge, 2005), p. 1.

9. Mike Marqusee, *Anyone but England* (Aurum Press, 2005), p. 206.

10. A multi-nation team from the Anglophone Caribbean region which was administered by Cricket West Indies.

11. 'History of ICC,' *ICC*, url: https://www.icc-cricket.com/about/the-icc/history-of-icc/1909-1963, accessed on 8 July 2021.

NOTES

12. Mike Marqusee, 'The Ambush Clause: Globalisation, Corporate Power and the Governance of World Cricket,' in Stephen Wagg (ed.), *Following On: Cricket and National Identity in the Postcolonial Age* (Routledge, 2005), p. 251.

13. Subhash Jaireth, 'Tracing Orientalism in Cricket: A Reading of Some Recent Australian Cricket Writing on Pakistani Cricket,' *Sporting Traditions* 12/1 (1995), p. 105.

14. In May 1961, South Africa, the third founding member, withdrew from the Commonwealth and was thus no longer eligible for ICC membership. They re-joined in 1991 following the deconstruction of apartheid—see 'History of ICC.'

15. Jaireth, 'Tracing Orientalism in Cricket.'

16. John Sainsbury, 'How the Taliban spin cricket,' *The Globe and Mail* (2 March 2015), url: https://www.theglobeandmail.com/opinion/how-the-taliban-spin-cricket/article23232635/, accessed on 8 July 2021.

17. Richard Cashman, *Patrons, Players and the Crowd* (Orient Longman, 1979), p. 37.

18. Clifford Geertz, *The Interpretation of Cultures* (Basic Books, 1973).

19. Stuart Hall, 'The West and the Rest: Discourse and Power,' in Stuart Hall and Bram Gieben (eds.), *Formations of Modernity* (Polity Press, 1992).

20. The remark was made to Pat Murphy in an interview to the BBC (mentioned in Henry Blofeld, *One Test after Another: Life in International Cricket* (Stanley Paul and Co Ltd., 1985), p. 109.

21. In Jaireth, 'Tracing Orientalism in Cricket,' p. 108.

22. Ian Healy, *Hands and Heals: The Autobiography* (HarperCollins, 2000), pp. 160–61.

23. Bob Willis and Alan Lee, *The Captain's Diary: England in Fiji, New Zealand, and Pakistan 1983–84* (Collins, 1984), p. 106.

24. Jack Russell, *A Wicket-Keeper's Life* (HarperCollins, 1997), p. 73.

25. Brian Close touring England cricketer—quoted in Oborne, *Wounded Tiger*, p. 114.

26. Healy, *Hands and Heals*, p. 160.

27. Derek Pringle, 'The special tensions of England v Pakistan,' *The Independent* (23 July 1996), url: https://www.independent.co.uk/sport/the-special-tensions-of-england-v-pakistan-1330199.html, accessed on 8 July 2021.

28. Russell, *A Wicket-Keeper's Life*, p. 73.

29. Vic Marks, writing in the *Cricketer* (May 1984).

30. Mike Coward, *Beyond the Bazaar* (Allen and Unwin, 1990), pp. 64–5.

31. Steve Waugh, *Out of My Comfort Zone: The Autobiography* (Penguin Books, 2005), p. 327.

32. Nasser Hussain, *Playing with Fire: The Autobiography* (Michael Joseph, 2004), p. 137.

33. Botham was injured on the tour and returned early.

34. Bob Willis, *The Captain's Diary*, p. 140.

35. Valiotis, 'Sporting Nations'; and Jaireth, 'Tracing Orientalism in Cricket.'

36. Jaireth, 'Tracing Orientalism in Cricket,' pp. 108–109.

37. Lutfi Sunar, 'The Long History of Islam as a Collective "Other" of the West and the Rise of Islamophobia in the U.S. after Trump,' *Insight Turkey* 19/3 (2017), pp. 35–52.

38. Valiotis, 'Sporting Nations.'

39. Bob Willis, *Lasting the Pace* (HarperCollins, 1985), p. 90.

40. Willis, *The Captain's Diary*, p. 118.

41. See for example: Kevin Pietersen, *Crossing the Boundary* (Random House, 2006); Darren Gough, *Dazzler* (Michael Joseph, 2001); Andrew Strauss, *Driving Ambition: My Autobiography* (Hodder and Staughton, 2013); Willis, *Lasting the Pace*; Willis, *The Captain's Diary*; Hussain, *Playing with Fire*.

42. Wisden (John Etheridge tour report, 2006), p. 1020.

43. Cricket did not introduce neutral umpires officially until 1994, depending instead on local umpires for all home series.

44. *Wisden Cricketers' Almanack* (John Wisden and Co. Ltd., 1988).

45. He was to take this back on President Ziaul Haq's request a few months later.

46. Simon Wilde, *England: The Biography: The Story of English Cricket* (Simon and Schuster, 2018); Scyld Berry, *Cricket Odyssey* (Pavilion Books, 1988).

47. Stephen Chalke, *Micky Stewart and the Changing Face of Cricket* (Fairfield Books, 2012).

48. John Crace, *Wasim and Waqar: Imran's Inheritors* (Boxtree Ltd., 1992).

49. Mihir Bose, 'Conflicting Loyalties: Nationalism and Religion in India–Pakistan cricket relations,' in A. Bateman and J. Hill (eds.), *The Cambridge Companion to Cricket* (Cambridge University Press, 2011).

50. Bill Athey in: Marqusee, *Anyone but England*, p. 172.

51. Javed Miandad, *Cutting Edge* (Oxford University Press, 2003), p. 251.

52. 'There has been one miscarriage of justice after another,' *ESPN Cricinfo* (February 1988), url: http://www.espncricinfo.com/wcm/content/story/226916.html, accessed on 8 July 2021.

53. Ibid.

54. Ibid.

55. Ibid.

56. See for example: documentary by Stevan Riley (dir.), *Fire in Babylon* (Cowboy Films/ Passion Pictures, director, 2010); Simon Lister, *Fire in Babylon: How the West Indies Cricket Team Brought a People to its Feet* (Yellow Jersey, 2016); Vivian Richards, *Hitting Across the Line* (Headline Book Publishing, 1992)—all of which speak of the racism faced by West Indian cricketers of the 1970s and 1980s.

57. Derek Birley, *Social History of English Cricket* (Aurum Press, 2003), p. 333.

58. Kishore Bhimani, *Director's Special Book of Cricketing Controversies* (Allied Publishers Limited, 1996), p. 77.

59. Paul Kelso and Rob Evans, 'Gatting's bust-up with umpire just wasn't cricket, said British envoy,' *The Guardian* (19 December 2005), url: https://www.theguardian.com/uk/2005/ dec/19/cricket.freedomofinformation, accessed on 8 July 2021.

60. Kelso and Evans, 'Gatting's bust-up.'

61. Neil Robinson, *Long Shot Summer: The Year of 4 England Captains 1988* (Amberley Publishing, 2015).

62. 'There has been one miscarriage of justice after another,' *ESPN Cricinfo*.

63. For a detailed account of the incident, see: Shaharyar Khan and Ali Khan, *Cricket Cauldron: The Turbulent Politics of Sport in Pakistan* (Harper Sport, 2013).

64. Jack Williams, *Cricket and Race* (Berg, 2001), p. 162.

65. Oborne, *Wounded Tiger*, p. 231.

66. *Wisden Cricketers' Almanack 1985* (John Wisden, 1985), p. 54.

67. Williams, *Cricket and Race*, p. 162.

68. *Daily Mirror* (10 December 1987) in: Williams, *Cricket and Race*, p. 163.

69. Marqusee, *Anyone but England*, p. 226.

70. See either Marqusee, *Anyone but England*, Chapter 5, or Williams, *Cricket and Race*, Chapter 6, for details on the 1996 World Cup bid.

71. Headline in *The Sun* (28 August 1992).

72. Chris Searle, *Pitch of Life: Writings on Cricket* (The Parrs Wood Press, 2001), p. 23.

73. Javed Miandad, quoted in: Williams, *Cricket and Race*, p. 139.

74. Quoted in: Marqusee, *Anyone but England*, p. 175.

75. Miandad was not a Pathan but a Muhajir—a migrant from India who settled in Karachi.
76. *The Sun* (22 July 1992).
77. *The Sun* (15 December 1987).
78. See Simon Barnes's article for example for a glowing tribute to how the Australian captain Steve Waugh shaped the 'modern' game—Simon Barnes, 'Steve Waugh: The Captain who Transformed Test Cricket—Almanack,' *Wisden India* (2 June 2019), url: https://www. wisden.com/almanack/steve-waugh-wisden-tribute, accessed on 8 July 2021.
79. Williams, *Cricket and Race*, p. 140.
80. Marqusee, *Anyone but England*, p. 195.
81. Ibid., p. 182.
82. *The Daily Mirror* (26 August 1992).
83. Searle, *Pitch of Life*, p. 32.
84. Marqusee, *Anyone but England*, p. 202.
85. Williams, *Cricket and Race*.
86. *The Guardian* (28 July 1992).
87. Quoted in: Adam Licudi and Wasim Raja, *Cornered Tigers: A History of Pakistan's Test Cricket* (Hansib Publishing, 1997), p. 48.
88. In: Marqusee, *Anyone but England*, p. 176.
89. Simon Heffer (*The Sunday Telegraph*, 12 July 1992).
90. Searle, *Pitch of Life*, p. 23.
91. Marqusee, *Anyone but England*, p. 184.
92. *The Times* (29 August 1992).
93. Marqusee, *Anyone but England*, p. 197.
94. The umpire who reported the tampering was removed from England's umpiring Test panel following that incident—see this link for a recording of the interview: http:// thecricketcouch.com/couch-talk/transcript-couch-talk-with-john-holder-former-international-umpire/. John Holder has recently taken the England Cricket Board to court for alleged racial discrimination—Barney Ronay, 'Former Test umpire John Holder sues ECB for alleged racial discrimination,' *The Guardian* (29 December 2020), url: https://www.theguardian.com/sport/2020/dec/29/former-test-umpire-john-holder-sues-ecb-for-alleged-racial-discrimination, accessed on 8 July 2021.
95. For a few prominent examples, see: 'Ball-tampering: Five memorable cricketing controversies from Atherton to Du Plessis,' *BBC Sport* (25 March 2018), url: https:// www.bbc.com/sport/cricket/43532624, accessed on 8 July 2021.
96. Chris Pringle, *Save the Last Ball for Me* (Celebrity Books, 1998).
97. For example, 'Cricket: Akhtar tossed out for ball tampering,' *NZHerald* (21 May 2003), url: https://www.nzherald.co.nz/sport/news/article.cfm?c_id=4&objectid=3503261, accessed on 8 July 2021; 'Afridi banned for two T20s for ball-tampering,' *ESPN Cricinfo* (31 January 2010), url: https://www.espncricinfo.com/story/_/id/22636034/shahid-afridi-banned-two-t20s-ball-tampering, accessed on 8 July 2021.
98. Shoaib Akhtar, *Controversially Yours* (HarperCollins, 2011), p. 124.
99. Williams, *Cricket and Race*, p. 160; Marqusee, *Anyone but England*, p. 178.
100. Claire Westall and Neil Lazarus, 'The Pitch of the World: Cricket and Chris Searle,' *Race and Class* 51/2 (2009), p. 57.
101. Marqusee, *Anyone but England*, p. 190.
102. For an analysis of the racist narrative used during the West Indies tour, see: Searle, *Pitch of Life*; Marqusee, *Anyone but England*; and Williams, *Cricket and Race*.
103. Gough, *Dazzler*, p. 301.

104. Hussain, *Playing with Fire*, pp. 294–95.

105. Nasser Hussain, quoted in: Ben Dirs, *Everywhere We Went: Top Tales from Cricket's Barmy Army* (Simon and Schuster, 2012).

106. Wasim Akram, with Patrick Murphy, *Wasim: The Autobiography of Wasim Akram* (Piatkus Books, 1998), p. 138.

107. Michael Atherton, *Athers: Authorised Biography of Michael Atherton* (Headline Book Publishing, 1996), p. 257.

108. Andrew Flintoff, *Being Freddie: My Story So Far* (Hodder and Stoughton, 2005).

109. Peter Oborne, 'Are We Wrong about Pakistan?,' *The Telegraph* (28 February 2012), url: https://www.telegraph.co.uk/travel/destinations/asia/pakistan/articles/Are-we-wrong-about-Pakistan/, accessed on 8 July 2021.

110. Moeen Ali, with Mihir Bose, *Moeen* (Allen and Unwin, 2018), p. 257.

111. For a detailed account of the incident, see: Khan and Khan, *Cricket Cauldron*.

112. See for example: Simon Barnes, 'Hair today, gone tomorrow—at least we hope so for sake of game,' *The Times* (22 August 2006), url: https://www.thetimes.co.uk/article/hair-today-gone-tomorrow-at-least-we-hope-so-for-sake-of-game-zfcn6tvv2gl, accessed on 8 July 2021. 'Hussain: I'd have done the same if I had been in Inzy's shoes,' *The Daily Mail* (21 August 2006); Mike Selvy: 'Umpires acting in such cavalier fashion brings shame on the game,' *The Guardian* (21 August 2006); Mike Masqusee, 'The Pakistanis were right to protest at a rank injustice,' *The Guardian* (22 August 2006); Geoffrey Boycott, 'Hair cuts an over-officious figure in the game,' *The Daily Telegraph* (21 August 2006).

113. 'I blame the ICC says Ian Botham,' *The Mirror* (21 August 2006), url: https://www.mirror.co.uk/news/uk-news/i-blame-the-icc-says-ian-botham-638824, accessed on 8 July 2021.

114. Robert Padmore died of a heart attack. Phil Long, 'Death of a fan,' *BBC Sport* (25 November 2005), url: http://news.bbc.co.uk/sport1/hi/cricket/england/4470766.stm, accessed on 8 July 2021.

115. 'Butt defends not suspending spot-fixing trio,' *The Independent* (22 October 2011), url: https://www.independent.co.uk/sport/cricket/butt-defends-not-suspending-spot-fixing-trio-2091765.html, accessed on 8 July 2021.

116. 'Ijaz Butt accuses England of accepting money to lose Pakistan match,' *The Guardian* (19 September 2010), url: https://www.theguardian.com/sport/2010/sep/19/ijaz-butt-england-pakistan, accessed on 8 July 2021.

117. 'Anger over Ijaz Butt Remarks,' *The National* (21 September 2010), url: https://www.thenational.ae/sport/anger-over-ijaz-butt-remarks-1.504169, accessed on 8 July 2021.

118. Owen Gibson, 'Ijaz Butt withdraws accusations of match fixing against England team,' *The Guardian* (29 September 2010), url: https://www.theguardian.com/sport/2010/sep/29/ijaz-butt-england-pakistan, accessed on 8 July 2021.

119. *The Guardian* (26 March 2007).

120. Dominic Malcolm, Alan Bairner, and Graham Curry, '"Woolmergate:" Sport and the Representation of Islam and Muslims in the British Press,' *Journal of Sport and Social Issues* 34/2 (2010), pp. 215–235.

121. Writing in: *The Sun* (23 March 2007).

122. Writing in: *The Independent* (19 March 2007).

123. Malcolm, Bairner, and Curry, 'Woolmergate', p. 222.

124. 'Islamic fanatics may have killed Woolmer,' *Daily Star* (30 April 2007); 'Murdered after angering radical Muslims,' *Daily Mail* (30 April 2007); 'Was Woolmer facing a Fatwa?'

Daily Mail (30 April 2007); 'Did Muslim radicals order the murder of Woolmer?' *Daily Mirror* (30 March 2007).

125. 'Woolmer "died of natural causes",' *BBC News* (12 June 2007), url: http://news.bbc. co.uk/1/hi/world/americas/6745589.stm, accessed on 8 July 2021.

Chapter 5: Pakistan in the Global Cricketing Order – South Asia I

1. 'India's Most Legendary of Figures,' *ESPN Cricinfo* (Auguste 1994), url: http://www. espncricinfo.com/cricketer/content/story/141740.html, accessed on 8 July 2021.
2. Peter Oborne, *Wounded Tiger: A History of Cricket in Pakistan* (Simon & Schuster, 2014); Ian Talbot and Tahir Kamran, 'Poets, Wrestlers and Cricketers: Patronage and Performance in Lahore and Beyond,' in Ian Talbot and Tahir Kamran (eds.), *Colonial Lahore: A History of the City and Beyond* (Oxford Scholarship Online, 2017).
3. Oborne, *Wounded Tiger*.
4. Oborne, *Wounded Tiger*, p. 69.
5. Nadeem F. Paracha, 'The Pakistan zeitgeists: A nation through the ages,' *Dawn* (29 May 2014), url: https://www.dawn.com/news/1109105, accessed on 8 July 2021; Rajendra Amarnath, *Lala Amarnath Life and Times: The Making of a Legend* (Sportsbooks Ltd., 2007).
6. Amarnath, *Lala Amarnath*, p. 214.
7. Ibid., p. 212.
8. Ibid., p. 212.
9. Ibid., p. 213.
10. 'India's Most Legendary of Figures,' *ESPN Cricinfo*.
11. Imtiaz Ahmed, 'Pakistan cricketers pay rich tribute to Lala,' *ESPN* (9 August 2000), url: https://www.espn.co.uk/cricket/story/_/id/23242977/pakistan-cricketers-pay-rich-tribute-lala, accessed on 8 July 2021; Imtiaz Ahmed, 'More tributes to Lala Amarnath from Pakistan,' *ESPN* (10 August 2000), url: https://www.espn.com.sg/cricket/story/_/id/23242079/more-tributes-lala-amarnath-pakistan, accessed on 8 July 2021; Omar Kureishi, 'Amarnath's death a sad moment in cricket,' *ESPN Cricinfo* (9 August 2000), url: https://www.espncricinfo.com/story/_/id/23241718/amarnath-death-sad-moment-cricket, accessed on 8 July 2021.
12. Mihir Bose, 'Conflicting Loyalties: Nationalism and Religion in India–Pakistan Cricket Relations,' in A. Bateman and J. Hill (eds.), *The Cambridge Companion to Cricket* (Cambridge University Press, 2011).
13. Bose, 'Conflicting Loyalties.'
14. Fazal Mahmood with Asif Sohail, *From Dusk to Dawn: Autobiography of a Pakistan Cricket Legend* (Oxford University Press, 2003), p. 106.
15. Rahul Bhattacharya, 'Hope and Fear,' *ESPN Cricinfo* (27 March 2004), url: https://www. espncricinfo.com/story/hope-and-fear-140425, accessed on 8 July 2021.
16. Bhattacharya, 'Hope and Fear.'
17. C. Valiotis, 'Sporting Nations of the Imagination: Pakistani Cricket and Identity in Pakistan and Anglo Pakistan,' Unpublished PhD dissertation, University of New South Wales, 2006, p. 118.
18. *The Times of India* (11 August 1947), quoted in: Oborne, *Wounded Tiger*, p. 17.
19. 'History of ICC,' *ICC*, url: https://www.icc-cricket.com/about/the-icc/history-of-icc/1909-1963, accessed on 8 July 2021.

20. Valiotis, 'Sporting Nations,' p. 122.
21. Oborne, *Wounded Tiger*, p. 18; Valiotis, 'Sporting Nations,' p. 122.
22. C. Jaffrelot, *The Pakistan Paradox: Instability and Resilience* (Random House, 2016), p. 7.
23. T.V. Paul, 'Causes of the India Pakistan Enduring Rivalry,' in T.V. Paul (ed.), *The India Pakistan Conflict: An Enduring Rivalry* (Cambridge University Press, 2005), p. 6.
24. Peter Lavoy, 'Pakistan's Foreign Relations,' in D. Hagerty (ed.), *South Asia in World Politics* (Roman and Littlefield Publishers, 2005), p. 50.
25. Jaffrelot, *The Pakistan Paradox*, p. 100; Shaharyar Khan, 'Rivalry and Diplomacy,' in Shashi Tharoor and Shaharyar Khan (eds.), *Shadows Across a Playing Field* (Roli Books, 2009), pp. 107–108.
26. Jaffrelot, *The Pakistan Paradox*, p. 99; Ian Talbot, *Pakistan: A Modern History* (Hurst and Company, 2005), p. 99.
27. Talbot, *Pakistan*, pp. 112–113.
28. 'Pakistan: End of the Water Dispute,' *The Round Table: The Commonwealth Journal of International Affairs* 51/201 (1960), pp. 72–75.
29. Minutes of the MCC Committee Meeting—10 March 1952.
30. Yasmin Khan, *The Great Partition* (Yale University Press, 2007), p. 129.
31. Jaffrelot, *The Pakistan Paradox*, p. 2; Talbot, *Pakistan*, pp. 101–106; Vazira Fazila-Yacoobali Zamindar, *The Long Partition and the Making of Modern South Asia: Refugees, Boundaries, Histories* (Columbia University Press, 2007), p. 6.
32. See for example: Urvashi Butalia, *The Other Side of Silence: Voices from the Partition of India* (Penguin, 1998); Gyanendra Pandey, *Remembering Partition: Violence, Nationalism and History in India* (Cambridge University Press, 2003); Ashutosh Varshney, *Ethnic Conflict and Civil Life: Hindus and Muslims in India* (Yale University Press, 2002); Khan, *The Great Partition*; Zamindar, *The Long Partition*.
33. Kausik Bandyopadhyay, *Sport, Culture and Nation: Perspectives from Indian Football and South Asian Cricket* (Sage Publications, 2015), p. 101.
34. See for example: S. Raghavan, *War and Peace in Modern India* (Palgrave Macmillan, 2010); Ayesha Jalal, *The Struggle for Pakistan: A Muslim Homeland and Global Politics* (Harvard University Press, 2017).
35. Khan, 'Rivalry and Diplomacy,' p. 112.
36. T.V. Paul, 'Causes,' p. 8.
37. Oborne, *Wounded Tiger*, p. 78.
38. Mahmood, *From Dusk to Dawn*, p. 26.
39. Waqar Hasan and Qamar Ahmed, *For Cricket and Country: An Autobiography* (CricketPrint Publication, 2002), p. 15.
40. Ramachandra Guha, *A Corner of a Foreign Field: The Indian History of a British Sport* (Picador, 2002), p. 372.
41. Oborne, *Wounded Tiger*, p. 81.
42. Shashi Tharoor, 'Fantasies and Realities,' in Shashi Tharoor and Shaharyar Khan (ed.), *Shadows Across a Playing Field* (Roli Books, 2009), p. 25.
43. Hanif Mohammed, with Qamar Ahmed and Afia Salam, *Playing for Pakistan: An Autobiography* (Hamdard Press, 1999).
44. Mahmood, *From Dusk to Dawn*.
45. Hasan and Ahmed, *For Cricket and Country*.
46. Guha, *Corner*, p. 369.
47. Mahmood, *From Dusk to Dawn*, p. 29.

48. Bose, 'Conflicting Loyalties,' p. 204; Bhattacharya, 'Hope and Fear'; Amarnath, *Lala Amarnath*, pp. 172–173.
49. Guha, *Corner*, p. 374.
50. Guha, *Corner*; Khan, 'Rivalry and Diplomacy.'
51. Guha, *Corner*, p. 374.
52. Mahmood, *From Dusk to Dawn*, p. 32.
53. Hasan and Ahmed, *For Cricket and Country*, p. 16.
54. Amarnath, *Lala Amarnath*, p. 170.
55. Khan, 'Rivalry and Diplomacy,' p. 113; Paul, 'Causes,' p. 14.
56. Guha, *Corner*, p. 384.
57. Mahmood, *From Dusk to Dawn*, p. 57.
58. Bose, 'Conflicting loyalties,' p. 205.
59. Mahmood, *From Dusk to Dawn*, p. 54.
60. Guha, *Corner*, p. 385.
61. Quoted in: Guha, *Corner*, p. 388.
62. Oborne, *Wouned Tiger*, p. 110.
63. Talbot, *Pakistan*, p. 175.
64. Qamaruddin Butt, *Playing for a Draw: Covering Pakistan's Tour of India 1960–61* (Jahaniasons, 1962), p. 252.
65. For further details on the debate over Muslim loyalty and belonging, see Gyanendra Pandey, 'Can a Muslim be an Indian?,' *Comparative Studies in Society and History* 41/4 (1999), pp. 608–29.
66. Bose, 'Conflicting Loyalties,' p. 205.
67. The Tebbit Test derives its name from Norman Tebbit, a British Conservative minister, who in 1990 argued that South Asian and Caribbean immigrants in the UK should support the English cricket team rather than the Indian or Pakistani teams, as proof of their commitment to the UK.
68. Guha, *Corner*, p. 410.
69. Bose, 'Conflicting Loyalties.'
70. He received hate mail for underperforming against Pakistan—James Astill, *The Great Tamasha: Cricket, Corruption and the Turbulent Rise of Modern India* (Wisden, 2013), p. 114.
71. Mike Marqusee, *War Minus the Shooting: Journey Through South Asia During Cricket's World Cup* (Heinemann, 1996), p. 210.
72. Jishnu Dasgupta, 'Manufacturing Unison: Muslims, Hindus and Indians during the India–Pakistan Match,' in Boria Majumdar and J.A. Mangan (eds.), *Sport in South Asian Society: Past and Present* (Routledge, 2005), p. 244.
73. Emily Crick, 'Can cricket be used as multi-track diplomacy in the context of Indo-Pakistani relations? With particular reference to the period between 1999 and 2005,' MSc Thesis in Development and Security, 2006, p. 39.
74. Crick, 'Can cricket be used,' p. 41.
75. '19 arrested for cheering Pakistan's Champions Trophy victory,' *Times of India* (21 June 2017), url: https://timesofindia.indiatimes.com/india/19-arrested-for-cheering-pakistans-champions-trophy-victory/articleshow/59243368.cms, accessed on 10 July 2021; 'University suspends cricket fans for cheering Pakistan's win over India,' *The Guardian* (6 March 2014), url: https://www.theguardian.com/world/2014/mar/06/university-expels-cricket-fans-pakistan-india, accessed on 10 July 2021; 'India drops

sedition charges against "Pakistan cricket fans",' *BBC* (22 June 2017), url: https://www.
bbc.co.uk/news/world-asia-india-40364164, accessed on 10 July 2021.

76. Paul, 'Causes,' p. 12.
77. Stephen Philip Cohen, *The Idea of Pakistan.*
78. Dasgupta, 'Manufacturing Unison'; and Crick, 'Can cricket be used.'
79. Dasgupta, 'Manufacturing Unison' p. 240.
80. Devin T. Hagerty and Herbert G. Hagerty, 'India's Foreign Relations,' in D. Hagerty
    (ed.), *South Asia in World Politics* (Roman & Littlefield, 2005), p. 34. Rajni Kothari
    and Mushirul Hasan in fact both argue that the Nehruvian Consensus disappeared
    by the 1960s. But any remnants of the ideology appear to have been wiped out some
    decades later—Rajni Kothari, 'Political Consensus in India: Decline and Reconstruction,'
    Economic and Political Weekly 4/41 (1969), pp. 1635, 1637, 1639, 1641–1644; Mushirul
    Hasan, *Legacy of a Divided Nation: India's Muslims From Independence to Ayodhya*
    (Routledge, 1997).
81. Shankar Gopalakrishnan, 'Defining, Constructing and Policing a "New India":
    Relationship between Neoliberalism and Hindutva,' *Economic and Political Weekly* 41/26
    (2006), pp. 2803–2813; Iain McDonald, 'Between Saleem and Shiva: The Politics of
    Cricket Nationalism in a "Globalising" India,' in John Sugden and Alan Bairnier (eds.),
    Sport in Divided Societies, (Meyer and Meyer Sport, 2000), p. 218.
82. McDonald, 'Between Saleem and Shiva,' pp. 219–220.
83. Thomas Blom Hansen, 'Globalisation and Nationalist Imaginations: Hindutva's Promise
    of Equality Through Difference,' *Economic and Political Weekly* 31/10 (9 March 1996),
    pp. 603–605, 607, 616.
84. G. Aloysius, 'Trajectory of Hindutva,' *Economic and Political Weekly* 29/24 (11 June
    1994), pp. 1450–1452. See also Badri Narayan, *Fascinating Hindutva: Saffron Politics and
    Dalit Mobilisation* (Sage, 2019), for an examination of how the promise of democracy
    and equal opportunity has been used by Hindutva politics in order to mobilize the lower
    castes to their ideology.
85. C. Jaffrelot, *Hindu Nationalism: A Reader* (Princeton University Press, 2007), p. 3;
    Varshney, *Ethnic Conflict*, p. 72.
86. Crick, 'Can cricket be used.'
87. Dexter Filkins, 'Blood and Soil in Narendra Modi's India,' *The New Yorker* (2 December
    2019), url: https://www.newyorker.com/magazine/2019/12/09/blood-and-soil-in-
    narendra-modis-india, accessed on 10 July 2021.
88. Zamindar, *The Long Partition*, p. 235.
89. O. Khalidi, 'From torrent to trickle: Indian Muslim migration to Pakistan, 1947–97,'
    Islamic Studies 37/3 (1998), pp. 339–352.
90. Tharoor, 'Fantasies and Realities,' p. 39; Oborne, *Wounded Tiger*, p. 270.
91. Ajit Wadekar, 'My Tour of Pakistan,' IWI (January 1977) in: Guha, *Corner*, p. 394.
92. Marqusee, *War*, p. 209.
93. *Wisden Cricketer's Almanack* (1980), p. 963.
94. Rahul Bhattacharya, *Pundits from Pakistan: On Tour with India 2003–04* (Picador, 2005),
    p. 308.
95. Imran Khan with Patrick Murphy, *Imran: The Autobiography of Imran Khan* (Pelham
    Books, 1983), p. 77.
96. Khan, *Imran*, p. 94.
97. *Wisden Cricketer's Almanack* (1980), p. 994.

98. Guha, Corner, p. 330; Marqusee, *War*, p. 79; Osman Samiuddin, *The Unquiet Ones: A History of Pakistan Cricket* (Harper Collins, 2014), pp. 301–302.
99. Marqusee, *War*, pp. 16–17; Jack Williams, *Cricket and Race* (Berg, 2001), pp. 162–163.
100. Marqusee, *War*, p. 16.
101. Williams, *Cricket and Race*, p. 163.
102. In Marqusee, *War*, p. 54.
103. Hagerty & Hagerty, 'India's Foreign Relations,' pp. 30–31.
104. Hagerty & Hagerty, 'India's Foreign Relations,' p. 33.
105. Stuart Croft, 'South Asia's Arms Control Process: Cricket Diplomacy and the Composite Dialogue,' *International Affairs* 81/5 (2005), pp. 1039–60.
106. Tharoor, 'Fantasies and Realities,' p. 57.
107. Bandyopadhyay, *Sport*, p. 101.
108. Khan, 'Rivalry and Diplomacy,' p. 117; Marqusee, *War*, p. 211.
109. Bhattacharya, *Pundits*, pp. 252–253.
110. Tharoor, 'Fantasies and Realities,' p. 85.
111. Guha, *Corner*, p. 396.
112. Guha, *Corner*, p. 427; Jayanta Sengupta, '2003 World Cup: Globalizing Patriotism,' in Boria Majumdar and J.A. Mangan (eds.), *Sport in South Asian Society* (Routledge, 2005), p. 270.
113. Hagerty & Hagerty, 'India's Foreign Relations,' p. 37.
114. Barbara Metcalf, 'Madrasas and Minorities in Secular India,' in Robert W. Hefner, Muhammad Qasim Zaman (eds.), *Schooling Islam: The Culture and Politics of Modern Muslim Education* (Princeton University Press, 2006), p. 31.
115. McDonald, 'Between Saleem and Shiva,' p. 216.
116. Sengupta, '2003 World Cup,' p. 250.
117. Ibid., p. 265.
118. McDonald, 'Between Saleem and Shiva,' p. 219; Marqusee, *War*, pp. 209–212.
119. Jaffrelot, *The Hindu Nationalist Movement*, in: Kingshuk Chatterjee, 'To Play of Not to Play: Fabricating Consent Over the Indo-Pak Cricket Series,' in Boria Majumdar and J.A. Mangan (eds.), *Sport in South Asian Society* (Routledge, 2005), p. 288.
120. Stephen Philip Cohen, 'India, Pakistan and Kashmir,' *Journal of Strategic Studies* 24/4 (2002), p. 43.
121. Talbot, *Pakistan*, p. 288.
122. Chatterjee, 'To Play or Not to Play,' p. 277.
123. Bandyopadhyay, *Sport*.
124. Marqusee, *War*, p. 212.
125. Marqusee, *War*, pp. 209–212.
126. Ibid., p. 215.
127. McDonald, 'Between Saleem and Shiva,' p. 221.
128. Marqusee, *War*, in Crick, 'Can cricket be used,' p. 47.
129. McDonald, 'Between Saleem and Shiva,' p. 229.
130. *Outlook* (24 March 1997), p. 64.
131. Guha, *Corner*; Sengupta, '2003 World Cup,' p. 265.
132. Marqusee, *War*.
133. Chatterjee, 'To Play or Not to Play,' p. 289.
134. Rifaat Hussain, 'Pakistan's Relations with Azad Kashmir and the Impact on Indo-Pakistani Relations,' in Rafiq Dossani and Henry S. Rowen (eds.), *Prospects for Peace in South Asia*, edited by (Stanford University Press, 2005), p. 130.

135. Ibid., p. 130.
136. Nicholas J. Wheeler, *Trusting Enemies: Interpersonal Relationships in International Conflict* (Oxford University Press, 2018), p. 198.
137. Wheeler, *Trusting Enemies*, pp. 198–199; Jaswant Singh, *Jinnah: India, Partition, Independence* (Oxford University Press, 2010), p. 161.
138. Nabiha Gul, 'Pakistan-India Peace Process 1990–2007: An Appraisal,' *Pakistan Horizon* 60/2 (2007), pp. 47–64.
139. Shaharyar M. Khan, *Cricket: A Bridge of Peace* (Oxford University Press, 2005), p. 5.
140. Khan, 'Rivalry and Diplomacy,' pp. 122–125.
141. Khan, *Cricket*, p. 6.
142. Guha, *Corner*, p. 409.
143. Guha, *Corner*, p. 411; Khan, 'Rivalry and Diplomacy,' pp. 122–125.
144. The incident is also recounted in Khan's dairy of the tour—Khan, *Cricket*, pp. 9–10.
145. Filkins, 'Blood and Soil.'
146. 'Karachi: Advani visits his birthplace, Mohatta Palace,' *Dawn* (6 June 2005), url: https://www.dawn.com/news/142259, accessed on 10 July 2021.
147. Randeep Ramesh, 'From Conflict to Conciliation,' *The Guardian* (16 June 2005), url: https://www.theguardian.com/world/2005/jun/16/worlddispatch.kashmir, accessed on 10 July 2021.
148. The Test match was recently overwhelmingly voted Pakistan's greatest ever win in a Test match—'Fans vote 1999 Chennai clash with India as Pakistan's "greatest Test match",' *Dawn* (29 July 2019), url: https://www.dawn.com/news/1496891, accessed on 10 July 2021.
149. Siddhartha Vaidyanathan, 'India. Pakistan. Chennai. 1999,' *The Cricket Monthly* (31 January 2019), url: https://www.thecricketmonthly.com/story/1172609/india--pakistan--chennai--1999, accessed on 10 July 2021.
150. Khan, *Cricket*, p. 40.
151. Kausik Bandyopadhyay, 'Pakistani Cricket at Crossroads: An Outsider's Perspective,' *Sport in Society* 10/1 (2017), p. 115.
152. Hagerty & Hagerty, 'India's Foreign Relations'; Talbot, *Pakistan*.
153. Hagerty & Hagerty, 'India's Foreign Relations,' p. 40.
154. Hagerty & Hagerty, 'India's Foreign Relations,' p. 40.
155. D. Hagerty, 'US Policy and the Kashmir Question: Prospects for Resolution,' in Sumit Ganguly (ed.), *The Kashmir Question Retrospect and Prospect* (Frank Cass and Company Ltd., 2003), p. 105.
156. Talbot, *Pakistan*, p. 397.
157. Sengupta, '2003 World Cup'; Chatterjee, 'To Play or Not to Play'; Bandyopadhyay, 'Pakistani Cricket at Crossroads,' pp. 101–119.
158. Sengupta, '2003 World Cup'; p. 270.
159. Chatterjee, 'To Play or Not to Play,' p. 290.
160. Talbot, *Pakistan*, pp. 396–397.
161. Subhash Shukla, 'Indo-Pak relations, Gujral to Manmohan Singh,' *The Indian Journal of Political Science* 69/4 (2008), pp. 904–905.
162. Layaslalu M., 'The First Vajpayee Government: Golden Years of Non-Military Confidence Building Measures Between India and Pakistan,' *IOSR Journal of Humanities and Social Science* 22/4 (2017), pp. 36–37.
163. Layaslalu, 'Vajpayee Government,' pp. 36–37.

164. Shaharyar Khan and Ali Khan, *Cricket Cauldron: The Turbulent Politics of Sport in Pakistan* (Harper Sport, 2013), p. 38.
165. Chatterjee, 'To Play or Not to Play,' p. 279.
166. Crick, 'Can cricket be used,' p. 36.
167. Khan & Khan, *Cricket Cauldron*, p. 45; Bhattacharya, *Pundits*, p. 13.
168. K. Bandyopadhyay, 'Pakistani Cricket at Crossroads: An Outsider's Perspective,' in Jon Gemmell and Boria Majumdar (eds.), *Cricket, Race and the 2007 World Cup* (Routledge, 2008); Bhattacharya, *Pundits*.
169. Crick, 'Can cricket be used,' p. 84; Bhattacharya, *Pundits*, p. 11.
170. Kausik Bandyopadhyay, 'Feel Good, Goodwill and India's Friendship Tour of Pakistan, 2004: Cricket, Politics and Diplomacy in Twenty-First-Century India,' *The International Journal of the History of Sport* 25/12 (2008), pp. 1654–1670; p. 1663.
171. Shaharyar Khan is from the Bhopal royal family and cousin to Indian cricket captain Mansur (Tiger) Ali Khan Pataudi.
172. Khan & Khan, *Cricket Cauldron*, p. 57.
173. Saskia Sassen, *Expulsions: Brutality and Complexity in the Global Economy* (Harvard University Press, 2014), pp. 149–151.
174. Mohammed Hanif, 'The Partition Goes On: A Pakistani Perspective,' *AlJazeera* (15 August 2017), url: https://www.aljazeera.com/indepth/features/2017/08/partition-pakistani-perspective-170807064330685.html, accessed on 2 April 2021.
175. Khan, 'Rivalry and Diplomacy,' pp. 131–132.
176. Bandyopadhyay, 'Pakistani Cricket,' p. 100.
177. Bhattacharya, *Pundits*, p. 71.
178. Khan, 'Rivalry and Diplomacy,' p. 135.
179. Bhattacharya, *Pundits*, pp. 265–66.
180. Bhattacharya, *Pundits*, p. 156.
181. Mushtaq Mohammed, *Inside Out: An Autobiography* (Uniprint, 2006), p. 193.
182. Bhattacharya, *Pundits*, pp. 128–129.
183. Khan & Khan, *Cricket Cauldron*, p. 70.
184. Bhattacharya, *Pundits*, p. 308.
185. Ibid., p. 28.
186. I had transcribed the story then and it appears in Khan & Khan, *Cricket Cauldron*, p. 63.
187. Saurav Ganguly with Gautam Bhattacharya, *A Century Is Not Enough: My Roller-coaster Ride to Success* (Juggernaut Publication, 2018), pp. 147–149.
188. Ibid., p. 160.
189. Ibid., p. 150.
190. This is the line taken by Shaharyar Khan and Varun Sahni who both indicate that poverty, unemployment, education, and health were issues of concern to populations in both India and Pakistan rather than Indo-Pak hostility. Sahni carried out a review of opinion polls in India in the print and television media between 1996 and 2004 and he concluded that poverty, unemployment, and education were consistently ranked as the highest issues of concern; Indo-Pak or Hindu–Muslim relations were rarely mentioned. See: Varun Sahni, 'The Protean Polis and Strategic Surprises: Do Changes within India Affect South, Asian Strategic Stability?,' *Contemporary South Asia* 14/2 (2005), pp. 219–31.
191. Singh, *Jinnah: India, Partition, Independence*, p. 413.
192. Bhattacharya, *Pundits*.
193. Khan & Khan, *Cricket Cauldron*, p. 70.
194. Ibid.

195. Emily Crick, 'Contact Sport: Cricket in India–Pakistan Relations Since 1999,' *South Asian Survey* 16/1 (2009), p. 77.
196. Ibid., p. 73.
197. Guha, *Corner*, p. 385.
198. Marqusee, *War*.
199. Marqusee, *Anyone but England*.
200. Mike Marqusee, 'The Lovable Marquee,' *Outlook India* (21 March 2005), url: https://www.outlookindia.com/magazine/story/this-lovable-marquee/226831, accessed on 10 July 2021.
201. Mike Marqusee, 'A Committed Neutral Speaks,' *Outlook India* (17 March 2005).
202. S. Croft, 'South Asia's arms control process: cricket diplomacy and the composite dialogue,' *International Affairs* 81/5 (2005), pp. 1055–1056.
203. Crick, 'Can cricket be used,' p. 46.
204. Croft, 'South Asia's arms control process,' p. 1041.
205. 'Reunited Kashmiris' tears of joy,' *BBC News* (7 April 2005), url: http://news.bbc.co.uk/1/hi/world/south_asia/4419109.stm, accessed on 10 July 2021.
206. Aftab Borka, 'Indian films breathe life into Pakistani cinemas,' *Reuters* (25 April 2008), url: https://www.reuters.com/article/us-pakistan-bollywood/indian-films-breathe-life-into-pakistani-cinemas-idUSISL17078720080425, accessed on 10 July 2021.
207. Nandini Ramnath, 'A brief history of Pakistan-India cultural ties,' *Dawn* (27 September 2016), url: https://images.dawn.com/news/1176320, accessed 10 July 2021.
208. Gyanendra Pandey, *Remembering Partition: Violence, Nationalism and History in India* (Cambridge University Press, 2003).
209. Pandey, *Remembering Partition*, p. 2.
210. Javeed Alam (1998) in: Gyanendra Pandey, *Remembering Partition: Violence, Nationalism and History in India* (Cambridge University Press, 2003).
211. Pandey, *Remembering Partition*, p. 64.
212. Barbara D. Metcalf, 'Introduction,' in *Islam in South Asia in Practice* (Princeton University Press, 2010).
213. Varshney, *Ethnic Conflict*, p. 68.
214. Ashfaque Swapan, 'Hate Not Last Word in Partition: Nandy,' *US Indian News* (13 March 2009), url: https://southasia.berkeley.edu/sites/default/files/Hate%20Not%20Last%20Word%20in%20Partition_India%20West_Ashis%20Nandy_Mar%2009%281%29.pdf, accessed on 10 July 2021.

Chapter 6: Pakistan in the Global Cricketing Order – South Asia II

1. Anatol Lieven, *Pakistan: A Hard Country* (Penguin Books, 2011), p. 417.
2. Christophe Jaffrelot, *The Pakistan Paradox* (Random House, 2016), p. 569.
3. Fatalities include civilians, terrorists, and security personnel.
4. 'Fatalities in Terrorist Violence in Pakistan 2000–2019,' *South Asia Terrorism Portal*, url: https://www.satp.org/satporgtp/countries/pakistan/database/casualties.htm, accessed on 18 July 2021. For a detailed analysis of violence in Pakistan during this period, see for example: *Pakistan the Militant Jihadi Challenge* (International Crisis Group, 2009); or Ethan Bueno de Mesquita, C. Christine Fair, Jenna Jordan, Rasul Baksh Rais, Jacob N. Shapiro, 'Measuring political violence in Pakistan: Insights from the BFRS Dataset,' *Conflict Management and Peace Science* (2014), pp. 1–23.

5. Matthew Allen, 'PCB saved by India windfall,' *BBC Sport* (28 February 2004), url: http://news.bbc.co.uk/sport1/hi/cricket/3495720.stm, accessed on 18 July 2021.

6. The four Asian Test nations signed an agreement in Sharjah in 2002 vowing to boycott any country that refused to tour any one of them—'Pakistan threatens boycott if Australia refuses to tour,' *The Sydney Morning Herald*, url: https://www.smh.com.au/sport/cricket/pakistan-threatens-boycott-if-australia-refuses-to-tour-20020802-gdfich.html, accessed on 18 July 2021.

7. Allen, 'PCB saved by India windfall.'

8. Declan Walsh, 'Suicide bombings in Lahore kill at least 31,' *The Guardian*, url: https://www.theguardian.com/world/2008/mar/12/pakistan, accessed on 18 July 2021.

9. Prem Mahadevan, *A Decade on from the 2008 Mumbai Attack: Reviewing the Question of State-Sponsorship* (International Centre for Counter Terrorism Publications, 2019); Somini Sengupta, 'Dossier Gives Details of Mumbai Attacks,' *The New York Times* (6 January 2009).

10. 'India cancel 2009 tour of Pakistan,' *CNN* (18 December 2008), url: http://edition.cnn.com/2008/SPORT/12/18/india.pakistan.cricket.tour/index.html, accessed on 18 July 2021.

11. Peter Oborne, *Wounded Tiger: A History of Cricket in Pakistan* (Simon & Schuster, 2014), p. 481.

12. Ibid., p. 482.

13. Ishtiaq Ahmed, 'Attack on Sri Lanka's Cricket Team: Is Pakistan in Total Chaos and Anarchy?,' ISAS Brief No. 99 (Institute of South Asian Studies, National University of Singapore, 4 March 2009).

14. 'Broad angry at security failure,' *BBC Sport* (4 March 2009), url: http://news.bbc.co.uk/sport1/hi/cricket/7923654.stm, accessed on 18 July 2021.

15. James Traub, 'Can Pakistan Be Governed?,' *The New York Times Magazine* (4 April 2009).

16. Oborne, *Wounded Tiger*, p. 482.

17. Osman Samiuddin, 'PCB keen on UAE venues despite ICC snub,' *ESPN Cricinfo* (26 June 2009), url: https://www.espncricinfo.com/story/_/id/22789023/pcb-continue-pushing-uae-venues, accessed on 18 July 2021.

18. 'Full statement of PCB chairman Ijaz Butt,' *ESPN Cricinfo* (9 May 2009), url: https://www.espncricinfo.com/story/_/id/22808350/full-statement-pcb-chairman-ijaz-butt, accessed on 18 July 2021.

19. Osman Samiuddin, 'All emotion, no logic,' *ESPN Cricinfo* (11 May 2009), url: https://www.espncricinfo.com/story/_/id/22807738/all-emotion-no-logic, accessed on 18 July 2021.

20. Mihir Bose, 'Conflicting loyalties: nationalism and religion in India–Pakistan cricket relations,' in A. Bateman and J. Hill, *The Cambridge Companion to Cricket* (Cambridge University Press, 2011), p. 215.

21. Bose, 'Conflicting loyalties,' p. 215.

22. Ibid.

23. Moeed Yusuf, 'How the India–Pakistan Conflict Leaves Great Powers Powerless,' *Foreign Policy* (10 December 2018), url: https://foreignpolicy.com/2018/12/10/954587-india-pakistan-mumbai-terror/, accessed on 18 July 2021.

24. In: Steve Coll, 'The Back Channel: India and Pakistan Secret Kashmir Talks,' *The New Yorker* (2 March 2009).

25. Moeed Yusuf, 'India–Pakistan equation,' *Dawn* (10 September 2012).

26. Moeed Yusuf, 'Small window of opportunity,' *Dawn* (23 September 2013).

27. Andrew Buncombe, 'Narendra Modi sworn in as India's new PM with Pakistani counterpart Nawaz Sharif looking on,' *The Independent* (27 May 2014), url: https://www.independent.co.uk/news/world/asia/indias-new-pm-narendra-modi-to-meet-with-pakistani-premier-nawaz-sharif-after-being-sworn-in-9436226.html, accessed on 18 July 2021.

28. 'India PM Modi in surprise Pakistan visit,' *BBC News* (25 December 2015), url: https://www.bbc.co.uk/news/world-asia-35178594, accessed on 18 July 2021.

29. Sameer Lalwani & Hannah Haegeland, 'Anatomy of a Crisis: Explaining Crisis Onset in India–Pakistan Relations,' *Stimson Centre* (2018), url: https://www.stimson.org/wp-content/files/InvestigatingCrisesOnset.pdf, accessed on 18 July 2021.

30. Burhan Wani was a commander of the Pro-Pakistani militant group Hizbul Mujahideen. Wani was popular on social media for his advocacy against Indian rule in Kashmir and his calls suggesting violent insurrection against the Indian state and has been credited for reinvigorating the Kashmiri uprising. He was 22 when he was killed with reports suggesting that his funeral was attended by so many supporters that there was no space for funeral prayers, Shujaat Bukhari, 'Why the death of militant Burhan Wani has Kashmiris up in arms,' *BBC News* (11 July 2016), url: https://www.bbc.co.uk/news/world-asia-india-36762043, accessed on 18 July 2021.

31. Bukhari, 'Why the death of militant Burhan Wani has Kashmiris up in arms.'

32. Vijayta Lalwani, 'Data check: Ceasefire violations along Line of Control this year are already more than all of 2017,' *Scroll.in* (7 August 2018), url: https://scroll.in/article/888719/data-check-already-more-ceasefire-violations-along-line-of-control-this-year-than-all-of-2017, accessed on 19 July 2021.

33. Lalwani and Haegland, 'Anatomy of a Crisis.'

34. Global Conflict Tracker, *Council on Foreign Relations*, url: https://www.cfr.org/interactive/global-conflict-tracker/conflict/conflict-between-india-and-pakistan, accessed on 18 July 2021.

35. Yusuf, 'How the India–Pakistan Conflict Leaves Great Powers Powerless.'

36. Moeed Yusuf, 'The Pulwama Crisis: Flirting With War in a Nuclear Environment,' *Arms Control Association* (May 2019), url: https://www.armscontrol.org/act/2019-05/features/pulwama-crisis-flirting-war-nuclear-environment, accessed on 18 July 2021.

37. Suparno Sarkar, 'IMPPA passes resolution to temporarily ban Pakistani artists in India; Twitter reacts,' *IB Times* (29 September 2016).

38. 'Bollywood divided on Pakistani actors ban issue,' *Times of India* (29 January 2017), url: https://timesofindia.indiatimes.com/entertainment/hindi/bollywood/news/Bollywood-divided-on-Pakistani-actors-ban-issue/articleshow/54735039.cms, accessed on 18 July 2021.

39. 'Uri attack aftermath,' *First Post* (23 September 2016), url: http://www.firstpost.com/sports/bcci-chief-anurag-thakur-says-no-question-of-playing-cricket-with-pakistan-after-uri-attack-3018372.html, accessed on 18 July 2021.

40. For example, Michael Kugelman, 'Mumbai terror attacks,' *CNN* (26 November 2018), url: https://edition.cnn.com/2018/11/25/opinions/10-year-anniversary-mumbai-terror-attacks-intl/index.html, accessed on 18 July 2021; Arundhati Roy, 'The monster in the mirror,' *The Guardian* (12 December 2008), url: https://www.theguardian.com/world/2008/dec/12/mumbai-arundhati-roy, accessed on 18 July 2021; James Glanz, Sebastian Rotella, and David E. Sanger, 'In 2008 Mumbai Attacks, Piles of Spy Data, but an Uncompleted Puzzle,' *The New York Times* (21 December 2014), url: https://

www.nytimes.com/2014/12/22/world/asia/in-2008-mumbai-attacks-piles-of-spy-data-but-an-uncompleted-puzzle.html, accessed on 18 July 2021.

41. Mahadevan, *Decade*.

42. Moeed Yusuf, 'Difficult Ties,' *Dawn* (3 June 2014).

43. 'India's Modi threatens to "isolate Pakistan" after Kashmir attack,' *Financial Times*, url: https://www.ft.com/content/bb7592de-82e3-11e6-8897-2359a58ac7a5, accessed on 18 July 2021.

44. For example, BJP loyalist Gajendra Chauhan's nomination as Chairman of FTII; the replacement of Gopalkrishna Gandhi at Simla's Indian Institute of Advanced Study by Chandrakala Padia; Lokesh Chandra (who claims Modi is a greater leader than Gandhi) as head of the Indian Council of Cultural Relations; and Sudershan Rao's ('Ramayana-is-history') designation as head of the Indian Council of Historical Research; Girish Chandra Tripathi, a state level RSS functionary, was appointed as Vice-Chancellor of Banaras Hindu University; and Baldev Sharma, former editor of the extremist RSS mouthpiece *Panchjanya*, was appointed as chairman of the National Book Trust. See: Girish Shahane, 'Why the BJP is appointing C-listers to head top institutions,' *Scroll.in* (22 July 2015), url: https://scroll.in/article/743006/why-the-bjp-is-appointing-c-listers-to-head-top-institutions, accessed on 18 July 2021; Soumya Shankar, 'The Takeover: How the Modi Government has Filled Key Positions in 14 Institutions,' *Catch News*, url: http://www.catchnews.com/india-news/the-takeover-how-the-modi-govt-has-filled-key-positions-in-14-institutions-.

45. Soutik Biswas, 'Ramachandra Guha: How the right wing hounded out a Gandhi biographer,' *BBC News* (3 November 2018), url: https://www.bbc.co.uk/news/world-asia-india-46069120, accessed on 18 July 2021; 'Amartya Sen's 9-year-long association with Nalanda University ends,' *Economic Times* (23 November 2016), url: https://economictimes.indiatimes.com/news/politics-and-nation/amartya-sens-9-year-long-association-with-nalanda-university-ends/articleshow/55586972.cms?from=mdr, accessed on 18 July 2021.

46. Soumya Shankar 'The Takeover.'

47. Moeed Yusuf, 'Difficult Equation,' *Dawn* (9 October 2018).

48. Iain McDonald, 'Between Saleem and Shiva: The Politics of Cricket Nationalism in a 'Globalising' India,' in John Sugden and Alan Bairnier (eds.), *Sport in Divided Societies*, (Meyer and Meyer Sport, 2000), p. 221.

49. 'Anurag Thakur becomes first serving BJP MP to join Territorial Army,' *Indian Express* (29 July 2016), url: https://indianexpress.com/article/india/india-news-india/anurag-thakur-territorial-army-bjp-mp-2942887/, accessed on 18 July 2021. Thakur was removed from the BCCI in 2017 by the Supreme Court: 'Anurag Thakur: India cricket board chief ordered to resign,' *BBC News* (2 January 2017), url: https://www.bbc.co.uk/news/world-asia-india-38487340, accessed on 18 July 2021.

50. 'Watch: Union minister Anurag Thakur leads "goli maaro saalon ko" slogans at rally,' *Scroll.in* (27 January 2020), url: https://scroll.in/video/951289/watch-anurag-thakur-minister-of-state-for-finance-lead-goli-maaro-saalon-ko-slogans-at-rally, accessed on 18 July 2021.

51. Gideon Haigh, 'The great carve-up of world cricket,' *ESPN Cricinfo*, url: http://www.espncricinfo.com/wisdenalmanack/content/story/735865.html, accessed on 18 July 2021.

52. Gideon Haigh, *Divide and Rule at the ICC: The Great Carve up of World Cricket* (Wisden and Bloomsbury, 2014).

53. Nabeel Hashmi, 'Pakistan receives major share of "Big Three" spoils,' *The Express Tribune* (26 June 2014), url: https://tribune.com.pk/story/727501/pakistan-receives-major-share-of-big-three-spoils?print=true, accessed on 18 July 2021.

54. Daniel Brettig, 'New ICC finance model breaks up Big Three,' *ESPN Cricinfo* (27 April 2017), url: https://www.espncricinfo.com/story/_/id/19253630/new-icc-finance-model-breaks-big-three, accessed on 18 July 2021.

55. Nagraj Gollapudi, 'PCB's case against BCCI dismissed by ICC dispute panel,' *ESPN Cricinfo* (20 November 2018), url: https://www.espncricinfo.com/story/_/id/25328942/pcb-case-bcci-dismissed-icc-dispute-panel, accessed on 18 July 2021.

56. 'Pakistan players hurt and angered by snub,' *ESPN Cricinfo* (19 January 2010), url: https://www.espncricinfo.com/story/_/id/22686959/pakistan-players-hurt-angered-snub-auction, accessed on 18 July 2021.

57. Bose, 'Conflicting loyalties,' p. 215.

58. Neil Perera, 'Pakistan: A True Fried of Sri Lanka Cricket,' *The Island* (7 October 2017).

59. Hassan Cheema, 'Pakistan playing Scotland? That's no surprise,' *ESPN Cricinfo* (13 June 2018), url: https://www.espncricinfo.com/story/_/id/23777527/pakistan-playing-scotland-no-surprise, accessed on 18 July 2021.

60. P. Venkateshwar Rao, 'Ethnic Conflict in Sri Lanka: India's Role and Perception,' *Asian Survey* 28/4 (1988), p. 425.

61. Maj. Gen. (Retd) Raj Mehta, *Lost Victory: The Rise & Fall of LTTE Supremo, V. Prabhakaran* (Pentagon Press, 2010), p. 317.

62. Maseeh Rahman, 'Schoolgirls killed in attack on orphanage,' *The Guardian* (15 August 2006), url: https://www.theguardian.com/world/2006/aug/15/schools.schoolsworldwide, accessed on 18 July 2021.

63. Oborne, *Wounded Tiger*, p. 311.

64. Sa'adi Thawfeeq, 'Lanka's tour to Pakistan will there be repercussions,' *Daily News* (25 September 2019), url: https://www.dailynews.lk/2019/09/25/sports/197934/lanka's-tour-pakistan-will-there-be-repercussions?page=4, accessed on 18 July 2021.

65. 'Sri Lankan cricket board warned over terrorist threat to Pakistan tour,' *The Guardian* (11 September 2019), url: https://www.theguardian.com/sport/2019/sep/11/sri-lankan-cricket-board-warned-over-terrorist-threat-to-pakistan-tour, accessed on 18 July 2021.

66. Kamran Yousaf, 'Rajapaksa's victory a setback for India but good for Pakistan,' *The Express Tribune* (17 November 2019), url: https://tribune.com.pk/story/2101463/1-rajapaksas-victory-setback-india-good-pakistan/, accessed on 18 July 2021.

67. Yousaf, 'Rajapaksa's victory.'

68. Sa'adi Thawfeeq, 'Lanka's tour to Pakistan.'

69. Oborne, *Wounded Tiger*, p. 276.

70. Ibid., p. 230.

71. Chandra Schaffter, 'Cricket and the Commonwealth,' *The Round Table* 108/1 (2019), pp. 67–79.

72. Cheema, 'Pakistan playing Scotland?.'

73. Kausik Bandyopadhyay, *Sport, Culture and Nation* (Sage Publications, 2015), p. 143.

74. Mohammad Isam, 'India v Pakistan, a Bangladeshi View,' *The Cricket Monthly* (17 October 2019).

75. Kaushik Basu, 'Why is Bangladesh booming?,' *Brookings* (1 May 2018), url: https://www.brookings.edu/opinions/why-is-bangladesh-booming/, accessed on 18 July 2021.

76. V.M. Hewitt, *The International Politics of South Asia* (Manchester University Press, 1992), p. 31.

77. Zahid Shahab Ahmed and Musharaf Zahoor, 'Bangladesh-Pakistan relations: hostage to a traumatic past,' *Commonwealth & Comparative Politics* 57/1 (2019), p. 34.

78. Ibid., p. 38.

79. Ibid.

80. Mohammad Isam, 'Tour postponed after court order,' *ESPN Cricinfo* (19 April 2012), url: https://www.espncricinfo.com/story/_/id/22319618/dhaka-high-court-puts-four-week-tour-embargo, accessed on 18 July 2021.

81. Umar Farooq, 'Zaka Ashraf reacts sternly to Bangladesh delaying tour,' *ESPN Cricinfo* (31 December 2012), url: https://www.espncricinfo.com/story/_/id/22103182/zaka-ashraf-reacts-sternly-bangladesh-delaying-tour, accessed on 18 July 2021.

82. Mohammad Isam, 'No Pakistan players in BPL,' *ESPN Cricinfo* (16 January 2013), url: https://www.espncricinfo.com/story/_/id/22097106/no-pakistan-players-bangladesh-premier-league, accessed on 18 July 2021.

83. 'Bangladesh reject invitation to tour Pakistan,' *ESPN Cricinfo* (31 March 2017), url: https://www.espncricinfo.com/story/_/id/19043732/bangladesh-reject-invitation-tour-pakistan, accessed on 18 July 2021.

84. Peter Lavoy, 'Pakistan's Foreign Relations,' in D. Hagerty (ed.), *South Asia in World Politics* (Roman and Littlefield Publishers, 2005), p. 66.

85. Ian Talbot, *Pakistan: A Modern History* (Hurst and Company, 2005), p. 99.

86. 'UNHCR welcomes new government policy for Afghans in Pakistan,' *UNHCR Pakistan* (7 February 2017), url: https://unhcrpk.org/unhcr-welcomes-new-government-policy-for-afghans-in-pakistan/, accessed on 18 July 2021.

87. Stephen Wagg, *Cricket: A Political History of the Global Game, 1945–2017* (Routledge, 2018), p. 290.

88. 'Cricket: Politics spices up ahead of Pakistan-Afghanistan match,' *TRT World* (28 June 2019), url: https://www.trtworld.com/sport/cricket-politics-spices-up-ahead-of-pakistan-afghanistan-match-27879, accessed on 18 July 2021.

89. 'Disgruntled Afghan Cricket Chief lashes out at Pakistan Cricket Board,' *Times of Islamabad* (30 June 2019), url: https://timesofislamabad.com/30-Jun-2019/disgruntled-afghan-cricket-chief-lashes-out-at-pakistan-cricket-board, accessed on 18 July 2021.

90. Muhammad Asif Khan, 'Cricket: The Rise of the Afghans,' *Dawn* (14 October 2018).

91. Khan, 'Cricket: The Rise of the Afghans.'

92. Wagg, *Cricket*, p. 292.

93. Sidharth Monga, 'An opportunity to keep the Afghanistan-Pakistan rivalry dignified,' *ESPN Cricinfo* (28 June 2019), url: https://www.espncricinfo.com/story/_/id/27075656/an-opportunity-keep-afghanistan-pakistan-rivalry-dignified, accessed on 18 July 2021.

94. Umar Farooq, 'Shahzad fined, asked to relocate to Afghanistan,' *ESPN Cricinfo* (14 April 2018), url: https://www.espncricinfo.com/story/_/id/23170364/mohammad-shahzad-fined-asked-relocate-afghanistan, accessed on 18 July 2021.

95. 'India helping us more than Pakistan: Afghan board CEO,' *Times of India* (21 January 2018), url: https://timesofindia.indiatimes.com/sports/cricket/news/india-helping-us-more-than-pakistan-afghan-board-ceo/articleshow/62593984.cms, accessed on 18 July 2021.

96. 'Afghanistan cancel Pakistan series,' *Cricket.com.au* (1 June 2017), url: https://www.cricket.com.au/news/pakistan-afghanistan-t20-friendly-series-cancelled-bomb-blast-kabul-intelligence-pcb-acb/2017-06-01, accessed on 18 July 2021.

97. Jack de Menezes, 'Pakistan and Afghanistan cricket fans involved in fight outside Headingley after plane flew over ground with 'Justice for Balochistan' message,' *The*

Independent (29 June 2019), url: https://www.independent.co.uk/sport/cricket/pakistan-afghanistan-fans-fight-video-cricket-world-cup-outside-ground-plane-justice-for-balochistan-a8980421.html, accessed on 18 July 2021.

98. 'Kashmir Attack: Tracing the path that led to Pulwama,' *BBC News* (1 May 2019), url: https://www.bbc.co.uk/news/world-asia-india-47302467, accessed on 18 July 2021.

99. Abhinav Pandya, 'The Future of Indo-Pak Relations after the Pulwama Attack,' *Perspectives on Terrorism* 13/2 (2019), pp. 65–68.

100. 'Pulwama attack: What are Modi's options?,' *BBC News* (19 February 2019), url: https://www.bbc.co.uk/news/world-asia-india-47278145, accessed on 18 July 2021.

101. 'All Indian Cine Workers Association Announces Complete Ban On Pakistani Artists, Actors Amid Pulwama Attack,' *Outlook India* (18 February 2019), url: https://www.outlookindia.com/website/story/entertainment-news-all-indian-cine-workers-association-announces-complete-ban-on-pakistani-artists-actors-amid-pulwama-attack/325699, accessed on 18 July 2021.

102. 'Team India wear special army caps in ODI against Australia,' *The Telegraph* (8 March 2019), url: https://www.telegraphindia.com/sport/team-india-wear-special-army-caps-in-odi-against-australia/cid/1686420, accessed on 18 July 2021.

103. Nagraj Gollapudi and Sidharth Monga, 'BCCI mulls asking for Pakistan World Cup ban,' *ESPN Cricinfo* (21 February 2019), url: https://www.espncricinfo.com/story/_/id/26045366/bcci-mulls-asking-pakistan-world-cup-ban, accessed on 18 July 2021.

104. 'Pulwama attack: BCCI calls on ICC to act following Kashmir incident,' *BBC Sport* (22 February 2019), url: https://www.bbc.co.uk/sport/cricket/47333834, accessed on 18 July 2021; 'India vs Pakistan: Yuzvendra Chahal wants action against those guilty in Pulwama attack,' *Hindustan Times* (22 February 2019), url: https://www.hindustantimes.com/cricket/india-vs-pakistan-yuzvendra-chahal-wants-action-against-those-guilty-in-pulwama-attack/story-7bBHV4Ihz3ovM2EoqtjuvI.html, accessed on 18 July 2021.

105. 'PCB files damages claim against IMG-Reliance for PSL pull-out,' *ESPN Cricinfo* (19 November 2019), url: https://www.espncricinfo.com/story/_/id/28114967/pcb-files-damages-claim-img-reliance-psl-pull-out, accessed on 18 July 2021.

106. https://www.aljazeera.com/news/2019/02/indian-broadcaster-pulls-pakistan-cricket-league-190218082302541.html (link no longer valid as of 18 July 2021).

107. Omer Farooq Khan, 'Pakistan bans broadcast of IPL matches,' *Times of India* (2 April 2019), url: https://timesofindia.indiatimes.com/sports/cricket/ipl/top-stories/pakistan-bans-broadcast-of-ipl-matches/articleshow/68693272.cms, accessed on 18 July 2021.

108. 'Kashmir under lockdown: All the latest updates,' *Al Jazeera* (27 October 2019), url: https://www.aljazeera.com/news/2019/08/india-revokes-kashmir-special-status-latest-updates-190806134011673.html, accessed on 18 July 2021.

109. Lindsay Maizland, 'Kashmir: What to Know about the Disputed Region,' *Council on Foreign Relations* (7 August 2019), url: https://www.cfr.org/in-brief/kashmir-what-know-about-disputed-region, accessed on 18 July 2021.

110. Hannah Ellis-Petersen, '"Many lives have been lost": five-month internet blackout plunges Kashmir into crisis,' *The Guardian* (5 January 2020), url: https://www.theguardian.com/world/2020/jan/05/the-personal-and-economic-cost-of-kashmirs-internet-ban, accessed on 18 July 2021.

111. 'Kashmir dispute: Pakistan downgrades ties with India,' *BBC News* (7 August 2019), url: https://www.bbc.co.uk/news/world-asia-49267912, accessed on 20 July 2021.

112. Julian Borger, 'Imran Khan warns UN of potential nuclear war in Kashmir,' *The Guardian* (26 September 2019), url: https://www.theguardian.com/world/2019/sep/26/imran-khan-warns-un-of-potential-nuclear-war-in-kashmir, accessed on 18 July 2021.

113. Rahul Rao, 'Test of faith: The CAA protests shake the old bounds of Indian secular morality,' *Caravan Magazine* (29 January 2020), url: https://caravanmagazine.in/politics/caa-protests-shake-old-bounds-indian-secular-morality, accessed on 18 July 2021.

114. Supriya Sharma, 'We knew Adityanath was hostile to Muslims. But did we expect his regime to be so savage?,' *Scroll.in* (30 December 2019), url: https://scroll.in/article/948194/we-knew-adityanath-was-hostile-to-muslims-but-did-we-expect-his-regime-to-be-so-savage?fbclid=IwAR1-jHJ6sZHPuQnIrbvZpNnxql_agi9RtZO4eBRLLCAVNi5P_BJ_IfvAw_M, accessed on 18 July 2021.

115. Sharda Ugra, 'Why Aren't Our Sports Celebrities Speaking Out?,' *The India Forum* (6 March 2020), url: https://www.theindiaforum.in/article/why-aren-t-sports-celebrities-speaking-about-caanrc-protests, accessed on 18 July 2021.

116. Gideon Haigh, 'Ugly Trend that can Poison Indian Cricket,' *The Australian* (2021), url: https://www.theaustralian.com.au/sport/cricket/ugly-trend-that-can-poison-indian-cricket/news-story/27588950568a90ea586d2607cbb61370, accessed on 18 July 2021.

117. Khushwant Singh, *The End of India* (Penguin Books, 2003), p. 72.

118. 'Keep my daughter out of this, says Sourav after "Sana's CAA post",' *Times of India* (19 December 2019), url: https://timesofindia.indiatimes.com/india/keep-my-daughter-out-of-this-says-sourav-after-sanas-caa-post/articleshow/72878319.cms?frmapp=yes&from=mdr, accessed on 18 July 2021.

119. Sharda Ugra, 'In cricket gear, a snapshot of India today,' *The Hindu* (17 February 2021), url: https://www.thehindu.com/opinion/op-ed/in-cricket-gear-a-snapshot-of-india-today/article33854390.ece, accessed on 18 July 2021; Ugra, 'Why Aren't Our Sports Celebrities Speaking Out?'; Haigh, 'Ugly Trend that can Poison Indian Cricket.'

120. Sanjay Ruparelia, 'Modi's Saffron Democracy,' *Dissent* 66/2 (2019), pp. 94–106.

121. '"Virat Kohli" spotted in Lahore donning Pakistan World Cup kit,' *The News* (9 June 2019), url: https://www.thenews.com.pk/latest/482201-virat-kohli-in-pakistani-kit-roaming-in-lahore, accessed on 18 July 2021.

122. 'Virat Kohli, come to Pakistan and play cricket: India captain's fan in Lahore wins hearts,' *India Today* (10 October 2019), url: https://www.indiatoday.in/sports/cricket/story/virat-kohli-pakistan-cricket-fan-lahore-gaddafi-stadium-banner-pak-vs-sl-1607889-2019-10-10, accessed on 18 July 2021.

123. '"Can trade onion, tomatoes then why not play cricket": Shoaib Akhtar on India–Pakistan bilateral series,' *Hindustan Times* (18 February 2020), url: https://www.hindustantimes.com/cricket/can-trade-onion-tomatoes-then-why-not-play-cricket-shoaib-akhtar-on-india-pakistan-bilateral-series/story-BQmMDWKAEKa8OZd5yw2QfL.html, accessed on 18 July 2021; 'Mushtaq Ahmed Calls for Resumption of India–Pakistan Cricketing Ties,' *NDTV* (17 November 2019), url: https://sports.ndtv.com/cricket/mushtaq-ahmed-calls-for-resumption-of-India–Pakistan-cricketing-ties-2133978, accessed on 18 July 2021.

124. Sreshth Shah, 'Indian and Pakistani players go about their business, game faces on, blinkers in place,' *ESPN Cricinfo* (3 February 2020), url: https://www.espncricinfo.com/story/_/id/28625641/indian-pakistani-players-go-their-business-game-faces-blinkers-place, accessed on 18 July 2021.

125. Marie Lall, 'Educate to Hate: the use of education in the creation of antagonistic national identities in India and Pakistan,' *Compare* 38/1 (2008), pp. 103–119.

126. Qtd. In: Ramachandra Guha, *A Corner of a Foreign Field: The Indian History of a British Sport* (Picador, 2002), p. 371.

127. Ibid.

Chapter 7: Conclusion—The Future

1. Anatol Lieven, *Pakistan: A Hard Country* (Penguin Books, 2011); S.K. Saini, 'Storming of Lal Masjid in Pakistan: An Analysis,' *Strategic Analysis* 33/4 (2009), pp. 553–565.

2. *Pakistan Security Report* (Pak Institute for Peace Studies, 2009), p. 12.

3. Justine Fleischner, *Governance and Militancy in Pakistan's Swat Valley* (Centre for Strategic and International Studies, Washington, 2011), p. 1.

4. *Pakistan Security Report* (Pak Institute for Peace Studies, 2009).

5. Basim Usmani, 'Pakistan at the crossroads,' *The Guardian* (10 March 2009), url: https://www.theguardian.com/commentisfree/2009/mar/09/pakistan-sri-lanka-cricket-team-attack, accessed on 23 July 2021.

6. Christophe Jaffrelot, *The Pakistan Paradox* (Random House, 2016), p. 278.

7. Mohammed Hanif, 'Our reward for appeasing the militants,' *The Guardian* (3 March 2009), url: https://www.theguardian.com/commentisfree/2009/mar/03/sri-lanka-cricket-pakistan, accessed on 23 July 2021.

8. Angelos Kanas, 'Pure Contagion Effects in International Banking: The Case of BCCI's Failure,' *Journal of Applied Economics* 8/1 (2005), pp. 101–123.

9. '62pc cut in war on terror losses,' *Dawn* (27 April 2018), url: https://www.dawn.com/news/1404161, accessed on 23 July 2021.

10. Neta C. Crawford, *Human Cost of the Post-9/11 Wars: Lethality and the Need for Transparency* (Watson Institute of International and Public Affairs, Brown University, 2018).

11. 'Human Development Report 2020: The Next Frontier: Human Development and the Anthropocene,' url: http://hdr.undp.org/sites/all/themes/hdr_theme/country-notes/PAK.pdf, accessed on 23 July 2021; 'UNDP Human Development Reports,' url: http://hdr.undp.org/en/countries/profiles/PAK, accessed on 23 July 2021.

12. 'Polio eradication a UN priority, says Guterres in Pakistan visit,' *United Nations*, url: https://news.un.org/en/story/2020/02/1057641, accessed on 23 July 2021.

13. 'Why Pakistan cricket is desperate to enjoy the comforts of home after 10 years in exile,' *The Telegraph* (19 May 2018), url: https://www.telegraph.co.uk/cricket/2018/05/19/pakistan-cricket-desperate-enjoy-comforts-home-10-years-exile/, accessed on 23 July 2021.

14. Sam Morshead, 'Winning hearts, changing minds: The inside story of the PSL's homecoming,' *The Cricketer* (6 March 2020), url: https://www.thecricketer.com/Topics/peshawarzalmi/winning_hearts_changing_minds_the_inside_story__psl_homecoming.html, accessed on 25 July 2021.

15. Shakeel Ahmad, 'Unleashing the potential of a young Pakistan,' *UNDP Human Development Reports* (24 July 2018), url: http://hdr.undp.org/en/content/unleashing-potential-young-pakistan, accessed on 23 July 2021.

16. Harsha Bhogle, 'Does our society breed corrupt sportsmen?,' *ESPN Cricinfo* (3 November 2011), url: https://www.espncricinfo.com/story/_/id/22374894/does-our-society-breed-corrupt-sportsmen, accessed on 23 July 2021.

17. Umer Farooq, 'Terror incidents continued to decline in 2018,' *The Express Tribune* (1 January 2019), url: https://tribune.com.pk/story/1878671/1-terror-incidents-continued-decline-2018/, accessed on 23 July 2021; Kathy Gannon, 'Terror attacks drop,

but Pakistan "not out of the woods",' *Associated Press* (30 January 2020), url: https://apnews.com/fca536aebf9b70141f22d99d4f94ba9b, accessed on 23 July 2021.

18. 'Bangladesh v England,' *BBC Sport* (12 September 2016), url: https://www.bbc.co.uk/sport/cricket/37331990, accessed on 23 July 2021.

19. This was reduced to twenty-three days because of the Covid-19 pandemic. The final and semi-finals were postponed indefinitely.

20. Martin Williamson, 'When Sylvester Clarke bricked it,' *ESPN Cricinfo* (13 May 2006), url: https://www.espncricinfo.com/story/_/id/21144653/when-sylvester-clarke-bricked-it, accessed on 23 July 2021.

21. Sam Morshead, 'Multan's message to the world on seismic opening night,' *The Cricketer* (Feb. 26, 2020), url: thecricketer.com/Topics/peshawarzalmi/multans_message_to_the_world.html, accessed on Jul. 23, 2021.

22. Morshead, 'Multan's message.'

23. 'Sultan' and 'Zalmi' refer to the two competing PSL teams—Multan Sultans and Peshawar Zalmi.

24. Ammara Maqsood, *The New Pakistani Middle Class* (Cambridge, MA: Harvard University Press, 2017), p. 35.

25. Taha Hashim, 'Leaps of faith: MCC send their message to the world,' *Wisden* (14 February 2020), url: https://wisden.com/stories/features/leaps-of-faith-mcc-send-their-message-to-the-world, accessed on 23 July 2021.

26. Ibid.

27. Kashif Abbasi, 'Previous PCB regime paid extra money to West Indies for series in Pakistan: Mani,' *Dawn* (7 March 2020), url: https://www.dawn.com/news/1539074, accessed on 23 July 2021.

28. 'Former Pakistan cricketer Nasir Jamshed jailed over fixing scandal,' *The Guardian* (8 February 2020), url: https://www.theguardian.com/sport/2020/feb/08/nasir-jamshed-former-pakistan-cricket-batsman-jailed-17-months-over-fixing-scandal, accessed on 23 July 2021.

29. "There was no way we could stay in the country' – New Zealand Cricket chief David White,' *ESPN Cricinfo* (19 September 2021), url: https://www.espncricinfo.com/story/new-zealand-tour-of-pakistan-nzc-chief-david-white-says-there-was-no-way-team-could-stay-1278454, accessed on 19 September 2021; "Cricket threat'" Black Caps arrive in Dubai after aborting Pakistan tour,' The *Guardian* (19 Sep. 2021), url: https://www.theguardian.com/sport/2021/sep/19/specific-credible-threat-black-caps-new-zealand-cricket-arrive-in-dubai-after-aborting-pakistan-tour, accessed on 19 Sep. 2021.

30. Shaharyar Khan and Ali Khan, *Cricket Cauldron: The Turbulent Politics of Sport in Pakistan* (Harper Sport, 2013), pp. 120–121.

31. Kamila Shamsie, 'Strong arms: The story of Pakistan women's cricket,' *The Cricket Monthly* (16 October 2019), url: https://www.thecricketmonthly.com/story/1202296/the-story-of-pakistan-women-s-cricket--from-the-khan-sisters-to-sana-mir, accessed on 23 July 2021.

32. Khan and Khan, *Cricket Cauldron*, p. 121.

33. Amber Rahim Shamsi, 'Why Haleema Rafique's death should matter, and why it won't,' *Dawn* (17 July 2014), url: https://www.dawn.com/news/1119734, accessed on 23 July 2021; M. Ilyas Khan, 'Family tells of Pakistan teen cricketer's 'suicide' after sex-pest row,' *BBC News* (17 July 2014), accessed on 23 July 2021.

34. The two divorced amicably in 2004 and have two sons from their marriage.

35. 'Handsome alert,' *Dunya News* (2 August 2018), url: https://dunyanews.tv/en/
Pakistan/450645-Handsome-alert-Khan-to-debut-in-the-list-of-good-looking-heads-of-,
accessed on 23 July 2021.

36. Apart from being the cricketing superpower of the world, Indian firms have increasingly
acquired a series of high profile British companies including Jaguar and Land Rover from
Ford Motors, Tetley Tea, Corus Hotels, and a host of IT firms, 'India's rise in reverse
imperialism: Forbes,' *IBEF* (12 June 2008), url: https://www.ibef.org/news/19325, accessed
on 23 July 2021.

37. Taha Hashim, 'Misbah-ul-Haq: "I was a bit worried about taking both roles",' *Wisden* (12
March 2020), url: https://www.wisden.com/stories/interviews/misbah-ul-haq-exclusive-
interview, accessed on 23 July 2021.

38. Mike M. Wood, 'India v Pakistan ...,' *Forbes* (14 June 2019), url: https://www.forbes.
com/sites/mikemeehallwood/2019/06/14/india-v-pakistan-at-the-cricket-world-cup-is-
the-biggest-sporting-event-in-the-world-this-weekend/, accessed on 23 July 2021.

39. Arjun Appadurai, 'Playing with Modernity: The Decolonization of Indian Cricket,' *Altre
Modernita* 14 (2015), p. 19.

40. 'Coronavirus: ECB recommends all recreation cricket is suspended indefinitely,' *BBC
Sport* (18 March 2020), url: https://www.bbc.co.uk/sport/cricket/51949526, accessed on
23 July 2021.

Epilogue: Cricket in the Time of Covid

1. 'Troubling projections,' *Dawn* (16 June 2020), url: https://www.dawn.com/news/1563859,
accessed on 6 August 2021.

2. 'Covid-19 Health Advisory Platform,' *Government of Pakistan*, url: https://covid.gov.pk.

3. 'PM Imran hopeful Pakistan's "hot and dry" weather will mitigate virus threat,' *Dawn* (20
March 2020), url: https://www.dawn.com/news/1542413, accessed on 7 August 2021.

4. 'Pakistan: Covid 19 – Situation Report (As of 10 June 2020),' *Reliefweb*, url: https://
reliefweb.int/report/pakistan/pakistan-covid-19-situation-report-10-june-2020, accessed
on 6 August 2021.

5. Asif Shahzad, '"God is with us": Many Muslims in Pakistan flout the coronavirus ban
in mosques,' *Reuters* (13 April 2020), url: https://www.reuters.com/article/us-health-
coronavirus-pakistan-congregat/god-is-with-us-many-muslims-in-pakistan-flout-the-
coronavirus-ban-in-mosques-idINKCN21V0T4, accessed on 6 August 2021.

6. Asif Chaudhry, 'Tableeghi Jamaat in hot water in Pakistan too for Covid-19 spread,' *Dawn*
(8 April 2020), url: https://www.dawn.com/news/1547354, accessed on 7 August 2021.

7. 'The global normalcy index,' *The Economist* (1 July 2021), url: https://www.economist.
com/graphic-detail/tracking-the-return-to-normalcy-after-covid-19, accessed on 6 August
2021.

8. Humayoun Ahmed Khan, 'Pakistan is safe for international cricket, says Atherton,' *Dawn*
(12 April 2020), url: https://www.dawn.com/news/1548429, accessed on 6 August 2021.

9. Stephan Shemilt, 'England v Pakistan: Ten players from touring squad have coronavirus,'
BBC Sport (23 June 2020), url: https://www.bbc.com/sport/cricket/53149897, accessed
on 6 August 2021.

10. 'How denial and conspiracy theories fuel coronavirus crisis in Pakistan,' *DW*, url:
https://www.dw.com/en/how-denial-and-conspiracy-theories-fuel-coronavirus-crisis-in-
pakistan/a-53913842, accessed on 6 August 2021.

11. Ameya Barve, 'Fans bash Pakistan players for not wearing masks or maintaining social distancing during Eid al-Adha celebrations,' *CricTracker* (1 August 2020), url: https://www.crictracker.com/fans-bash-pakistan-players-for-not-wearing-masks-or-maintaining-social-distancing-during-eid-al-adha-celebrations/, accessed on 6 August 2021.

12. 'Cricket: 'Behave yourself' – Pakistan cricket legend Shoaib Akhtar slams NZ Cricket over Black Caps tour threat,' *NZHerald* (27 November 2020), url: https://www.nzherald.co.nz/sport/cricket-behave-yourself-pakistan-cricket-legend-shoaib-akhtar-slams-nz-cricket-over-black-caps-tour-threat/PSS2GI2AWKST2BBCIWXCIEOEYY/, accessed on 6 August 2021.

13. Shubhajit Roy, 'India to supply Covid vaccines to Pakistan,' *The Indian Express* (10 March 2021), url: https://indianexpress.com/article/india/india-to-supply-covid-vaccines-to-pakistan-7221680/, accessed on 6 August 2021.

14. Praveen Swami, 'A Secret ISI-RAW Channel, Talks Since 2018: What Led to India–Pakistan LoC Ceasefire,' *News18* (23 March 2021), url: https://www.news18.com/news/india/a-secret-isi-raw-channel-talks-since-2018-what-led-to-india-pakistan-ceasefire-3563711. html, accessed on 6 August 2021; Khurshid Kasuri and Radha Kumar, 'There is hope for Pakistan-India peace process,' *Dawn* (24 March 2021), url: https://www.dawn.com/news/1614187/there-is-hope-for-pakistan-india-peace-process, accessed on 6 August 2021.

15. Baqir Sajjad Syed, 'Pakistan, India agree on LoC ceasefire,' *Dawn* (26 February 2021), url: https://www.dawn.com/news/1609468, accessed on 6 August 2021.

16. Swami, 'A Secret ISI-RAW Channel.'

17. 'India–Pakistan T20 series in the offing: Report,' *The Times of India* (25 March 2021), url: https://timesofindia.indiatimes.com/sports/cricket/news/india-pakistan-t20-series-in-the-offing-report/articleshow/81684414.cms, accessed on 6 August 2021.

Bibliography

'19 arrested for cheering Pakistan's Champions Trophy victory.' *Times of India* (21 June 2017) <https://timesofindia.indiatimes.com/india/19-arrested-for-cheering-pakistans-champions-trophy-victory/articleshow/59243368.cms>.

'62pc cut in war on terror losses.' *Dawn* (27 April 2018) <https://www.dawn.com/news/1404161>.

Abbasi, Ansar. 'Is Pakistan More Corrupt Than Before?.' *Geo TV* (13 October 2019) <https://www.geo.tv/latest/251054-v>.

Abbasi, Kashif. 'Previous PCB regime paid extra money to West Indies for series in Pakistan: Mani.' *Dawn* (7 March 2020) <https://www.dawn.com/news/1539074>.

'Afghanistan cancel Pakistan series.' *Cricket.com.au* (1 June 2017) <https://www.cricket.com.au/news/pakistan-afghanistan-t20-friendly-series-cancelled-bomb-blast-kabul-intelligence-pcb-acb/2017-06-01>.

'Afridi banned for two T20s for ball-tampering.' ESPNcricinfo (31 January 2010) <https://www.espncricinfo.com/story/_/id/22636034/shahid-afridi-banned-two-t20s-ball-tampering>.

Afridi, Shahid (w/ Wajahat S. Khan). *Game Changer* (HarperCollins, 2019).

Ahmad, Sadaf. 'Al-Huda and Women's Religious Authority in Urban Pakistan.' *The Muslim World* 103/3 (2013), pp. 363–374.

Ahmad, Sadaf. 'Pakistani policewomen: questioning the role of gender in circumscribing police corruption.' *Policing and Society* 8 (2019), pp. 890–904.

Ahmad, Shakeel. 'Unleashing the potential of a young Pakistan.' *UNDP Human Development Reports* (24 July 2018) <http://hdr.undp.org/en/content/unleashing-potential-young-pakistan>.

Ahmed, Imtiaz. 'More tributes to Lala Amarnath from Pakistan.' *ESPN* (10 August 2000) <https://www.espn.com.sg/cricket/story/_/id/23242079/more-tributes-lala-amarnath-pakistan>.

Ahmed, Imtiaz. 'Pakistan cricketers pay rich tribute to Lala.' *ESPN* (9 August 2000) <https://www.espn.co.uk/cricket/story/_/id/23242977/pakistan-cricketers-pay-rich-tribute-lala>.

Ahmed, Ishtiaq. ISAS Brief No. 99 (Institute of South Asian Studies, National University of Singapore, 4 March 2009).

Ahmed, Mushtaq. *Twenty20 Vision: My Life and Inspiration* (Methuen Publishing Ltd., 2006).

Ahmed, Zahid Shahab, and Musharaf Zahoor. 'Bangladesh-Pakistan Relations: Hostage to a Traumatic Past.' *Commonwealth & Comparative Politics* 57/1 (2019), pp. 31–51.

Akhtar, Shoaib. *Controversially Yours* (HarperCollins, 2011).

Akram, Wasim, (with Patrick Murphy). *Wasim: The Autobiography of Wasim Akram* (Piatkus Books, 1998).

Ali, Moeen. *Moeen* (Allen and Unwin, 2018).

Ali, Sameen A. Mohsin. 'Governance Amid Crisis: Delegation, Personal Gain, and Service Delivery in Pakistan.' In Mariam Mufti, Sahar Shafqat, and Niloufer Siddiqui (eds.),

Pakistan's Political Parties: Surviving Between Dictatorship and Democracy (Georgetown University Press, 2020).

'All Indian Cine Workers Association Announces Complete Ban on Pakistani Artists, Actors Amid Pulwama Attack.' *Outlook India* (18 February 2019) <https://www.outlookindia.com/website/story/entertainment-news-all-indian-cine-workers-association-announces-complete-ban-on-pakistani-artists-actors-amid-pulwama-attack/325699>.

Allen, David and Hubert Doggart (eds.), *'A Breathless Hush ...': The MCC Anthology of Cricket Verse* (Methuen Publishing, 2007).

Allen, Matthew. 'PCB saved by India windfall.' *BBC Sport* (28 February 2004) <http://news.bbc.co.uk/sport1/hi/cricket/3495720.stm>.

Aloysius, G. 'Trajectory of Hindutva.' *Economic and Political Weekly* 29/24 (11 June 1994), pp. 1450–1452.

Amarnath, Rajendra. *Lala Amarnath Life and Times: The Making of a Legend* (Sportsbooks Ltd., 2007).

'Amartya Sen's 9-year-long association with Nalanda University ends.' *Economic Times* (23 November 2016) <https://economictimes.indiatimes.com/news/politics-and-nation/amartya-sens-9-year-long-association-with-nalanda-university-ends/articleshow/55586972.cms?from=mdr>.

Anderson, Benedict. *Imagined Communities: Reflections on the Origin and Spread of Nationalism* (Verso, 1991).

Angelos, Kanas. 'Pure Contagion Effects in International Banking: The Case of BCCI's Failure.' *Journal of Applied Economics* 8/1 (2005), pp. 101–123.

'Anger over Ijaz Butt Remarks.' *The National* (21 September 2010) <https://www.thenational.ae/sport/anger-over-ijaz-butt-remarks-1.504169>.

'Anurag Thakur becomes first serving BJP MP to join Territorial Army.' *Indian Express* (29 July 2016) <https://indianexpress.com/article/india/india-news-india/anurag-thakur-territorial-army-bjp-mp-2942887/>.

'Anurag Thakur: India cricket board chief ordered to resign.' *BBC News* (2 January 2017) <https://www.bbc.co.uk/news/world-asia-india-38487340>.

Appadurai, Arjun. 'Playing with modernity: The decolonization of Indian Cricket.' *Altre Modernita* 14 (2015), pp. 1–24.

Appadurai, Arjun. *Modernity at Large: Cultural Dimensions of Globalization* (University of Minnesota Press, 1996).

Astill, James. *The Great Tamasha: Cricket, Corruption and the Turbulent Rise of Modern India* (Wisden, 2013).

Atherton, Michael. *Athers: Authorised Biography of Michael Atherton* (Headline Book Publishing, 1996).

'Ball-tampering: Five memorable cricketing controversies from Atherton to Du Plessis.' *BBC Sport* (25 March 2018) <https://www.bbc.com/sport/cricket/43532624>.

Bandyopadhyay, Kausik. 'Pakistan Cricket at the Crossroads: An Outsider's Perspective.' In Jon Gemmel and Boria Majumdar (eds.), *Cricket, Race and the 2007 World Cup* (Routledge, 2008).

Bandyopadhyay, Kausik. *Sport, Culture and Nation* (Sage Publications, 2015).

Bandyopadhyay, Kausik. 'Pakistani Cricket at Crossroads: An Outsider's Perspective.' *Sport in Society* 10/1 (2017), pp. 101–119.

'Bangladesh reject invitation to tour Pakistan.' ESPNcricinfo (31 March 2017) <https://www.espncricinfo.com/story/_/id/19043732/bangladesh-reject-invitation-tour-pakistan>.

'Bangladesh v England.' *BBC Sport* (12 September 2016) <https://www.bbc.co.uk/sport/cricket/37331990>.

Barnes, Simon. 'Hair today, gone tomorrow—at least we hope so for sake of game.' *The Times* (22 August 2006) <https://www.thetimes.co.uk/article/hair-today-gone-tomorrow-at-least-we-hope-so-for-sake-of-game-zfcn6tvv2gl>.

Barnes, Simon. 'Steve Waugh: The captain who transformed Test cricket—Almanack.' *Wisden India* (2 June 2019) <https://www.wisden.com/almanack/steve-waugh-wisden-tribute> accessed on 8 July 2021.

Barve, Ameya. 'Fans bash Pakistan players for not wearing masks or maintaining social distancing during Eid al-Adha celebrations.' *CricTracker* (1 August 2020) <https://www.crictracker.com/fans-bash-pakistan-players-for-not-wearing-masks-or-maintaining-social-distancing-during-eid-al-adha-celebrations/>.

Bass, B.M., and B.J. Avolio. *MLQ Multifactor Leadership Questionnaire* (Mind Garden, 2000).

Basu, Kaushik. 'Why is Bangladesh booming?.' *Brookings* (1 May 2018) <https://www.brookings.edu/opinions/why-is-bangladesh-booming/>.

Bateman, Anthony, and Jeffrey Hill. *The Cambridge Companion to Cricket* (Cambridge University Press, 2011).

Beckles, Hilary McDonald. 'The Detachment of West Indies Cricket from the Nationalist Scaffold.' In Anthony Bateman and Jeffrey Hill (eds.), The Cambridge Companion to Cricket (Cambridge University Press, 2011), pp. 160-173.

Beckles, Hilary. *Cricket without a Cause: Fall and Rise of the Mighty West Indian Cricketers* (Ian Randle, 2017).

Belmekki, Belkacem. 'Sir Sayyid Ahmad Khan's Framework for the Educational Uplift of the Indian Muslims during British Raj.' *Anthropos* 104/1 (2009), pp. 165–172.

Berry, Scyld. *Cricket Odyssey* (Pavilion Books, 1988).

Berry, Scyld. *Cricket: The Game of Life* (Hodder & Stoughton, 2015).

Bhattacharya, Rahul. 'Hope and Fear.' ESPNcricinfo (27 March 2004) <https://www.espncricinfo.com/story/hope-and-fear-140425>.

Bhattacharya, Rahul. 'Indians in Pakistan: Brothers, Not in Arms.' In John Stern and Marcus Williams (eds.), *The Essential Wisden: An Anthology of 150 Years of Wisden Cricketers' Almanack* (Bloomsbury, 2013).

Bhattacharya, Rahul. *Pundits from Pakistan* (Picador, 2005).

Bhimani, K. *Director's Special Book of Cricketing Controversies* (Allied Publishers Limited, 1996).

Bhogle, Harsha. 'Does our society breed corrupt sportsmen?.' ESPNcricinfo (3 November 2011) <https://www.espncricinfo.com/story/_/id/22374894/does-our-society-breed-corrupt-sportsmen>.

Birley, Derek. *A Social History of English Cricket* (Aurum Press, 1999; 2003).

Biswas, Soutik. 'Ramachandra Guha: How the right wing hounded out a Gandhi biographer.' *BBC News* (3 November 2018) <https://www.bbc.co.uk/news/world-asia-india-46069120>.

Blofeld, Henry. *One Test after Another* (Stanley Paul and Co Ltd., 1985).

Boardley, Ian D., and Maria Kavussanu. 'The Moral Disengagement in Sport Scale–Short.' *Journal of Sports Sciences* 26/14 (2008), pp. 1507–1517.

Boardley, Ian, and Maria Kavussanu. 'Moral Disengagement in Sport.' *International Review of Sport and Exercise Psychology* 4 (2011), pp. 93–108.

'Bollywood divided on Pakistani actors ban issue.' *Times of India* (29 January 2017) <https://timesofindia.indiatimes.com/entertainment/hindi/bollywood/news/Bollywood-divided-on-Pakistani-actors-ban-issue/articleshow/54735039.cms>.

Borger, Julian. 'Imran Khan warns UN of potential nuclear war in Kashmir.' *The Guardian* (26 September 2019) <https://www.theguardian.com/world/2019/sep/26/imran-khan-warns-un-of-potential-nuclear-war-in-kashmir>.

Borka, Aftab. 'Indian films breathe life into Pakistani cinemas.' *Reuters* (25 April 2008) <https://www.reuters.com/article/us-pakistan-bollywood/indian-films-breathe-life-into-pakistani-cinemas-idUSISL17078720080425>.

Bose, Mihir. 'Conflicting loyalties: nationalism and religion in India–Pakistan cricket relations.' In A. Bateman and J. Hill (eds.), *The Cambridge Companion to Cricket* (Cambridge University Press, 2011).

Bose, Mihir. *A History of Indian Cricket* (Andre Deutsch Ltd., 1980; 2002).

Bose, Mihir. *The Nine Waves* (Rupa Publications, 2019).

Bowen, Rowland. *Cricket: A History of its Growth and Development* (Eyre & Spottiswoode, 1970).

Brearley, Mike. *On Cricket* (Little, Brown Book Group, 2018).

Brettig, Daniel. 'New ICC finance model breaks up Big Three.' ESPNcricinfo (27 April 2017) <https://www.espncricinfo.com/story/_/id/19253630/new-icc-finance-model-breaks-big-three>.

Britain, Gerald M., and Ronald Cohen (eds.). *Hierarchy and Society: Anthropological Perspectives on Bureaucracy* (Institute for the Study of Human Issues, 1980).

'Broad angry at security failure.' *BBC Sport* (4 March 2009) <http://news.bbc.co.uk/2/hi/south_asia/7924210.stm>.

Brown, Bernardo. 'From Guru Gama to Punchi Italia: Changing Dreams of Sri Lankan Transnational Youth.' *Contemporary South Asia* 22 (2014), pp. 335–349.

Bull, Andy. 'The tension between Test cricket and Twenty20.' *The Guardian* (6 January 2015) <https://www.theguardian.com/sport/2015/jan/06/the-spin-cricket-big-bash-tensions-tests-twenty20>.

Buncombe, Andrew. 'Narendra Modi sworn in as India's new PM with Pakistani counterpart Nawaz Sharif looking on.' *The Independent* (27 May 2014) <https://www.independent.co.uk/news/world/asia/indias-new-pm-narendra-modi-to-meet-with-pakistani-premier-nawaz-sharif-after-being-sworn-in-9436226.html>.

Butalia, Urvashi. *The Other Side of Silence: Voices from the Partition of India* (Penguin, 1998).

'Butt defends not suspending spot-fixing trio.' *The Independent* (22 October 2011) <https://www.independent.co.uk/sport/cricket/butt-defends-not-suspending-spot-fixing-trio-2091765.html>.

Butt, Qamaruddin. *Playing for a Draw: Covering Pakistan's Tour of India 1960–61* (Jahaniasons, 1962).

'Can trade onion, tomatoes then why not play cricket': Shoaib Akhtar on India–Pakistan bilateral series.' *Hindustan Times* (18 February 2020) <https://www.hindustantimes.com/cricket/can-trade-onion-tomatoes-then-why-not-play-cricket-shoaib-akhtar-on-india-pakistan-bilateral-series/story-BQmMDWKAEKa8OZd5yw2QfL.html>.

Cashman, Richard. 'The Paradox that is Pakistani Cricket: Some Initial Reflections.' *The Sports Historian* 14/1 (1994), pp. 21–37.

Cashman, Richard. *Patrons, Players and the Crowd* (Orient Longman, 1979).

'CBI Report on Cricket Match Fixing and Related Malpractices.' *Cricinfo India* (2000) <http://www.aus.cricket.org/link_to_database/NATIONAL/IND/NEWS/CBI-REPORT.html>.

Chalke, Stephen. *Micky Stewart and the Changing Face of Cricket* (Fairfield Books, 2012).

Chatterjee, Kingshuk. 'To Play of Not to Play: Fabricating Consent Over the Indo-Pak Cricket Series.' In Boria Majumdar and J.A. Mangan (eds.), *Sport in South Asian Society* (Routledge, 2005).

Chaudhary, Vivek. 'Wide boy.' *The Cricket Monthly* (March 2015) <http://www. thecricketmonthly.com/story/836893/wide-boy>.

Chaudhry, Asif. 'Tableeghi Jamaat in hot water in Pakistan too for Covid-19 spread.' *Dawn* (8 April 2020) <https://www.dawn.com/news/1547354>.

Cheema, Hassan. 'Pakistan playing Scotland? That's no surprise.' ESPNcricinfo (13 June 2018) <https://www.espncricinfo.com/story/_/id/23777527/pakistan-playing-scotland-no-surprise>.

Chêne, M. 'Overview of corruption in Pakistan' (U4 Anti-Corruption Resource Center, Chr. Michelsen Institute, 2008).

Clifton et al. '"Staggering" trade in fake degrees revealed.' *BBC News* (16 January 2018) <https:// www.bbc.com/news/uk-42579634>.

Cohen, Stephen Philip. 'India, Pakistan and Kashmir.' *Journal of Strategic Studies* 24/4 (2002), pp. 32–60.

Cohen, Stephen. *The Idea of Pakistan* (Vanguard Books, 2005).

Coll, Steve. 'The Back Channel: India and Pakistan Secret Kashmir Talks.' *The New Yorker* (2 March 2009).

Condon, Sir Paul. *Report on Corruption in International Cricket* (Anti-Corruption Unit, 2001).

Corbin, Eddie. 'Leadership Issues in West Indies Cricket: A Theoretical Analysis of Leadership Styles of a Purposive Group of Captains.' *Journal of Eastern Caribbean Studies* 30/1 (2005), pp. 31–53.

'Coronavirus: ECB recommends all recreation cricket is suspended indefinitely.' *BBC Sport* (18 March 2020) <https://www.bbc.co.uk/sport/cricket/51949526>.

Corrigan, Peter. 'Imran Khan: The Road from Cricket to Politics.' In David L. Andrews, Steven J. Jackson (eds.), *Sports Stars: The Cultural Politics of Sporting Celebrity* (Routledge, 2002).

'Covid-19 Health Advisory Platform.' *Government of Pakistan* <https://covid.gov.pk>.

Coward, Mike. *Cricket Beyond the Bazaar* (Allen and Unwin, 1990).

Crace, John. *Wasim and Waqar: Imran's Inheritors* (Boxtree Ltd., 1992).

Crawford, Neta C. *Human Cost of the Post-9/11 Wars: Lethality and the Need for Transparency* (Watson Institute of International and Public Affairs, Brown University, 2018).

Crick, Emily. 'Can cricket be used as multi-track diplomacy in the context of Indo-Pakistani relations? With particular reference to the period between 1999 and 2005.' M.Sc. Thesis in Development and Security, 2006.

Crick, Emily. 'Contact Sport: Cricket in India–Pakistan Relations Since 1999.' *South Asian Survey* 16/1 (2009), pp. 59–79.

'Cricket: "Behave yourself" – Pakistan cricket legend Shoaib Akhtar slams NZ Cricket over Black Caps tour threat.' *NZHerald* (27 November 2020) <https://www.nzherald.co.nz/sport/cricket-behave-yourself-pakistan-cricket-legend-shoaib-akhtar-slams-nz-cricket-over-black-caps-tour-threat/PSS2GI2AWKST2BBCIWXCIEOEYY/>.

'Cricket: Akhtar tossed out for ball tampering.' *NZHerald* (21 May 2003) <https://www.nzherald.co.nz/sport/news/article.cfm?c_id=4&objectid=3503261>.

'Cricket: Politics spices up ahead of Pakistan-Afghanistan match.' *TRT World* (28 June 2019) <https://www.trtworld.com/sport/cricket-politics-spices-up-ahead-of-pakistan-afghanistan-match-27879>.

Croft, Stuart. 'South Asia's Arms Control Process: Cricket Diplomacy and the Composite Dialogue.' *International Affairs* 81/5 (2005), pp. 1039–60.

Dalrymple, William. 'The Great Divide.' *The New Yorker* (22 June 2015) <https://www.newyorker.com/magazine/2015/06/29/the-great-divide-books-dalrymple>.

Dasgupta, Jishnu. 'Manufacturing Unison: Muslims, Hindus and Indians during the India–Pakistan Match.' In Boria Majumdar and J.A. Mangan (eds.), *Sport in South Asian Society: Past and Present* (Routledge, 2005).

'Did Muslim radicals order the murder of Woolmer?.' *Daily Mirror* (30 March 2007).

Dirs, Ben. *Everywhere We Went: Top Tales from Cricket's Barmy Army* (Simon and Schuster, 2012).

'Disgruntled Afghan Cricket Chief lashes out at Pakistan Cricket Board.' *Times of Islamabad* (30 June 2019) <https://timesofislamabad.com/30-Jun-2019/disgruntled-afghan-cricket-chief-lashes-out-at-pakistan-cricket-board>.

'Donald Carr: "Few in cricket have been so close to so much for so long"—Almanack.' *Wisden* (12 July 2019) <https://www.wisden.com/almanack/donald-carr-almanack-tribute>.

Ellis-Petersen, Hannah. '"Many lives have been lost": Five-Month Internet Blackout Plunges Kashmir Into Crisis.' *The Guardian* (5 January 2020) <https://www.theguardian.com/world/2020/jan/05/the-personal-and-economic-cost-of-kashmirs-internet-ban>.

'England's Jonathan Trott shocked by Pakistan spot-fixing allegations.' *The Telegraph* (4 September 2010) <https://www.telegraph.co.uk/sport/cricket/international/england/7981536/Englands-Jonathan-Trott-shocked-by-Pakistan-spot-fixing-allegations.html>.

'Fans vote 1999 Chennai clash with India as Pakistan's "greatest Test match"'. *Dawn* (29 July 2019) <https://www.dawn.com/news/1496891>.

Farooq, Umer. 'Shahzad fined, asked to relocate to Afghanistan.' ESPNcricinfo (14 April 2018) <https://www.espncricinfo.com/story/_/id/23170364/mohammad-shahzad-fined-asked-relocate-afghanistan>.

Farooq, Umer. 'Terror incidents continued to decline in 2018.' *The Express Tribune* (1 January 2019) <https://tribune.com.pk/story/1878671/1-terror-incidents-continued-decline-2018/>.

Farooq, Umer. 'Zaka Ashraf reacts sternly to Bangladesh delaying tour.' ESPNcricinfo (31 December 2012) <https://www.espncricinfo.com/story/_/id/22103182/zaka-ashraf-reacts-sternly-bangladesh-delaying-tour>.

'Fatalities in Terrorist Violence in Pakistan 2000–2019.' *South Asia Terrorism Portal* <https://www.satp.org/satporgtp/countries/pakistan/database/casualties.htm>.

Filkins, Dexter. 'Blood and Soil in Narendra Modi's India.' *The New Yorker* (2 December 2019) <https://www.newyorker.com/magazine/2019/12/09/blood-and-soil-in-narendra-modis-india>.

Fleischner, Justine. *Governance and Militancy in Pakistan's Swat Valley* (Centre for Strategic and International Studies, Washington, 2011).

Flintoff, Andrew. *Being Freddie* (Hodder and Stoughton, 2005).

'Former Pakistan cricketer Nasir Jamshed jailed over fixing scandal.' *The Guardian* (8 February 2020) <https://www.theguardian.com/sport/2020/feb/08/nasir-jamshed-former-pakistan-cricket-batsman-jailed-17-months-over-fixing-scandal>.

Frith, David. 'Corruption in Cricket.' In Anthony Bateman and Jeffrey Hill (eds.), *The Cambridge Companion to Cricket* (Cambridge University Press, 2011).

'Full statement of PCB chairman Ijaz Butt.' ESPNcricinfo (9 May 2009) <https://www.espncricinfo.com/story/_/id/22808350/full-statement-pcb-chairman-ijaz-butt>.

'Full transcript of Mohammad Amir interview.' ESPNcricinfo (20 March 2012) <https://www.espncricinfo.com/story/_/id/21284462/full-transcript-mohammad-amir-interview>.

Gammell, Caroline. 'Pakistan's captain "raised concerns about Mazhar Majeed Two Months Ago".' *The Telegraph* (31 August 2010) <https://www.telegraph.co.uk/news/

uknews/7971839/Pakistans-captain-Shahid-Afridi-raised-concerns-about-Mazhar-Majeed-two-months-ago.html>.

Ganguly, Saurav. *A Century Is Not Enough: My Roller-coaster Ride to Success* (Juggernaut Publication, 2018).

Gannon, Kathy. 'Terror attacks drop, but Pakistan "not out of the woods".' *Associated Press* (30 January 2020) <https://apnews.com/fca536aebf9b70141f22d99d4f94ba9b>.

Geertz, Clifford. *The Interpretation of Cultures* (Basic Books, 1973).

Gemmell, Jon, and Boria Majumdar (eds.). *Cricket, Race and the 2007 World Cup* (Routledge, 2008).

Gemmell, Jon. 'Cricket, Race and the 2007 World Cup.' In Jon Gemmell and Boria Majumdar (eds.), *Cricket, Race and the 2007 World Cup* (Routledge, 2008).

Gibson, Owen. 'Ijaz Butt withdraws accusations of match fixing against England team.' *The Guardian* (29 September 2010) <https://www.theguardian.com/sport/2010/sep/29/ijaz-butt-england-pakistan>.

Giulianotti, Richard. *Sport: A Critical Sociology* (Polity Press, 2016).

Glanz, James, Sebastian Rotella, and David E. Sanger. 'In 2008 Mumbai Attacks, Piles of Spy Data, but an Uncompleted Puzzle.' *The New York Times* (21 December 2014) <https://www.nytimes.com/2014/12/22/world/asia/in-2008-mumbai-attacks-piles-of-spy-data-but-an-uncompleted-puzzle.html>.

Global Conflict Tracker, *Council on Foreign Relations* <https://www.cfr.org/interactive/global-conflict-tracker/conflict/conflict-between-india-and-pakistan>.

Gneezy, Uri, and Aldo Rustichini. 'A Fine is a Price.' *Journal of Legal Studies* 29/1 (2000), pp. 1–17.

Gollapudi, Nagraj, and Sidharth Monga. 'BCCI mulls asking for Pakistan World Cup ban.' ESPNcricinfo (21 February 2019) <https://www.espncricinfo.com/story/_/id/26045366/bcci-mulls-asking-pakistan-world-cup-ban>.

Gollapudi, Nagraj. 'PCB's case against BCCI dismissed by ICC dispute panel.' ESPNcricinfo (20 November 2018) <https://www.espncricinfo.com/story/_/id/25328942/pcb-case-bcci-dismissed-icc-dispute-panel>.

Gopalakrishnan, Shankar. 'Defining, Constructing and Policing a "New India": Relationship between Neoliberalism and Hindutva.' *Economic and Political Weekly* 41/26 (2006), pp. 2803–2813.

Gorvine, Albert. 'The Civil Service under the Revolutionary Government in Pakistan.' *Middle East Journal* 19/3 (1965), pp. 321–336.

Gough, Darren. *Dazzler* (Michael Joseph, 2001).

Guha, Ramachandra. 'Cricket and Politics in Colonial India.' *Past & Present* 161 (1998), pp. 155–190.

Guha, Ramachandra. *A Corner of a Foreign Field: The Indian History of a British Sport* (Picador, 2002).

Gul, Nabiha. 'Pakistan-India Peace Process 1990–2007: An Appraisal.' *Pakistan Horizon* 60/2 (2007), pp. 47–64.

Hagerty, Devin T. (ed.). *South Asia in World Politics* (Roman & Littlefield Publishers, 2005).

Hagerty, Devin. 'US Policy and the Kashmir Question: Prospects for Resolution.' In Sumit Ganguly (ed.), *The Kashmir Question Retrospect and Prospect* (Frank Cass and Company Ltd., 2003).

Hagerty, Devin T., and Herbert G. Hagerty. 'India's Foreign Relations.' In D. Hagerty (ed.), *South Asia in World Politics* (Roman & Littlefield, 2005).

Haigh, Gideon. 'The Great Carve-Up of World Cricket.' ESPNcricinfo, <http://www.espncricinfo.com/wisdenalmanack/content/story/735865.html>.

Haigh, Gideon. 'Ugly Trend that can Poison Indian Cricket.' *The Australian* (2021) <https://www.theaustralian.com.au/sport/cricket/ugly-trend-that-can-poison-indian-cricket/news-story/27588950568a90ea586d2607cbb61370>.

Haigh, Gideon. *Divide and Rule at the ICC: The Great Carve up of World Cricket* (Wisden and Bloomsbury, 2014).

Haigh, Gideon. *The Cricket War: The Story of Kerry Packer's World Series Cricket* (Wisden, 2017).

Hall, Stuart. 'The West and the Rest: Discourse and Power.' In Stuart Hall and Bram Gieben (eds.), *Formations of Modernity Polity Press* (Cambridge, 1992).

Hall, Stuart. *Stereotyping as a Signifying Practice* (Sage Publications, 1997).

'Handsome alert.' *Dunya News* (2 August 2018) <https://dunyanews.tv/en/Pakistan/450645-Handsome-alert-Khan-to-debut-in-the-list-of-good-looking-heads-of->.

Hanif, Mohammed. 'Our reward for appeasing the militants.' *The Guardian* (3 March 2009) <https://www.theguardian.com/commentisfree/2009/mar/03/sri-lanka-cricket-pakistan>.

Hanif, Mohammed. 'The partition goes on: A Pakistani perspective.' *AlJazeera* (15 August 2017) <https://www.aljazeera.com/indepth/features/2017/08/partition-pakistani-perspective-170807064330685.html>.

Hansen, T.B. 'Globalisation and Nationalist Imaginations: Hindutva's Promise of Equality Through Difference.' *Economic and Political Weekly* 31/10 (9 March 1996), pp. 603–605, 607, 616.

Hasan, Mushirul. *Legacy of a Divided Nation: India's Muslims From Independence to Ayodhya* (Routledge, 1997).

Hasan, P. 'Learning from the past: a fifty-year perspective on Pakistan's development.' *The Pakistan Development Review* 36/4 (1997), pp. 355–402.

Hasan, P. 'Poverty and social justice: some challenges for Islamization in Pakistan.' In R.M. Hathaway & W. Lee (eds.), *Islamization and the Pakistani Economy* (Woodrow Wilson International Centre for Scholars, 2004).

Hasan, Waqar, and Qamar Ahmed, *For Cricket and Country* (CricketPrint Publication, 2002).

Hashim, Taha. 'Leaps of faith: MCC send their message to the world.' *Wisden* (14 February 2020) <https://wisden.com/stories/features/leaps-of-faith-mcc-send-their-message-to-the-world>.

Hashim, Taha. 'Misbah-ul-Haq: 'I was a bit worried about taking both roles'.' *Wisden* (12 March 2020) <https://www.wisden.com/stories/interviews/misbah-ul-haq-exclusive-interview>.

Hashmi, Nabeel. 'Pakistan receives major share of 'Big Three' spoils.' *The Express Tribune* (26 June 2014) <https://tribune.com.pk/story/727501/pakistan-receives-major-share-of-big-three-spoils?print=true>.

Hawkins, Ed. *Bookie Gambler Fixer Spy: A Journey to the Heart of Cricket's Underworld* (Bloomsbury, 2013).

Healy, Ian. *Hands and Heals* (Harper Collins, 2000).

Heller, Richard, and Peter Oborne. *White on Green: A Portrait of Pakistan Cricket* (Simon Schuster, 2016).

Hewitt, V.M. *The International Politics of South Asia* (Manchester University Press, 1992).

Hill, C.R. *Olympic Politics* (Manchester University Press, 1992).

'History of ICC.' *ICC* <https://www.icc-cricket.com/about/the-icc/history-of-icc/1909-1963>.

Houlihan, Barry. *Sport and International Politics* (Harvester Wheatsheaf, 1994).

'How denial and conspiracy theories fuel coronavirus crisis in Pakistan.' *DW* <https://www. dw.com/en/how-denial-and-conspiracy-theories-fuel-coronavirus-crisis-in-pakistan/ a-53913842>.

Hughes, Geoffrey; Chiara Bresciani; Megnaa Mehtta; and Stuart Strange, 'Introduction: Ugly Emotions and the Politics of Accusation.' In 'Envy and Greed: Ugly Emotions and the Politics of Accusation,' Special issue of the *Cambridge Journal of Anthropology* 37/2 (2019), pp. 1–20.

'Human Development Report 2020: The Next Frontier: Human Development and the Anthropocene' <https://hdr.undp.org/sites/all/themes/hdr_theme/country-notes/PAK.pdf>.

Hussain, Abid. 'Tape Ball Tales.' *The Cricket Monthly* (November 2015) <http://www. thecricketmonthly.com/story/929545/tape-ball-tales>.

Hussain, Nasser. *Playing with Fire* (Michael Joseph, 2004).

Hussain, Rifaat. 'Pakistan's Relations with Azad Kashmir and the Impact on Indo-Pakistani Relations.' In Rafiq Dossani and Henry S. Rowen (eds.), *Prospects for Peace in South Asia* (Stanford University Press, 2005).

Hutchins, Brett. 'Unity, Difference and the 'National game': Cricket and Australian National Identity.' In Stephen Wagg (ed.), *Cricket and National Identity in the Postcolonial Age: Following On* (Routledge, 2005).

'I blame the ICC says Ian Botham.' *The Mirror* (21 August 2006) <https://www.mirror.co.uk/ news/uk-news/i-blame-the-icc-says-ian-botham-638824>.

'Ijaz Butt accuses England of accepting money to lose Pakistan match.' *The Guardian* (19 September 2010) <https://www.theguardian.com/sport/2010/sep/19/ijaz-butt-england-pakistan>.

'India cancel 2009 tour of Pakistan.' *CNN* (18 December 2008) <https://edition.cnn.com/2008/ SPORT/12/18/india.pakistan.cricket.tour/index.html>.

'India drops sedition charges against 'Pakistan cricket fans'.' *BBC* (22 June 2017) <https://www. bbc.co.uk/news/world-asia-india-40364164>.

'India helping us more than Pakistan: Afghan board CEO.' *Times of India* (21 January 2018) <https://timesofindia.indiatimes.com/sports/cricket/news/india-helping-us-more-than-pakistan-afghan-board-ceo/articleshow/62593984.cms>.

'India PM Modi in surprise Pakistan visit.' *BBC News* (25 December 2015) <https://www.bbc. co.uk/news/world-asia-35178594>.

'India vs Pakistan: Yuzvendra Chahal wants action against those guilty in Pulwama attack.' *Hindustan Times* (22 February 2019) <https://www.hindustantimes.com/cricket/india-vs-pakistan-yuzvendra-chahal-wants-action-against-those-guilty-in-pulwama-attack/story-7bBHV4Ihz3ovM2EoqtjuvI.html>.

'India's Modi threatens to "isolate Pakistan" after Kashmir attack.' *Financial Times* <https:// www.ft.com/content/bb7592de-82e3-11e6-8897-2359a58ac7a5>.

'India's Most Legendary of Figures.' ESPNcricinfo (August 1994) <http://www.espncricinfo. com/cricketer/content/story/141740.html>.

'India's rise in reverse imperialism: Forbes.' *IBEF* (12 June 2008) <https://www.ibef.org/ news/19325>.

'India–Pakistan T20 series in the offing: Report.' *The Times of India* (25 March 2021) <https:// timesofindia.indiatimes.com/sports/cricket/news/india-pakistan-t20-series-in-the-offing-report/articleshow/81684414.cms>.

Iqbal, Nasir. '1,027 civilian posts occupied by servicemen.' *Dawn* (3 October 2003) <https:// www.dawn.com/news/118233>.

Iqtidar, Humeira. *Secularising Islamists? Jama'at-e-Islami and Jam'at-ud-Da'wa in Urban Pakistan* (University of Chicago Press, 2012).

Isam, Mohammad. 'India v Pakistan, a Bangladeshi View.' *The Cricket Monthly* (17 October 2019).

Isam, Mohammad. 'No Pakistan players in BPL.' ESPNcricinfo (16 January 2013) <https://www.espncricinfo.com/story/_/id/22097106/no-pakistan-players-bangladesh-premier-league>.

Isam, Mohammad. 'Tour postponed after court order.' ESPNcricinfo (19 April 2012) <https://www.espncricinfo.com/story/_/id/22319618/dhaka-high-court-puts-four-week-tour-embargo>.

'Islamic fanatics may have killed Woolmer.' *Daily Star* (30 April 2007).

Jaffrelot, Christophe. *Hindu Nationalism* (Princeton University Press, 2007).

Jaffrelot, Christophe. *The Pakistan Paradox* (Random House, 2016).

Jaireth, Subhash. 'Tracing Orientalism in Cricket: A Reading of Some Recent Australian Cricket Writing on Pakistani Cricket.' *Sporting Traditions* 12/1 (1995), pp. 103–120.

Jalal, Ayesha. *The Struggle for Pakistan* (Harvard University Press, 2017).

James, C.L.R. *Beyond a Boundary* (Yellow Jersey Press, 2005 [1963]).

Javaid, Umbreen. 'Corruption and its Deep Impact on Good Governance in Pakistan.' *Pakistan Economic and Social Review* 48/1 (2010), pp. 123–134.

Kanas, Angelos. 'Pure Contagion Effects in International Banking: The Case of BCCI's Failure.' *Journal of Applied Economics* 8/1 (2005), pp. 101–123.

'Karachi: Advani visits his birthplace, Mohatta Palace.' *Dawn* (6 June 2005) <https://www.dawn.com/news/142259>.

'Kashmir Attack: Tracing the path that led to Pulwama.' *BBC News* (1 May 2019) <https://www.bbc.co.uk/news/world-asia-india-47302467>.

'Kashmir dispute: Pakistan downgrades ties with India.' *BBC News* (7 August 2019) <https://www.bbc.co.uk/news/world-asia-49267912>.

'Kashmir under lockdown: All the latest updates.' *Al Jazeera* (27 October 2019) <https://www.aljazeera.com/news/2019/08/india-revokes-kashmir-special-status-latest-updates-190806134011673.html>.

Kasuri, Khurshid, and Radha Kumar. 'There is hope for Pakistan-India peace process.' *Dawn* (24 March 2021) <https://www.dawn.com/news/1614187/there-is-hope-for-pakistan-india-peace-process>.

Kaufman, J., and O. Patterson. 'Cross-National Cultural Diffusion: The Global Spread of Cricket.' *American Sociological Review* 70/1 (2005), pp. 82–110.

'Keep my daughter out of this, says Sourav after 'Sana's CAA post.' *Times of India* (19 December 2019) <https://timesofindia.indiatimes.com/india/keep-my-daughter-out-of-this-says-sourav-after-sanas-caa-post/articleshow/72878319.cms?frmapp=yes&from=mdr>.

Kelso, Paul, and Rob Evans. 'Gatting's bust-up with umpire just wasn't cricket, said British envoy.' *The Guardian* (19 December 2005) <https://www.theguardian.com/uk/2005/dec/19/cricket.freedomofinformation>.

Keys, Barbara. 'International Relations.' In S.W. Pope and John Nauright (eds.), *The Routledge Companion to Sports History* (Routledge, 2009).

Khalidi, O. 'From torrent to trickle: Indian Muslim migration to Pakistan, 1947–97.' *Islamic Studies* 37/3 (1998), pp. 339–352.

Khan, Ali. 'Cricket, society and religion: a study of increasing religiosity in the national cricket team of Pakistan.' *Sport in Society* (online, 1 February 2019).

Khan, Humayoun Ahmed. 'Pakistan is safe for international cricket, says Atherton.' *Dawn* (12 April 2020) <https://www.dawn.com/news/1548429>.

Khan, M. Ilyas. 'Family tells of Pakistan teen cricketer's "suicide" after sex-pest row.' *BBC News* (17 July 2014).

Khan, Muhammad Asif. 'Cricket: The Rise of the Afghans.' *Dawn* (14 October 2018).

Khan, Naveeda. *Muslim Becoming: Aspiration and Scepticism in Pakistan* (Duke University Press, 2012).

Khan, Omer Farooq. 'Pakistan bans broadcast of IPL matches.' *Times of India* (2 April 2019) <https://timesofindia.indiatimes.com/sports/cricket/ipl/top-stories/pakistan-bans-broadcast-of-ipl-matches/articleshow/68693272.cms>.

Khan, Shaharyar M. *Cricket: A Bridge of Peace* (Oxford University Press, 2005).

Khan, Shaharyar M., and Ali Khan. *Cricket Cauldron: The Turbulent Politics of Sport in Pakistan* (HarperSport, 2013).

Khan, Shaharyar. 'Rivalry and Diplomacy.' In Shashi Tharoor and Shaharyar Khan (eds.), *Shadows Across a Playing Field* (Roli Books, 2009).

Khan, Shaharyar. *Shadows Across the Playing Field* (Roli Books, 2009).

Khan, Yasmin. *The Great Partition: The Making of India and Pakistan* (Yale University Press, 2007).

Kidambi, P. *Cricket Country* (Oxford University Press, 2019).

Kothari, Rajni. 'Political Consensus in India: Decline and Reconstruction.' *Economic and Political Weekly* 4/41 (1969), pp. 1635, 1637, 1639, 1641–1644.

Kothari, Shuchi. 'From genre to *zanaana*: Urdu television drama serials and women's culture in Pakistan.' *Contemporary South Asia* 14/3 (2005), pp. 289–305.

Kudaisya, Gyanesh. 'The demographic upheaval of partition: Refugees and agricultural resettlement in India, 1947–67.' *South Asia: Journal of South Asian Studies* 18/1 (1995), pp. 73–94.

Kugelman, Michael. 'Mumbai terror attacks.' *CNN* (26 November 2018) <https://edition.cnn.com/2018/11/25/opinions/10-year-anniversary-mumbai-terror-attacks-intl/index.html>.

Kugelman, Michael. 'Remembering Pakistan's Biggest and Baddest Fraud Scandal.' *Foreign Policy* (22 May 2015) <https://foreignpolicy.com/2015/05/22/remembering-pakistans-biggest-and-baddest-fraud-scandal/>.

Kureishi, Omar. 'Amarnath's death a sad moment in cricket.' ESPNcricinfo (9 August 2000) <https://www.espncricinfo.com/story/_/id/23241718/amarnath-death-sad-moment-cricket>.

Lall, Marie, and Tania Saeed. *Youth and the National Narrative: Education, Terrorism and the Security State in Pakistan* (Bloomsbury, 2019).

Lall, Marie. 'Educate to Hate: the use of education in the creation of antagonistic national identities in India and Pakistan.' *Compare* 38/1 (2008), pp. 103–119.

Lalwani, Sameer, and Hannah Haegeland. 'Anatomy of a Crisis: Explaining Crisis Onset in India–Pakistan Relations.' *Stimson Centre* (2018) <https://www.stimson.org/wp-content/files/InvestigatingCrisesOnset.pdf>.

Lalwani, Vijayta. 'Data check: Ceasefire violations along Line of Control this year are already more than all of 2017.' *Scroll.in* (7 August 2018) <https://scroll.in/article/888719/data-check-already-more-ceasefire-violations-along-line-of-control-this-year-than-all-of-2017>.

Lambert, Simon. 'How much do top cricketers learn?.' *This Is Money* (3 September 2010) <https://www.thisismoney.co.uk/money/article-1702948/How-much-do-top-cricketers-earn.html>.

'Lanka's tour to Pakistan will there be repercussions.' *Daily News* (25 September 2019) <https://www.dailynews.lk/2019/09/25/sports/197934/lanka's-tour-pakistan-will-there-be-repercussions?page=4>.

Lavoy, Peter. 'Pakistan's Foreign Relations.' In D. Hagerty (ed.), *South Asia in World Politics* (Roman and Littlefield Publishers, 2005).

Layaslalu, M. 'Vajpayee Government: Golden Years of Non-Military Confidence Building Measures Between India and Pakistan.' *IOSR Journal of Humanities and Social Science* 22/4, ver. 5 (2017), pp. 31–39.

Levitt, Steven, and Stephen Dubner. *Freakonomics: A Rogue Economist Explores the Hidden Side of Everything* (William Morrow, 2005).

Licudi, Adam, and Wasim Raja. *Cornered Tigers: A History of Pakistan's Test Cricket* (Hansib Publishing, 1997).

Lieven, Anatol. *Pakistan: A Hard Country* (Penguin Books, 2011).

Lister, Simon. *Fire in Babylon: How the West Indies Cricket Team Brought a People to its Feet* (Yellow Jersey, 2016).

Little, Charles, and Chris Valiotis. 'Cricket in Pakistan.' In John Nauright and Charles Parrish (eds.), *Sports Around the World: History, Culture, and Practice*, vol. 1 (ABC-CLIO, 2012).

Long, Phil. 'Death of a fan.' *BBC Sport* (25 November 2005) <http://news.bbc.co.uk/sport1/hi/cricket/england/4470766.stm>.

Lutfi, Sunar. 'The Long History of Islam as a Collective "Other" of the West and the Rise of Islamophobia in the U.S. after Trump.' *Insight Turkey* 19/3 (2017), pp. 35–52.

Magazine, Pradeep. *Not Quite Cricket* (Penguin Books, 1999).

Mahadevan, Prem. *A Decade on from the 2008 Mumbai Attack: Reviewing the question of state sponsorship* (International Centre for Counter Terrorism Publications, 2019).

Mahmood, Fazal (w/ Asif Sohail). *From Dusk to Dawn* (Oxford University Press, 2003).

Maizland, Lindsay. 'Kashmir: What to Know about the Disputed Region.' *Council on Foreign Relations* (7 August 2019) <https://www.cfr.org/in-brief/kashmir-what-know-about-disputed-region>.

Majumdar, Boria, and J.A. Mangan (eds.). *Sport in South Asian Society* (Routledge, 2005).

Majumdar, Boria. 'Prologue: Stepping Stones Across a Stream.' In B. Majumdar and J.A. Mangan (eds.), *Sport in South Asian Society* (Routledge, 2005).

Majumdar, Boria. *Eleven Gods and a Billion Indians: The On and Off the Field Story of Cricket in India and Beyond* (S&S Publications, 2018).

Majumdar, Boria. *The Illustrated History of Indian Cricket* (Roli Books, 2006).

Majumdar, Boria. *Twenty-two Yards to Freedom: A Social History of Indian Cricket* (Viking, 2004).

Malcolm, Dominic, Alan Bairner, and Graham Curry. '"Woolmergate": Sport and the Representation of Islam and Muslims in the British Press.' *Journal of Sport and Social Issues* 34/2 (2010), pp. 215–235.

Malcolm, Dominic, Jon Gemmell, and Nalin Mehta. 'Cricket and modernity: international and interdisciplinary perspectives on the study of the Imperial Game.' *Sport in Society* 12/4/5 (2009), pp. 431–446.

Malcolm, Dominic. '"It's Not Cricket": Colonial Legacies and Contemporary Inequalities.' *Journal of Historical Sociology* 14 (2001), pp. 253–75.

Malec, M., and H. Beckles. 'Baseball, Cricket and Social Change: Jackie Robinson and Frank Worrell.' In Robert R. Sands (ed.), *Anthropology, Sport and Culture* (Westport, 1999), pp. 137–144.

Maqsood, Ammara. *The New Pakistani Middle Class* (Harvard University Press, 2017).

Marqusee, Mike. 'A committed neutral speaks.' *Outlook India* (17 March 2005).

Marqusee, Mike. 'The Ambush Clause: Globalisation, Corporate Power and the Governance of World Cricket.' In Stephen Wagg (ed.), *Following On: Cricket and National Identity in the Postcolonial Age* (Routledge, 2005).

Marqusee, Mike. 'The Lovable Marquee.' *Outlook India* (21 March 2005) <https://www.outlookindia.com/magazine/story/this-lovable-marquee/226831>.

Marqusee, Mike. *Anyone but England* (Aurum Press, 2005).

Marqusee, Mike. *War Minus the Shooting* (Heinemann, 1996).

Marsden, Magnus. *Living Islam: Muslim Religious Experience in Pakistan's North-West Frontier* (Cambridge University Press, 2005).

'Match-fixing is more common than ever.' *The Economist* (23 September 2017) <https://www.economist.com/international/2017/09/23/match-fixing-is-more-common-than-ever>.

McDonald, Iain. 'Between Saleem and Shiva: The Politics of Cricket Nationalism in a 'Globalising' India.' In John Sugden and Alan Bairnier (eds.), *Sport in Divided Societies* (Meyer and Meyer Sport, 2000).

Mehta, Raj. *Lost Victory: The Rise and Fall of LTTE Supremo, V. Prabhakaran* (Pentagon Press, 2010).

Menezes, Jack de. 'Pakistan and Afghanistan cricket fans involved in fight outside Headingley after plane flew over ground with 'Justice for Balochistan' message.' *The Independent* (29 June 2019) <https://www.independent.co.uk/sport/cricket/pakistan-afghanistan-fans-fight-video-cricket-world-cup-outside-ground-plane-justice-for-balochistan-a8980421.html>.

Mesquita, Ethan Bueno de; C. Christine Fair; Jenna Jordan; Rasul Baksh Rais; and Jacob N. Shapiro. 'Measuring political violence in Pakistan: Insights from the BFRS Dataset.' *Conflict Management and Peace Science* (2014), pp. 1–23.

Metcalf, Barbara D. 'Introduction.' In Barbara D. Metcalf (ed.), *Islam in South Asia in Practice* (Princeton University Press, 2010).

Metcalf, Barbara. 'Madrasas and Minorities in Secular India.' In Robert W. Hefner and Muhammad Qasim Zaman (eds.), *Schooling Islam: The Culture and Politics of Modern Muslim Education* (Princeton University Press, 2006).

Miandad, Javed. *Cutting Edge* (Oxford University Press, 2003).

'Mohammad Amir interview with Sky Sports in full.' *The Telegraph* (19 March 2012) <https://www.telegraph.co.uk/sport/cricket/international/pakistan/9154012/Mohammad-Amir-interview-with-Sky-Sports-in-full.html>.

Mohammad, Hanif. *Playing for Pakistan* (Hamdard Press, 1999).

Mohammad, Mushtaq. *Inside Out* (Uniprint, 2006).

Monga, Sidharth. 'An opportunity to keep the Afghanistan-Pakistan rivalry dignified.' ESPNcricinfo (28 June 2019) <https://www.espncricinfo.com/story/_/id/27075656/an-opportunity-keep-afghanistan-pakistan-rivalry-dignified>.

Moro, Pamela; James Myers, and Arthur Lehmann. *Magic, Witchcraft and Religion: A Reader in the Anthropology of Religion* (McGraw Hill, 2008).

Morshead, Sam. 'Multan's message to the world on seismic opening night.' *The Cricketer* (26 February 2020) <https://www.thecricketer.com/Topics/peshawarzalmi/multans_message_to_the_world.html>.

Morshead, Sam. 'Winning hearts, changing minds: The inside story of the PSL's homecoming.' *The Cricketer* (6 March 2020) <https://www.thecricketer.com/Topics/peshawarzalmi/winning_hearts_changing_minds_the_inside_story__psl_homecoming.html>.

Murdered after angering radical Muslims.' *Daily Mail* (30 April 2007).

'Mushtaq Ahmed Calls for Resumption of India–Pakistan Cricketing Ties.' *NDTV* (17 November 2019) <https://sports.ndtv.com/cricket/mushtaq-ahmed-calls-for-resumption-of-india-pakistan-cricketing-ties-2133978>.

Nandy, A. *A Very Popular Exile: An Omnibus, comprising The Tao of Cricket; An Ambiguous Journey to the City; Traditions, Tyranny, and Utopias* (Oxford University Press, 2020).

Narayan, Badri. *Fascinating Hindutva* (Sage, 2019).

National Corruption Perception Survey, 2010.' Transparency International (19 March 2013).

Oborne, Peter. 'Are we wrong about Pakistan?.' *The Telegraph* (28 February 2012) <https://www.telegraph.co.uk/travel/destinations/asia/pakistan/articles/Are-we-wrong-about-Pakistan/>.

Oborne, Peter. *Wounded Tiger: A History of Cricket in Pakistan* (Simon & Schuster, 2014).

'Pakistan players hurt and angered by snub.' ESPNcricinfo (19 January 2010) <https://www.espncricinfo.com/story/_/id/22686959/pakistan-players-hurt-angered-snub-auction>.

Pakistan Security Report (Pak Institute for Peace Studies, 2009).

Pakistan the Militant Jihadi Challenge (International Crisis Group, 2009).

'Pakistan threatens boycott if Australia refuses to tour.' *The Sydney Morning Herald* <https://www.smh.com.au/sport/cricket/pakistan-threatens-boycott-if-australia-refuses-to-tour-20020802-gdfich.html>.

'Pakistan: Covid 19 – Situation Report (As of 10 June 2020).' *Reliefweb*, <https://reliefweb.int/report/pakistan/pakistan-covid-19-situation-report-10-june-2020>.

'Pakistan: End of the water dispute.' *The Round Table: The Commonwealth Journal of International Affairs* 51/201 (1960), pp. 72–75.

Pandey, Gyanendra. 'Can a Muslim be an Indian?.' *Comparative Studies in Society and History* 41/4 (1999), pp. 608–29.

Pandey, Gyanendra. *Remembering Partition: Violence, Nationalism and History in India* (Cambridge University Press, 2003).

Pandya, Abhinav. 'The Future of Indo-Pak Relations after the Pulwama Attack.' *Perspectives on Terrorism* 13/2 (2019), pp. 65–68.

Papanek, Gustav F. *Pakistan's Development* (Harvard University Press, 1967).

Paracha, N.F. 'The 'swinging seventies' in Pakistan: An urban history.' *Dawn* (22 August 2013) <https://www.dawn.com/news/1037584>.

Paracha, N.F. 'The Pakistan zeitgeists: A nation through the ages.' *Dawn* (29 May 2014) <https://www.dawn.com/news/1109105>.

Paul, T.V. 'Causes of the India Pakistan Enduring Rivalry.' In T.V. Paul (ed.), *The India Pakistan Conflict: An Enduring Rivalry* (Cambridge University Press, 2005).

Payne, Gary. 'Pakistan refuse to suspend 'spot-fixing' players without proof.' *The Guardian* (31 August 2010) <https://www.theguardian.com/sport/2010/aug/31/pakistan-england-spot-fixing>.

'PCB files damages claim against IMG-Reliance for PSL pull-out.' ESPNcricinfo (19 November 2019) <https://www.espncricinfo.com/story/_/id/28114967/pcb-files-damages-claim-img-reliance-psl-pull-out>.

Perera, Neil. 'Pakistan: A True Friend of Sri Lanka Cricket.' *The Island* (7 October 2017).

Pietersen, Kevin. *Crossing the Boundary* (Random House, 2006).

'PM Imran hopeful Pakistan's "hot and dry" weather will mitigate virus threat.' *Dawn* (20 March 2020) <https://www.dawn.com/news/1542413>.

'Polio eradication a UN priority, says Guterres in Pakistan visit.' *United Nations* <https://news.un.org/en/story/2020/02/1057641>.

Pringle, Chris. *Save the Last Ball For Me* (Celebrity Books, 1998).

Pringle, Derek. 'The special tensions of England v Pakistan.' *The Independent* (23 July 1996) <https://www.independent.co.uk/sport/the-special-tensions-of-england-v-pakistan-1330199.html>.

'Pulwama attack: BCCI calls on ICC to act following Kashmir incident.' *BBC Sport* (22 February 2019) <https://www.bbc.co.uk/sport/cricket/47333834>.

'Pulwama attack: What are Modi's options?.' *BBC News* (19 February 2019) <https://www.bbc.co.uk/news/world-asia-india-47278145>.

Radford, Brian. 'Call girls to be questioned in cricket scandal.' *The Guardian* (21 January 2001) https://www.theguardian.com/uk/2001/jan/21/sport.theobserver.

Raghavan, S. *War and Peace in Modern India* (Palgrave Macmillan, 2010).

Rahman, Maseeh. 'Schoolgirls killed in attack on orphanage.' *The Guardian* (15 August 2006) <https://www.theguardian.com/world/2006/aug/15/schools.schoolsworldwide>.

Ramesh, Randeep. 'From Conflict to Conciliation.' *The Guardian* (16 June 2005) <https://www.theguardian.com/world/2005/jun/16/worlddispatch.kashmir>.

Ramnath, Nandini. 'A brief history of Pakistan-India cultural ties.' *Dawn* (27 September 2016) <https://images.dawn.com/news/1176320>.

Rao, P. Venkateshwar. 'Ethnic Conflict in Sri Lanka: India's Role and Perception.' *Asian Survey* 28/4 (1988), pp. 419–436.

Rao, Rahul. 'Test of faith: The CAA protests shake the old bounds of Indian secular morality.' *Caravan Magazine* (29 January 2020) <https://caravanmagazine.in/politics/caa-protests-shake-old-bounds-indian-secular-morality>.

Rashid, Ahmed. *Descent into Chaos: The United States and the Failure of Nation Building in Pakistan, Afghanistan, and Central Asia* (Penguin Random House, 2008).

Rashid, Ahmed. *Pakistan On the Brink* (Penguin Random House, 2012).

Raza, Syed Irfan. 'Ex-chief of Wapda held in Bosnia on corruption charges.' *Dawn* (10 May 2013), url: https://www.dawn.com/news/1010570.

'Reunited Kashmiris' tears of joy.' *BBC News* (7 April 2005) <http://news.bbc.co.uk/1/hi/world/south_asia/4419109.stm>.

Richards, Huw. 'After 5-Year Ban for Fixing, Player Returns to Pakistan.' *The New York Times* (13 January 2016) <https://www.nytimes.com/2016/01/14/sports/cricket/after-5-year-ban-for-fixing-amir-returns-for-pakistan.html>.

Richards, Vivian. *Hitting Across the Line* (Headline Book Publishing, 1992).

Robinson, Neil. *Long Shot Summer: The Year of 4 England Captains 1988* (Amberley Publishing, 2015).

Robinson, Peter. 'For the love of money, says Cronje.' ESPNcricinfo (21 June 2000) <https://www.espncricinfo.com/story/_/id/23232893/for-love-money-says-cronje>.

Ronay, Barney. 'Former Test umpire John Holder sues ECB for alleged racial discrimination.' *The Guardian* (29 December 2020) <https://www.theguardian.com/sport/2020/dec/29/former-test-umpire-john-holder-sues-ecb-for-alleged-racial-discrimination>.

Roy, Arundhati. 'The monster in the mirror.' *The Guardian* (12 December 2008) <https://www.theguardian.com/world/2008/dec/12/mumbai-arundhati-roy>.

Roy, Shubhajit. 'India to supply Covid vaccines to Pakistan.' *The Indian Express* (10 March 2021) <https://indianexpress.com/article/india/india-to-supply-covid-vaccines-to-pakistan-7221680/>.

Rumford, Chris. 'More than a game: globalization and the post-Westernization of world cricket.' *Global Networks 7*, no. 2 (2007), pp. 202–214.

Ruparelia, Sanjay. 'Modi's Saffron Democracy.' *Dissent* 66/2 (2019), pp. 94–106.

Russell, Jack. *A Wicket-Keeper's Life* (Harper Collins, 1997).

Sahni, Varun. 'The Protean Polis and Strategic Surprises: Do Changes within India Affect South, Asian Strategic Stability?.' *Contemporary South Asia* 14/2 (2005), pp. 219–31.

Saini, S.K. 'Storming of Lal Masjid in Pakistan: An Analysis.' *Strategic Analysis* 33/4 (2009), pp. 553–565.

Sainsbury, John. 'How the Taliban spin cricket.' *The Globe and Mail* (2 March 2015) <https://www.theglobeandmail.com/opinion/how-the-taliban-spin-cricket/article23232635/> accessed on 8 July 2021.

Samiuddin, Osman, et al. 'Who gets paid what in cricket.' *The Cricket Monthly* (17 October 2017) <https://www.thecricketmonthly.com/story/1123792/who-gets-paid-what-in-cricket>.

Samiuddin, Osman. 'All emotion, no logic.' ESPNcricinfo (11 May 2009) <https://www.espncricinfo.com/story/_/id/22807738/all-emotion-no-logic>.

Samiuddin, Osman. 'Clean up your act, ICC tells PCB.' *ESPN* (13 October 2010) <https://www.espn.co.uk/cricket/story/_/id/22378298/clean-your-act-icc-tells-pcb>.

Samiuddin, Osman. 'PCB keen on UAE venues despite ICC snub.' ESPNcricinfo (26 June 2009) <https://www.espncricinfo.com/story/_/id/22789023/pcb-continue-pushing-uae-venues>.

Samiuddin, Osman. 'The Imran Khans I've Known.' *The Cricket Monthly* (10 August 2018) <http://www.thecricketmonthly.com/story/1154531/the-imran-khans-i-ve-known>.

Samiuddin, Osman. 'The Miracle of 1992.' *The Cricket Monthly* (November 2014) <http://www.thecricketmonthly.com/story/793785/the-miracle-of--92>.

Samiuddin, Osman. *The Unquiet Ones: A History of Pakistan Cricket* (Harper Collins, 2014).

Sandel, Michael J. *What Money Can't Buy: The Moral Limits of Markets* (Farrar, Straus and Giroux, 2012).

Sandiford, Keith A.P. 'Cricket and the Victorian Society.' *Journal of Social History* 17/2 (1983), pp. 303–317.

Sanghvi, Vir. 'The transformation of the image of the global Pakistani.' (2010) <https://virsanghvi.com/Article-Details.aspx?key=540>.

Sarkar, Suparno. 'IMPPA passes resolution to temporarily ban Pakistani artists in India; Twitter reacts.' *IB Times* (29 September 2016).

Sassen, Saskia. *Expulsions: Brutality and Complexity in the Global Economy* (Harvard University Press, 2014).

Sayeed, Asad. 'Contextualising Corruption in Pakistan.' *Social Science and Policy Bulletin* 2/1 (2010), pp. 10–18.

Schaffter, Chandra. 'Cricket and the Commonwealth.' *The Round Table* 108/1 (2019), pp. 67–79.

Scott, Matt. 'Cricket agent accuses Salman Butt of recruiting spot-fixing players.' *The Guardian* (2 November 2011) <https://www.theguardian.com/sport/2011/nov/02/mazhar-majeed-accusations-salman-butt>.

Scott, Matt. 'Cricket spot-fixing: How the Pakistan three fell into a trap.' *The Guardian* (1 November 2011) <https://www.theguardian.com/sport/2011/nov/01/cricket-spot-fixing-pakistan-trial-guilty>.

Scott, Matt. 'Pakistan cricketers wanted to sabotage Afridi captaincy, agent claimed.' *The Guardian* (11 October 2011) <https://www.theguardian.com/sport/2011/oct/11/pakistan-cricket-sabotage-captaincy-claim>.

Scott, William G. 'Organization Theory: An Overview and Appraisal.' *Journal of the Academy of Management* 4 (1961), pp. 7–26.

Searle, Chris. *Pitch of Life: Writings on Cricket* (The Parrs Wood Press, 2001).

Selvey, Mike. 'Pakistan clears its players of match-fixing.' *The Guardian* (11 May 2000) <https://www.theguardian.com/sport/2000/may/11/cricket2>.

Sen, Sataduru. 'History without a Past in Postcolonial Pakistan.' In Stephen Wagg (ed.), *Cricket and National Identity in the Postcolonial Age* (Routledge, 2005).

Sengupta, Jayanta. '2003 World Cup: Globalizing Patriotism.' In Boria Majumdar and J.A. Mangan (eds.), *Sport in South Asian Society* (Routledge, 2005).

Sengupta, Somini. 'Dossier Gives Details of Mumbai Attacks.' *The New York Times* (6 January 2009).

Shah, Sreshth. 'Indian and Pakistani players go about their business, game faces on, blinkers in place.' ESPNcricinfo (3 February 2020) <https://www.espncricinfo.com/story/_/id/28625641/indian-pakistani-players-go-their-business-game-faces-blinkers-place>.

Shahane, Girish. 'Why the BJP is appointing C-listers to head top institutions.' *Scroll.in* (22 July 2015) <https://scroll.in/article/743006/why-the-bjp-is-appointing-c-listers-to-head-top-institutions>.

Shahzad, Asif. '"God is with us": Many Muslims in Pakistan flout the coronavirus ban in mosques.' *Reuters* (13 April 2020) <https://www.reuters.com/article/us-health-coronavirus-pakistan-congregat/god-is-with-us-many-muslims-in-pakistan-flout-the-coronavirus-ban-in-mosques-idINKCN21V0T4>.

Shamsi, Amber Rahim. 'Why Haleema Rafique's death should matter, and why it won't.' *Dawn* (17 July 2014) <https://www.dawn.com/news/1119734>.

Shamsie, Kamila. 'Strong arms: The story of Pakistan women's cricket.' *The Cricket Monthly* (16 October 2019) <https://www.thecricketmonthly.com/story/1202296/the-story-of-pakistan-women-s-cricket--from-the-khan-sisters-to-sana-mir>.

Sharma, Supriya. 'We knew Adityanath was hostile to Muslims. But did we expect his regime to be so savage?.' *Scroll.in* (30 December 2019) <https://scroll.in/article/948194/we-knew-adityanath-was-hostile-to-muslims-but-did-we-expect-his-regime-to-be-so-savage?fbclid=IwAR1-jHJ6sZHPuQnIrbvZpNnxql_agi9RtZO4eBRLLCAVNi5P_BJ_IfvAw_M>.

Shemilt, Stephan. 'England v Pakistan: Ten players from touring squad have coronavirus.' *BBC Sport* (23 June 2020) <https://www.bbc.com/sport/cricket/53149897>.

Shukla, Subhash. 'Indo-Pak relations, Gujral to Manmohan Singh.' *The Indian Journal of Political Science* 69/4 (2008), pp. 897–910.

Sikand, Y.S. 'The Tablighi Jama'at and Politics: A Critical Re-Appraisal.' *The Muslim World* 96/1 (2006), pp. 175–195.

Sikand, Y.S. *The Origins and Development of the Tablighi Jama'at (1920–2000), A Cross-country Comparative Study* (Orient Blackswan, 2002).

Singh, Jaswant. *Jinnah: India, Partition, Independence* (Oxford University Press, 2010).

'Sri Lankan cricket board warned over terrorist threat to Pakistan tour.' *The Guardian* (11 September 2019) <https://www.theguardian.com/sport/2019/sep/11/sri-lankan-cricket-board-warned-over-terrorist-threat-to-pakistan-tour>.

Stern, John, and Marcus Williams (eds.). *The Essential Wisden: An Anthology of 150 Years of Wisden Cricketers' Almanack* (Bloomsbury, 2014).

Strauss, Andrew. *Driving Ambition: My Autobiography* (Hodder and Stoughton, 2013).

Swami, Praveen. 'A Secret ISI-RAW Channel, Talks Since 2018: What Led to India–Pakistan LoC Ceasefire.' *News18* (23 March 2021) <https://www.news18.com/news/india/a-secret-isi-raw-channel-talks-since-2018-what-led-to-india-pakistan-ceasefire-3563711.html>.

'Swann slams 'aloof and arrogant' Butt.' *ESPN* (2 November 2011) <http://en.espn.co.uk/cricket/sport/story/119211.html>.

Swapan, Ashfaque. 'Hate Not Last Word in Partition: Nandy.' *US Indian News* (13 March 2009) <https://southasia.berkeley.edu/sites/default/files/Hate%20Not%20Last%20Word%20in%20Partition_India%20West_Ashis%20Nandy_Mar%2009%281%29.pdf>.

Syed, Baqir Sajjad. 'Pakistan, India agree on LoC ceasefire.' *Dawn* (26 February 2021) <https://www.dawn.com/news/1609468>.

Talbot, Ian, and Tahir Kamran, 'Poets, Wrestlers and Cricketers: Patronage and Performance in Lahore and Beyond.' In Ian Talbot and Tahir Kamran (eds.), *Colonial Lahore: A History of the City and Beyond* (Oxford Scholarship Online, 2017).

Talbot, Ian. *A History of Modern South Asia* (Oxford University Press, 2017).

Talbot, Ian. *Pakistan: A Modern History* (Hurst and Company, 2005).

'Team India wear special army caps in ODI against Australia.' *The Telegraph* (8 March 2019) <https://www.telegraphindia.com/sport/team-india-wear-special-army-caps-in-odi-against-australia/cid/1686420>.

Tennant, Ivo. *Imran Khan* (Gollancz/Witherby, 1995).

Tharoor, Shashi. 'Fantasies and Realities.' In Shashi Tharoor and Shaharyar Khan (eds.), *Shadows Across a Playing Field* (Roli Books, 2009).

'The global normalcy index.' *The Economist* (1 July 2021) <https://www.economist.com/graphic-detail/tracking-the-return-to-normalcy-after-covid-19>.

'The Takeover: How the Modi Government has Filled Key Positions in 14 Institutions.' *Catch News* <http://www.catchnews.com/india-news/the-takeover-how-the-modi-govt-has-filled-key-positions-in-14-institutions->.

'There has been one miscarriage of justice after another.' ESPNcricinfo (February 1988) <http://www.espncricinfo.com/wcm/content/story/226916.html>.

Thompson, James D. *Organizations in Action* (McGraw Hill, 1967).

Tiwari, Manas. 'IPL Economy: What the cash-rich league adds to India's GDP.' *Financial Express* (22 January 2018), <https://www.financialexpress.com/sports/ipl/ipl-economy-what-the-cash-rich-league-adds-to-indias-gdp/1025063/>.

'Top 3 Pakistani Cricketers Involved in Spot Fixing Scam.' *YouTube* (7 October 2011) <https://www.youtube.com/watch?v=jWWCTni1oTM>.

Transparency International. 'Corruption Perceptions Index.' <https://www.transparency.org/en/cpi/2020/index/pak>.

Traub, James. 'Can Pakistan Be Governed?.' *The New York Times Magazine* (4 April 2009).

'Troubling projections.' *Dawn* (16 June 2020), url: https://www.dawn.com/news/1563859.

Ugra, Sharda. 'In cricket gear, a snapshot of India today.' *The Hindu* (17 February 2021) <https://www.thehindu.com/opinion/op-ed/in-cricket-gear-a-snapshot-of-india-today/article33854390.ece>.

Ugra, Sharda. 'Play Together, Live Apart: Religion, Politics and Markets in Indian Cricket since 1947.' In Stephen Wagg (ed.), *Cricket and National Identity in the Postcolonial Age* (Routledge, 2005).

Ugra, Sharda. 'What makes sportsmen go corrupt?.' ESPNcricinfo (4 November 2010) <https://www.espncricinfo.com/story/_/id/21284459/makes-sportsmen-go-corrupt>.

Ugra, Sharda. 'Why Aren't Our Sports Celebrities Speaking Out?.' *The India Forum* (6 March 2020) <https://www.theindiaforum.in/article/why-aren-t-sports-celebrities-speaking-about-caanrc-protests>.

'UNDP Human Development Reports' <http://hdr.undp.org/en/countries/profiles/PAK>.

'UNHCR welcomes new government policy for Afghans in Pakistan.' *UNHCR Pakistan* (7 February 2017) <https://unhcrpk.org/unhcr-welcomes-new-government-policy-for-afghans-in-pakistan/>.

'University suspends cricket fans for cheering Pakistan's win over India.' *The Guardian* (6 March 2014) <https://www.theguardian.com/world/2014/mar/06/university-expels-cricket-fans-pakistan-india>.

'Uri attack aftermath.' *First Post* (23 September 2016) <http://www.firstpost.com/sports/bcci-chief-anurag-thakur-says-no-question-of-playing-cricket-with-pakistan-after-uri-attack-3018372.html>.

Usmani, Basim. 'Pakistan at the crossroads.' *The Guardian* (10 March 2009) <https://www.theguardian.com/commentisfree/2009/mar/09/pakistan-sri-lanka-cricket-team-attack>.

Vaidyanathan, Siddhartha. 'India. Pakistan. Chennai. 1999.' *The Cricket Monthly* (31 January 2019) <https://www.thecricketmonthly.com/story/1172609/india--pakistan--chennai--1999>.

Valiotis, Chris. 'Cricket in a "Nation Imperfectly Imagined": Identity and Tradition in Postcolonial Pakistan.' In Stephen Wagg (ed.), *Cricket and National Identity in the Postcolonial Age* (Routledge, 2005).

Valiotis, Chris. Sporting Nations of the Imagination: Pakistani Cricket and Identity in Pakistan and Anglo Pakistan. PhD dissertation, University of New South Wales. Unpublished, 2006.

Varshney, Ashutosh. *Ethnic Conflict and Civil Life: Hindus and Muslims in India* (Yale University Press, 2002).

'Virat Kohli, come to Pakistan and play cricket: India captain's fan in Lahore wins hearts.' *India Today* (10 October 2019) <https://www.indiatoday.in/sports/cricket/story/virat-kohli-pakistan-cricket-fan-lahore-gaddafi-stadium-banner-pak-vs-sl-1607889-2019-10-10>.

'"Virat Kohli" spotted in Lahore donning Pakistan World Cup kit.' *The News* (9 June 2019) <https://www.thenews.com.pk/latest/482201-virat-kohli-in-pakistani-kit-roaming-in-lahore>.

Wagg, Chris. 'Introduction.' In Stephen Wagg (ed.), *Cricket and National Identity in the Postcolonial Age: Following On* (Routledge, 2005).

Wagg, Stephen. *Cricket: A Political History of the Global Game, 1945–2017* (Routledge, 2018).

Walsh, Declan. 'Suicide bombings in Lahore kill at least 31.' *The Guardian* <https://www.theguardian.com/world/2008/mar/12/pakistan>.

'Was Woolmer facing a Fatwa?.' *Daily Mail* (30 April 2007).

'Wasim Akram, Sohaib Akhtar criticize Amir's decision to retire from Test cricket.' *The News* (27 July 2019) <https://www.thenews.com.pk/latest/504478-wasim-akram-shoaib-akhtar-criticize-amirs-decision-to-retire-from-test-cricket>.

'Watch: Union minister Anurag Thakur leads "goli maaro saalon ko" slogans at rally.' *Scroll.in* (27 January 2020) <https://scroll.in/video/951289/watch-anurag-thakur-minister-of-state-for-finance-lead-goli-maaro-saalon-ko-slogans-at-rally>.

Waugh, Steve. *Out of My Comfort Zone* (Penguin Books, 2005).

Weber, Max. *Economy and Society*, ed. Guenther Roth and Clauss Wittich (University of California Press, 1978).

Webster, Rudi V. 'Would a code of honour help?.' ESPNcricinfo (14 November 2010) <http://www.espncricinfo.com/magazine/content/story/486861.html>.

Westall, Claire, and Neil Lazarus. 'The Pitch of the World: Cricket and Chris Searle.' *Race and Class* 51/2 (2009), pp. 44–58.

Wheeler, Nicholas J. *Trusting Enemies* (Oxford University Press, 2018).

'Why Pakistan cricket is desperate to enjoy the comforts of home after 10 years in exile.' *The Telegraph* (19 May 2018) <https://www.telegraph.co.uk/cricket/2018/05/19/pakistan-cricket-desperate-enjoy-comforts-home-10-years-exile/>.

'Why the death of militant Burhan Wani has Kashmiris up in arms.' *BBC News* (11 July 2016) <https://www.bbc.co.uk/news/world-asia-india-36762043>.

Wilde, Simon. *Caught: The Full Story of Cricket's Match-Fixing Scandal* (Aurum Press, 2000; 2001).

Wilde, Simon. *England: The Biography: The Story of English Cricket* (Simon and Schuster, 2018).

Williams, Jack. *Cricket and Race* (Berg, 2001).

Williamson, Martin. 'When Sylvester Clarke bricked it.' ESPNcricinfo (13 May 2006) <https://www.espncricinfo.com/story/_/id/21144653/when-sylvester-clarke-bricked-it>.

Willis, Bob, and Alan Lee. *The Captain's Diary: England in Fiji, New Zealand and Pakistan 1983–4* (Collins, 1984).

Wisden Cricketer's Almanack (John Wisden and Co. Ltd., 1980).

Wisden Cricketers' Almanack (John Wisden and Co. Ltd., 1988).

Wisden Cricketers' Almanack 1985 (John Wisden and Co. Ltd., 1985).

Wood, Mike Meehall. 'India v Pakistan At The Cricket World Cup Is The Biggest Sporting Event In The World This Weekend.' *Forbes* (14 June 2019) <https://www.forbes.com/sites/mikemeehallwood/2019/06/14/india-v-pakistan-at-the-cricket-world-cup-is-the-biggest-sporting-event-in-the-world-this-weekend/>.

'Woolmer "died of natural causes".' *BBC News* (12 June 2007) <http://news.bbc.co.uk/1/hi/world/americas/6745589.stm>.

World Bank. 'Worldwide Governance Indicators.' <https://info.worldbank.org/governance/wgi/Home/Reports>.

Wright, Susan (ed.). *Anthropology of Organizations* (Routledge, 1994).

Yousaf, Kamran. 'Rajapaksa's victory a setback for India but good for Pakistan.' *The Express Tribune* (17 November 2019) <https://tribune.com.pk/story/2101463/1-rajapaksas-victory-setback-india-good-pakistan/>.

Yusuf, Moeed. 'Difficult Equation.' *Dawn* (9 October 2018).

Yusuf, Moeed. 'Difficult Ties.' *Dawn* (3 June 2014).

Yusuf, Moeed. 'How the India–Pakistan Conflict Leaves Great Powers Powerless.' *Foreign Policy* (10 December 2018) <https://foreignpolicy.com/2018/12/10/954587-india-pakistan-mumbai-terror/>.

Yusuf, Moeed. 'India–Pakistan equation.' *Dawn* (10 September 2012).

Yusuf, Moeed. 'Small window of opportunity.' *Dawn* (23 September 2013).

Yusuf, Moeed. 'The Pulwama Crisis: Flirting with War in a Nuclear Environment.' *Arms Control Association* (May 2019) <https://www.armscontrol.org/act/2019-05/features/pulwama-crisis-flirting-war-nuclear-environment>.

Zamindar, Vazira Fazila-Yacoobali. *The Long Partition and the Making of Modern South Asia: Refugees, Boundaries, Histories* (Columbia University Press, 2007).

Index